More Praise for *Game of Queens*

'Gristwood handles multiple narrative strands with tremendous finesse… Densely packed with fascinating material, this immensely ambitious undertaking succeeds triumphantly.'

Literary Review

'A magnificent exploration of a most remarkable group… Gristwood gives us impeccable research, incisive attention to detail and exquisite writing as she investigates these truly fascinating women and their lives of courage, tribulation and determination. Absolutely unputdownable.'

Kate Williams, author of *The Storms of War*

'Gristwood interweaves the drama of monarchy with its more domestic moments.'

Telegraph

'The complete portrait that emerges reveals a complexity of inter actions and relationships among these exceptional, now legendary women, their families, and their nations that greatly contributed to the political, intellectual, and cultural achievements as well as the climate of the Renaissance era. A fascinating work of world and women's history.'

Booklist

'Gristwood brings them all to life with her usual mix of character study and pacy narrative.'

History Revealed

'A fast-paced chronological narrative bursting with intrigue.'

Publishers Weekly

'Readers of popular history, especially of Tudor England, and of women's history will find much to ⸻.'

Library Journal

About the Author

Sarah Gristwood has written bestselling biographies of Arbella Stuart and Elizabeth & Leicester. Her book *Blood Sisters*, a dramatic portrait of the women whose dynastic ambitions and rivalries fuelled the Wars of the Roses, was published in 2012. She lives in Camden, north London, and Kent.

Game *of* Queens

The Women Who Made
Sixteenth-Century Europe

SARAH GRISTWOOD

ONEWORLD

First published ... First published 16

The moral ... ... to be identified as the Author of this work has been
asserted ... ... in accordance with the Copyright, Designs, and Patents Act 1988

... ... All rights re...
... ... copyright under Berne Convention.
A CIP record for this title is available from the British Library

ISBN 978-1-78607-100-2
eISBN 978-1-78074-995-2

Every effort has been made to trace copyright holders for the use of
materials in this book. The publisher apologises for any errors or omissions
herein and would be grateful if they were notified of any corrections that
should be incorporated in future reprints or editions of this book.

Typeset by Hewer Text UK Ltd, Edinburgh
Printed and bound by Clays Ltd, St Ives plc

Oneworld Publications
10 Bloomsbury Street
London WC1B 3SR
England

Stay up to date with the latest books,
special offers, and exclusive content from
Oneworld with our monthly newsletter

Sign up on our website
www.oneworld-publications.com

FSC
www.fsc.org
MIX
Paper from
responsible sources
FSC® C018072

For my eldest niece, Emily West

Contents

Illustration Credits

Game of Chess, 1555, Anguissola, Sofonisba (c.1532–1625): Museum Narodowe, Poznan, Poland/Bridgeman Images.

Isabella of Castile, Ms 604/1339 f.64v King Ferdinand II of Aragon and Isabella of Castile, from the 'Devotionary of Queen Juana the Mad', c.1482 (vellum): Musee Conde, Chantilly, France/Bridgeman Images.

Anne de Beaujeu, detail of the right leaf of the Triptych of the Virgin in glory, 1498–1499, by Jean Hey or Hay (ca.1475–ca.1505), known as the Master of Moulins, sacristy of the church of Notre-Dame in Moulins, France: DeAgostini/Getty Images.

The Field of the Cloth of Gold: Wikimedia Commons.

Margaret of Austria, c.1490 (oil on oak panel), Master of Moulins (Jean Hey), (fl.c.1483–c.1529): Metropolitan Museum of Art, New York, USA/Bridgeman Images.

Manuscript miniature showing french queen Louise of Savoy: PVDE/Bridgeman Images.

Marguerite of Navarre, c.1527, by Jean Clouet (c.1485–1541), found in the collection of Walker Art Gallery: Fine Art Images/Heritage Images/Getty Images.

Margaret Tudor: Sir Francis Ogilvy/The National Library of Scotland.

Anne Boleyn, 1534 (oil on panel), English School: Hever Castle, Kent, UK/Bridgeman Images.

Katherine of Aragon: Universal History Archive/Getty Images.

Elizabeth I when a Princess, c.1546, attributed to William Scrots (1537–53): Royal Collection Trust/© Her Majesty Queen Elizabeth II 2016.

Queen Mary I (1516–58) 1554 (oil on panel), Mor, Anthonis van

Dashorst (Antonio Moro) (c.1519–1576/77): Prado, Madrid, Spain/ Bridgeman Images.

An Allegory of Tudor Succession: The Family of Henry VIII: Wikimedia Commons.

Mary of Guise (1515–1560), 1537, found in the collection of the National Gallery of Scotland, Edinburgh: Fine Art Images/Heritage Images/Getty Images.

Mary of Austria (a.k.a. Mary of Hungary), c.1520 (oil on vellum on panel), Maler, Hans or Johan (fl.1510–1523): Society of Antiquaries of London, UK/Bridgeman Images.

Margaret of Parma: Stedelijk Museum 'Het Prinsenhof', Delft, Netherlands/Lessing Images.

Jeanne d'Albret: Peter Horree/Alamy Stock Photo.

Catherine de Medici (1519–89) (oil on panel), French School: Musee Conde, Chantilly, France/Bridgeman Images.

François Dubois (1529–1584) – St. Bartholomew's Night, August 24, 1572: DEA/G. DAGLI ORTI/De Agostini/Getty Images.

Elizabeth I: His Grace the Duke of Bedford and the Trustees of the Bedford Estates, from the Woburn Abbey Collection.

Portrait of Mary Queen of Scots by François Clouet (1510–1572): World History Archive/Alamy Stock Photo.

Game of Queens: Who's Who

Spain and the Habsburg Empire

Isabella of Castile (1451–1504)

Queen Regnant of Castile from 1474, Isabella's marriage to Ferdinand II of Aragon (1452–1516) united the two main Spanish kingdoms. They famously ruled together as the mighty Catholic monarchs, producing only a short-lived son but several influential daughters. On Isabella's death Castile was inherited by their eldest surviving daughter, Juana 'the Mad' (1479–1555), but Ferdinand proved reluctant to lose his power in that kingdom.

Maximilian I, Holy Roman Emperor (1459–1519)

After his marriage to Mary of Burgundy (1457–1482), ruling duchess of what would later be known as the Netherlands, Maximilian's ambition was to unite as much of Europe as possible under the hands of his Habsburg family. The marriage of his son Philip of Burgundy (1478–1506) to Ferdinand and Isabella's daughter Juana produced (among other children) the future Charles V.

Margaret 'of Austria' (1480–1530)

Maximilian and Mary of Burgundy also had a daughter, Margaret. Contracted to the young French king Charles VIII, she was sent as a toddler to be raised in that country. When that alliance collapsed she married Isabella and Ferdinand's son and heir Juan and then, after his early death, the Duke of Savoy. But when he too died she returned to the Netherlands, which she ruled as regent for many years on behalf of her nephew Charles; the twelve-year-old Anne Boleyn was one of her maids.

Charles V (1500–1558)

Charles inherited the Austrian lands of his paternal grandfather Maximilian, as well as the elective title of Holy Roman Emperor, which Maximilian also held, the Burgundian inheritance of his father Philip (the Netherlands), the Castile of his mother Juana and the Aragon of his maternal grandfather Ferdinand, to say nothing of lands in the New World. He found the inheritance personally wearing and ultimately ceded the Austrian lands, power in Eastern Europe and eventually leadership of the Holy Roman Empire to his younger brother Ferdinand (1503–1564). This concentration of territories into the hands of one family established the Habsburg dominance of the sixteenth century.

Mary 'of Hungary' (1505–1558)

Another sibling of Charles V and Ferdinand, Mary was married to the King of Hungary until the Battle of Mohacs made her a youthful widow. She then held Habsburg power on Ferdinand's behalf against the advance of the Ottoman Turks. The niece of Margaret of Austria, who brought her up, she then became Margaret's successor as Regent of the Netherlands. Mary's three sisters all became queens consort: Eleanor (1498–1558) first of Portugal, then of France, Isabella (1501–1526) of Denmark, Norway and Sweden and Catherine (Catalina, 1507–1578) of Portugal, which she later ruled as regent.

Christina of Denmark (1521–1590)

Daughter of Isabella and her husband King Christian of Denmark, after her father was deposed Christina was raised by Isabella's aunt Margaret of Austria and sister Mary of Hungary. Married first to the Duke of Milan and then the Duke of Lorraine, she was considered as a possible bride for Henry VIII of England. She was a determined player on the European political scene, attempting to regain her father's Scandinavian kingdoms, and a key negotiator of the important Peace of Cateau-Cambrésis.

Margaret 'of Parma' (1522–1586)

The illegitimate daughter of Charles V, Margaret was also raised by Mary of Hungary, whom she in turn succeeded in 1555 as Regent of the Netherlands, ruling on behalf of her half-brother Philip of Spain. Her son Alexander Farnese, Duke of Parma, was Philip's great general.

Philip II (1527–1598)

Philip 'of Spain' was also hereditary ruler of the Netherlands, as well as the increasingly important New World territories. Early in his life, his marriage to Mary Tudor made him King Consort of England; late in it, he inherited Portugal, through his mother. He is of course famous, or infamous, for the Armada he sent against Elizabeth of England in 1588.

France

Anne de Beaujeu (Anne of France) (1461–1522)

The oldest daughter of the French king Louis XI (1423–1483), Anne acted as regent of France in all but name during the minority of her younger brother Charles VIII (1470–1498). A powerful and influential figure, author of a manual of advice for noblewomen that has been compared to Machiavelli's *The Prince*, she helped bring up both Margaret of Austria and Louise of Savoy.

Anne of Brittany (1477–1515)

Inheriting the independent duchy of Brittany from her father in 1488, Anne's hope was to preserve the independence of Brittany in the face of pressure from France. After some months of armed conflict, in 1492 she found herself forced to marry the young French king Charles VIII who, with the help of his sister Anne de Beaujeu, kept her largely powerless. By the terms of the marriage, she was forced on Charles's death to marry his successor, the next King of France, Louis XII (1462–1515).

Louise of Savoy (1476–1531)

Initially a poor relation of Anne de Beaujeu, Louise's status rose steadily as several French kings in succession died without heir until the closest in line to the throne was François, her son by the Count d'Angoulême. After François I (1494–1547) became king in 1515, Louise was widely regarded as the power behind his throne.

Marguerite of Navarre
(Marguerite d'Angoulême, 1492–1549)

As well as François, Louise also bore a daughter, Marguerite. The three were so close they were known as 'the Trinity'. Neither of Marguerite's two marriages (to the Duc d'Alençon and to Henri II of Navarre) impeded her devotion to her brother or her sway over his court. An author, an intellectual, and a reformer of the Catholic church, Marguerite may have been a role model for the young Anne Boleyn.

Bonnivet (Guillaume Gouffier,
Seigneur de Bonnivet 1488?–1525)

A soldier and nobleman, Bonnivet was raised in company with the future François I, whose tutor was Bonnivet's older brother, Artus Gouffier. Made Admiral of France in 1515, François's favour placed him in charge of a number of important military and diplomatic campaigns. He has been identified as the predatory hero of sections of Marguerite of Navarre's *Heptaméron*.

Catherine de Medici (1519–1589)

Daughter of the great Florentine banking family, with all too bitter a personal experience of the wars of the early sixteenth century,

Catherine's marriage to the future Henri II (1519–1559) made her Queen Consort of France. But only after Henri's death in 1559 did she became the powerful figure behind the three of her sons who successively occupied the French throne: François II (1544–1560), Charles IX (1550–1574) and Henri III (1551–1589).

Guise (Francis, Duc de Guise, 1519–1563, Henri, Duc de Guise, 1550–1558, and the Guise family)

Catherine de Medici's chief rivals for power in France were the members of the powerful Guise family. As uncles of the young Mary, Queen of Scots, the soldier duke Francis and his brother the Cardinal of Lorraine exercised particular influence over Mary and her husband, the French king François II. After Francis was assassinated in 1563 his son Henri became the leader of the Catholic faction in the French Wars of Religion.

Jeanne d'Albret (1528–1572)

The daughter of Marguerite 'of Navarre', in 1555 she inherited her father's Navarrese kingdom. Reared in her mother's reforming tradition, in 1560 she publicly converted to the Protestant faith and became the first great heroine of the Reformation. Her marriage to Antoine de Bourbon (1518–1562) produced a son, Henri of Navarre (1553–1610) who eventually became Henri IV of France.

Scotland

Margaret Tudor (1489–1541)

The older sister of Henry VIII, Margaret was married to James IV (1473–1513), the King of Scots, only to see him killed by her brother's army at Flodden, leaving her regent for her baby son, James V (1512–1542). Determined to hold on to power, Margaret was, nevertheless, insecure about her ability to wield it alone and made two futher disastrous marriages.

Angus (Archibald Douglas, sixth Earl of Angus, 1489?–1557)

Margaret Tudor married Angus as her second husband in 1514, perhaps to claim the support of his powerful Douglas clan. The marriage soon turned sour and Angus became one of Margaret's chief rivals for control of her son, the young king. The marriage also produced a daughter, Lady Margaret Douglas (Countess of Lennox, 1515–1578), whose bloodline produced the future monarchs of a united British Isles.

Albany (John Stuart, second Duke of Albany, 1481?–1536)

Reared in France, and married to a French heiress, Albany was, nonetheless, a grandson of the fifteenth-century King of Scotland, James II. He was thus an obvious choice to replace Margaret Tudor as regent for her infant son James V. He acted with considerable ability as Regent of Scotland from 1515 but never altogether came to terms with the country.

Marie de Guise (1515–1560)

A French noblewoman from the powerful Guise family, in 1538 Marie married James V of Scotland. He died in 1542, days after the birth of their only child, the future Mary, Queen of Scots. From that time Marie's life was dedicated to trying to preserve the Scottish throne for her daughter.

Arran (James Hamilton, second Earl of Arran and Duke of Châtelherault, 1519?–1575)

Arran's descent from an earlier Scottish king, James II, left him convinced he had the right to take a leading part in Scottish affairs. Vacillating (or perhaps pragmatic) after James V's death he nevertheless contended for power with Marie de Guise and was a thorn in the side of her daughter Mary Stuart.

James Stewart (first Earl of Moray, 1531/2–1570)

The illegitimate son of James V, Lord James had, before the return of his young half-sister Queen Mary, established himself in a position of power in Scotland; a position he had no desire to relinquish. A committed Protestant, he moved from being Mary's advisor to one of the agents of her downfall and regent for the son who replaced her.

Mary Stuart (Mary, Queen of Scots 1542–1587)

Queen of Scotland from her earliest infancy, Mary spent most of her youth in France, awaiting marriage to Catherine de Medici's eldest son, François. After his early death, she returned to Scotland in 1561 and set about trying to rule that turbulent country. Her mistakes are notorious and all male: Rizzio, Darnley and Bothwell. But just as significant in her final downfall and execution at Fotheringhay was the fact that her bloodline made her a Catholic rival for Elizabeth Tudor's English throne.

Darnley (Henry Stuart, or Stewart, Lord Darnley, 1545–1567)

The son of Lady Margaret Douglas, Margaret Tudor's daughter, Darnley thus had a claim to the English throne. This may be the rationale behind his marriage in 1565 to Mary, Queen of Scots. His personality soon showed Mary, however, that the marriage had been misguided, while his murder at Kirk o'Field besmirched her reputation and led indirectly to her overthrow.

Bothwell (James Hepburn, fourth Earl of Bothwell, 1534?–1578

The direct cause of Mary's downfall was her third marriage, to the Earl of Bothwell, made in May 1567 while Bothwell was still widely suspected of Darnley's murder. Mary's hand may have been forced by Bothwell's abduction and rape of her. Fleeing abroad after her defeat and deposition, he died a prisoner in Denmark, reputedly insane.

James VI (1566–1625)

The son of Mary, Queen of Scots and Lord Darnley, James (like several of his predecessors on the Scottish throne) was crowned while still in his cradle, his mother having been forced to abdicate. Reared in the harsh traditions of the Scottish reformed church, he was taught to see Mary as an example of bad management and perhaps womanly weakness. He was on good terms with Elizabeth I, upon whose death in 1603 he became James I, King of England.

England

Henry VII (1457–1509)

The first Tudor monarch won the crown of England at the Battle of Bosworth in 1485. His marriage to the Yorkist heiress Elizabeth united the Yorkist and Lancastrian claims, ending the Wars of the Roses but there seems, even on the Yorkist side, to have been no thought that Elizabeth of York could herself assume the crown. Marrying his heir Prince Arthur to Ferdinand and Isabella's daughter Katherine was a coup for his fragile new dynasty.

Katherine of Aragon (1485–1536)

The youngest daughter of Ferdinand and Isabella of Spain, she was first married to Henry VII's oldest son Arthur. After Arthur's early death, Katherine famously and controversially married Arthur's younger brother, Henry VIII. It was a love match that endured for over a decade into Henry's reign but foundered on her failure to give him a son.

Henry VIII (1491–1547)

Most widely known for his six wives and for the break with Rome to which his desire for a male heir led him, Henry was a Renaissance monarch. The rival of François I and Charles V, he was anxious to play a role on the wider European stage. His older sister Margaret was already married to the King of Scots when he came to the throne in 1509 but he arranged the marriage of his younger sister Mary (1496–1533) to Louis XII of France and tolerated her second marriage to his favourite Charles Brandon (Lord Lisle, Duke of Suffolk, 1484–1545).

Wolsey (Thomas, Cardinal 1473?–1530)

A meteoric rise through the ranks of the church brought Wolsey, a butcher's son, from humble origins to a pre-eminent position in the government of Henry VIII. Lord chancellor of England, and a cardinal after 1515, he exercised a controlling hand over the diplomacy of much of Henry's early reign, but fell as dramatically as he had risen over his failure to win Henry his divorce from Katherine of Aragon.

Cromwell (Thomas, 1485?–1540)

A protégé of Wolsey, Cromwell survived his master's fall and, from even more humble origins, rose to have his finger in even more of the nation's pies. A layman committed to religious reform, he was given unique powers over the nascent Church of England, which he used to mastermind the dissolution of the monasteries. Cromwell first supported and then broke with Anne Boleyn and was instrumental in her downfall. His own downfall came through another of Henry's wives, when the king turned against his fourth wife, Anne of Cleves whose marriage Cromwell had promoted.

Anne Boleyn (1501?–1536)

Anne was born in comparative obscurity. She was brought up, however, first under the tutelage of Margaret of Austria and then at the French court. Despite her disgrace and death on the scaffold, English Protestantism, and the reign of her daughter Elizabeth, are her enduring legacies.

Edward VI (1537–1553)

Henry VIII's third wife Jane Seymour at last gave him the longed-for son but Edward survived only six years after inheriting his father's throne at the age of nine. The zealous Protestantism of his reign culminated in the boy-king's attempt to will the throne not to either of his half-sisters, Elizabeth and Mary but to his second cousin Lady Jane Grey (1537–1554), the granddaughter of Henry VIII's younger sister Mary.

Mary Tudor (1516–1558)

The daughter of Katherine of Aragon and Henry VIII, Mary Tudor suffered acutely from the break-up of her parents' marriage, refusing to follow her father's move towards the reformed faith. She endured years of real hardship before, in 1553, the death of her younger brother Edward brought her to the throne. Once on it, however, her efforts to restore Catholicism, and her marriage to Philip of Spain, brought her the sobriquet 'Bloody' Mary.

Elizabeth Tudor (1533–1603)

Anne Boleyn's daughter had an equally difficult path to the English throne, for all that her long reign has left her remembered as our greatest monarch. History tells of her long rivalry with her kinswoman, Mary Stuart, across the Scottish border but it is less often that we think to see her in relation to other European female rulers.

Dudley (Robert, first Earl of Leicester, 1532–1588)

The son of the man who promoted Lady Jane Grey to the throne, Robert Dudley nevertheless became Elizabeth I's great favourite, some said her lover, and the longest-lasting contender for her hand in marriage. Her reputation and his suffered when his wife Amy Dudley died in suspicious circumstances but he remained her close advisor and friend.

Burghley (William Cecil, first Baron Burghley, 1520–1598)

The great statesman of Elizabeth Tudor's reign, Cecil became principal secretary of state immediately upon her accession and subsequently lord treasurer. Like his rival Dudley he was a committed

Protestant, urging the queen to aid her co-religionists in Europe and was a particularly determined enemy to the Catholic Mary, Queen of Scots.

Reformers

Martin Luther (1483–1546)

The German theologian and former monk is credited with having launched the Protestant Reformation when, in 1517, he reputedly nailed his Ninety-five Theses, complaints of corrupt practices within the Catholic church, to a church door in Wittenberg. His refusal to recant sparked a great divide in Europe but Luther's ideas (which still shared some key points of Catholic doctrine) would be superseded in many territories by a new and more severe generation largely made up of Swiss reformers.

John Calvin (1509–1564)

Best known as leader of the Protestant church in Geneva, Calvin was born in France but fled after a clampdown in 1534 forced a distinction between those seeking reform of the Catholic church and those at odds with its central tenets. The doctrines of what became known as Calvinism include the belief that the fate of each human soul is predestined and the absolute sovereignty of God in its salvation, without reference to ritual or good works.

John Knox (1513?–1572)

The Scottish reformer and firebrand, once sentenced to row the French galleys as a prisoner for his part in a rebellion, found life in English and European exile hardened his virulent anti-Catholicism. An outspoken critic of the Catholic Mary, Queen of Scots, his most famous work, *The first blast of the trumpet against the monstrous regiment of women*, set him also at odds with the Protestant Elizabeth Tudor.

England and Scotland

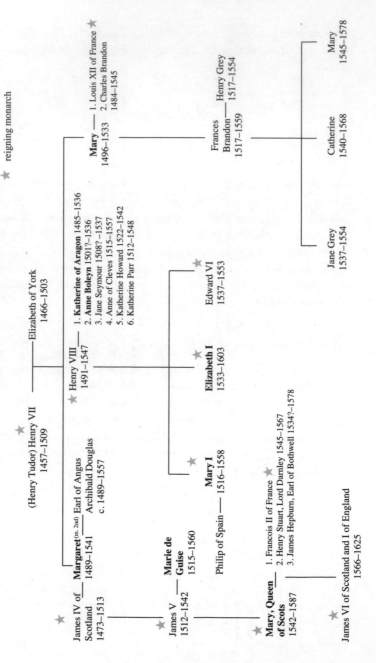

⭐ reigning monarch

France

Louis XI
1423–1483

Charles VIII
1470–1498

Anne de Beaujeau
1461–1522

1. Margaret of Austria
2. Anne of Brittany (m. 2nd)
1477–1514

Louis XII
1462–1515

Claude
1499–1524

François I
1494–1547

Louise of Savoy
1476–1531

Charles d'Orléans
1459–1496

Marguerite
1492–1549

1. Charles d'Alençon
1489–1525
2. Henri d'Albret (Henri II of Navarre)
1503–1555

Jeanne d'Albret (Jeanne III of Navarre)
1529–1572

Antoine de Bourbon
1518–1562

Henri III of Navarre (Henri IV of France)
1553–1610

Henri II
1519–1559

Catherine de Medici
1519–1589

François II
1544–1560

Mary, Queen of Scots

Charles IX
1550–1574

Henri III
1551–1589

Margot
1553–1615

Spain and the Habsburg Empire

★ reigning monarch

Maximilian I
1459–1516

Mary of Burgundy
1457–1482

Ferdinand of Aragon
1452–1516

Isabella of Castile
1451–1504

Margaret of Austria
1480–1530

1. Charles VIII of France
2. Juan of Spain (see right)
3. Philibert of Savoy
1480–1504

Philip of Burgundy
1478–1506

Juana of Castile
1479–1555

Juan
1478–1497

Margaret of Austria
1482–1517

Isabella — Manuel I
1470–1498   of Portugal

Eleanor — (m. 2nd)* Francois I of France
1498–1558

Isabella — Manuel I (m. 2nd) Maria
of Portugal   1482–1517

Katherine
1485–1536

Henry VIII
of England

Mary Tudor

Christian
of Denmark

Isabella
1501–1526

Ferdinand — Anne of Bohemia
1503–1563   & Hungary

Mary
1505–1558

Louis II
of Hungary

Charles V
1500–1558

Catalina — Juan III of Portugal
1507–1578

Isabella
of Portugal

Juana — Prince Juan
1535–1573   of Portugal

Christina of Denmark
1521–1590

(illegitimate)

Margaret of Parma
1522–1586

Philip of Spain
1527–1598

* Eleanor first married Manuel I of Portugal

Chronology

1474 December 11   Isabella I becomes Queen Regnant of Castile, succeeding her half-brother whose putative daughter, La Beltraneja, also claimed the throne.

1479 January 20   Isabella's husband Ferdinand becomes King of Aragon, succeeding his father. He and Isabella exercise effective joint rule as the 'Catholic Kings' of Spain.

1482 March 27   Mary, ruling Duchess of Burgundy, dies, to be succeeded by her young son Philip.

1483 August 30   Charles VIII becomes King of France, succeeding his father Louis XI. Charles's sister Anne de Beaujeu becomes regent in all but name during the thirteen-year-old's minority.

1486 February 16   Maximilian I (Maximilian of Austria), widower of Mary of Burgundy, is elected Holy Roman Emperor.

1491 December 6   Anne, the ruling Duchess of Brittany, is forced to marry the French king Charles, beginning what would become a permanent attachment of Brittany to France's interests.

1492   Ferdinand and Isabella conquer Granada (2 January) and end the Moorish rule of southern Spain, expel the Spanish Jews (31 March) at the demand of Grand Inquisitor Tomás de Torquemada and (17 April) sign an agreement with Italian navigator Christopher Columbus, allowing him to claim any new lands discovered on their behalf.

1498 April 7   Louis XII becomes King of France, succeeding his kinsman Charles VIII.

1504 November 26   Juana 'the Mad' becomes titular Queen Regnant of Castile, succeeding her mother Isabella. Her father Ferdinand and husband Philip of Burgundy contest control of the country.

1506 September 22   Philip of Burgundy dies, leaving his widow Juana to spend most of her life in incarceration and leaving control of Castile to Ferdinand of Aragon. Philip's Netherlands territories pass to his six-year-old son Charles.

1507 March 18   Margaret of Austria appointed Regent of the Netherlands for her nephew Charles.

1509 April 21   Henry VIII becomes King of England, succeeding his father Henry VII. He immediately marries Katherine of Aragon.

1513 September 9   The Battle of Flodden between England and Scotland. James IV of Scotland dies, to be succeeded by his infant son James V, whose mother Margaret Tudor is left as regent.

1515 January 1   François I becomes King of France, succeeding his cousin and father-in-law Louis XII.

1516 January 23   The death of Ferdinand leaves Aragon to his grandson Charles, already ruler of the Netherlands. On 14 March it is announced that Charles will assume rule of all Spanish territories, nominally sharing that rule with his incarcerated mother Juana, official Queen Regnant of Castile.

1517 October 31   Martin Luther posts Ninety-five Theses on the door of the Palast Church at Wittenberg, condemning corrupt practices in the Catholic church.

1519 June 28   Charles V is elected Holy Roman Emperor, succeeding his grandfather Maximilian.

1521 January 3	Pope Leo X (the first pope from the Florentine banking family, the Medici) excommunicates Martin Luther.
April 18	Luther appears before the Diet of Worms but refuses to recant.
April 8	Charles V gives control of his hereditary Habsburg Austrian lands to his brother Ferdinand (also his regent in the Holy Roman Empire) keeping control of his Spanish, New World and Netherlands territories himself.
1525 February 24	Battle of Pavia sees the crushing defeat of the French by Charles V's army and the capture of King François.
1526 August 29	Battle of Mohacs; the Ottoman army under Suleiman the Magnificent defeats the Hungarian forces, which causes the subsequent reorganisation of Hungary. The Turkish threat to the east becomes an ever-greater factor in European politics through the following decades.
1527 May 6	Rome plundered by imperial troops, Pope Clement VII (a second Medici pope, uncle of Catherine de Medici) is forced to flee. This has serious consequences for the papal inquiry into the validity of the marriage of Henry VIII to Katherine of Aragon.
1529 August 3	Ladies' Peace of Cambrai signed by Margaret of Austria (on behalf of her nephew Charles V) and Louise of Savoy (on behalf of her son François I).
October 1	The Marburg Colloquy, a discussion between Martin Luther and the more radical Swiss reformer Ulrich Zwingli, illustrates important theological differences between different branches of the new Reforming faith. The following year, 1530, sees the 'Protestant' princes of Germany form the Schmalkaldic

	League, a defensive alliance against the over-lordship of Holy Roman Emperor Charles V.
1531 January 3	Mary of Hungary requested by her brother Charles V to assume regency of the Netherlands, following the death of their aunt Margaret of Austria.
1533 ?January?	Henry VIII of England secretly marries Anne Boleyn, who is crowned queen 1 June before the birth of their daughter Elizabeth on 7 September.
1534 March 23	First Act of Succession secures the English succession to King Henry's children by Anne Boleyn and declares Princess Mary a bastard. In November, the Act of Supremacy declares Henry the 'only supreme head on earth' of the English church.
1536 January 7	Katherine of Aragon, Henry VIII's first wife, dies.
May 19	Anne Boleyn, Henry VIII's second wife, executed.
May 30	Henry VIII marries his third wife, Jane Seymour.
October 13	The Pilgrimage of Grace protests against Henry's break with Rome and the dissolution of the monasteries but is harshly repressed.
1542 April 15	James V of Scotland dies, to be succeeded by his infant daughter Mary, beginning the slow rise to power of James's widow Marie de Guise.
1545 December 13	Pope Paul III convenes the Council of Trent, the twenty-five sessions of which would be held off and on until 1563. The ecumenical council both consolidated the doctrines of the Catholic church and condemned those of Protestantism. This can be seen as the start of the Counter-Reformation.
1547 January 28	Henry VIII dies, succeeded as King of England by his son Edward VI.

March 31	Henri II becomes king of France, succeeding his father François I.
1553 July 6	The early death of Edward VI sees the throne pass for a mere nine days to Lady Jane Grey before being seized by Edward's half-sister Mary Tudor. Crowned as Mary I, she sets about returning England to the Catholic faith.
1555 May 25	Jeanne d'Albret becomes Queen Regnant of Navarre.
1555 October 25	Mary of Hungary resigns regency of the Netherlands.
1556 January 16	Charles V abdicates the crown of Spain to his son Philip II, to whom he had already handed over the Netherlands the previous October.
1558 November 17	Elizabeth I becomes Queen of England, succeeding her half-sister Mary.
1559 April 3	Treaty of Cateau-Cambrésis, orchestrated by Christina of Denmark, ends sixty-five years of intermittent warfare, much of it centring on rival claims to the Netherlands.
May 2	John Knox returns to Scotland from exile. In Geneva, where he had worked closely with John Calvin, he published the pamphlet *The first blast of the trumpet against the monstrous regiment of women*.
July 10	François II (husband of Mary, Queen of Scots) becomes King of France, succeeding his father Henri II. Rise to power of the Guise family.
1560 December 5	Charles IX becomes King of France, succeeding his brother François II. His mother Catherine de Medici assumes power during his minority, in rivalry with the Guises.
1561 August 9	Mary, Queen of Scots returns to her country to assume active rule.
1562 March 1	The Massacre of Vassy, the killing of French Protestants by the Duc de Guise's men, triggers the start of the French Wars of Religion.

1564 July 25	Maximilian II becomes Holy Roman Emperor, following his father Ferdinand.
1567 February 10	Lord Darnley, second husband of Mary, Queen of Scots, is murdered.
May 15	Mary marries Lord Bothwell, widely held responsible for Darnley's murder.
July 24	Mary is forced by her rebellious nobles to abdicate in favour of her infant son James VI.
September 5	The Duke of Alba, arriving in the Netherlands to put down iconoclastic riots, establishes the 'Council of Troubles'. Margaret of Parma resigns her regency and Alba's harshness signals the start of the long Dutch revolt against Spanish rule.
1568 May 16	Mary, Queen of Scots flees south over the border into England, to begin almost twenty years of captivity.
1571 October 7	The Battle of Lepanto gives a league of European Catholic powers a great naval victory against the Ottoman Turks.
1572 June 9	Jeanne d'Albret dies, to be succeeded as ruler of Navarre by her son Henri.
August 24	Celebrations for Henri of Navarre's marriage to Catherine de Medici's daughter, intended to heal religious divides, instead herald the terrible anti-Protestant slaughter of the Massacre of St Bartholomew's Day.
1574 May 30	Henri III becomes King of France, succeeding his brother Charles IX.
1581 July 26	Seven northern (and largely Protestant) provinces of the Netherlands formally declare independence from Spain.
1587 February 8	Mary, Queen of Scots is executed at Fotheringhay.
1588 August 8	The approach of the Armada fleet, sent by Philip of Spain against England, provokes Elizabeth I's address to the troops at Tilbury. Much of the fleet is destroyed by adverse weather.

| 1589 August 2 | Henri of Navarre becomes Henri IV of France, succeeding his kinsman and brother-in-law Henri III. This ends the line of Valois kings and brings in the Bourbon dynasty. |
| 1603 March 24 | Elizabeth I dies, leaving the throne of England to James VI of Scotland, Mary, Queen of Scots's son. |

Preface

The Queene is queint and quick conceit,
Which makes hir walke which way she list,
And rootes them up, that lie in waite
To work hir treason, ere she wist
Hir force is such, against her foes,
That whom she meetes, she overthrows.

The Chesse Play,
Nicholas Breton, 1593

I N   T H E   E A S T E R N lands where chess was first played, all the human figures were male, with the king flanked by his general or chief counsellor; his vizier. As the game spread through Europe, after the Arabs invaded in the eighth century, the queen first appeared but still as a comparatively impotent figure, able to advance only one diagonal square at a time. It was in the Spain ruled by Isabella of Castile that the chess queen took on the almost unbounded power of movement we accord her today.

Two books written in Spain in the last years of the fifteenth century describe these new powers, referring to 'lady's chess' or 'queen's chess'. True, in 1493 the Italian translator of Jacobus de Cessolis's *Game of Chess* queried whether the queen could really assume the knight's powers, 'because it is uncharacteristic of women to carry arms, on account of their frailty'. Two decades earlier, William Caxton's English translation had stressed above all else the queen's 'shamefastedness' and chastity.

But the translators can never have met the 'warrior queen' Isabella, herself an impassioned player of the game. It is probable that it was largely the example of Isabella and the real-life ruling women who came before her that finally provoked an echo on the board.[1]

The allegorical significance of the game was obvious to contemporaries: it was, as many an illustration can testify, this which had made it a staple of courtly love play. But the change of moves would not be without controversy. The new game became known as mad queen's chess – *scacchi de la donna* or *alla rabiosa* in Italian, *esches de la dame* or *de la dame enragée* in French. But it was here to stay.

The time from the accession of Isabella of Castile to the throne in 1474 to France's Massacre of St Bartholomew almost a century later (a horror which ruptured loyalties across the continent) was an Age of Queens. The period saw an explosion of female rule scarcely equalled in even the twentieth century. These years saw the birth of the new reformed religion, as well as the dawn of the world we know today and for much of them, large swathes of Europe were under the firm hand of a reigning queen or a female regent. This was a sisterhood which recognised both their bonds as women and their ability to exercise power in a specifically feminine way.

This book will follow the passage of power from mother to daughter, from mentor to protégée. From Isabella of Castile to her daughter Katherine of Aragon and from Katherine to her daughter Mary Tudor. From the French dowager Louise of Savoy to her daughter the writer and reformer Marguerite of Navarre; from Marguerite not only to her own daughter Jeanne d'Albret but to her admirer Anne Boleyn and thence Elizabeth Tudor.

As the century wore on, the daughters of the first powerful women found themselves at the forefront of the great religious divides that racked the sixteenth century. Most, though not all, attempted to exercise a measure of religious tolerance before those hopes foundered in the face of other, more extreme, opinions.

Religion helped bring many of them into prominence; religion, in the end, would drive them apart and bring the Age of Queens to an end. But the sheer scale on which the women of the sixteenth century exercised power (as well as the challenges they faced) remains both a spectacle and a warning to our own day.

Throughout the century the Habsburgs would prove doughty, if unexpected, promoters of female authority. With some notable exceptions, the Habsburg Empire, which in the course of the century came to stretch from the Mediterranean to the English Channel; from the glories of the Alhambra to the grey skies of Antwerp, knew women as regents, rather than as queens regnant. The Netherlands passed from the hands of a ruling duchess into those of an almost unbroken succession of authoritative female governors, each the niece of her predecessor, that endured for sixty years. The Habsburg's great rival in Europe – France – subscribed to the Salic Law, which forbad women from inheriting the throne. It had, however, a formidable tradition of women exercising rule on behalf of an absent husband or under-age son.

At the start of this era England was perhaps the least female-friendly of all the European powers. It had no Salic Law; yet when Henry Tudor became Henry VII of England, he subsumed into his claim the blood rights of two women: his mother Margaret Beaufort and his wife Elizabeth of York. No one, including the women themselves, seems to have found his action extraordinary. Yet it was England, of course, which saw a woman – Anne Boleyn – tip a nation into religious revolution. It was England which, in Anne's daughter, would go on to produce perhaps the most admired female ruler in history.

That, in a sense, is an impetus for this book. I have written about two royal Elizabeths – Elizabeth of York and Elizabeth I – and I want to join up the dots: to discover what lessons England had learnt in those seventy years that meant it could accept a queen regnant? (And, as a corollary, why did it then cease to do so?) The answer may lie in Europe.

The female rulers of Europe recognised bonds of sisterhood that crossed the borders, and sometimes even ran contrary to the interests, of their countries. They consciously invoked their status as women to conduct business in a different way. In 1529, the famous Ladies' Peace of Cambrai, a halt in the long war between Spain and France, was struck between Margaret of Austria, the Habsburg emperor's aunt and regent, and Louise of Savoy, mother of the French king. The princes might fear loss of honour in making peaceful overtures but (as Margaret wrote) 'ladies might well come forward' in such an undertaking.

This was an ideal which would echo through their century. There were a number of attempts, however abortive, to revive the idea of a ladies' peace in subsequent decades.[2] Sixteen years before Cambrai, in fact on the eve of the Battle of Flodden that cost her her husband, the King of Scots, Margaret Tudor had wished she might meet with her sister-in-law Katherine of Aragon, then ruling England while her husband Henry VIII was away: 'if we shall meet, who knows what God by our means may bring to pass?' Mary Stuart always hoped England and Scotland could find lasting peace, if only she and Elizabeth Tudor could meet.

The line of descent from mother to daughter, whether physical or spiritual, runs like an artery through sixteenth-century Europe. And the connections between the women form a complex web. Margaret 'of Austria', born the daughter of the ruling Duchess of Burgundy, was sent as a toddler to the French court, where she fell under the influence of the formidable Anne de Beaujeu and then, as a teenager, to the court of Castile, where she became Isabella's daughter-in-law and sister-in-law of Katherine of Aragon. She was then, as an adult, herself instrumental in bringing up Anne Boleyn.

But the powerful women in the later decades of the sixteenth century found themselves in a very different climate from that which their predecessors had enjoyed. Elizabeth I, at the end of this story, has many affinities with Margaret of Austria at the beginning; but while Margaret of Austria had lived in four realms by her early twenties, Elizabeth Tudor never set foot outside her own land. Neither woman bore a living child, yet Margaret would become known as 'La Grande Mère de l'Europe', while Elizabeth's preferred identity was famously that of virgin.

The Reformation drove fault lines across the continent, while conversely giving to some of these women a fame more enduring than they might otherwise have enjoyed. This book was born, though I didn't realise it, when as a teenager I read Garrett Mattingly's classic The Defeat of the Spanish Armada and noted his passing comment that in 1587, the year of the execution of Mary, Queen of Scots, sixty years had passed since the parties of religion had begun to form, the old versus the new, 'and always by some trick of Fate one party or the other and usually both, had been rallied and led by a woman'.

In the so-called gynocracy debate, concerning women's fitness for authority, two writers influenced the political thinking of the times to a degree that requires special mention. One, of course, was Niccolò Machiavelli, whose *The Prince* was first privately distributed in 1513. The second is Christine de Pizan, the French-Italian author and some would argue, early feminist: the first woman to become a professional writer. Her work of the early fifteenth century, *The Book of the City of Ladies*, had lost none of its relevance by the sixteenth century (or even, perhaps, the twenty-first), as the interest demonstrated by a number of women in this story goes to prove. Anne de Beaujeu and Louise of Savoy inherited copies of Christine's work, while Margaret of Austria's three-volume set would have passed to her niece, Mary of Hungary. Anne of Brittany and Margaret of Austria also owned suites of tapestries based on the *City of Ladies*, as did Elizabeth Tudor. All too aware of the clerical portrayal of women as Eve's daughters, weak and essentially untrust-worthy, Christine gives into the mouth of Justice a rebuttal of 'certain authors' who 'criticise women so much', pointing out that there is 'little criticism of women in the holy legends and the stories of Jesus Christ and his Apostles', despite what Christ's later servants might say.

Machiavelli, who portrayed fickle Fortune as a woman, saw war as a prince's first duty, as well as pleasure. By contrast, Christine's model of the virtuous ruler downplayed the ruler's role as warlord (a practical problem for the female ruler, leaving aside the question of any innately pacific tendencies) and stressed the 'prudence' which, in the Aristotelian concept, was the entry point of all the other virtues. Prudence was a virtue attributed to the majority of these women, and *The Book of the City of Ladies* made a point of describing a number of women from both ancient and more recent French history who had successfully governed nations or territories.

The continuity of experience – the repetition of tropes and patterns through the century – is something of a theme of this book. Most can be allowed to manifest themselves through the course of the narrative but one is so insistent as to require special note: the question of how frequently debate about these powerful women centres on their bodies. Each of these women would prove to have a role beyond the usual consort's function of a breeding machine but nonetheless the story abounds with questions of debated virginity and fertility, of women most easily attacked through querying their chastity or their desirability. Questions, even, as to whether the division of a sovereign's body natural and body politic might not be the best way to allow female rule. This was perhaps the idea behind Elizabeth I's famous speech at Tilbury: 'I know I have the body of a weak and feeble woman but I have the heart and stomach of a king . . .'

Though the forceful women of fifteenth-century Italy are sadly beyond the scope of this story, Caterina Sforza may be the most striking of 'the ones that got away' (as well as being another suggested as a model for the new chess queen). Machiavelli, who encountered Caterina when sent on an embassy, described how, besieged, with her children taken hostage, Caterina pulled up her skirts and showed the besiegers 'her genital parts', telling them she had the means to make more children if necessary. Caterina was perhaps unique even among contemporaries but nonetheless, the stress on a powerful woman's physicality is something that endures.

Modern comparisons are often invidious and will largely be excluded from this book. Nonetheless, at this of all moments, they cannot be ignored completely. A decade ago as I write – on 19 January 2006, to be precise – the *New York Times* paid an international group of women a backhanded compliment. It was, it said, 'the most interesting and accomplished group of female leaders' ever assembled – 'with the possible exception of when Queen Elizabeth I dined alone'.

A good deal has changed in the last ten years concerning women's role on the international stage. But a lot has *not* changed – and that includes the visibility of much of women's history. Elizabeth and her kinswomen apart, the female rulers of sixteenth-century Europe are not always familiar to the general reader in English-speaking countries. In the attempt to change that, this book must be regarded as an opening gambit. But one thing at least it can hope to do: prove that Elizabeth I could dine in some extraordinary company.

Author's Note

Of the sixteen protagonists in this book, four are called some version of 'Margaret' and another four variants of 'Mary'. I therefore make no apology for distinguishing them as clearly as possible, even at the cost of some consistency. Thus while Margaret of Austria keeps her natal title despite her three marriages, Marguerite 'of Navarre' is so described even before her marriage to the king of that small country. It is the title under which she is most familiar, the title under which her writings are still published today. Also in the interests of clarity, spelling, punctuation and capitalisation have sometimes been modernised.

PART I

1474–1513

'Since you have given women letters and continence and magnanimity and temperance, I only marvel that you would not also have them govern cities, make laws and lead armies...'

The Magnifico replies, also laughing:

'Perhaps even that would not be amiss ... Do you not believe that there are many to be found who would know how to govern cities and armies as well as men do? But I have not laid these duties on them, because I am fashioning a Court Lady, not a Queen.'

The Book of the Courtier, Baldassare Castiglione 1528

Entrance

The Netherlands, 1513

THE GIRL WHO arrived at the court of the Netherlands in the summer of 1513 was a courtier's daughter, bred to know the steps of the dangerous courtly dance; a life where assets were exchanged for attendance, where favour was won by flattery. She knew how the pageantry of a Christmas masque could spell a message, how a family's fortune could rise or fall on a ruler's whim and that in the great chess game of European politics, even she might have a part to play.

No one, of course, had yet any idea just how great a part that would be. She arrived as the latest of the eighteen maids of honour waiting on Margaret of Austria, the Regent of the Netherlands. At just twelve years old, she had been handed over to a stranger (one of the regent's esquires) and escorted from her manor house home in the Weald of Kent, in England, to make the rare journey across the sea. She would have been keyed up to a pitch of excitement, but scared, too, surely. Perhaps no arrival in her life, not even her arrival at the Tower of London more than twenty years later, would be quite as alienating as this one.

Twelve years old; or about that, anyway. We do not know the date of Anne Boleyn's birth with certainty. We deduce it, in fact, partly from the knowledge that she came to Margaret of Austria's court in 1513 and that twelve was the youngest age at which a girl would normally take up such duties.

'I find her so bright and pleasant for her young age that I am more beholden to you for sending her to me than you are to me', Margaret wrote to Anne's father. The tribute meant the more for the fact that

Margaret had herself served a European-wide political apprenticeship unparalleled even in the sixteenth century. At thirty-three, after six years ruling the Netherlands on behalf of her father Maximilian and his grandson, her nephew Charles, she was a figure of international authority. To follow the early career of Margaret of Austria is to read a *Who's Who* of sixteenth-century Europe. And Margaret would come to play a significant role in the lives of two of the most controversial queens in English history.

'Whatever you do, place yourself in the service of a lady who is well regarded, who is constant and who has good judgement', one of Margaret's mentors, the French governor Anne de Beaujeu, had advised in a manual of instruction for her daughter. If Anne Boleyn were to learn the lesson that a woman could advance ideas, exercise authority and control her own destiny, she could hardly have fallen into better hands.

The controversial German scholar Cornelius Agrippa dedicated *On the Nobility and Excellence of the Feminine Sex* to Margaret of Austria. Agrippa said the differences between men and women were merely physical: 'the woman hath that same mind that a man hath, the same reason and speech, she goeth to the same end of blissfulness, where shall be no exception of kind', and that the only reason women were subordinate was lack of education and masculine ill-will.

In schoolgirl French – French being the chosen language of Margaret of Austria's court – Anne Boleyn wrote to her father of her determination to make the most of her opportunities. She wrote with distinctly idiosyncratic grammar and spelling (she would strive, she wrote in that letter, to learn to speak French well 'and also spell') but under a tutor's eye. Margaret's court might be a centre both of power and of pleasure but it was also Europe's finest seminary. The French diplomat, Lancelot de Carles, later described how the young Anne 'listened carefully to honourable ladies, setting herself to bend all her endeavour to imitate them to perfection and made such good use of her wits that in no time at all she had command of the language'.

Portraits of the woman Anne Boleyn met in 1513 display a subtle mixture of messages. Since the end of her third and last marriage, Margaret of Austria had made a point of having herself painted always in a widow's coif, with only the white of the headdress and the sleeves of her costume relieving the inky black. At first sight, no more sombre figure could be imagined. But appearances can be deceptive. To appear as a widow was on the surface a statement of self-abnegation, almost of weakness, a plea for pity. But in fact it allowed a woman both moral and practical authority; the only role that allowed her to operate independently, as neither child nor chattel.

In heraldry, black was the colour of trustworthiness, or '*loyaute*'. Margaret of Austria had a name for reliability but one Italian visitor noted that as well as 'a great and truly imperial presence', she had 'a certain most pleasing way of laughing'. Black fabric, which needed much expensive dye and labour to produce its depth of colour, was the luxury material of the sixteenth century. And in the portrait, now in Vienna, the pale fur on Margaret's sleeves is costly ermine. The court to which Anne Boleyn had come, whether at the summer palace of Veure (La Veuren), or at Margaret's main base of Mechelen, was a place of culture and luxury. Among the illustrated books Anne Boleyn could have seen in Margaret's library was the already-famous *Trés Riches Heures du Duc de Berry* (a legacy from Margaret's last husband), as well as newer books decked with flowers in the margins. Anne would later exchange notes with Henry VIII in the margins of just such a book.

Erasmus was just one of the artists and thinkers Margaret of Austria welcomed to Mechelen. Outwardly large, but by palace standards an unostentatious, brick-built house, Margaret's home was a place where devotional works jostled Renaissance nudes. A *mappa mundi* that Van Eyck had made for her great-grandfather, Philip the Good, sat beside more recent acquisitions. One was what Margaret's inventories describe as '*Ung grant tableau*' (a large picture) '*qu'on appelle, Hernoul-le-fin*'; what is now called the Arnolfini portrait. This had, said her inventories of 1516, 'been given to Madame by Don Diego'. Don Diego de Guevara, a Spaniard who had come into the service of Margaret's family, was another courtier with a young female relation to place in the ducal household and the Arnolfini portrait ('*fort exquis*', exquisite, as one of Margaret's later inventories describes it) may have been a token of his gratitude and a sign of just how highly these places were sought.

Mechelen's walls were hung with blue and yellow damask, with green taffeta, or with Margaret's legendary collection of the tapestries for which the Netherlands was famous. Later, after the conquistador

Cortés returned from Mexico, Margaret's collection included Montezuma's feather cloak, Aztec mosaic masks and a stuffed bird of paradise. As a northern pioneer of the kind of cabinet of curiosities beloved of Italian patrons, she employed a curator and two assistants to look after her collection.

Those in charge of young girls, Anne de Beaujeu wrote, should:

> make sure they serve God, hear the Mass every day, observe the Hours and other devotions, pray for their sins, go to confession and frequently give alms. And to console them and enliven their youth and the better to maintain their love for you, you must sometimes let them frolic, sing, dance and amuse themselves happily but honestly, without groping, hitting, or quarrelling.[1]

A *fille d'honneur* had no specific duties, which makes it all the likelier that Anne would have witnessed and perhaps participated in Margaret of Austria's pleasures. Margaret kept close by her a paintbox, covered in purple velvet and disguised as a book, which she herself used frequently. Music was another important recreation. Her choir was legendary and she herself was a notable keyboard performer and composer of songs. The masses, motets and *chansons* in her music books were by the composers Anne herself later favoured when her interest in music formed a bond with Henry VIII.

Margaret also played chess for recreation, with sets of chalcedony and jasper, and silver and gilt. (Her godmother, Margaret of York, who owned Mechelen before her, had kept volumes on chess in the study she hung with violet taffeta.) But Margaret of Austria played the same game also on a wider stage, as, in the years ahead, would Anne Boleyn.

The thriving, merchant-led community of the Netherlands had a tradition of social mobility. The Arnolfini portrait features not an aristocratic but an aspirational merchant couple. This too, perhaps, was not without its effect on Anne. The Boleyns themselves, you might say, were an example of English social mobility. Not that Anne came from such humble stock as has often been claimed. There was merchant money in the Boleyn family but it was Anne's great-grandfather who had made the family fortune and become Lord Mayor of London. In the go-getting Tudor age many great families had connections closer than hers with trade. Anne was better-born than two of Henry's other wives; her mother was a scion of the mighty Howard family, eldest daughter of the Earl of Surrey, later Duke of Norfolk and her father, Thomas, had a connection to the Irish earldom of Ormonde and his mother was heiress to half the Ormonde fortune.

But Thomas's career in royal service began as a comparatively impe-cunious young man on the make. He rose rapidly, however. He was present when Katherine of Aragon was married to Henry VII's heir in 1501 and was one of the escort that took the king's eldest daughter Margaret Tudor to marry the King of Scots in 1503. By the time Henry VIII came to the throne in 1509 Thomas Boleyn was in his early thir-ties, perhaps a little too old to be one of the king's close cronies but as an accomplished man at the joust, as well as a linguist and a clever courtier, the sort of man Henry was glad to have about him.

In 1512 Thomas was sent on his first diplomatic mission, to the court of Margaret of Austria. Anne Boleyn's appointment there was proof of how well, in the course of a ten-month stay, the two had got on. There is a record of them shaking hands on a bet that they could advance in their negotiations in ten days, both wagering different types of horse: her Spanish courser against his hobby. In her letter to Thomas about Anne's progress Margaret told him that if the young girl went on as well as she was doing, then 'on your return the two of us will need no intermediary other than she'.

Beyond a general, faintly sexualised, reference to her cosmopolitan gloss and Frenchified ways, Anne's early experience abroad does not perhaps feature as strongly as it should in our understanding of her. She is more usually placed against a background of Hever, the lovely fortified manor house in the Weald of Kent bought and remodelled by her great-grandfather and inherited by her father Thomas in 1505. Hever is where she spent most of her childhood. There – preparing to go abroad for what was always likely to be a stay of years – she would have walked around the ravishing springtime orchards and gardens, taking, with an intelligent adolescent's intensity, a last look.

But though Mechelen too, under Margaret's rule, had fine gardens aplenty, the contemporary image of court life dwelt on the snares and tares amid the plants. The Tudor rising classes both feared and needed the court. It was the only place where real secular preferment might be won but also the place where any slip of tongue or tactics, any over-weening ambition or misplaced allegiance, could be, quite literally, fatal. This was the world into which Anne Boleyn was sent by her rela-tions, aimed like any missile.

On the one hand she was there as her family's agent and ambassador, as surely as her father was England's. On the other, what would this long separation do to her relationship with that family? She would at times be in company with her father and other family members in the decade ahead, when their careers brought them, too, across the Channel. But for long periods she must often have been forced on her own resources. In later years she was perceived as not showing a proper womanly reliance on the guidance of her family – the wider Howard clan – but after this decade largely on her own recognisance, why should she?

At the court, where Margaret of Austria consulted with her council every day, Anne – with the wits, the determination and above all the power of observation de Carles noticed – surely learnt more than the French tongue. She might have observed a woman exercising power and perhaps even, within careful confines, enjoying her sexuality.

For there was another lesson Anne Boleyn could have learnt in Margaret's glamorous, cultivated sphere. The Netherlands (the old Burgundian) court was home to all the pageantry and parade of courtly love; that great game of sexual role playing that dominated upper-class Europe for three centuries and still influences us today.* This too was a game Anne learnt how to play.

'Sir', Anne wrote to her father, 'I understand from your letter that you desire me to be a woman of good reputation [toufs onette fame] when I come to court . . .' But the lessons she could learn at Mechelen were many and varied. The English court had long borrowed its best

---

* The duchy of Burgundy had come to comprise not only the southerly territory we today think of as Burgundy but also much of modern Belgium and Holland. Since the original 'Burgundy' was indeed almost immediately to be yielded to France under the terms of Margaret of Austria's marriage treaty, it will be more convenient to speak at once of 'the Netherlands'. These Netherlands would themselves be split into the Catholic Spanish Netherlands and the seven independent Protestant provinces before the end of the sixteenth century.

ideas from Burgundy. On the one hand, Margaret maintained a strict etiquette. Anne and her fellow maids were guarded carefully. On the other, Margaret wrote a poem for her young attendant ladies, warning them against taking the game too seriously:

> Trust in those who offer you service,
> And in the end, my maidens,
> You will find yourselves in the ranks of those
> Who have been deceived.

A girl's best defence lay in wit and confidence. 'Fine words' were a game that two could play. It was, of course, a game in which Anne Boleyn became the expert and which no one in Europe played more significantly.

Margaret, for all her widow's wear, allowed those around her to play the game of courtly love to an extent that could indeed be misunderstood by those from a less flexible culture. But – as events would shortly prove – Margaret knew when it was time to stop. Anne Boleyn should have taken heed.

Fifteen years later, Europe would hear of Anne Boleyn as the rival of Katherine of Aragon, Queen of England and Margaret of Austria's former sister-in-law. Theirs was a struggle in which the power of personality (and of personal appeal) was just another side of the coin to questions of policy.

Anne's time at the courts of the Netherlands, and later France, gave her the cosmopolitan polish that so captivated Henry VIII. But it also made her Katherine's match in another sense. To watch a woman exercising power, in a way still unfamiliar to England, gave Anne a taste of the kind of European training Katherine herself had enjoyed as the daughter of Isabella, the Queen Regnant of Castile.

The story of Anne Boleyn and Katherine of Aragon, and of their daughters, was part of a much larger European picture. In the years ahead the royal women of the British Isles would be woven, or sometime weave themselves, into a web of rivalry and mutual reliance with Habsburg, Valois and Medici women every bit as colourful as they. But to understand *that*, it is first necessary to briefly look at the decades that went before.

2

'Lessons for my Daughter'

Spain, France, 1474–1483

THE THIRTEENTH OF December 1474; the day after Isabella of Castile received news of King Enrique, her half-brother's, death. She entered the great church of Castile's capital, Segovia, dressed in plain mourning white; she emerged, after the Mass, decked with jewels and blazing with colour. In the porch, on a hastily built platform draped in brocade, she was proclaimed Castile's queen. Isabella would become the first, and more famous, of two women who would set a precedent for the female rulers of the sixteenth century.

As the coronation procession wound its way through the streets, Isabella of Castile rode on horseback, with nobles on foot bearing the train of her gown. Ahead of her went a lone horseman holding a drawn sword pointing upwards; the traditional symbol of kingship. When he heard the news, in distant Zaragosa, even Isabella's husband Ferdinand of Aragon was shocked that she had taken to herself the symbolic sword. His advisors had assured him he could tame his wife 'by satisfying assiduously the demands of conjugal love'. But Ferdinand protested in horror that he had never heard of a queen who usurped this masculine attribute.

After five years of marriage, Ferdinand should have known his Isabella better. She had, after all, broken with precedent in herself arranging her marriage to him. The heir to a neighbouring kingdom edging the Pyrenees, he was a useful ally in Isabella's battle for her own disputed throne.

Isabella was not born to inherit Castile. There were two male heirs ahead of her; first her half-brother, Enrique, and then her full brother,

Alfonso. But when Enrique succeeded to the throne with no sign of a child to follow him, and when Alfonso died suddenly during Enrique's reign, Isabella's position changed. It was then she made her alliance with Ferdinand, with the terms of the marriage ensuring that she would continue to outrank him in Castile. He was an experienced soldier who could fight her battles, as well as sire her children. A match made on practical grounds, it was nonetheless to become one of the most famously successful partnerships in Christendom.

Ferdinand's potential as stud was proven, although when Isabella took the throne the couple had only a daughter, not a son. His abilities as a soldier were also to prove useful, since Isabella was not the only candidate for queen regnant of Castile. Her sister-in-law, Enrique's wife, had eventually born a daughter, Juana, although rumour said she was sired by a lover, Béltran, rather than by Enrique. That gave Isabella the chance to stake her own claim above that of the child, 'la Beltraneja', who would eventually retire defeated to a convent, while still in her teens. In 1470s Spain (as in England, some seventy years later) the twists of heredity decreed that it would be two women disputing a throne – and worth querying whether or not a woman trying to challenge a man would still have won her victory. But Isabella had also received the sanction of one theoretician, Fray Martin de Cordoba, in his *Jardin de nobles doncellas*:

> Some people, My Lady . . . take it badly when a kingdom or other
> state comes under the rule of a woman. But, as I will explain below,
> I disagree, since, from the very beginning of the World to the
> present, we see that God always gave women responsibility for
> humanity's salvation, so that life would emerge from death.

The struggle against the supporters of la Beltraneja (the War of the Castilian Succession) went on for another five years and it was almost the end of the 1470s before Ferdinand and Isabella could feel sure of Castile. By this time Isabella had also borne a son, Juan. Three more daughters would follow: Juana, Maria and Katherine.

The crusade was now to drive out the Moors, who had for many years colonised Spain's southern tip. Contemporaries varied in their opinions as to whether Ferdinand or Isabella was the most significant partner in their alliance, after Ferdinand succeeded his father in 1479. Despite the marriage agreement, Ferdinand had more authority in Isabella's kingdom than she did in his. (Ferdinand's Aragon was, unlike Castile, governed by a variant of the Salic Law that prohibited female rule although it did, unlike that prevailing in France, allow inheritance through the female line.) But her territory was by far the larger and richer and a Venetian diplomat said that she was the one most spoken of.[1]

Ferdinand and his advisors took some time to accept this unusual situation but in the end the pair did much to live up to their famous slogan: that they would 'command, govern, rule and exercise lordship as one'. Their motto was *'Tanto monta, monta tanto, Isabel como Ferdinand'* – to stand as high, as high to stand, Isabel as Ferdinand.

Famously, Isabella of Castile accompanied her armies to the battle-field – clad in armour and mounted on a warhorse – if not actually into the fray. She was an efficient organiser of supply and provisions, and of armaments, recruiting thousands of workmen to build roads along which the guns could pass. A mobile hospital comprising six huge tents was another of her innovations but her contribution was signifi-cant in two other ways. The first was the talismanic importance she had for her soldiers, so that her presence was said to spur on the Castilian troops to certain victory. (Interestingly, the troops cried out for 'King' Isabella.) The second was as a tactician but Isabella's role can be hard to assess with certainty, since in military matters she was care-ful to defer to her husband, at least publicly.

Isabella did not hesitate to take her daughters with her from one siege to another but it was her son Juan, and he alone, who was given the training of a future ruler. Isabella (like Elizabeth Tudor after her) may have regarded herself as an exception to the usual role allocated to women, as opposed to seeking a general expansion of that role. But nonetheless, as the fifteenth century drew towards its close, hers was a formidable example of female monarchy.

In 1483 another woman came to join Isabella at the forefront of European politics: Anne de Beaujeu, ruling France on behalf of her thirteen-year-old brother, the new king. France had a tradition of royal women assuming responsibility on behalf of a male relative. Christine de Pizan's *City of Ladies* had been written, at the beginning of the century, as an argument that an earlier French queen, Isabeau of Bavaria, should be allowed to act as regent during her husband's bouts of insanity. (The *City of Ladies*, moreover, figured the Virgin Mary as exercising a regent's powers on behalf of her heavenly son.)

Born in 1461, Anne de Beaujeu (also known as Anne of France) could never have succeeded to the throne, because France subscribed to the Salic Law. Instead she had, at thirteen, been married to a brother of the Duc de Bourbon, a gentle soul twenty-one years older than herself. Anne, at twenty-two, had escaped damage from the inbreeding which weakened so many of her family. Her father Louis XI had called her 'the least foolish of women'; refusing to admit that there could be a clever one. And on his death he broke with tradition by giving her (and, nominally, her husband) charge of the young king Charles VIII, in preference to the normal combination that would have included his widow, the boy's mother, as guardian and his male relatives forming a regency council. Instead, Louis's widow, Queen Charlotte, was forbidden to have any contact with her son.

Though the Salic Law debarred women from inheriting, or even transmitting, a claim to the throne, in one sense it favoured female authority in a limited sphere. As one contemporary writer, Jean de Saint-Gelais, put it, the person of an under-age king should be placed in the hands 'of those nearest to him who are not entitled [*non capables*] to succeed'. It might seem less dangerous to give a measure of authority to a woman, since there could be no question of her snatching the final authority of monarchy itself, than to a male relative.

Anne de Beaujeu – '*Madame la Grande*' – was a controversial figure, a true daughter of the father she revered.[2] Louis had, not without cost to his people, done much to increase the power and the territories of the French crown. Anne was likewise undoubtedly able, working within the confines of a position that was not always easy. One contemporary called her a 'virago . . . a woman truly superior to the female sex . . . who did not cede to the resolution and daring of a man'. She would have been born to the height of sovereignty 'had nature not begrudged her the appropriate sex'.

Time and again, exceptional women would be praised as being hardly women at all and would sometimes seem to accede to the verdict themselves. Christine de Pizan described herself, when widowed, as metamorphosed into a man to provide for her family. But it was noted of Anne de Beaujeu that one of her most effective techniques was not to flaunt her position, being content usually to operate from behind the scenes.

She was also a notable chess player.

The volume of advice, *Enseignements* ('Lessons for my Daughter') that Anne wrote later in life warns a girl: 'you should have eyes to notice everything yet to see nothing, ears to hear everything yet to know nothing and a tongue to answer everyone yet to say nothing prejudicial to anyone'. Keep your own counsel, she wrote, about 'that which can affect your honour', unless 'it is something that strains your heart to conceal'; and then confide only inside the family.

Anne advocated the virtues urged on women – piety and docility – but less for their own sake, if you look closely, than as a technique. Perhaps this is why the *Enseignements* has been compared to Machiavelli's *The Prince*. The perfections and the ploys urged on men and on women may be different but each volume comes from the pen of a writer who sees virtue as a tool.[3]

In the century ahead, France would see several notable instances of a woman's authority coming from women who, directly or indirectly, had profited from Anne de Beaujeu's example. Both Anne and Isabella of Castile were cited when successful women rulers were discussed in Baldassare Castiglione's famous *Book of the Courtier* (published in Venice in 1528), for both would prove to have an influence which extended far beyond their own lands.

3

Youthful experience

The Netherlands, France, 1483–1493

MORE IMMEDIATELY, BOTH Anne de Beaujeu and Isabella of Castile were mentors to another significant woman: Margaret of Austria. Margaret would grow up to be the third example of a successful female ruler cited by Castiglione. But Margaret was only a child when in 1483 she, like another young girl, Louise of Savoy, with whom as an adult she would sit across a conference table, came into Anne de Beaujeu's care.

Margaret's mother Mary, the ruling Duchess of Burgundy, had inherited that territory from her father Charles 'the Bold' in the cold early spring of 1477. The nineteen-year-old Mary faced huge challenges. As soon as her father died, the French king, Louis XI, laid claim to a significant part of her lands, while the city-states of Flanders seized the chance to claim ever more autonomy. But Mary had support in the form of her stepmother, Charles's widow, Margaret of York; sister of the English king, Edward IV, and the future king, Richard III. Together, the two women acted to resist the French invaders. They reached an accommodation with the Netherlands parliament, the Estates General, although not before the Estates had arrested and brutally executed some of the two women's most trusted advisors. And they were able to bring about Mary's long-planned marriage to Maximilian, Archduke of Austria and son of the Holy Roman Emperor.*

---

* The ancient title of Holy Roman Emperor – though it had for the last century been held by members of the Habsburg family – was an elective office for which the rulers of

The marriage took place the same summer and was blessed with two healthy children: Margaret 'of Austria' and her brother Philip. But in March 1482, Mary of Burgundy died after a riding accident. On a domestic level, Mary left her children to the care of her stepmother, Margaret of York. Duchess Mary had written of her stepmother that she had always held 'our person and our lands and lordships in such complete and perfect love and goodwill that we can never sufficiently repay and recompense her' and the younger Margaret – god-daughter to the elder – would come to feel the same way. But the ducal family of Burgundy was royal in all but name and for royal children, and especially royal girls, things were never that easy.

Duchess Mary willed her lands to her children, with the regency to be held by her husband Maximilian during their minority. But the degree to which the Netherlanders were prepared to accept foreign Habsburg dominance would be a growing source of conflict. The city of Ghent wrested away Maximilian the right to bring up the young Philip, the new Duke of Burgundy. As for little Margaret of Austria, two days before Christmas 1482 the Treaty of Arras, which made peace between France and Burgundy, promised her in marriage to the thirteen-year-old Charles VIII, soon to be King of France under his sister Anne's care. Territories such as Mâcon became the property of France as Margaret's dowry, on condition that she should not make any further claims on her mother's lands. She, of course, was too young to object. Her father – ambitious, aggressive and intensely hostile to France's expansionism – was furious at seeing the lands given away. But Maximilian was cut off from power in his dead wife's lands by a regency council appointed to take control during his son's minority.

Just a year after her mother's death, resplendent in adult black velvet and pearls, the three-year-old Margaret was sent towards France, escorted to the border by a great retinue. Only a tiny handful, however, was allowed

---

Europe could compete. Created for Charlemagne in 800, it carried special responsibility for, and prestige within, the Catholic church; a secular counterpart of the pope's religious authority. It also, crucially, carried with it not only overlordship of the conglomeration of ecclesiastical and temporal principalities which made up Germany but also an ever-shifting degree of influence in certain other areas, most notably Italy. The Empire was not abolished until the Napoleonic era.

to remain with her as she was carried through France on a triumphal progress. Margaret was met at the border by Anne de Beaujeu, whose status, as a mere daughter during her father's reign, was still lower than Margaret's. The three-year-old Margaret was given a ceremonial entry into Paris, where just two months earlier Anne had been denied one.

On 22 June 1483, at the Loire chateau of Amboise that would become her principal residence, Margaret of Austria met and was formally engaged to her prospective husband, to whom, indeed, she was officially married the next day. She was now Dauphine of France. Two months later, on 30 August, old King Louis XI died. Margaret became, nominally, France's queen and Anne de Beaujeu became effectively its ruler; not merely guardian of the young king but the country's regent in all but name.

Anne de Beaujeu's assumption of power met with resistance. One of her concerns was that the disgruntled French nobles would try to kidnap the young king. Conversations reported between France's princes spoke of sending Anne back to her household duties. But, slowly, she won most of the dissenters round, to ratify a status quo which, while declaring that in his early teens Charles VIII was sufficiently mature not to require a regency, yet left Anne and her husband in control of his person.[1]

One noble not won round, however, was the Duc d'Orléans, who might otherwise have expected to lead a regency council. A kinsman of the king, he was moreover married to Anne's humpbacked younger sister, Jeanne. The match had been made in cynicism by the old king who hoped thus to keep the ambitious d'Orléans without heir, saying callously that 'any children they have will not cost them much to keep'.

In the winter of 1484–85, offering to free the young king Charles from his sister Anne's 'clutches', d'Orléans launched a rebellion. Anne de Beaujeu and the royal forces successfully put it down, always with the young king as their figurehead, to mask the unpalatable thought of a woman leading a military campaign. D'Orléans's wife Jeanne (like Anne de Beaujeu a daughter of the dead King Louis) sided with her sister against her husband, while their mother Queen Charlotte, King Louis's widow, sided with d'Orléans. But it was time to curb the ambitions of the Orléans clan through any means available. One means was marriage, made easier by the fact that Anne de Beaujeu was bringing up not only Margaret of Austria but a number of other aristocratic girls whose families were bound to her by ties of influence or family.

One such girl was the eight-year-old Louise of Savoy, later Margaret of Austria's adversary and ally, now a pawn to be deployed against the d'Orléans clan. Louise was born in 1476, the daughter of a younger son of the Duke of Savoy, a man his contemporaries knew as '*Monsieur sans terre*' (Mr Lackland). Her mother dying when she was seven, Louise (and her younger brother Philibert) went to be raised by Anne de Beaujeu, a cousin on her father's side as well as her aunt by marriage on her mother's.

In this extensive family, Louise of Savoy was very far from being an important member, and was certainly treated in a very different way than Margaret of Austria. While Margaret's household accounts record a queenly entourage: twenty ladies and six lords in waiting, chaplain and treasurer, physician and secretaries, ponies and parrots, falcons and hounds, clothing even for her dolls, those around her had a significantly lower status. Louise was given eighty *livres* a year to buy a court gown for state occasions. Who would have guessed Margaret and Louise would one day meet as equals across the conference table?

Louise of Savoy had, since she was two years old, nominally been betrothed to Charles d'Angoulême, a junior scion of the d'Orléans family almost twenty years older than she. Being tied to the penniless Louise was – another humiliation for her – a way for the French king Louis to clip the d'Orléans's wings. When in 1487 Angoulême followed the example of his kinsman by joining another rebellion (an attempt so abortive it was known as the 'Mad War') he was ordered, by way of curbing his ambitions, to proceed with the marriage to Louise, on terms very favourable to the young bride. The ceremony went ahead on 16 February 1488. A surviving letter from Louise's peripatetic father, making a rare appearance at her side, displays the eleven-year-old's concerns.

Her father wrote jocularly to his own new wife that Louise had questioned him about the wedding night in a way that showed her eagerness. But a look at the context of the phrase reveals a darker story:

> my daughter says that she is still too narrow and she does not know whether she might die of it; so much so that she asks every day

how big and how long his thing is and whether it is as big and long as her arm, which shows that she is already itching to be at the business of you other old married women . . .

When she was finally sent to live with her husband, in his château in the Loire valley and Cognac, Louise of Savoy had to come to terms with the facts that Charles d'Angoulême's establishment was ruled by his mistress, the daughter of one of his officials, Jean de Polignac, and that his illegitimate children by several women would be reared with Louise's own. Angoulême's mistress, however, appears to have taken his young wife under her wing and Louise accepted her friendship; Anne de Beaujeu's lessons in discretion and pragmatism had been well-learned. There were compensations. Louise had been raised in a family that valued books and the cultured Charles possessed a notable two hundred or more volumes. His library held romances, theological texts, Boethius and Ovid and the works of the ubiquitous Christine de Pizan, while his court was home to artists, notably the illuminator Robinet Testard, and men of letters such as the Saint-Gelais brothers.

But every aristocratic girl learnt one lesson: that to raise her status in her husband's household, she needed a male heir. Just three years into her marriage, still a young teenager but already concerned, Louise turned to a saintly hermit to pray for fertility. He reassured her not only of her prospect of bearing a son but also (she later said) of that son's glorious prospects.

The following year, 1492, Louise gave birth to a girl, Marguerite but in 1494 there followed the all-important boy. As Louise's *Journal* later had it: 'François, by the Grace of God, King of France, my pacific Caesar took his first sight of the light of day at Cognac, about ten hours after midday 1494, the 12th day of September.'[2]

Change had also come, by now, for the most prominent of Louise of Savoy's playmates. In 1491, Margaret of Austria's secure and indulged life as Queen of France came to an abrupt end. The important dukedom of Brittany had, three years before, been inherited by a young ruling duchess, just as Margaret's mother Mary had inherited the duchy of Burgundy. Anne of Brittany was not yet twelve when she inherited but she was, nonetheless, determined to rule. In pursuit of that aim, she had undergone a proxy marriage ceremony with Margaret of Austria's father Maximilian, decades her senior but delighted to be thus striking a blow against the hated French, and one that would give the Habsburgs, with territory both to France's east and west, something of a stranglehold on that country.

But Anne de Beaujeu, still a dominant force in France, had other plans for Brittany. She was determined to annexe the duchy, whether by force of arms, or in some other way. Anne of Brittany was persuaded – or forced by the French troops encircling her borders – to renounce Maximilian and marry Charles VIII but it was noted the ceremony had no show of joy. (Hardly likely, perhaps, after the bride was, allegedly, forced to parade naked in front of her groom's advisors to demonstrate her fitness for child-bearing.) Charles's existing marriage to Margaret of Austria was annulled; not an unusual arrangement when a match made between two minors was unconsummated.

Margaret of Austria had been dumped for a richer heiress; the victim of France's quarrel with her father Maximilian. She was, nonetheless, kept in France for another two years; there was, after all, the question of what would happen to the dowry lands she had brought with her. Eventually, in May 1493, by a new treaty, her father Maximilian won them back but in the meantime Margaret had been moved out of royal Amboise and into conditions she clearly found humiliating. She had become attached to Charles VIII, and he to her, and now felt isolated. A desperate letter survives from Margaret to Anne de Beaujeu, pleading against the removal of a cousin and companion: 'All the pastime I have and when I have lost her I do not know what I shall do'.

Anne of Brittany would also become attached to her unenthusiastic husband Charles but found herself sidelined, with no voice in the affairs of her duchy, receiving ambassadors only with Anne de Beaujeu at her side. Anne de Beaujeu and her husband enjoyed less influence than once they had and spent more time on their estates. Nonetheless, when the time came for Charles to go to war in Italy, it was once again Anne de Beaujeu who was recalled to power, with Anne of Brittany left in her charge. There was perhaps always a concern as to what the young queen-duchess – who never gave up her dream of Brittany's independence – might do if left unsupervised.

Anne of Brittany quickly gave Charles VIII a son and when, finally, the thirteen-year-old Margaret of Austria was sent home, the future of France at least seemed assured. Margaret took with her a farewell gift made by Anne of Brittany's most skilful embroideress. The two women kept up a connection but Margaret remained lastingly angry towards the country that had rejected her. On the way home she cracked a bitter joke when offered wine from that year's worthless vines (*sarments*). They fitted in well, she said, with the king's oaths, or *serments*.

Margaret of Austria had experienced something of the twists and turns of Fortune that loomed so large in the late medieval mind. 'Always remember that, as Saint Augustine says, you cannot be certain of even a single hour', Anne de Beaujeu wrote. For the moment Fortune seemed to be favouring Louise of Savoy, now the mother of an important son, but perhaps she too had learnt that it was not easy for a woman to control her destiny.

4

'Fate is very cruel to women'

Spain, Savoy, France, 1493–1505

MARGARET OF AUSTRIA and Louise of Savoy were now young women, looking to find their place in the world. But Margaret's future was not yet clear. In June 1493, at Cambrai (the scene of several important later encounters) she again met her godmother and step-grandmother Margaret of York, for whom she had been named. The next few years were to be spent in the older Margaret's company. But another marriage was always going to be on the board.

In 1493, Margaret's father Maximilian succeeded his father as Holy Roman Emperor. Margaret, like her brother Philip, was to be used to cement his great project: an anti-French alliance. Philip was to marry Juana, daughter of the rulers of Spain, Ferdinand and Isabella; Margaret was to marry Juan, their heir.* The grand scheme comprised plans for the youngest daughter of the Spanish monarchs, Katherine of Aragon, to marry the heir to the English throne, thus cementing another useful alliance.

On 5 November 1495, at Malines, Margaret of Austria underwent a proxy marriage with her Spanish prince. The discussions over whether she should set sail for Spain before Juana arrived in Flanders resemble, in a modern scenario, nothing so much as the exchange of hostages. Nonetheless, in late January 1497 she was under way. The weather was

---

* Again it will often be convenient to speak of 'Spain', although official unification of the Spanish kingdoms would not happen until the eighteenth century.

so bad her ship had to take refuge on the English coast, in Southampton, to the delight of the English king Henry VII, who sent letters urging her to lodge in the town long enough for him to visit and for her to avoid the 'movement and roaring of the sea'. She might have wished she had, for in the Bay of Biscay her ship ran into storms so severe that Margaret composed a rueful epitaph:

> Here lies Margot, the willing bride,
> Twice married – but a virgin when she died
> (Cy-gist Margot la gentil' damoiselle
> Qu'ha deux marys et encor est pucelle)

Safely landed in Spain, Margaret met her new mother-in-law, Isabella of Castile. It was a chance to witness a woman exerting regal force in the most direct way. Margaret met a woman who, as she advanced in years, was most at ease in the rough habit of a Franciscan monk but who, in public, could appear decked in rubies the size of pigeons' eggs. Isabella commissioned a female professor of Latin to remedy the defects in her education but nonetheless, educated her daughters as consorts, not as rulers.

Five years earlier, in 1492, a single triumphant year had seen Isabella of Castile riding into the palace of the Alhambra, victorious at last over the Moors who had long occupied southern Spain, her expulsion of the Jews and the discovery of the New World by her protégé Christopher Columbus. But even more significant, perhaps, would be Isabella's work in supporting – but also, crucially, in reforming – the Catholic church in Spain.

In 1478 Isabella had applied to the pope for permission to launch the Inquisition in Spain. Her and Ferdinand's officers acted so harshly that the pope felt impelled to intervene; they were replaced, ironically, with the now-infamous Tomás de Torquemada, who soon established not only an authoritarian spiritual rule but an efficient network of tribunals across all the territories of the Catholic kings. This impetus fuelled action against Moor and Jew. Isabella's Castile had been front-line territory, with Islam on its very boundaries. But her efforts would prove something of a pre-emptive strike, explaining why Protestantism would never make any real incursion on the Spanish peninsula.

The impetus for change came from Isabella herself. She boasted that in her eagerness to root out other, heretical strands of faith: 'I have caused great calamities and depopulated towns, lands, provinces and kingdoms'. The human cost of her actions was high. A priest who observed the expulsion of Jews, whose families had lived in Spain for centuries, recorded the emigrants collapsing, giving birth, dying by the roadside 'so that there was no Christian who was not sorry for them'. Nevertheless, after her death, there were moves for Isabella's canonisation.

This was the spirit and the lesson that her daughters carried abroad, as they were married off to spread the influence of Isabella and Ferdinand's dynasty. Margaret of Austria, as she arrived in Spain, had the chance to meet at least some of her new sisters-in-law. The eldest – named Isabella for the mother whose heir she was – had years earlier been married to the heir of the King of Portugal. Her young spouse was killed in a riding accident after they had been married a mere seven months, and after years of family pressure Isabella was persuaded in 1497 to marry Manuel, who had replaced her first husband as Portugal's king. As Margaret of Austria arrived in the country, Isabella was departing, while Juana had already left for the Netherlands.[1]

Margaret of Austria certainly met her youngest sister-in-law, who was preparing to eventually leave the Spanish court. The marriage of Katherine of Aragon to the English Prince Arthur was becoming ever more pressing. On July 1498, Spain's ambassador in England wrote that:

> The Queen and the mother of the King [Elizabeth of York and Margaret Beaufort] wish that the Princess of Wales [Katherine] should always speak French with the Princess Margaret [of Austria] who is now in Spain, in order to learn the language and to be able to converse in it when she comes to England. This is necessary, because these ladies do not understand Latin and much less, Spanish.

Margaret was warmly welcomed in Spain despite a certain clash of cultures. The seventeenth-century Jesuit author Pedro Abarca, in his *Reyes de Aragon*, wrote that although Margaret was allowed all her habitual servants, freedom and diversions, she was warned not to treat grandees 'with the familiarity and openness usual with the houses of

Austria, Burgundy and France but with the gravity and measured dignity of the kings and realms of Spain'.

Just months after his marriage to Margaret, in the autumn of 1497, the frail, over-solemn Juan died and Margaret ('so full of sorrow', as she described herself, 'that there was no room for any more griefs') lost the baby she was carrying. Her court poet Jean Lemaire, in *Couronne Margaritique*, later wrote that she endured a labour of twelve days and nights without food or sleep.[2]

Margaret told her father that Queen Isabella never left her and that she would have died were it not for her mother-in-law's care. Ferdinand and Isabella wrote to Maximilian that Margaret was 'as strong and full of courage as you would wish her to be and we try to console her . . . we have and will have as much care of her as we would have if her husband were alive'. A generous reaction, given that many contemporaries believed Juan had been killed by overindulgence in 'the pleasures of marriage' with the hot-blooded Margaret.

Margaret of Austria now had no real role in Spain, any more than she had had in France after Charles VIII abandoned her. Again, however, Margaret stayed for a time in her new country, where she had found great popularity. Her departure was delayed while her father-in-law and her father haggled over her dowry, her future marriage possibilities, her best deployment in the ongoing tug-of-war with France, and finally over the route and timing of her journey. But early in 1499 – crossing by land the France of which she had once been called queen – she returned to Flanders. Nineteen years old and once again cheated of married life.

She arrived just in time to stand godmother (alongside her own godmother Margaret of York) to her brother Philip of Burgundy's son by Juana of Aragon, the eventual heir to both Spain, through his mother, and to his father's Netherlands territories. For the Habsburg dynasty the birth of baby Charles was a triumph but on a personal level the marriage of Philip and Juana was a disaster. Not perhaps for the husband, who had from the first treated his wife with a contempt bordering on cruelty but for Juana, who responded to this harsh treatment with a devotion to Philip so slavish – and if hostile reports are to be believed, so hysterically jealous – that it became the chief grounds for the allegations of her insanity.

Margaret's personal sympathies were probably torn. In any case, she was soon given her own residence at the castle of le Quesnoy, away from the court. Politically, in March 1501 the Spanish ambassador Fuensalida was able to report disgruntledly that Madame Margaret 'simply follows her brother's fancies in all things'. When later asked by the Spanish to mediate between the warring couple, she sent word to Ferdinand that there was nothing she could do. As the Spanish ambassador reported ominously, 'she is returning to her own lands now because she is not able to suffer here the things that she sees going on . . .'

Margaret of Austria was not going to remain in the Netherlands forever. Discussions, conducted by her father and brother, about yet another marriage had begun while she was still in Spain, with mentions of the Duke of Milan, the kings of Scotland, Hungary and even France, since Margaret's childhood husband Charles VIII had died and a new king held the French throne. In the end, the choice of Margaret's next husband fell on the young Duke of Savoy, Philibert, brother of Margaret's erstwhile playmate Louise of Savoy.

The duchy of Savoy was the gateway to Italy, the stage of much of the competitive fighting between the great European powers, and so the match gave Margaret of Austria's relatives access to a strategically vital territory. Moreover while Philibert was technically a vassal of Maximilian's, his French upbringing at Anne de Beaujeu's hands meant he was very much under the sway of that country. This was something Margaret's father and brother may have been eager to change.

Margaret showed no eagerness to remarry. But although this third marriage would prove to be the least important on the great European stage, it would be the one which gave her most happiness. Philibert, a party-loving daredevil just a few months younger than she, shared, with Margaret's brother, the sobriquet of 'the Handsome'. The marriage contract was signed in Brussels on 26 September 1501 and Margaret of Austria set off in October (accompanied for the first half league by Margaret of York, the last time they would meet). At the beginning of December she met Philibert near Geneva and was received enthusiastically. For the first time Margaret had a partner who shared her vitality. Touring the duchy together, they settled down at the castle of Pont l'Aine near Borg in the spring of 1503.

But there was another side to Philibert's gaiety. His time was occupied in hunting, jousting and dancing; he had no interest in attending to the business of the duchy. That was dealt with by his illegitimate half-brother, René, until the advent of Margaret, who had no intention of leaving the 'Bastard of Savoy' his authority. Whether or not her hostility was justified, she used every weapon at her disposal against him, even involving her father to have René stripped of the letters of legitimacy that gave him, a bastard, the right to his property.

Her motives may have been political; she had her family's interests to follow, or they may have been personal. Perhaps past experiences had soured her of (usually masculine) authority. Perhaps, even, she had seen in her sister-in-law Juana's fate what happened when a royal wife abnegated public responsibility. Either way, the Bastard was declared a traitor. He took refuge in France, where he was welcomed by his half-sister Louise of Savoy.

While Philibert hunted, Margaret of Austria took up the reins of government, effectively telling him not to worry his pretty head. She summoned the council, appointed officers, discussed foreign policy with her brother when he visited and approved his plans for a contin-ued *rapprochement* with France. She never neglected the parties or the hunting; there is an account of her appearing at one masque as Queen of the Amazons, with a crimson headdress and jewelled cuirass and with (one thinks of Isabella of Castile) a naked sword in hand. But her experience in Savoy was the final stage of her political apprenticeship; a rehearsal for activities on the wider European stage, to which fate was about to return her.

The summer of 1504 was scorchingly hot. Even Philibert was unable to hunt. So in the first days of September he returned to his avocation with even more enthusiasm. After a frenetic morning pursuing a wild boar, he flung himself down in the shade, gulping from a fountain, only to be seized by a sudden chill. At the palace, doctors were summoned but despaired. Margaret ordered her valuable pearls to be ground up for medicine but to no avail; Philibert died on the morning of 10 September. The story goes that Margaret's attendants had to restrain her from flinging herself from the window.

She did fling herself into the rebuilding of the family church at Brou, where Philibert was buried, causing her self-invented motto: 'FORTUNE. INFORTUNE. FORT. UNE' to be carved all over it. This can be translated to imply that 'fate is very cruel to women' or, conversely, that 'Fortune. Misfortune. Strengthens. One'. The 'e' of '*une*' makes it clear that it is a woman in question.[3] In the years ahead Margaret of Austria's palace at Mechelen was to feature wooden busts of herself and Philibert, in which Margaret, although she commissioned them after his death, wore the loose hair of a bride, rather than the widow's cap. At twenty-four, she was cheated of married life for yet a third time. Her father and brother were at first anxious to marry her off yet again but after three such ill-fated attempts at matrimony, Margaret declared herself 'much disinclined to make another trial'.

But as well as her husband, she had lost her new-found role. Or had she? Philibert was succeeded by an eighteen-year-old half-brother whose youth made it seem, for a while, as though Margaret might manage to hold on to a measure of power. The new young duke, however, reneged on the deal, leaving Margaret furious. If he thought 'that by such unmannerly treatment he can reduce us and put his intentions through, he has the wrong idea', she wrote later. 'For all that we are a woman, our heart is of a different nature . . .'*

In France, Louise of Savoy was also now a youthful widow. The little dauphin, the son that Anne of Brittany had borne to Charles VIII of France at the start of their marriage, had died in 1495. Louise's husband Charles d'Angoulême fell sick of a fever and died on his way to the dauphin's funeral. Resisting, like a striking number of these women, any attempt to marry her off again, Louise concentrated on keeping control of her son, François.

As the boy's leading kinsman, the Duc d'Orléans had claimed that Louise of Savoy could not take guardianship of her two children, being herself a minor, as France set twenty-five as the age of legal majority for women. But the young widow argued that in Cognac, where François was born, women were allowed to exercise rights of guardianship at fourteen. The royal council decided more or less in her favour, with the Duc d'Orléans (provided Louise did not remarry) given merely a supervisory role.

Louise of Savoy settled down in Cognac to administer her extensive lands. There she set about bringing up her two children in the strong-minded and scholarly tradition she had learnt in Anne de Beaujeu's

---

* Impossible not to think, in comparison and contrast, of the 'heart and stomach of a king' and Elizabeth I at Tilbury.

household. 'Also, my daughter, if at some point in the future God takes your husband, leaving you a widow, then you will be responsible for your children, like many other young women; have patience, because it pleases God, and govern wisely', Anne wrote in her *Enseignements*. Louise's motto (borrowed from Lorenzo de Medici and written on the wall of her room at Angoulême) was *'libris et liberis'*: books and children.

Her daughter, Marguerite, had the same teachers as her son. Both learnt Spanish and Italian from their mother, and Latin and biblical history from two humanist scholars, while a miniature shows Marguerite and her brother playing chess. But there was no doubt which of the two children occupied more of their mother's attention.

Louise of Savoy has been blamed for her focus on François but Marguerite herself would share that obsessive interest. And perhaps it was inevitable, as the childlessness of successive short-lived French kings brought François ever closer to the throne. When, in 1498, Charles VIII suddenly died, after hitting his head on the lintel of a doorway, the throne passed to Louis, Duc d'Orléans, the cousin of Louise's husband Angoulême. And Louis was still childless, the cynical predictions about his marriage to the crippled Jeanne having proved all too accurate.[4]

After Charles VIII's death, his widow Anne of Brittany threw herself into hysterical mourning but also immediately took steps to resume her rights in her duchy. Her first marriage contract stipulated that if King Charles died, the only person she could remarry was the next King of France; a way to continue France's annexation of Brittany. The new king Louis XII accordingly took steps to set aside his existing wife, the barren Jeanne, on the grounds of non-consummation. Jeanne was asked to undergo a humiliating physical examination, a papal decree was granted and Jeanne retired to a convent, eventually to be canonised.

While the marriage of Louis and Anne of Brittany was politically necessary for both sides, this was no guarantee it would solve the problem of the succession. The groom was thirty-six and in poor health, while Anne's repeated pregnancies by Charles had not yet produced an heir.

Unless or until a son was born to King Louis and his new queen, Louise of Savoy's boy François was heir presumptive. Under these circumstances, Louise had to battle to be allowed to bring up François herself. She did have to bring her son rather more closely under Louis's eye, to Amboise on the Loire, where François and the gang of young

men placed around him could enjoy the hunting and mock tournaments that were so much to his taste. She had also to submit to the
surveillance of Louis's trusted man, the Seigneur de Gié, whose aggressive concept of his duties made the family feel like prisoners at times.
Louise's children slept in her bedroom and an officer had to be present
at the *lever*, the ceremonial rising of the young heir. One day, when
Louise declared her children were still sleeping, an official went so far
as to break down the door.

Anne of Brittany endured repeated pregnancies and Louise's journal
makes no bones about her feelings. In 1502, 'Anne, Queen of France, on the
twenty-first of January, Saint Agnes Day, gave birth at Blois to a son; however,
stillborn, he was no threat to my Caesar's rise to power.' There continued to
be no sign of a living boy. In 1499 Louise and her children were at
Romorantin, where Queen Anne joined their seclusion to avoid the plague,
and there gave birth to a daughter, Claude. Was the idea of a match between
this royal daughter and Louise's son François also born at Romorantin?

Perhaps neither mother wanted the match: Anne of Brittany because
she secretly hoped to marry Claude, Brittany's heiress, to the imperial
Habsburgs (Anne had always kept in touch with Margaret of Austria)
and thus maintain her duchy's independence, while Louise of Savoy
may have reflected that Claude came from a family with a poor record
of fertility and was, like so many of her inbred clan, including Louis's
first wife Jeanne, mildly deformed. Louise and Anne of Brittany were
always in enmity, although in 1504 they had briefly collaborated to rid
themselves of the overbearing Seigneur de Gié.

But in 1505, when Louis XII fell desperately ill, it made imperative
what had long been discussed: the marriage of twelve-year-old
François, the heir, to King Louis's seven-year-old daughter Claude.
Louis's will placed the guardianship of Claude with her mother Anne
but gave Louise a seat alongside her on the regency council. Both
women swore to execute the will with their hands resting on a piece of
the True Cross. King Louis recovered but the betrothal ceremony went
ahead, with the pair then separating to grow up. The following spring
another formal ceremony acknowledged François as Louis's heir.

Margaret of Austria and Louise of Savoy were now both young
widows. But while Margaret was again plunged into uncertainty,
Louise's path lay clear ahead.

5

Princess Brides

England, Scotland, 1501–1505

A PRINCESS'S FATE WAS to be married for her family's benefit. Her own happiness, or otherwise, was a matter of fortune. Across the Channel, in England and in Scotland, two other royal girls were feeling the force of that lesson.

Katherine of Aragon finally arrived in England in 1501. Her marriage to its heir Prince Arthur was celebrated with extraordinary festivities. Isabella of Castile and her husband had displayed some qualms at sending their youngest to distant England, where the Tudor regime was still a fragile new arrival but Isabella was not the woman to let sentiment stand in the way of dynastic advantage.

Any foreign princess faced a terrifying prospect as she arrived, exhausted and travel-worn, on the shores of a foreign land after a long and dangerous journey, knowing her entire future depended on pleasing the man (or boy) she was about to meet, and that, at best, she faced a future of juggling her loyalties to him and her responsibilities to her native country. It must have taken all the festivities – the tournaments and the tumblers, the pageants and the parades between the river palaces – to pin the ritual smile on Katherine of Aragon's face. And she may, as Isabella's daughter, have been taken aback to discover the limitations on a royal Englishwoman's power.

True, Henry VII's mother, Margaret Beaufort – 'My Lady the King's Mother' – exercised a good deal of influence but the same could not be said of his wife, Elizabeth of York. Moreover, both Margaret Beaufort and Elizabeth of York had been required to set aside their blood rights to let Henry ascend his throne. There was no thought that a woman could rule in England, as she could in Castile, although Katherine could not have known how this assumption would come to haunt her.

In January 1502 the young couple set out for Ludlow, Arthur's seat as Prince of Wales. But less than five months after the wedding came tragedy. On 2 April 1502 Prince Arthur died after a short illness, leaving his parents devastated and his wife in the most painful uncertainty. Another royal bride widowed early; another princess left stranded in a foreign country without an obvious role to play.

But marriage abroad was a princess's lot. At the English court, one of Katherine's new Tudor sisters-in-law was preparing for that destiny. Margaret Tudor had been born in 1489, the eldest daughter of Henry VII and Elizabeth of York. She was not quite four when her elder brother Arthur was sent to Ludlow at six years old, to assume his role as Prince of Wales, leaving Margaret to be raised with her younger siblings Henry and Mary. The royal children largely grew up at Eltham Palace, just outside London. Desiderius Erasmus, the great humanist from the Netherlands, accompanying the English scholar Thomas More to pay his respects in 1499, portrays them as happy, although his report makes it clear the eight-year-old Henry ('already with a certain royal demeanour') expected, and was given, precedence over the two girls.

There had already been discussions about Margaret Tudor's future. In 1498 the Spanish ambassador reported to Ferdinand and Isabella on the proposed marriage between the eight-year-old Margaret and the 25-year-old James IV of Scotland but added that there were many 'inconveniences' involved. Henry VII said that his wife and his mother Margaret Beaufort had joined forces to protect little Margaret:

> The Queen and my mother are very much against this marriage. They say if the marriage were concluded, we should be obliged to send the Princess directly to Scotland, in which case they fear the King of Scots would not wait but injure her and endanger her health.

Wait: as in wait to consummate the marriage. Here, Margaret Beaufort knew all too well what she was talking about. She had been married at twelve and a mother at thirteen; the birth had permanently damaged her slight physique. If the granddaughter named for her had inherited Margaret Beaufort's small stature, this was a real and vivid concern. Nonetheless, on the 25th of January 1502 (just weeks after Arthur and Katherine set out for Ludlow) Richmond Palace saw the formal celebration of Margaret Tudor's marriage to the King of Scots. Representatives of both countries signed the three agreements which made up the optimistically-named Treaty of Perpetual Peace, aimed at ending disputes between the ever-squabbling neighbours, and arranging the details of Margaret's match and her £10,000 dowry.[1]

The following day, after Mass was celebrated in the new royal chapel, a proxy wedding ceremony was performed in the queen's great chamber, with the Earl of Bothwell standing in for the absent King James. Henry, his wife Elizabeth and Margaret herself were asked whether they knew of any impediment and whether Margaret were acting 'without compulsion and of her own free will'. She affirmed that 'if it please my Lord and Father the King and my Lady Mother the Queen', she was content. A full and unqualified affirmation, in the eyes of the sixteenth century.

After the business was concluded and the trumpets sounded, Queen Elizabeth 'incontinently' (as a contemporary chronicle of the proceedings describes it) took her daughter by the hand and, two queens together, they 'dined both at one mess covered'; a covered dish indicating their regal status. Jousts and a supper banquet followed and the *Te Deum* was sung at St Paul's. The next morning the twelve-year-old Queen of Scots came into her mother's great chamber and 'by the voice of' the officer of arms gave thanks to all the noblemen who had jousted for her and distributed prizes 'by the advice of the ladies of the court'. Praise went to one young gentleman, Charles Brandon, of whom more would be heard a few years later. It was agreed Margaret should be sent north not later than September 1503 but for the moment, she was to be left in her mother's charge.

There is a story that Prince Henry wept with rage when he realised his sister, as a queen, now outranked him. But Henry was about to become much more important in the scheme of things. Barely two months after Margaret Tudor's wedding came news of their brother Arthur's death in Wales. And worse was to follow. As Margaret's sombre mourning clothes were softened by sleeves of white and then of orange, she would have known her mother was pregnant again. Elizabeth of York had thought she had put her childbearing years behind her but with Arthur gone, there was an heir but no spare. In February 1503, just days after bearing a short-lived daughter, Queen Elizabeth died.

Margaret Tudor had, that coming summer, to travel north towards her new life without her mother behind her. On 8 July she set off, as the 'Somerset Herald' recorded, 'richly dressed, mounted upon a fair palfrey . . . very nobly accompanied, in fair order and array', to be crowned Queen of Scotland in Edinburgh. She was not yet fourteen years old.

She met her thirty-year-old husband at Haddington, just inside Scotland. The Herald's account shows, with unusual clarity, the stages of two people getting to know each other under these trying circumstances. When James IV was brought to what was now Margaret's great chamber she met him at the door and the two 'made great reverences, the one to the other, his head being bare, and they kissed together'. The greeting to the rest of her party being made, they 'went aside and communed together by long space'.

Returning the next day, James found Margaret playing cards in her room and she kissed him 'of good will'. When bread and wine were brought to him, he served her before himself and played for her on the clarichords and the lute, 'which pleased her very much'. The next day, seeing the stool on which she was seated for supper 'was not for her ease', he gave her his chair. A letter to her father Henry in England, sent in the early days of her marriage, breathes homesickness and the uncertainties of an adolescent trying to negotiate her path through the power plays of a foreign court. 'I would I were with your Grace now and many times more', she told her father, as many another princess must have wished to do. All the same, it sounds as if, by the standards of the day, Margaret had been lucky.

Katherine of Aragon's situation, by contrast, was the worse for the death of her kindly mother-in-law Elizabeth of York, although for a brief time it seemed that new, if controversial, possibilities might open. King Henry was a widower, just as his son's wife, Katherine of Aragon, was a widow. Marriage between the two looked, for a moment, a good way of resolving the equation and keeping Katherine's dowry and the Spanish connection: good to Henry, at least. But Katherine's mother Isabella of Castile was horrified when she heard the rumours; such a marriage between father and daughter-in-law would be 'a very evil thing – one never before seen and the mere mention of which offends the ears – we would not for anything in the world that it should take place'.

Instead, in June 1503, the seventeen-year-old Katherine of Aragon was betrothed to Arthur's eleven-year-old brother Prince Henry, amid some confusion as to whether she was betrothed as Arthur's widow in the fullest sense, or as the virgin survivor of an unconsummated marriage. But there was another extended row between Henry VII and Ferdinand over the question of Katherine's dowry, with Katherine caught between her father's and her father-in-law's diplomacy. Events in Spain, moreover, were about to make Katherine less attractive as a marital possibility.

In November 1504 Isabella of Castille died, leaving questions about what would happen to her country. From the English perspective, this meant that an alliance with Katherine now represented only an alliance with her father's Aragon, rather than also one with the more important Castile. In June 1505, Prince Henry was instructed by his father to repudiate his betrothal to her. While her sister-in-law Margaret Tudor seemed comparatively secure in Scotland, Katherine was once again left without clear prospects in a strange land.

6

Repositioning

The Netherlands, Spain, England, Scotland, 1505–1512

THERE WERE OTHERS on the far side of the English Channel whose place on the political board would be affected even more directly by the death of Isabella of Castile. One was Katherine of Aragon's former sister-in-law Margaret of Austria, and another was Katherine's sister, Juana.

Juana was her mother Isabella's heir, but from the first she showed little sign of taking the reins of power into her own hands. The tussle was between Juana's husband Philip of Burgundy – Margaret's brother – and Juana's father Ferdinand of Aragon, Isabella's widower, who was reluctant to relinquish the larger part of the lands he had co-ruled for many years.

News of her inheritance reached Juana as she was with her husband in the Netherlands and the couple set about making preparations for their return to Spain. Storms forced Philip and Juana into harbour on the coast of England, which gave Katherine of Aragon the thrilling possibility of seeing her sister, but Philip purposely kept Juana away from Henry's court until he himself was firmly established as the star visitor, which left Katherine only a few hours to spend with the sister she was likely never to see again.

But back in Spain, in September 1506, Philip of Burgundy died suddenly of a fever. The comportment of his widow Juana made it easy for her male relatives to outmanoeuvre her. Juana would shortly be declared incapable (insane), although the diagnosis is now suspect. Juana herself had written to her father that while the Castilians 'want to make out that I am not in my right mind . . . if I did fly into passions and failed to keep up my proper dignity, it is well known that the only cause of my doing so was jealousy'. It is however possible that her husband forced her to write the letter.

Juana would be no player in the game of queens. Most of her life was spent incarcerated; it remains uncertain to what degree this was inevitable. Certainly she was effectively the victim of a stitch up, in which her husband had been at least as complicit as her father. A deal was struck whereby Castile would be controlled by Juana's father Ferdinand during the minority of her six-year-old son, Charles.

But what of the Netherlands, which Charles had also inherited on his father's death and where Philip and Juana had left him when they sailed to Spain? Regency of the Netherlands passed to Charles's other grandfather, Maximilian, but Maximilian resided in his own, Austrian, lands. Instead, with the approval of all involved, he devolved his powers on to his Netherlands-born, recently widowed (and thus fortuitously available) daughter, Margaret of Austria. In the weeks before Philip of Burgundy's death, Maximilian's agent described how he 'daily pressed [Margaret] during a whole month' to consent to marriage with England's Henry VII. Maximilian had assured the English king that he himself would travel to Savoy to persuade her. But now her family had found another use for her, and at twenty-seven, Margaret had found the part she was born to play.

When fate, and her brother's death, placed the government of the Netherlands in her hands, she took to the role with ability. Margaret of York had died in 1503 but Margaret of Austria set up court in her godmother's old home, Mechelen, where council meetings were held twice a week, though most of the hundred and fifty people who made up her household lived around the city.*

Sworn in as governess-general in March 1507, Margaret took her nephew Charles on a tour of his domain, promising on his behalf to preserve the rights and privileges of each of the seventeen provinces, receiving their oath of fidelity and convening the Estates-General to raise

---

* There she was to bring up not only her nephew Charles but also three of his sisters. Charles's younger brother Ferdinand, however, was raised in Spain by the grandfather for whom he was named, while a younger sister Catalina, born after Juana had returned to Spain, shared her mother's captivity.

a tax with which to redeem Charles's mortgaged lands, since Philip had left his territories in very poor array. A good deal of her time was occupied in international diplomacy and the pursuance of her father's policies.

Her own hand in marriage was a pawn Maximilian was still attempting to play. But Margaret of Austria continued to resist all blandishments, resolutely refusing to marry Henry VII of England, although her father assured her that she would be able to return to her own domains for three or four months of every year and thus 'will not feel yourself a prisoner in England . . . with a headstrong man'. She was, however, persuaded to write Henry a number of flattering letters and thus keep up her father's alliance with England.

The death of Philip of Burgundy brought potential benefits to another woman. Henry VII now sought a marriage with the widowed Juana, unperturbed, so the Spanish ambassador reported, by any thought of insanity, 'especially since I have assured them [the English] that her derangement of mind would not prevent her from bearing children'. As Juana's sister, Katherine of Aragon became involved, at Henry's request, in the negotiations. Katherine had every reason to long for Juana's presence at Henry's side, which might not only help her free herself from limbo but also relieve her endless money worries. The disputes about her dowry had dragged on, and she sent frantic pleas to her father that she was spending not on frivolities but on necessities. (The Spanish ambassador, de Puebla, was famous for eating at court to save money.) It was at this point that she was able to deliver a 'letter of credence' to her father-in-law that made her officially her father Ferdinand's ambassador

But Ferdinand was never going to give Henry VII the controlling hand in Spanish affairs he might have had as Juana's husband. Katherine of Aragon's minor triumph notwithstanding, the desperate tone of her letters in the final years of Henry VII's reign is more pathetic than anything later in her story.

Margaret Tudor's life in Scotland, by contrast, continued for some time on the same gracious note with which it had begun, and she had probably her husband to thank for that. James was a complex character – devote and romantic – determined some day to go on crusade but meanwhile amusing himself with a variety of studies, including the practice of dentistry.* But James IV was also an ardent practitioner of the amatory arts and from the very first Margaret had to cope with evidence of his infidelity. In the autumn, James took her (and her ladies and her musicians and eighteen wagons of 'gear') on a tour of her traditional dower land, starting at the romantic loch-side palace of Linlithgow. When they moved on to Stirling, however, Margaret found that her dower castle was a nursery for the king's half a dozen illegitimate children.

But James's long devotion to his mistress Janet Kennedy may have made it easier for him to show restraint in other directions. It was more than three years after her arrival in Scotland that in 1507, by then seventeen, Margaret gave birth to a son. James was ecstatic, and not forgetful of Margaret, who after the birth lay dangerously ill. James went on pilgrimage to the shrine of St Ninian, on the Galloway coast, to pray for her recovery: on foot, taking seven days for the 120-mile journey. At exactly the moment he knelt at the tomb, Margaret's fever abated. Or so it was reported through all Christian countries.

Tragically, just over a year later, the baby died but Margaret Tudor was again pregnant. However, when she gave birth (to a girl) in July 1508, the baby died the same day. It was, of course, too soon to see how closely events in England would replicate this story. But Margaret's fertility, or lack thereof, had implications for England; since the death of Prince Arthur, she was second in line to the English throne.

Margaret Tudor was, like so many princesses, a living pledge of an international alliance, and the Anglo-Scottish accord had at first seemed to being going well. But by 1508 James IV was receiving embassies from Louis XII of France, whose alliance with Maximilian against the growing power of Venice did not include England. James was, moreover, irritated when his father-in-law arrested his cousin, the Earl of Arran, for passing through his kingdom without official permission. Henry VII sent north, to kiss and make up, an able new young English official by the name of Thomas Wolsey. Margaret was tasked with winning Wolsey an audience, since her husband declared, ominously, that he was too busy 'shooting guns and making gunpowder'. After five days, she managed it; albeit with an inexperience in the smooth ways of diplomacy that had her

---

* He paid those who allowed him to take out their teeth, rather than the reverse; a practice that might endear him to many today.

contradicting any Scot who said her father in England had done anything wrong.

When Henry VII died, on 21 April 1509, Margaret Tudor (once again pregnant) was now the heir to the English throne. While James and the new king Henry VIII confirmed the Treaty of Perpetual Peace, Margaret's baby, born in October at Holyrood, was christened Arthur, a name of great significance in recent and legendary English history. This Arthur was to die at a year old but of course, there was by that point every reason to hope that Henry VIII and his new queen would have children of their own.

When Henry VII of England died, his son Henry VIII instantly marked his accession by marrying Katherine of Aragon, his brother's widow. Henry wrote to Margaret of Austria in the Netherlands, truly or falsely, that this was by the dying Henry VII's 'express command'. The wedding took place quickly and privately but their joint coronation, less than a fortnight later, was huge and public. That ceremony took place on 24 June 1509 and although a sudden shower forced the drenched queen to shelter under the awning of a draper's stall, Katherine's dreary years were at an end – for the moment, anyway.

Her world had gone from darkness into light. It was, on the surface, a fairy-tale piece of romanticism. Katherine, at twenty-four, still had the sunny good looks noted when she first came to England. She was described by ambassadors as being buxom, amiable and lively, inclined to smile even in adversity. Interestingly, however, letters between Katherine of Aragon and her father Ferdinand before the marriage suggest a more pragmatic agenda behind the love match, and a more active role for Katherine. Ferdinand urged his daughter to use 'all your skill and prudence' so as swiftly to 'close the deal'.[1] And Katherine, once safely wed, told Ferdinand that she loved her new husband so well firstly because he was the 'so true son of your highness', who desired to serve Ferdinand 'with greater love and obedience' than even a blood son might. This identification of Katherine of Aragon with Spain's interests was a potential source of danger. But for the moment, this marriage gave the young Henry a partner more experienced in the ways of the world than he.

Perhaps there was a hint of trouble to come when in January 1510 Katherine suffered her first miscarriage. But this was in itself not an uncommon occurrence. More worrying, in hindsight, with our knowledge of both Katherine's and her daughter Mary's gynaecological history, was the fact that her doctors seem to have convinced Katherine she had miscarried one of twins and was still pregnant, although even the Spanish ambassador reported she had resumed her menstrual cycle. She remained in seclusion, preparing for childbirth, until forced to emerge, discreetly, in the spring. By that time, however, she was able to announce that she was pregnant once again.

On the morning of New Year's Day 1511, Katherine gave birth to a boy, christened Henry, amid great rejoicing. After just seven weeks, the baby died, but again, such misfortunes were not uncommon in the sixteenth century. Certainly Katherine of Aragon's relationship with Henry remained strong; strong enough so that by 1513 she was able to influence her husband and steer his country in the direction of an alliance with the Habsburgs and her birth family. She had obviously not forgotten her connection with Margaret of Austria, who had been one of the godparents of that short-lived baby boy.

Margaret of Austria's role as Governor of the Netherlands was not always easy; indeed, she wrote that she often wished herself back in her mother's womb. She had to tread carefully around her father: 'I know that it is not my business to interfere in your said affairs, as I am an inexperienced woman in such matters, nevertheless the great duty I have towards you emboldens me to beg of you . . . to take care whilst there is still time', she wrote on one occasion. ('Rude and ungracious' was how he described the advice so carefully hedged around.) She had, moreover, to stand up for the needs of the Netherlands themselves, as distinct from her father's grandiose policies. But she scored an early victory for those Netherlands when she succeeded in overturning a trade agreement with England that was highly detrimental to its interests: the '*Malus Intercursus*'.

Five years before Anne Boleyn arrived in the Netherlands, moreover, Margaret of Austria had been a major player in the League of Cambrai, trusted in 1508 to represent her father, Emperor Maximilian, and her former father-in-law Ferdinand to negotiate an alliance with the French to aid the papacy against the encroachments of Venice. Maximilian wrote to advise her to engage all the houses on one side of Cambrai,[2] leaving the other to the French king's representative. Meanwhile the French king, Louis, himself wrote chattily to remind her of how he had played with her when she was a little girl at Amboise. Even the pope, another partner in this alliance against the encroachments of the Venetian republic, was in the habit of sending Margaret devotional objects and relics of great value, while Henry VII ordered his ambassador to speak to Margaret about English interests. As her court poet Jean Lemaire put it: 'Madame Margaret has seen and experienced more at her youthful age . . . than any lady on record, however long her life.'

Commentators spoke of her 'courteous and caressing manners'. Although Margaret wrote to her ambassador in England that the negotiations gave her a headache and that she and her opponent frequently 'got into each other's hair', she was willing to bring all her various abilities to the fight. Was it at Margaret of Austria's court that Anne Boleyn learnt that her gender – femininity, sex itself – could be a weapon; could be a gambit in the great game that would set her against another woman – another queen – as surely as black and white face across the chessboard?

But the League of Cambrai did not long endure after the pope decided that France itself represented more of a threat than Venice. The year 1511 saw the pope organising a Holy League against France, to which he recruited Maximilian and Ferdinand, Venice and Henry VIII. Margaret's father wrote that French perfidy would teach her a lesson: 'We have more experience of the French than you have . . . and we would rather you were deceived by their fair speeches than ourselves, so that you would take more care in future.'

Faced with a long-running problem (the revolt of the Duke of Guelders, striving to win back the independence of his territory), at the end of 1510 Margaret wrote in agitation to her father: 'you know I am a woman and that it is not my place to meddle in war . . . I beseech you my lord to have good advice over all this . . .' Yet a few months later: 'My Lord, I am readying myself . . . in order to march before our army. The army makes a very good sight, together with the artillery . . .' Her father told her that she had fought 'with the courage of a man and not that of a woman'.

The year 1512 was particularly wearing. Guelders gained the backing of the French and Margaret had no money to fight either her own or her father's various campaigns. But in 1513 the new anti-French coalition was confirmed and Margaret was as central to the process as its very name, the Treaty of Mechelen, suggests. Margaret (in contrast to her former sister-in-law Juana) was at the heart of European diplomacy.

7

'False imputations'

France, the Netherlands, 1513

'A WOMAN', CASTIGLIONE WROTE, 'has not so many ways of defending herself against false imputations as has a man.' Margaret of Austria was one of several women about to prove the truth of that dictat. The first six years of Margaret's regency had left her looking like a woman with her hands very firmly on the reins. Anne de Beaujeu's perfect pupil, you might say; the sort of woman Anne meant when she wrote that noblewomen were, 'and should be, a pattern and an example for others in all things'.

But a great deal of Anne de Beaujeu's advice centred on one particular theme:

> Suffer no man to touch your body, no matter who he is . . . not one in a thousand escapes without her honour being attacked or deceived, however 'good' or 'true' her love. Therefore, for the greatest certainty in such situations, I advise you to avoid all private meetings, no matter how pleasant they are . . .

Even the slightest slip could incur blame. Or, as Anne de Beaujeu had written in an uncomfortable prophecy:

> There is no man of worth, however noble he may be, who does not use treachery, nor to whom it does not seem good sport to deceive or trick women of rank . . . there is no man so perfect who, in matters of love, is truthful or keeps his word.

The truth of that was about to be proved by Margaret of Austria herself, and perhaps also in France by the daughter of Anne de Beaujeu's protégée, Margaret's former playmate Louise of Savoy.

The early years of Louise's daughter Marguerite are inevitably known chiefly through accounts of her brother François, on whom centred all the hopes of the family 'trinity'.[1] But Marguerite's marriage had long been discussed. While still a child she had been offered as a bride for the future Henry VIII but the offer was declined, since it was felt that England's heir merited a daughter of the King of France, not a mere cousin.

As François's probable accession, and his marriage to King Louis XII's daughter Claude were established, England came back with a counter-offer: the suggestion that Marguerite might indeed marry the younger Henry if Louise of Savoy would marry his father, the widowed Henry VII. But Louis of France feared this double alliance might admit too much English influence into his country. When the English then suggested that Marguerite herself might marry the ageing Henry VII, she is reputed to have given a spirited refusal: 'When my brother becomes king I will marry a man who is young, rich and noble – without having to cross the Channel!' But in fact, in 1509, Marguerite was married off to the personally unimpressive Charles, Duc d'Alençon, thus settling a longstanding territorial dispute between the house of Alençon and Marguerite's house of Angoulême.

In 1513 it was not Marguerite of Navarre but the English who crossed the Channel. And not for matters of love but of war. In theory at least England's efforts were directed at regaining the power and the territories it had held on the continent for much of the Middle Ages, and lost only in the fifteenth century. But in fact war was recognised as the main business, as well as pleasure, of the ruler – Machiavelli had very explicitly said as much – and Henry VIII was delightedly flexing his muscles as a warrior king when his alliance with the pope and Emperor Maximilian against France brought him abroad at the head of a mighty army.

That August, the fall of the town of Thérouanne, near the borders of France and the Netherlands, was followed by the siege and triumphant capture of the wealthy walled city of Tournai. And when the treaty she struck between her father Maximilian and Henry VIII brought Henry across the English Channel, Margaret of Austria was there. Her father, quixotically, had declared his intention of serving as a volunteer in the English army. When he asked her to join him at the besieged town of Tournai, she replied that she would do so if it were really necessary, 'but otherwise, it is not fitting for a widow to be trotting about and visiting armies for pleasure . . .' Was she protesting too much? Perhaps.

Later, Margaret of Austria did take her nephew Charles to meet her father and Henry VIII at Lille, and went on to Tournai, with notable consequences. Although it might not be considered worthy of record in the chronicles of great European events, the small drama played in the summer of 1513 and the following months is worth anatomising, not only for the insight it gives into the protagonists (Henry VIII included) but as a test case of the way a powerful woman could be manipulated through her sexuality; the way in which, particularly where women were concerned, the personal became part of the political.

The Tudor chronicler Edward Hall described how Henry received Charles and Margaret outside Tournai and brought them into the town 'with great triumph. The noise went that the Lord Lisle made request of marriage to the Lady Margaret . . . but whether he proffered marriage or not she favoured him highly.' Lord Lisle was the recently ennobled Charles Brandon, a man on the make and already a man with a colourful marital history.

Born in the gentry, Brandon had been raised at court. His father died at Bosworth, bearing Henry's standard on the battlefield that gave Henry VII his crown. This sacrifice on the father's part ensured favour for the son. A star of the tiltyard, he first jousted publicly on the occasion of Katherine of Aragon's marriage to Henry VIII and had, crucially, quickly become the boon companion of the younger man. Contracted in youth to one of Elizabeth of York's gentlewomen, he made her pregnant before repudiating the match to marry her wealthy widowed aunt instead. He sold many of the aunt's lands before having that marriage annulled, on the grounds of consanguinity, and returning to marry the younger woman, who then died in 1510, leaving Brandon free. Made a Knight of the Garter in April 1513, he was created Viscount Lisle in May, when he was also betrothed to the eight-year-old Elizabeth Grey, heir to the Lisle barony.

He had raised fifteen hundred men for the 1513 campaign and, at the siege of Tournai, led a successful assault on one of the city gates, in reward for which Henry handed him the keys of the surrendering city. Margaret of Austria's agent with the English army reported to her that he was 'a second king'; but he was someone she would, in any case, have been watching carefully.

Margaret and her nephew Charles spent ten days with the English forces; ten days of 'great solace'. (In celebration of the victory, Margaret was presented with a six-piece tapestry depicting Christine de Pizan's *City of Ladies*.) It is likely that Anne Boleyn was in Margaret of Austria's train, observing the phenomenon that was the young Henry VIII. Spectators reported that one evening Henry danced 'from the time the banquet finished until nearly day, in his shirt [that is, without his doublet]' with Margaret and with Margaret's 'damsels'.

But Margaret of Austria may not have had eyes only for Henry. What she saw in those ten days was Brandon and King Henry answering all comers at the joust, Brandon and King Henry dressed identically in purple velvet decked with gold, Brandon coming in disguise with the king to the masque that followed a banquet of a hundred dishes. On 20 October Margaret and her nephew returned to Lille but talk of their visit to Tournai continued.

When Brandon was created Duke of Suffolk, it may have been in tribute to his prowess in France but such a leap, for such a man, attracted a great deal of international comment. Erasmus was among the shocked. Some said Brandon had been dramatically elevated so as to make him a more fitting match for Margaret: 'Gossip has it that Maximilian's daughter Margaret is to marry that new duke, whom the King has recently turned from a stableboy into a nobleman.' In May, Brandon and Henry were once again defenders at a tournament, bearing the motto 'Who can hold that will away', perhaps suggesting that Brandon might be about to make a foreign journey.

If Brandon indeed had pretensions to Margaret of Austria's hand, it looked as though Henry were encouraging them. But the king found it at least prudent to express annoyance, writing to Margaret to promise signal punishment of the rumour-mongers. He acknowledged, however, 'that the common report is in divers places that marriage is contemplated between you and our very dear and loyal cousin and councillor the Duke of Suffolk'. Margaret's feelings can be seen in two long letters, signed simply 'M'. [see note on sources] 'M' dared not write directly to king or duke, she said, 'because that I fear my letters to be evil kept'. Discretion was the watchword, for all this was a tardy slamming of the stable door, and Margaret sounds a repeated note of almost hysterical caution.

After having been some days at Tournai, she had been, she declared, struck by King Henry's love for Brandon and by 'the virtue and grace' of Brandon's person ('the which me seemed that I had not much seen gentleman to approach it'). Because of 'the desire the which he always showed me that he had to do me service', she forced herself 'to do unto him all honour and pleasure'. This seemed to be 'well agreeable' to King Henry, who indeed 'many time spake unto me, for to know if this goodwill . . . might stretch unto some effect of promise of marriage'. As Margaret tells it, it was Henry who urged that this (a love match, a woman making her own choice?) 'was the fashion of the ladies of England and . . . was not there holden for evil'. Margaret replied that 'it was not here the custom and that I should be dishonoured and holden for a fool and light'.

But Henry VIII would brook no argument. Margaret of Austria was forced to find another plea: that the English were so soon to leave the country. This went down better but Henry warned Margaret that she would surely have to marry somebody: 'that I was yet too young for to abide thus; and that the ladies of his country did remarry at fifty and threescore years'. Margaret insisted she had no desire to marry again: 'I was too much unhappy in husbands.' But the men would not believe her. Twice more, in Brandon's presence, Henry urged the match on Margaret, telling her again that she might well be forced into a marriage. Unconvinced by her protests, 'he made me to promise in his hand that howsoever I should be pressed of my father, or otherwise, I should not make alliance of marriage [with] prince of the world, at the least unto his return, or the end of the year'.

What was going on? Was Henry truly playing Cupid, sportingly trying to help his crony towards this great match? Was he trying to avoid Margaret making another match; one disadvantageous to England? And what of the feelings of the two people most involved?

In what sounds like a three-way conversation 'at Tournai in my chamber one night after supper, full late', Brandon told Margaret (she wrote) he would never marry, nor yet take 'lady nor mistress, without my commandment, but would continue all his life my right humble servant'. These were the tropes of courtly love; Margaret of Austria, that child of a determinedly chivalrous court, was perhaps taken in. She promised 'to be to him such mistress all my life as to him who me seemed desired to do me most of service'. And after that, said Margaret crossly, there was, nor should have been, any more said of the affair, if it had not been for some 'gracious letters' which had not been carefully and privately kept.

She was not, after all, quite swept away. Not too swept away to query whether King Henry, in his role of '*trwcheman*' or go-between, had (for whatever motive) perhaps protested even more than Brandon felt, or to note that many of the questions asked about the rumoured match seemed to be more concerned with Henry's part in it than her own.

Margaret had been told, she wrote, that Brandon had shown off a diamond ring of hers 'which I cannot believe, for I esteem him much a man of virtue and wise'. But one night at Tournai, 'after the banquet he put himself upon his knees before me and in speaking and him playing, he drew from my finger the ring and put it upon his and then showed it to me and I took to laugh'.

Margaret told Brandon he was a thief, a '*laron*' and that she hadn't thought the king kept thieves in his company. Brandon couldn't understand the word *laron*, so Margaret tried the Flemish word, '*dieffe*', and begged him (once that evening, when he seemed not to understand her and once next morning through the king) to return the ring to her 'because it was too much known'. She gave him one of her bracelets instead; a less incriminatingly familiar piece of jewellery.

But Brandon took the ring from her again at Lille and would not give it back, saying he would give her other, better, rings. He 'would not' understand her protests and Margaret could only beg that the jewel would never be shown to anybody. She had been carried beyond what her prudence would allow. But all the same, at bottom the matter of the ring was, or should have been, a courtly game. Fun, flattering, and genuinely warming, no doubt, to a woman who was still, as Henry VIII kept reminding her, too young to have given up on love, but not in itself to be taken seriously.

The serious part came in the second letter, in which Margaret of Austria promised to show 'all the inconveniences which may happen of this thing'. She had been horrified to discover the business was being spoken of at home, abroad, even in Germany 'so openly as in the hands of merchant strangers'. An English merchant had dared to make wagers upon it and though she was grateful for everything Henry had done to quash the story, 'yet I see the bruit is so imprinted in the fantasies of people . . . [that] I continue always in fear'.

The letter shows her not as the powerful fixer but as a very rattled, still-young, woman. Nonetheless, Margaret of Austria had made her choice: power over pleasure. But the same trap that had caught even the confident and experienced Margaret of Austria may in the same year have ensnared the more vulnerable Marguerite of Navarre.

Clever, complex, self-critical and conflicted, Marguerite was the author of a huge body of published writings that were highly unusual for her day in exploring, almost obsessively, a woman's inner journey. Most notable is the *Heptaméron*, a collection of stories about love and lust, supposedly told to each other by a group of stranded travellers, which Marguerite wrote later in life. Though modelled (like Christine de Pizan's *City of Ladies*) on Boccaccio's *Decameron*, parts of the *Heptaméron* display so many echoes of real life that the idea that it is to some degree autobiographical cannot entirely be dismissed [**see note on sources**].

Her near-contemporary, the writer Brantôme, identifies Marguerite and a young nobleman called Guillaume Gouffier, Seigneur de Bonnivet, as the protagonists of one particular story that describes a sexual assault. Although much of Brantôme's writing is scurrilous to the point of pornography, he is the better a witness for the fact that both his mother and his grandmother had been Marguerite's ladies-in-waiting.

The protagonists of novella ten of the *Heptaméron* are Floride and Amadour; the flowerily-named Marguerite and the amorous Bonnivet? In the novel Amadour had been married to Floride's favourite attendant, Avanturade, who died early; in real life Bonnivet married Marguerite's lady-in-waiting Bonaventure, who likewise died young. Floride had known Amadour in childhood; just so had the real-life Bonnivet come into Marguerite's family circle when his elder brother was appointed to oversee the education of her brother François. That was in Marguerite's youth but in 1513 Marguerite had been four years a married woman, which made her fair game in the essentially adulterous sport of courtly love.

In December 1513 Marguerite and her husband, Alençon, visited Louise in Cognac. The hapless Alençon had fallen from his horse and broken his arm when François came to join them, with Bonnivet in his train. And, if the events of the *Heptaméron* are in any sense autobiographical, Bonnivet was set on the path 'that leads to the forbidden goal of a lady's honour'. The protagonists of the novel have an encounter in which Amadour seizes Floride's hands and takes her feet 'in a vice-like grip'. 'His whole expression, his face, his eyes change as he speaks. The fair complexion flushes with a fiery red; the kind, gentle face contorts with a terrifying violence, as if there were a raging inferno belching fire in his heart and behind his eyes. When Floride repulses him he claims to have been merely testing her; a familiar trope of the courtly love story.[2]

Marguerite had a difficult and dramatic emotional history.* A letter to her spiritual advisor tells us than in her childhood Louise of Savoy had so 'beaten and berated' Marguerite for some 'folly and guile', that Marguerite could not believe her mother really loved her. But the continued prevalence of sexual violence in Marguerite's writing may suggest some specific concern or trauma. The narrator of the *Heptaméron*, Parlamente, warns her female listeners against men's treachery: 'A woman's love is rooted in God and founded on honour . . . But most [men's] love is based on pleasure, so much so that women not being aware of men's evil intentions, sometimes allow themselves to be drawn too far.'

Perhaps, like Margaret of Austria, Marguerite of Navarre had learnt a painful lesson. And there was a lesson there for Anne Boleyn too, surely, though only time would prove how well or badly she had learnt it.

---

* Marguerite's lifelong concern with the establishment of hospitals and the care of orphaned children makes it very hard not to think of another people's princess who compensated for lack of love closest to home by loving all the world in the hope it would love her.

8

Flodden

Scotland, England, 1513

T HE SAME QUARREL between France and its neighbours that had taken Charles Brandon across the Channel was also fought in the British Isles, and would continue to be fought through the first part of the century. Where France led, its old ally Scotland would usually follow, whereas in England, Katherine of Aragon had been one of the chief promoters of war against France, her Aragonese father's ancient enemy.

As the Venetian ambassador put it: 'the King is bent on war, the Council is averse to it; the Queen will have it and the wisest councillors in England cannot stand against the Queen'. But any resumption of the centuries-old conflict between England and Scotland would set Katherine of Aragon painfully at odds with her husband's sister, Margaret Tudor, wife of the King of Scots.

When Henry VIII set off on campaign in France in the summer of 1513, Katherine was left as 'Regent and Governess' of England, albeit with a council of noblemen to advise her. Her appointment might well have been controversial. Half a century earlier, when Henry VI's wife Margaret of Anjou had tried to exercise power during his incapacity, the result had been a power struggle culminating in civil war: the Wars of the Roses.

'Moreover it is a right great perversion / A woman of a land to be a regent' ran a popular ditty, while descriptions of Margaret of Anjou as a 'great and strong laboured woman' went hand in hand with slurs on her sexual morality. But since then, the mechanics of Henry VIII's accession had been (in the words of the Garter Herald) 'over seen by the mother of the said late king'; Henry VII's mother, Margaret Beaufort. Katherine's influence over her husband's policies was an accepted, if not necessarily a welcome, fact. And there was, in any case, a different tussle looming.

Scotland's 'auld alliance' with France had set it too on a collision course with the 'holy alliance' of which England was a part, dragging the two island neighbours into war with each other. Katherine herself – just as had her mother Isabella of Castile – accompanied the country's army northwards when the Scots took advantage of Henry's absence and invaded. Peter Martyr d'Anghiera, historian and tutor at the Spanish court, heard that 'in imitation of her mother Isabella', Katherine gave a moving speech to rally the troops, telling them that 'they should be ready to defend their territory, that the Lord smiled upon those who stood in defence of their own'.

She wrote to the Netherlands (her letter addressed to that rising man Thomas Wolsey, there with King Henry) that she was busy 'making standards, banners, and badges'. She also wrote to Margaret of Austria, asking her to send a physician to Henry. And, like her mother Isabella before her, Katherine immersed herself in the most fundamental preparations for war. She organised troops and money to go northwards – artillery, provisions and ships – and told Wolsey also that 'My heart is very good to it.'

The Earl of Surrey, in the north, was England's first line of defence and a second wave of troops was stationed across the Midlands. But Katherine herself (who carried in her luggage a light gold helmet with a crown) was prepared if necessary to command a third wave even further to the south, despite the fact that she was perhaps once again in the early stages of pregnancy. Events meant her force was not needed but the possibility was sufficiently realistic for the Venetian ambassador in London to report that, 'Our queen also took the field against the Scots with a numerous force one hundred miles from here.'

Katherine of Aragon's fervour was in sharp contrast to the feelings of Margaret Tudor, who Katherine had known a decade before, on her first arrival in England, and with whom, on a personal level, she felt considerable sympathy.

Margaret Tudor had always taken seriously the idea that it was her mission to bring about closer relations between England and Scotland, but that dream had looked fragile almost from the start of her brother's reign. Her husband, James IV, had been horrified by the anti-French league formed between England and its allies, including Spain, the Empire and the papacy. He wrote – and made Margaret write – to the crowned heads of Europe, beseeching them to keep the peace.

One welcome event in the spring of 1512 was the birth of another son. But Margaret Tudor's hopes of an Anglo-Scottish alliance seemed far from accomplishment, and further than ever when the French queen Anne of Brittany sent James her glove, with a letter begging him to be her champion. Margaret was horrified that her husband took so seriously a gesture from the games of chivalry. Later stories report that she dreamt of seeing him hurled from a cliff, while her own jewels, under her horrified gaze, changed from diamonds into a widow's pearls.

A kind of family relationship continued; the ambassador who came north to talk to James also brought a letter from Henry to Margaret. When Margaret had recently been pregnant with her surviving boy, Henry and Katherine had sent the girdle of Our Lady to her from Westminster Abbey. But when, dining with the ambassador, Margaret plied him with questions about the brother she had not seen for a decade – and also about the enthusiasm husband and brother shared for building up their navies – the man assumed she had been told by her husband to gather naval secrets. Small wonder the ambassador reported that she ended the meeting 'right heavy'.

The collapse of the Treaty of Perpetual Peace between England and Scotland – by now clearly inevitable – was all the more strange for the fact that Margaret Tudor and her Scottish son were still Henry VIII's heirs. Henry was in France when the Scottish herald arrived, bearing a declaration of war. Henry shouted that James IV was a man of no faith and that he himself was, harking back to a claim made centuries before, 'the very owner' of Scotland, which James held only by homage. It would 'become him, being married to the king of England's sister, to recount the king of England his ally,' Henry said. 'I care nothing but for the mistreating of my sister, that would God she were in England on a condition she cost the Scottish king not a penny.'

Presciently, James IV had not waited to hear Henry VIII's reply before he began to muster his armies. On his way to join them, he called at Linlithgow to see Margaret, now (like Katherine) in the early throes of another pregnancy. He dismissed her dreams of his death, her pleas that he should not go: 'It is no dream. Ye are to fight a mighty people.' If she really spoke those words, they could have been in pride as well as terror, since they had been her people too. There is a tower in Linlithgow from which, yet another romantic story says, Margaret strained her eyes southwards to watch for James's return. But they also say that, so certain had she been of what would happen that day, she did not send to search the battlefield at Flodden where, on 9 September, the armies met.

The loss of Scottish life was appalling; perhaps as many as ten thousand men. Katherine, in England, described the victory in triumphant terms to Henry, sending her husband the coat of the slain Scottish king, James IV. She would have sent the king himself (as a prisoner, or as a corpse?), she wrote, 'but our Englishmen's hearts would not suffer it'.

When the news of her husband's death, 140 rugged miles away, reached Margaret Tudor at Linlithgow, the 23-year-old pregnant widow acted both swiftly and decisively. Though the battle had been fought well south of the border, the English armies might yet advance into Scotland. Margaret took her eighteen-month-old son, the new James V, further inland, to her castle of Stirling, where the rocky crags below made the castle at least feel invulnerable. There, James V was crowned on 21 September, just twelve days after his father's death, in what became known as the Mourning Coronation.

After the catastrophe of Flodden, only fifteen temporal lords and a handful of bishops were left alive to help Margaret govern the country. A reeling council, a mere twenty-three men, hastily read and approved the will James had made before he left Linlithgow, which appointed Margaret as regent for their son. Just half a century earlier, after all, Scotland had seen another queen consort, Mary of Guelders, act as regent for her son, the nine-year-old James III. Margaret was to be 'testamentary tutrix' to the new James V, though she was not to act without a quorum of lords that would be permanently on hand to advise her.

In their wreck of a country, Margaret Tudor and the Scottish council acted swiftly to try to restore order. As September turned to October, royal proclamations were sent out forbidding the looting of houses and the molesting of women left (as so very many were) without a male protector. Stirling, and other fortresses, were strengthened, for all that there were hardly enough men left to garrison them.

Very quickly, however, cracks began to appear in the Scottish command. When Margaret wrote to the pope, suggesting her candidates for several bishoprics left vacant when their incumbents died at Flodden, there was anger that she had failed to consult the lords about her choices. More seriously, there was division over what line to pursue with England, whose troops were still, as a punitive measure, burning crops and raiding villages along the Scottish border. A number of younger lords wanted to continue the war and avenge their kinsmen. To do so, they wanted the help of their traditional ally, France. And they wanted a military leader, the obvious candidate being the man who was now (since the infant James V had as yet no siblings) Scotland's heir.

John Stuart, Duke of Albany, cousin of James IV, had spent his whole life in exile in France, his father having been exiled after trying to seize the Scottish throne. Now, many lords thought he should be recalled. On 26 November the council wrote to the French king, asking him to send Albany home to Scotland 'for its defence'. Margaret was to continue her role as regent and tutrix of the young king, whose person was to be 'kept as devised in the late King's will'. Henry VIII for one was horrified, convinced that Albany might easily depose a vulnerable baby monarch; might spirit him away to the Outer Isles and thence who knew where, much as his great-uncle Richard III was widely believed to have spirited away his nephews, the 'Princes in the Tower'. Henry saw himself as his Scottish nephew's natural protector. But that was not how the situation appeared to the Scots.

For Margaret Tudor, there must have been a clash of loyalties; a clash familiar to many royal consorts but surely in this case worse than most, since her husband had actually been killed by her brother's troops. Yet in the task that now came upon her so suddenly, Henry was the closest natural advisor she had left for the protection of herself and her son. For their part the Scottish lords must have looked at Margaret with double vision. On the one hand she was their queen, wife of one beloved Scottish king and mother of their present ruler. On the other, she was the sister of the man, Henry VIII, who had caused that same king's death and brought them defeat and disgrace. The message Henry sent north was tactfully mediated – that Margaret's sister-in-law, Katherine of Aragon, sent her love – but the more Margaret Tudor seemed to turn towards her brother for help, the more divided the perception of her grew.

For all her triumphalism, Katherine expressed herself personally sympathetic to Margaret. 'The Queen of England for the love she bears the Queen of Scots would gladly send a servant to comfort her.' Margaret wrote back asking Katherine to put her in Henry's remembrance. In the weeks after Flodden Katherine did indeed send Friar Bonaventure Langley to Stirling to discuss a truce. As can be seen time and again, the personal, the feminine, was a cover for the political. One story had Margaret claiming war might have been averted had she only been able to meet with the sister-in-law she had known at the English court: 'If we shall meet, who knows what God by our means may bring to pass?' But any closeness to the Queen of England could still be one strike against the Queen of Scotland.

Margaret Tudor suffered other disadvantages. Unlike her European contemporaries, or Katherine, she had been raised by a woman, Elizabeth of York, who had been kept away from power by her husband Henry VII. Margaret struggled to occupy a position to which, Tudor-like, she laid claim but for which nothing in her life had prepared her.

In the years ahead she would find herself caught in a different trap; the trap that lay in wait for powerful women. The trap that had entangled Marguerite of Navarre and Margaret of Austria and the trap that (not at the courts of France or the Netherlands but at that of England) would have one last deadly game to play. Meanwhile, the protagonist of that legendary drama was soon to move from the orbit of Margaret of Austria to that of Marguerite of Navarre, as the shifting landscape of the European scene sent the young Anne Boleyn her way.

PART II

1514–1521

When it comes to the government of their affairs, [widowed women] must depend only on themselves; when it comes to sovereignty, they must not cede power to anyone. And then, you must protect yourself from deceitful and presumptuous followers, especially those with whom you conduct business often, because of the suspicions that can arise . . .

Lessons for my Daughter, Anne of France
(Anne de Beaujeu), published 1517–1521

9

Wheel of Fortune

France, the Netherlands, 1514–1515

ACHIAVELLI ENVISAGED FORTUNE as a woman. But the events immediately following the traumatic year of 1513 made it clear no spirit of sisterhood would move Fortune to give her fellow women an easy ride. Louise of Savoy in France, and Margaret of Austria in the Netherlands, were both to find themselves spinning on her wheel.

On 9 January 1514, just before her thirty-seventh birthday, Anne of Brittany, Louis XII's queen, died. Her funeral saw an extended parade of ceremony suitable not just for a queen but for a king, as well as an outpouring of public grief; both recognising, perhaps, the doughty part she had played in trying against the odds to preserve the independence of her duchy.

But Anne of Brittany's death was like a stone dropped in a pond. And the ripples spreading from this stone would reach to touch Margaret of Austria, as well as Louise of Savoy's family.

Anne de Beaujeu played a prominent part in the funeral ceremonies, as did Louise of Savoy and her children. Louise's daughter Marguerite would assume an older sister's role towards the two daughters Anne of Brittany left: fourteen-year-old Claude (now Duchess of Brittany in her own right, thanks to the marriage agreement Anne had made with Louis XII before their marriage) and little Renée, who would come to absorb some of Marguerite's ideas. Louise noted in her *Journal*:

Anne, queen of France, passing from life to death, left me the administration of her goods, her fortune and her daughters . . . a charge of which I have acquitted myself honourably and kindly; this is known to all, a recognised and demonstrable truth and confirmed by public opinion.

Plans were carried out as arranged. On 14 May François underwent a binding marriage ceremony with Claude; a marriage that made him Duke of Brittany. François's friend Fleuranges wrote that Claude had inherited her mother Anne of Brittany's disapproval of François and his clan: 'never a day but those two houses were bickering'. Personal compatibility was not the point, however, and François must have felt confident as he went hunting the next day.

But the hopes of Louise and her family had been founded on the inability of the pair on the French throne to produce a son. Anne of Brittany's death – paving the way for a younger bride for King Louis XII – could yet prove worrying for them.

Henry VIII's younger sister, the eighteen-year-old Mary Tudor, had long been contracted to marry Margaret of Austria's nephew, Charles. Mary had only recently been in correspondence with Margaret about the style of dress the Flemish ladies preferred. But earlier, in 1514, as Margaret of Austria urged ever more desperately that her father should push ahead with the match between her nephew and the English princess, a match vital for fostering the peace in her Netherlands territories, her father Maximilian and her erstwhile father-in-law Ferdinand were conspiring to keep her in the dark about very different plans.

In 1514 Ferdinand wrote to his ambassador (was he supposed to show Margaret the letter?) that she was 'the most important person in Christendom, since she acts as mediator in almost all the negotiations between the princes'. In another letter, he wrote that 'Madam Margaret is the person on whom, more than anyone else on earth, peace or war depends.' But the flattery may have been intended to keep her in line.

He and Maximilian now proposed that instead of marrying Mary Tudor, as had been arranged, to cement the alliance between England and the Habsburgs, Charles should instead marry the French king's little daughter, Renée. Ferdinand was also offering the recently bereaved Louis XII a new bride of his own; either Margaret herself, or Margaret's niece Eleanor. Louis chose the nubile Eleanor and the marriage articles were drawn up.

'Madame Margaret', Ferdinand said:

> dwells on the great difference of age between the King of France [fifty-one] and Madame Eleanor [seventeen]. Lanuza [the ambassador] is to tell her that in marriage of great kings difference of age is never taken into account . . . Madame Margaret is mistaken if she thinks it a disadvantage that Madame Eleanor is so thin. Thin women generally . . . bear more children than stout ones . . .

As Margaret frantically wrote to Maximilian, it was all very well for Spain to make peace with France. They had the barrier of the mountains to protect them, and England had the sea. The Netherlands, long the object of France's rapacity, were protected by no such freak of geography. But no holds were barred in the attempt to unite the empire, France and Spain into one future 'family', of which Maximilian envisaged himself the head. And when England too made its peace with France, there was yet another change of marriage plans. The proposed marriage between Louis XII and Eleanor was off. Instead, he would marry the woman who had been promised to Margaret's nephew Charles: King Henry VIII of England's sister Mary.

In addition to the hastily assembled trousseau and to the immense 'Mirror of Naples' diamond the French king had sent as a wedding gift, Mary Tudor would, of course, take a number of English ladies in her train, and the Boleyns were never going to miss such an opportunity. In August 1514, Thomas Boleyn wrote to Margaret of Austria to ask that his daughter might be released from service in order – her French, thanks to Margaret, being now so good! – to transfer to the French court. The place Margaret had given Anne Boleyn as a great favour was to be put aside for an even more promising opportunity.

Anne's name is not on the list of those who accompanied Mary on her journey from England and she is not recorded as being in France until slightly later. Her whereabouts for those few months are unknown. Margaret of Austria and her court were in Zeeland when Thomas Boleyn's letter arrived and that may have caused the delay. Or Margaret may have stalled, either from reluctance to foster this Anglo-French marriage in even the smallest way, or out of sheer pique. And, as Margaret would feel acutely, Mary Tudor's was far from the only royal marriage that year.

In May, Margaret of Austria's niece Mary was summoned to Maximilian's court in Vienna, preparatory to a marriage with the son of the King of Hungary. In June, Margaret was called upon to arrange, at very short notice, the marriage of her niece Isabella, not yet thirteen, to King Christian of Denmark, twenty years Isabella's senior, whose ambassadors arrived on a Wednesday and, on the Saturday, declared their wish that the marriage should take place the next day, the day of Christian's coronation. 'But Monseigneur', Margaret wrote to her father, 'it was very difficult to arrange such a solemn function in so short a time . . . but, anxious to please them and gratify their desires, I agreed . . . and I did my best to have everything arranged and put in order.' The bride at least, she wrote touchingly, was a figure 'it certainly did one good to look at'. This marriage would end badly but for the next year Isabella, like her elder sister Eleanor (now re-betrothed to the heir of Portugal), was to be left in Margaret's care.[1]

Margaret of Austria also found herself under pressure from events within the Netherlands. Her nephew Charles was now in his teens and beginning to resent the government of an autocratic aunt. She had long been at odds with William de Croy, the Sieur de Chievres, the nobleman who had been left as governor of the country in her brother's absence, until Margaret replaced him. Chievres remained tutor and mentor to her young nephew Charles, working well enough with Margaret until the League against France she had helped to mould offended his strongly French sympathies. Things came to a head over a seemingly unrelated matter. Castile – one of the territories of which Charles would be ruler – was in the grip of a nationalist movement; the Castilians concerned alike about their current government by Ferdinand of Aragon and their future under a boy being reared wholly in the Netherlands. The Castilian faction at Margaret of Austria's court was headed by Don Juan Manuel de la Cerda, a political agitator whom Ferdinand was anxious to get into his hands. It seemed a comparatively minor matter to Margaret to have Don Juan arrested with the intention of sending him to Aragon, but she found she had gone too far.

Don Juan was a knight of the Order of the Golden Fleece, the glorious chivalric order of Burgundy to which even privileged foreign males such as Henry VIII were proud to belong. Now the knights – headed by Charles as their titular leader, and by Chievres – came to Margaret in a deputation, furiously brandishing the statutes which declared that one of the order could be tried only by his brother knights. Margaret was indignant and uncomprehending: 'Ah, Messeigneurs, if I were such a man as I am a woman I would make you bring your statutes to me and make you sing out passages from them!' (Perhaps she was aware that her former mother-in-law Isabella of Castile had persuaded the papacy to grant her administration of three such chivalric orders, although not without some masculine grumbling that this was 'a monstrous thing'.)

The affair ended when Maximilian (himself a former head of the order) had Don Juan brought to Germany for investigation. But Margaret of Austria had lost much goodwill among the local nobility.

Under the influence of Chievres, the Estates General demanded that Charles should be declared of age, offering Maximilian a large sum of money if he would agree. Maximilian did not even warn Margaret he was planning to do so. No wonder her letters to him complain that he does not take her fully into his confidence, so that the foreign ambassadors seem to know more of events than she.

In the spring of 1515, letters from Charles to the various provinces of the Netherlands declared 'it is fit and reasonable that all things which concern our rights, greatness, lordship and even the doing of justice and our other affairs, should be conducted henceforth in our name and under our title'.

Maximilian himself wrote to Charles (and sent a copy to Margaret) that: 'we make no doubt, because of the honour and love you owe to our very dear daughter, your aunt, that you communicate your chief and most arduous business to her and that you take and use her good advice . . .' But Maximilian was to find he too was no longer as important as he had been in Charles's country.

Now that Margaret of Austria was displaced, complaints about her rule came in thick and fast. She was blamed for having failed to maintain the alliance she had made with the Netherlands' trading partner, England and for having used Netherlands money for alien wars – although it might be more accurate to say that she had failed entirely to stop her father from doing so – and even for having illegitimately enriched herself.

Through all this Margaret had to put on a brave face, as she accompanied her nephew on the extended tour that marked the handover of power. But, as she wrote to her father, she asked herself whether she should not retire south to her own lands and devote herself to her own 'small interests'. Shortly after Charles's emancipation – while Maximilian nonetheless continued to bombard her with business – she replied that she had passed on his letter to de Chievres but could do no more, 'for now I do not meddle in any business'.

In fact, time would show that Margaret of Austria was too determined, too canny a politician to remain long in the shadows. Someone who could be circumvented, yes, but still someone around whom even the most alpha males moved carefully. After that six-month tour of the provinces with her nephew, at a meeting of the council she read aloud to Charles a memorandum refuting the accusations made against her, accusations planned, she said, 'to give you suspicions of me, your humble aunt, to withdraw from me your goodwill and confidence, which would indeed be a poor recompense for the services which I have rendered you until now . . .'

'Item: Madame has lent her money for State affairs and has greatly reduced the expenses of her own household . . . For three years, far from having a pension for her services, she spent her dowry as long as it lasted'. At the end of her oration it was agreed 'that Madame was held fully discharged from all things'. Margaret of Austria 'gracefully' retired for a time into her books, her estates, her ongoing plans for the building of her husband Philibert's tomb in Brou. But she did so without any shadow hanging over her head.

'a splendid New Year's gift'

France, 1514–1515

ANOTHER ROYAL DEATH in France would soon prove to be another turn of the wheel of Fortune. This one meant that while Margaret of Austria's star seemed to have fallen, that of her erstwhile playmate Louise of Savoy would rise dramatically. But not without some scares along the way.

The arrival in France of Mary Tudor – young, nubile, and presumably fertile – cannot have been welcome to Louise and her family, anxious lest the birth of a son to the old king should spoil François's chance of the throne. But old Louis XII seemed enchanted with his new bride and claimed to have performed great feats in the bedroom.

Perhaps no one quite believed it. François's friend, the courtier and adventurer Fleuranges, reported François had told him: 'unless people are lying very hard, I now know that the king and queen cannot possibly have children'. But there were other worrying possibilities. As the king's son-in-law and putative heir, François had led the party to welcome Mary Tudor and taken a starring role in the jousts in her honour. He got on notably well with his beautiful nineteen-year-old stepmother-in-law. Soon Louise was being warned to keep a close eye on her son, lest he himself father a male baby to supplant him. But Louise's anxieties were not to last.

Fleuranges reported rumours that the King of England had sent a filly to the King of France to gallop him off to heaven or to hell. It proved all too accurate a prophecy. Less than three months after Mary Tudor was married, on 1 January 1515, her husband Louis XII was dead.

Fleuranges described how the new François I put on mourning clothes and, 'coming to the palace in haste, informed all the princes and ladies of the kingdom, especially his mother, Madame Louise. It was a splendid New Year's gift, I must say . . .' Louise recorded: 'On the first day of January I lost my husband and on the first day of January my son became king of France.'

Technically, it was unclear whether François was king until it was confirmed that Mary Tudor was not pregnant. But the principle of 'the king is dead – long live the king' prevailed, the more so since no one thought a posthumous baby was likely. The official period of mourning was cut short and François was crowned at the end of the month.

For the new dynasty in France, Mary Tudor, the old king's widow, represented a loose thread. But Mary would find her own solution; another Tudor sister prepared to put passion before policy. Wolsey had urgently warned, from the earliest days of her widowhood, that she should give no heed to any new 'motion of marriage' that might be made to her. 'I trust the King my brother and you will not reckon in me such childhood', she replied, from her widow's seclusion, indignantly.

But there were 'motions' a-plenty. Rumours of the Duke of Lorraine, of François himself putting Claude away to marry her, of her brother cementing another foreign, this time Habsburg, alliance with her hand. It may have been this, and an awareness that disputes over her dowry would play a major part in her future, if it were negotiated between the two kings, that decided Mary Tudor to act.

Before she left England she had extracted an informal promise from her brother that if she married the aged King Louis, she would be allowed to choose her next husband. And she knew on whom her choice would light. Charles Brandon had escorted her to France; in January he was sent to negotiate her return to England. There was already an acknowledged attraction between the pair, and on Brandon's arrival Mary sent for him. 'I never saw woman so weep', wrote Brandon afterwards in excuse, telling Wolsey on 5 March that. 'The queen would never let me be in rest till I had granted her to be married and so, to be plain with you, I have married her heartily and lain with her.'

This was more than lèse-majesté, but the couple could rely on a measure of protection from the French, to whom this appeared a handy way of avoiding either the expense of a queen dowager permanently in France or of Mary's being used to cement some unwelcome political alliance. With Mary's brother Henry, it was a different story. But even he was not too angry to be placated by the couple's promising to make over to him Mary's dowry and any goods she had received through her marriage. (To François's fury, she sweetened the deal by smuggling back to her brother in England the fabulous Mirror of Naples.) Returning home, her marriage confirmed in a public English ceremony, Mary Tudor settled into a future of domesticity. Many of her English ladies returned home with her but Anne Boleyn (perhaps because her command of French was so good) remained behind.* In the early days of her French sojourn, Anne had, if later stories are to be believed, to witness her sister Mary's a brief relationship with the libidinous François, and to witness, too, its detrimental effect on Mary Boleyn's reputation. The lessons in love, and in the dangers it posed for women, were coming in thick and fast.

Mary Tudor's was not the future every royal woman would choose. Louise of Savoy's *Journal* noted coolly that Mary, on the last day of March, had married Brandon, 'a person of low estate'. Temperamentally, perhaps, Louise had more in common with Margaret of Austria. She too could vouch for Brandon's charms but she received word of such an illicit love match with incomprehension. Something, she wrote to Maximilian, so senseless that the idea would never have entered her head.

Louise of Savoy was almost forty, still in her prime, when her son François I inherited the French throne. There seems from the first to have been a sense that the business of government – at least in these early stages of his reign – was at least as much her concern as her son's. 'A boy's best friend is his mother' might have been the motto for early modern monarchs. England had recently seen two new rulers

---

* There has long been debate over whether Anne Boleyn, appointed to Queen Claude's household, remained there for the duration of her stay in France, or whether she was transferred to that of Marguerite, who seems a more likely mentor. But Marguerite's involvement in her brother's court perhaps makes the distinction unnecessary, and we can assume Anne would at the very least have been acutely conscious of the doings of so charismatic a figure.

– Edward IV and Henry VII – treat their mothers as mentors (and unlike those two, François had not had to fight for his crown).

As the main officers of state were confirmed in their office (as François's brother-in-law, Alençon, his sister Marguerite's husband, was declared second person of the realm and Bonnivet Admiral of France), several of Louise's trusted officials were also given important places. She herself was given estates – the duchy of Angoulême, that of Anjou, the counties of Maine and Beaufort and the barony of Amboise – that made her hugely wealthy.

Nor was the earlier governess of the French royal family, Anne de Beaujeu, forgotten. Her son-in-law, the Duc de Bourbon, was made Constable of France. This would be an appointment with consequences, since the amalgamation of Bourbon's own lands with those Anne's daughter Suzanne stood to inherit made a huge and potentially controversial land mass right in the centre of France. Anne, like Louise and Marguerite but unlike François's wife, the pregnant Claude, accompanied François to his coronation in Rheims.

As Louise of Savoy's *Journal* had it:

> This day of the Conversion of St Paul 1515 my son was anointed and consecrated in the church of Rheims. For this I hold myself grateful to the Divine Mercy, by which I am amply repaid for all the adversities and inconvenience which came to me in my early years and in the flower of my youth. Humility has borne me company and Patience has never abandoned me.

The humility was not evident to all. Charles Brandon wrote of Louise to Henry VIII: 'it is she who runs all and so may she well; for I never saw a woman like to her, both for wit, honour and dignity. She hath a great stroke in all matters with the King her son.'

A Venetian envoy asked the veteran Marshal Trivulzio who really held power in the land; who controlled the king? The answer was that Louise of Savoy,

> lays claim to managing everything, not allowing him to act without her concurrence . . . it is his mother, with Madame de Bourbon [the still-active Anne de Beaujeu] and Boisy [François's former

governor, Bonnivet's brother], who really manage everything. It is a great pity to see him under petticoat government. But what can you expect, the way he lives? He does not get out of bed until a little before noon. Then, after dressing and hearing mass, he goes straight to dinner. Immediately afterwards he withdraws to his mother. Then, after a short while with the council, he plunges into amusement which goes on incessantly until supper time.

Venice now knew to whom to apply. 'The Most Christian King's most illustrious mother' was soon assuring the Venetians her son would prove 'the greatest and most faithful friend' their city had ever had.

The year before her son's accession, Louise of Savoy had been at Blois when the ceiling of her room came down. 'I think it was a sign that the whole of this house was destined to rest on me', she wrote later in her *Journal*, 'and that I was divinely appointed to have charge of it.' But in many ways it would be a burden, as well as an opportunity. When the Venetian envoy added that François's mother 'applies all her energy to accumulating money', it was a reputation that would cling to Louise. But perhaps it was also the result of what one writer called Louise's avidity for security; something Louise shared with Henry VII's mother, Lady Margaret Beaufort. But Henry had shared his mother's close-fistedness, while Louise faced the very real problem of how freely her son could spend, not least on the expensive sport of war.

On Louise of Savoy, inevitably, fell much of the task of helping to sort out the difficult relationships of François I's reign. His relationship with Charles V, as ruler of the Netherlands, seemed in the short term to be assured by Charles's betrothal to Louis XII's four-year-old daughter Renée (yet another royal marriage destined never to take place). Louise hoped also to bring the pope to her side, by arranging the marriage of his Medici brother to her half-sister, Philiberte of Savoy.

But the three-way relationship between the French crown, the papacy and France's secular and religious bodies had long been edgy. In 1516 François, surely with Louise's advice behind the scenes, hammered out with Pope Leo an agreement known as the Concordat of Bologna, which gave François the right to nominate his own religious officials. This, however, put him into conflict with the Paris *parlement* and with the faculty of theology at the university, which had previously been involved in making such appointments.* The *parlement* was likewise outraged that the king's sister Marguerite and her husband Alençon had been given an annual pension of twenty thousand *livres* and the lucrative right to name the head of each of France's trade guilds, as well as the duchy of Armagnac, which the *parlement* held to be inalienably attached to the French crown itself.

Marguerite's role in her brother's quarrels with both his *parlement* and his religious authorities would have later consequences, not least for Marguerite. But for the moment, his generosity meant her husband Alençon accepted that her place would now be largely at her brother's court, where she took on many of the ceremonial duties of a queen, just as her mother accepted much of the workload of a king. In story four of the *Heptaméron* Marguerite wrote of a young prince ('fond of the ladies, of hunting and generally enjoying himself') whose wife 'was rather difficult and did not enjoy the same things as he did, so he always used to take his sister along as well'. Her letters to him were most often signed as François's most humble and most obedient subject and sister, or '*et mignonne*', darling.

Queen Claude was shy, plain and afflicted with a limp, and almost solidly pregnant, with deliveries in 1515, 1516, 1518, 1519, 1520, 1522 and 1523, though only two of the children outlived their parents. But it seems Louise of Savoy – and surely Marguerite too – valued Claude for what she could do for François and they could not. Though the near-contemporary biographer the Seigneur de Brantôme wrote that Claude was bullied by her mother-in-law as well as ignored by her husband, there is no evidence that she resented her treatment; she had, after all, grown up partly under Marguerite's and Louise's, wing.

The relationship between mother and son was so close that when François ran a thorn into his leg, Louise wrote that 'true love forced me to suffer the same pain'. So her feelings about her son's natural venturesomeness were mixed. She was terrified when he had a boar captured

---

* The Paris was by far the most powerful of France's seven *parlements* – a provincial high court, rather than a legislative assembly. François's voice in it was his chancellor, Duprat, a long-standing associate of Louise's.

and set loose in the courtyard at Amboise, only to kill it himself with one blow of the sword. It was infinitely worse when it became clear François was determined to pursue his ambitions for the disputed territory of Milan, to which he had an hereditary claim.

When François left for the Italian wars, taking all the nobles of his blood with him, he announced that his mother would act as regent while he was away:

> We have decided to leave the government of our realm to our well beloved and dear Lady and Mother, the Duchess of Angoulême and Anjou, in whom we have entire and perfect confidence who will by her virtue and prudence, know how to acquit this trust.

Though the Italian wars would prove to be an endlessly enduring business, François's efforts in 1515 met with impressive success. In September, the Battle of Marignano was, said one observer, a battle of giants, in which François's forces achieved an overwhelming victory over the army of Swiss mercenaries assembled by the Sforzas, the current rulers of Milan, in alliance with the Papal States. Never had there been seen so spirited and cruel a battle, François boasted to his mother. Louise, with Claude, immediately went on pilgrimage to Notre Dame de la Guiche to give thanks for the preservation of 'him, whom I love better than myself, my boy, glorious and triumphant Caesar, subjugator of the Swiss'. On 10 October, François entered Milan in triumph, the very model of a young warrior king.

When the news came of François's return from Marignano, Louise of Savoy, Marguerite and Claude set out to meet their 'triumphant Caesar', as Louise's journal describes him. 'God knows that I, poor mother, was overjoyed to see my son safe and whole after all he had suffered and endured to serve the common good.' By January 1516 they were with him for his triumphant entry into Marseille.

The pattern of Europe in the first half of the sixteenth century was one of three young men sowing their oats: François I, the Habsburg Charles and Henry VIII of England. Each had a woman – mother, aunt or wife – standing behind him. And if the last years had seen several women trying to juggle the demands of power with their female destiny, Louise seemed to have been the most successful.

'One of the lowest-brought ladies'

Scotland, England, 1515–1517

FOR HENRY VIII's elder sister, Margaret Tudor, things had long been going badly. But an event such the death of Louis XII in France had an effect far beyond his own country, even in distant Scotland, France's 'Auld Ally'.

As long ago as the autumn of 1513, Henry, in England, had been receiving agents' reports that the Scots lords 'were not pleased that the Queen should have rule, as they fear she will comply too much with England'. Even when, in February 1514, Margaret managed to push through an uneasy peace with England, not everyone on her council was happy.

But when in March 1514 the summoning of the Scottish parliament exhibited her to the people in the eighth month of her pregnancy, she was cheered to the rafters, the more so since her gracious speech left most of the real business of the session to others and allowed the parliament to take control of all the main fortresses in the country. As the madonna, the mother, the dead king's relict, she was welcome in the country. It was when she tried to overstep those bounds that there was a difficulty.

On 30 April she gave birth to a second son, Alexander, Duke of Ross. In England Henry and Katherine of Aragon, who had possibly suffered a miscarriage the previous autumn, still had no living child. That Margaret Tudor's offspring would succeed to the throne of England looked more likely than ever. In the summer she emerged from her confinement and on 12 July the Scottish nobles signed a unanimous statement in support of her regency. 'Madame,' it ran, 'we are content to stand in one mind and will to concur with all the lords of the realm to the pleasure of our master the King's grace, your grace and for the common weal . . .' Yet within a few weeks, the situation had changed completely.

On 14 August, in a secret ceremony, Margaret Tudor was married for a second time, to the Earl of Angus. Roughly her own age (twenty-four) he was a scion of the powerful but controversial Douglas clan, and hated by most of the other nobles.

History has often chosen to see Margaret as a fool for love, seduced by a pretty face, and so it might have been. Or she may, like other women in this story, have been determined to avoid her male relations marrying her off again for their own purposes. But it is also possible that she was trying to bolster her authority.[1] Throughout the last century the Douglases had almost rivalled the Scottish crown. But if that were her motive, then she could hardly have chosen more unwisely.

On 26 August the council demanded that Margaret Tudor should summon John Stuart, Duke of Albany, from France to become Governor of Scotland; to take her place, basically. Most councillors were behind a demand that she should surrender the Great Seal and issue no further proclamations. By the middle of September they were questioning whether it were even appropriate that she should remain in charge of her son, the baby king, James V. The provisions of her husband's will had been dependent upon her not remarrying. Now that was forfeit, as Lord Home trenchantly put it:

> We have shown heretofore our willingness to honour the Queen contrary to the ancient law and custom of this kingdom. We have suffered and obeyed her authority the whiles she herself kept her right by keeping her widowhood. Now she has quit it by marrying, why should we not choose another to succeed in the place she has voluntarily left?

The Lyon Herald was sent to inform Margaret that she was to be deposed from the regency. He addressed Margaret not as 'the Queen's Grace' but as 'My Lady the King's Mother', the title her grandmother and namesake Margaret Beaufort had borne so proudly. Margaret

Tudor took it less kindly. And her new husband's grandfather and mentor, old Lord Drummond, boxed the herald's ears, a staggering breach of propriety.

Margaret dismissed Drummond's insult to the Lyon Herald and, more seriously, nominated her husband Angus, whose own uncle called him a callow young fool, as her co-regent. Angus proved the truth of the description by attacking the lord chancellor, who had made clear his disapproval of the match, and seizing the Great Seal. The outraged nobility stopped Margaret's dower rents, while the lord chancellor and his followers rode to Edinburgh and took possession of the city.

This was civil war, or something very like it. Margaret and Angus promptly fled with Margaret's sons to Stirling Castle: 'my party adversary continues in their malice and proceed in their Parliament usurping the King's authority as I and my lords were of no reputation reputing us as rebels', was how she put it to her brother Henry VIII.

The Scottish lords would have allowed her to keep charge of her sons if she gave up her regent's powers but Margaret Tudor was having none of it. Her sons were 'right lifelike' (lively) she assured Henry. But she ended her letter: 'If you send not soon succours in men and money I shall be super extended.' She urged her brother to send an English army to where her husband was trying to relieve the besieged Castle of St Andrews. The army was to be proclaimed a peacekeeping force and the Scots told that 'their lands and goods shall not be hurt and they shall be recompensed double and treble'. But she was, essentially, inviting an enemy to occupy their country.

'Brother, all the welfare of me and my children rests in your hands', she wrote. She warned that her adversaries were forging her signature and Henry should take as genuine only those letters signed not just 'Margaret R' but 'your loving sister Margaret R'. In late January 1515, Henry VIII sent word that she should flee to the border but Margaret quailed at the practical difficulties, and at the implications for her and her son's power.

'God send I were such a woman that might go with my bairns in my arms', she wrote back. If that had been so, then 'I should not be long from you'. But she was a queen, and the death of the old French king, Louis XII, while making her sister Mary a merry widow, had dramatically weakened Margaret's position, depriving her a family connection to the French throne.

The promise King Louis had made to his bride's brother, Henry VIII, to keep the Duke of Albany in France, and away from rivalry with Margaret in Scotland, had died with him. On 2nd April 1515 Albany set out from the French court.

From the time Albany arrived in Scotland, in answer to the council's summons, to separate Margaret from her son, the king, it was, as the Venetian ambassador wrote, François I who was likely to be blamed 'for this cruelty'. The French ambassador in London wrote to François's mother, Louise of Savoy, asking to be recalled and warning that the opinion on the London streets was that Henry VIII should declare war on France to avenge the insult to his sister.

When Albany reached Scotland there came the inevitable tussle for control of the young king. A cultivated man, wealthy from his marriage to a great French heiress, Albany spoke little English, and less of the Scottish idiom than Margaret herself, but nonetheless, he set conscientiously and ably about his responsibilities.

Albany was to appoint four guardians from a selection of peers made by the council, and Margaret was to vet his choice. It was a dramatic public scene when the child was handed over to his new mentors. In the forecourt of Stirling Castle, Margaret Tudor stood, holding the young king by the hand, Angus by her side, her younger son in a nurse's arms. But as the representatives of the council approached, Margaret formally called on them to declare the cause of their coming, and ordered the portcullis dropped in their faces. Requesting six days to consider parliament's plan, ignoring her husband's urging that she should comply, she retreated into to the formidable and easily defensible bulk of Stirling, while her rattled husband Angus withdrew to his own lands.

Albany of course followed her, determined to take Stirling by siege, however long it took. When Margaret saw the forces and the heavy artillery Albany had assembled against her, she was frightened enough to comply. Even then she caused the little king to be the one who handed over the castle's keys; a defeat with dignity. While Albany set off after Angus and his family, Margaret was taken back to Edinburgh under guard. On 2 August she signed a statement declaring her wish that Albany should indeed 'have the charge and keeping' of both her sons; forced to do so, she later declared, by Albany's 'crafty and subtle ways'.

Once again her brother Henry VIII's representative urged her to flee south, to withdraw from Edinburgh 'with all the politic ways and wisdom you can use'. This time Margaret agreed. She was heavily pregnant with Angus's child and had told Albany that she proposed to 'take her chamber' for the child's birth at Linlithgow. Arriving there she claimed to be ill, so that Angus would be allowed to visit her. When darkness came, they slipped away with a handful of servants, riding hard despite Margaret's pregnancy. Before dawn they reached the Douglas's Tantallon Castle, close to the border.

With Albany in pursuit, the queen and her party had to flee so speedily that Margaret's clothes, even her precious jewels, were left behind. As Berwick Castle, in England, came into sight, adventure descended into bathos as its governor refused to admit them without orders. Finally Henry VIII's representative, Lord Dacre, arrived to escort Margaret instead to his headquarters, Harbottle Castle.

This was a military stronghold, and no place for a royal confinement. It was difficult even to get a midwife through the rough and bandit-infested country. But there, having arrived in a state of collapse, after an extended labour, Margaret gave birth to a daughter.[2]

Margaret would later charge Albany that she had been forced 'for fear and jeopardy of my life' to flee into England 'great with child and nigh my deliverance', so that eight days after crossing the border 'I was delivered of child fourteen days afore my time to my great spoil and extreme danger.' It was certainly ten days before she could sit up long enough to read letters from her brother Henry, and from Katherine of Aragon, and November before, at an agonisingly slow pace, she could be moved to the more comfortable castle of Morpeth.

At Morpeth, as the household began to prepare for Christmas, Margaret was at last shown the array of gifts Henry and Katherine had tried to send to her at Harbottle: dresses, bed-hangings, everything to deck her as a queen again. When she was carried in a chair from her room to see the dresses laid out in the great hall, she cried: 'ye may see the King my brother hath not forgotten me and that he would not that I should die for lack of clothes'. Clothes were of course an important signifier of status, regardless of any question of pleasure or practicality.

Margaret was still suffering from what seems to have been sciatica, unable to enjoy the resplendent Christmas festivities. Lady Dacre's cook prepared invalid's almond milk and broths alongside the Christmas baked meats, game and jellies but (wrote Sir Christopher Garnyshe, the man Henry had sent north with his gifts), 'Her grace hath such pain in her right leg that this three weeks she may not endure to sit up while her bed is a-making and when her grace is removed it would pity any man's heart to hear the shrieks and cries that her grace giveth.' Nevertheless, he added, Margaret 'hath a wonderful love of apparel', making her attendants display the dresses Henry had sent once or twice a day.

When she grew stronger, in the first months of the new year, it was only to hear dreadful news. Her second son, the Duke of Ross, had died in Scotland, while in Albany's charge, of a childhood illness. Her hosts had known since Christmas but decided to spare her while she herself was so ill; the more so since, Sir Christopher recorded, she loved to speak of this little boy, praising him 'even more than she doth her elder son the King.' Sir Christopher added: 'I think her one of the lowest-brought ladies'.

Her spirits would not be raised by the fact that her husband Angus, on returning to his own lands in Scotland, had decided to remain there. He preferred to make an accommodation with Albany rather than become a penniless exile by accompanying Margaret as she prepared to go south to the English court.

'When it comes to the government of their lands and affairs, [widows] must depend only on themselves', Anne de Beaujeu had written. Margaret Tudor – unlike Louise of Savoy and Margaret of Austria – had not lived up to that wise advice. But then she, unlike them, had not had the benefit of Anne's example.

In 'much heaviness', as Dacre put it, Margaret Tudor set out southwards on 8 April. Ambassadors from Scotland reached London before her but Henry VIII refused to see them until he had met his sister. From Stony Stratford she wrote to him that she was 'in right good health and as joyous of my said journey towards you as any woman may be in coming to her brother', and that she was 'most desirous now to come to your presence and to have a sight of your person'. She reached London on 3 May, entering the city in triumphal procession, riding a white palfrey sent by Queen Katherine.

There were now, with Henry VIII's sister Mary Tudor, the dowager of France, three queens at the English court. It was the first time the Tudor siblings had been together since 1503 and whatever Margaret's recent experiences, the news from the other two meant that this was a time of celebration. In March, at their London house, Mary Tudor gave birth to Brandon's son and in February Katherine of Aragon, for the first time, bore Henry a living child, 'a lively little daughter', as an Italian correspondent wrote to Erasmus: the Princess Mary.

The Venetian ambassador Giustinian wrote home bluntly that the birth of a mere girl 'has proved vexatious, for never had this entire kingdom ever so anxiously desired anything as it did a prince, it appearing to everyone that the state would be safe should his majesty leave an heir male, whereas, without a prince, they are of a contrary opinion'.

But Katherine of Aragon was triumphant and Henry convinced that a living daughter was at least a promise of better to come. As he told Giustinian: 'We are both young'. Although Katherine wanted to look after the child herself, Henry insisted that instead the whole panoply ratified by his grandmother Margaret Beaufort should swing into place, with a lady governess to take care of the baby from her christening and everything in accordance with tradition, down to the ermine quilt on the baby's 'cradle of estate'.

All of May was a party time, with a tournament at which Henry and men were decked in purple velvet embroidered with golden roses. But behind the scenes there were stresses. Both the Tudor sisters were alarmingly short of money. Mary Tudor and her husband Charles Brandon had worked out that the only way to cope with the expectations of the state a dowager queen of France should keep in public was for Mary to live largely in private on their country estates. Pending some arrangement about the receipt of income from her Scottish lands, Margaret Tudor was dependent on her brother's goodwill. There were rumours that her life in Scotland was over forever. Giustinian heard that Henry was to find a pretext to have her marriage to Angus annulled and marry her to the Emperor Maximilian.

In fact, Henry VIII was in negotiation with Albany and the Scottish authorities and as a first point in the bargaining, Margaret's wardrobe and jewels were returned to her, including pieces of crimson satin set with diamonds, white taffeta sewn with pearls, gold collars, and a red silk hat set with a diamond, given to her by the King of France. The Scottish lords even promised to retrieve from storage in Stirling the 'furrings' her late husband James had given her. They also promised to help Margaret's commissioners look into the matter of her rents. But somehow, no money arrived. By Christmas 1516 Margaret wrote that she had no money to give presents to the servants on New Year's Day, to the detriment of her brother's honour and her own.

Of the three queens in England, even Katherine of Aragon had her problems, despite the birth of her daughter. Katherine had long suffered from the policy of her relatives on the continent; the English alienation from Ferdinand and Emperor Maximilian that had seen Henry marry his sister into France. The Spanish ambassador found that 'strange words' were said to him as he went through the town and complained he felt like a bull at whom everyone threw darts. Katherine herself had been horrified by her father's ruthless shifts of loyalty. Or (so the Spanish ambassador hoped), found it prudent to pretend she was:

> The reason the queen is behaving so strangely is that her confessor, Friar Diego, has told her to act as though she has forgotten Spain and everything Spanish in order to win the English king's love and the love of the English. She has become so accustomed to doing this that she will not change.

In due course, political necessity brought Ferdinand and Henry VIII back into a somewhat edgy alliance and Katherine of Aragon once again found herself in the position of mediator, trying to explain the one to the other. But in January 1516, just weeks before Katherine gave birth to her daughter, Ferdinand died, his life shortened by his recklessness in 'following more the counsel of his falconers than of his physicians'. By then, however, Katherine's political stance was perhaps becoming less important than once it had been.

King Henry had always looked for support in the daily business of politics and now he found it in the portly shape of Thomas – or as he had become in the autumn of 1515, Cardinal – Wolsey. Wolsey's rise had been meteoric and he was now, in his early forties, reaching the position of power he would hold for more than a decade.

Born the son of a butcher, Wolsey was ordained after studying at Oxford and entered the service of Henry VII, who appointed him royal chaplain and then Dean of Lincoln. Henry VIII, on his accession, appointed him his almoner but even that did not explain what lay so close ahead. His rise in the church was dazzlingly rapid: Dean of York, Bishop of Tournai (for his work in organising Henry's army there), Bishop of Lincoln in March 1514 and Archbishop of York that September. A year later he was made a cardinal and appointed lord chancellor four months after that. Just six years after Henry's accession, he had a pudgy finger in every international as well as domestic pie. And already it was clear that Wolsey's view of England's interests would not always accord with Katherine of Aragon's naturally pro-Spanish policy.

Wolsey, inevitably, had been prominent in the negotiations with the Scottish lords carried out on Margaret Tudor's behalf, hammering out the arrangement by which, just a year after she arrived at her brother's court, Margaret would return north. But first, there was a dramatic scene to play. The spring of 1517 saw what came to be known as 'Evil May Day', when several hundred London apprentices, whipped up into a xenophobic frenzy by an irresponsible preacher, rioted through the streets attacking members of London's foreign community.

The riots were quickly put down and more than a dozen of the rioters hung, drawn and quartered but several hundred more remained in London's gaols. Popular pity was aroused by the fact that some of the 'poor younglings' were as young as thirteen. They were brought to trial on 7 May, in Westminster Hall, bound and haltered, expecting to have to face a dreadful fate. When Wolsey asked the king for mercy for them Henry sternly refused (as no doubt it had been agreed he would do) and then Katherine of Aragon, with both her Tudor sisters-in-law, dramatically made the same plea. Three queens on their knees before him. As Henry agreed and the tearful prisoners were set free, it was a scene straight from the pages of chivalry. An intercessory function, of course, had been traditional for queens, from the biblical Esther and Bathsheba to the Virgin Mary.

A week or so later, Margaret Tudor left the city; propelled in part by her brother's reluctance to maintain her forever and partly by her optimistic conviction that she could get back all the power she had lost in Scotland. Her hopes were the higher for the fact that, almost as she reached the Scottish border, her nemesis Albany was sailing back to France to visit his wife. Before he left he had agreed with Henry VIII and Wolsey that (for the next few months, at least) Margaret would have Stirling Castle and free access to her son. Greeted at the border by her husband Angus, and the nobleman who was carrying out Albany's duties, she must have felt optimistic about her return.

The first check came when she went, immediately, to Edinburgh Castle to find the son she had not seen for almost two years. She was denied entrance and told her son had been taken to Craigmillar because there was plague in the city. It was clear, as she finally got a limited measure of access, that some of the lords feared she might try to snatch him back to England.

Albany was far from eager to speed back to the taxing responsibilities of Scotland. He wrote to Margaret, suggesting the lords might allow her to resume the regency. But Margaret's idea was that her husband should rule with her as co-regent, and this the lords absolutely refused. She had once again been given the chance of a measure of power and, once again, her foolish decision threw it away.

And the lords, after all, knew more than she did. While Margaret was in England, her husband Angus had lived with the lady to whom he had formerly been betrothed, Lady Janet Stewart. And he had been doing it on the rents from Margaret's lands of Methven and Ettrick Forest. Nor was he prepared to refund the revenues he had seized and much of Margaret's energy over the next few years would be devoted to trying to reclaim them.

Just three months after she had arrived back in Scotland she wrote to Henry begging to return to England and separate from Angus. Henry's response was to send a friar north, to impress on her the importance of marriage.[3] The Scots lords themselves agreed with English observers that she was being badly treated, with 'no promise kept to her', as Henry's representative Lord Dacre reported. But if, as she complained, they gave her 'nothing but fair words', the same was true of her brother. Since England's best ally in Scotland was likely to be Angus's Douglas clan, Henry was determined that Margaret should remain his wife.

One moment Margaret seems to be moved more by Angus's iniquities in taking her revenues from Ettrick Forest than by his keeping a mistress. But to complain of that, after all, might meet with scant sympathy, since Katherine of Aragon was by now having to put up with her husband's relationship with one Elizabeth Blount. The revenues were a more concrete grievance.

The feuding of Margaret Tudor and her husband had vital political consequences, the more so since Albany showed no signs of coming back to Scotland, telling the Clarencieux Herald that he wished he had broken both his legs before ever he set foot in the country. In England, Henry and Katherine were both horrified to hear that Margaret now sought a formal separation from Angus, which he opposed, preferring to claim a husband's right to her income.

The following autumn Margaret would write to her brother that she and Angus had not been together 'this half year' and that she had been forced to pawn her jewels and silver. 'I am so minded that, an [if] I may by law of God and to my honour, to part with him, for I wit well he loves me not, as he shows me daily.' Her son was kept apart from her; she was personally humiliated and living in poverty. The years ahead would show Margaret Tudor dreaming always of regaining a measure of power, but coupling acts of energy and inventiveness with ones of utter folly.

'inestimable and praiseworthy services'

The Netherlands, France, 1516–1519

IN THE NETHERLANDS, another Margaret, of Austria, was managing her return to power more skilfully. A series of events would mean that – whether or not she wanted – she was never going to be left long in quietude. The first event had come quickly.

In January 1516 Ferdinand of Aragon died, and his grandson Charles added Ferdinand's territories to the Castile of which (during his mother Juana's enduring incarceration) he was the de facto ruler. As ruler also of the Netherlands, he was faced with the task of trying to govern two separate realms at opposite ends of the continental land mass.

It was imperative that Charles should visit Spain, and quickly, since the Spanish Cortes showed signs of resisting a ruler they had never seen and who did not speak a word of their language. To do so safely he needed to leave the Netherlands not only at peace with their neighbours, both France and England, but in experienced hands. Maximilian, for one, had no doubt whose hands those should be, writing to Charles of the virtues of his 'so good and virtuous aunt' and writing that Charles, Margaret and Maximilian himself were literally as one: *'une mêsme chose correspondant à ung mêsme désir et affection'*. Another trinity, in effect; if not in the passion of emotion the French one shared, then at least in practicality.

In February 1517 Maximilian came to the Netherlands in person, to effect a complete reconciliation of aunt and nephew and to discuss the future, since to the huge lands Charles already ruled, more might be added on Maximilian's death; not only his own hereditary Austrian lands but the Holy Roman Empire of which François and Louise also dreamt. When Charles set out in 1517 he left a turbulent Netherlands (northern parts of which were in revolt against Habsburg rule) in the hands of a regency council, nominally led by Maximilian. But one seat on it was assigned to Margaret, who was moving back towards power by slow degrees.

Early in 1518 two members of the Netherlands council, who were Margaret's strong opponents both died. In July, from Saragossa, Charles granted his 'very dear Lady and Aunt' the right to sign 'all letters, acts and documents with her own hand, which are issued for us', declaring that she 'alone' should 'provide and dispose of the appointments of this our country'. This was still not quite a full regency but Maximilian had every reason to write to Margaret in December of his hopes that 'as your good nephew he [Charles] will increase your said authority more and more'.

The steady accretion of territories and dignities to Charles and his Habsburg family led to a shift in European diplomacy. Through the years ahead François I and Charles would be great rivals, and this left England a delicate but often rewarding diplomatic game to play, adjusting the balance between the pair. In 1518 however – with the Habsburgs temporarily at peace with France – the most urgent job on England's international calendar was to improve relations between England and England's ancient enemy.

So in October 1518 there was once again an Anglo-French betrothal to be celebrated, as there had been four years earlier. This time the Princess Mary who was to be allied to France was not Henry VIII's sister, but his and Katherine's two-year-old daughter, who would be contracted to François I's son and heir, the seven-month-old French dauphin. Just as Margaret of Austria, four years before, had felt betrayed when her nephew's English alliance was replaced with a French betrothal, so Katherine of Aragon can only have been dismayed when her only daughter was promised to the old enemy of her natal country. But as Henry's wife and England's queen, her task was to put a good face on things, and she did it nobly.

In the Queen's Great Chamber at Greenwich on 5 October, Katherine was asked, as protocol required, whether she approved this match for the toddler Mary, seated in front of her. 'With great pleasure we give our royal word,' she said doughtily. Perhaps she found comfort in reflecting that any actual marriage would not take place for many years and that slips between cup and lip were a virtual certainty.

The French representatives – led by none other than the same Bonnivet who featured in Marguerite of Navarre's writings – were received with great honour. Wolsey, two days before the official ceremony, entertained them at York House, to a 'most sumptuous supper, the like of which, I fancy, was never given by Cleopatra or Caligula', wrote the Venetian envoy Giustinian, 'the whole banqueting hall being so decorated with huge vases of gold and silver that I fancied myself in the tower of Croesus'. George Cavendish, Wolsey's gentleman usher and biographer, noted that the aim was 'to make the French such triumphant cheer that they might not only wonder at it here but make a glorious report in their country'. As twelve masked gentlemen and twelve masked ladies began to dance after the feast, two were revealed as Henry and his sister Mary; a neat allegory since this was also the King of England partnering the dowager Queen of France. Katherine of Aragon, with the excuse of another visible pregnancy, had gone to bed early.

A meeting was to be arranged in 1519 between the kings of England and France. (It would be postponed until 1520.) But meanwhile Katherine had high hopes; as even the Venetian ambassador wrote, 'God grant she may give birth to a son'. She and Henry had spent the summer balancing the differing demands of her health: to stay away from London while the sweating sickness was there and yet during (as Henry wrote) 'her dangerous times', to move her as little as possible. Alas, the high hopes were not to be. In November 1518 Katherine was delivered of a daughter, who was either stillborn or lived only very briefly.

Katherine of Aragon's distress was the greater for another eventuality. In the summer of 1519, Henry VIII at last got his healthy boy. But the mother of his son was not Katherine but his mistress Elizabeth ('Bessie') Blount. The king acknowledged the boy and named him Henry Fitzroy. It was proof, if any were needed, in a century that assumed the woman's 'fault', that it was not the king but the queen who could not produce a boy. But it also perhaps gave Henry an option other than the succession of his daughter Mary, should the vexations of gender prove more worrying than those of illegitimacy.

Meanwhile, on the other side of the English Channel, in the great European power tussle and in another kind of succession struggle, a new factor had come into play.

The battle to become the next Holy Roman Emperor was no new thing. To avoid a prolonged interregnum, a certain amount of discreet campaigning for the next emperor went on before the death of the last. Another Habsburg to follow Maximilian was the likeliest candidate but there was technically no reason to assume this was certain. Early in her son's reign Louise of Savoy was in touch with her kinsman, the Elector of Bavaria, urging François's candidacy.

The question was vital. Charles feared incursions into his hereditary German states and even into the Netherlands, if François I won the imperial crown. More pressingly yet, François wrote that 'seeing the greatness of the kingdoms and lordships he [Charles] possesses, he might, in time, do me inestimable harm'. If Charles gained control of Germany, as well as Spain, Austria and the Netherlands, France would be almost completely surrounded on every landward side.

The race was about to get off the starting block. On 12 January 1519 Emperor Maximilian fell ill and died, ordering his attendants not to shed tears over so natural and inevitable an event, and desiring to be buried next to Mary of Burgundy. His daughter Margaret's personal grief was expressed, as so often in her life, by a long poem. Maximilian had been, she wrote, her Caesar, her only lord and father '*mon seul seigneur et pere*'. But Margaret was busy. The battle for Maximilian's title (and the attempt to influence the seven electors) suddenly gained heat and intensity.

Through the summer of 1518 Margaret of Austria was engaged in a new campaign, this time with the Fugger banking family. Even Charles himself was shocked at how much his aunt was spending on his campaign: more than a million gold guilders, on top of the half a million Maximilian, in his lifetime, had thrown into his grandson's cause. (The merchants of Antwerp, prudently, were forbidden at the same time to lend money to any foreign power.) Charles had, as Margaret allegorically put it:

written to us that the horse on which he wishes to come and see us is very dear. We know well that it is dear; but as matters stand, if he does not wish to have it, there is a buyer ready to take it and since he has broken it in, it seems a pity he should give it up, whatever it costs him.

François I (claiming he was motivated not by personal ambition but by a desire to lead Christendom against the Turks) was also openly determined to gain the imperial crown *'soit par amour, soit par argent, soit par force'* ('by love, by money, or by force'). Troops had to be recruited and border towns reinforced; one of Margaret's own ambassadors said that the baseness of the intrigues made the very bribers blush for shame. To counter France's attempts to the do the thing by *amour*, or sheer popularity, Margaret exchanged letters with the electors, distributed presents among their relatives and their staffs and sent out her secretary, Marnix, with promises and warnings. The imperial contest cast its shadow over everything in these months, even the response of the religious establishment to a new cloud on the horizon.

The 31st of October 1517 was celebrated afterwards as 'Reformation Day'; the day on which the German monk, Martin Luther, reputedly nailed a copy of his Ninety-five Theses, or points for disputation, to the church door in Wittenberg. Whether or not that is literally true, his rebuke to the church practice of indulgences gave voice to a wide spread chorus of complaint.*

But at this point Luther's own beliefs were considerably less radical than those that would later come to define 'reform'. He appeared, for example, still to believe in purgatory, to accept that good works and penance could contribute to man's salvation, and the first reaction of the Vatican was to instruct the German Augustinian order, to which Luther belonged, to sort out among themselves this routine and not unreasonable call for reform.

---

* The belief was that an indulgence gave the Christian the right to purchase – literally purchase, for money – the reduction of the time a soul would spend in Purgatory. The cost of the new building of St Peter's Basilica in Rome was the cue for a papal bull proclaiming the issue of a new indulgence in 1515.

In general terms the papacy, with the Turkish threat looming in the east of Europe, had plenty on its plate. Specifically, the pope's remonstrances of Luther were softened by his need not to antagonise Luther's protector, Frederick 'the Wise' of Saxony. The month of the Imperial election, June 1519, would prove to be the one in which Luther arrived at the University of Leipzig for the public debate that saw him pushed into a position that set him at odds with the whole Western church. But at the time, the Imperial election seemed the more exciting contest.

It was, to say the least, unconvincing for François to declare that there was no personal conflict between him and Charles; that the imperial crown was a mistress for whom they were both contesting and they could rival one another for her hand in all friendliness and chivalry. But there is an intriguing suggestion that the positions of the women – Margaret of Austria and Louise of Savoy – were less entrenched than those of the men for whom they campaigned. Both were painfully aware of the costs of the election.

François's friend Fleuranges reported an encounter between an ally of Louise's and the Spanish ambassador Naturelli, discussing the possibility of finding a third-party candidate acceptable to both sides. One who (as the Spanish ambassador put it) 'would not be profitable to one or the other but to the whole of Christendom and the unity of Germany'. Perhaps that was a quixotic thought but both women seem to have hailed with interest the idea of their young men ceasing to lock horns, feeling that an understanding was better than an overwhelmingly costly victory. Naturelli wrote to Margaret of Austria: 'I put before Madame [Louise] all the arguments which you wrote to me.' But it was to no avail. Even Henry VIII entered the lists, although he would, humiliatingly, in the end get not one vote.

François's campaign was in the hands of his old crony Bonnivet, who ran the gamut of electioneering antics. When the election began in Frankfurt in June he donned a disguise to try to smuggle himself in, because, while the election was running, foreigners were banned from the city. His campaign was conspicuous for its lack of success, however. The pope (whose hands alone could ultimately crown an emperor) had originally promised to support François but changed his mind. Charles was elected unanimously as 'Charles V', thanks less, perhaps, to his stronger family roots in the area than to the fact that, begged by the electors to protect them against France, he had a huge army of mercenaries surrounding the city.

Louise of Savoy recorded the event in her journal with stoicism, referring to the will of Christ. But she knew France was now dangerously close to being encircled by Habsburg territory, while the campaign had cost a fortune to both sides.

In October the Venetian Giustinian reported home that Louise of Savoy and her son 'were more unpopular all over France than words could express'. Louise 'is supposed to have invested much capital throughout the country and is intent on hoarding, for the purpose, it is said, of aiding the King in the event of any sudden need'. Bonnivet (possibly suffering from syphilis) wisely took himself for a cure before reappearing at the French court. His standing as one of François's cronies – as well as leading negotiator and fixer – was too well established for him to be permanently damaged. But it was the end of François's first heyday.

In the Netherlands, Margaret of Austria ordered bonfires, feasts and prayers to celebrate the fact that, 'inspired by the Holy Ghost', the electors had chosen her nephew. Unanimously. As for that nephew himself, he gave credit where credit was due. On 1 July, in Barcelona, in view of her 'great, inestimable and praiseworthy services', he signed letters naming his 'very dear lady and aunt' as regent and governess of the Low Countries, to be obeyed as he would himself. The world would see that Margaret of Austria had won.

There was, however, another great international competition in store.

13

The Field of Cloth of Gold

Calais, 1520

WHAT WAS THE 'Field of Cloth of Gold'? A celebration of Anglo-French amity (the official theory)? A chance for two of the young titans of Europe to compete face to face under an unconvincing mask of friendship? François I sought to ensure English neutrality in any war between himself and Charles V; Henry VIII was enjoying being courted by both sides. All of the above, perhaps. But one thing is for sure; it was the party of the century, which meant that the ladies had a role to play.

Henry would come to his proposed meeting with the French king accompanied by his wife Katherine of Aragon and by his sister Mary Tudor, the former Queen of France. François would bring his wife, Claude, of course, but also his mother Louise of Savoy and his sister Marguerite. It is a safe supposition that Anne Boleyn was present. Not only were linguists at a premium but her parents were certainly there, as was her sister and perhaps her brother George.

It is no surprise that the Boleyns were present in force. So was anybody who was anybody. The English train comprised almost six thousand people and more than three thousand horses. Although no comparable figures survive for the French party, every effort was made to ensure that the two kings and the two countries held equal status in every way.

Katherine of Aragon's preparations started early; she was under pressure to make an impressive display. Henry's ambassador in France wrote anxiously that:

Queen Claude, with the King's mother, make all the search possible to bring at the assembly the fairest ladies and demoiselles that may be found . . . I hope at the least, Sir, that the Queen's Grace shall bring such in her band, that the visage of England, which hath always had the praise, shall not at this time lose the same.

How might that go down with the Spanish Katherine, who despite her 'very beautiful complexion' was dubbed 'not handsome' in the cold clear eyes of European diplomacy? But Katherine of Aragon had also been working in another way; working with her nephew and her former sister-in-law Margaret of Austria to provide a framework for the Field of Cloth of Gold that would present Henry with a very different European possibility. She dreamed of an alliance with the new emperor Charles, instead of with France. As the Venetian ambassador noted, she had already 'as a Spaniard' been gratified by her nephew's success in the imperial election.

The French king's mother was all too aware of Katherine's influence. Henry and François had made a pact, months earlier, not to shave their beards before they met. Henry broke the pact, 'by the queen's desire', Thomas Boleyn assured Louise of Savoy, perhaps only meaning to suggest that this was not serious; the queen had, after all, made Henry 'great instance' about getting rid of his beard on various earlier occasions. But Louise of Savoy took it differently. 'Is not the queen's grace aunt to the king of Spain [Charles]?', Louise pointedly asked Thomas Boleyn. She seemed to accept Boleyn's reassurances, affirming politely that 'their love is not in the beards but in the hearts'.

But later she asked another English ambassador whether Katherine of Aragon had 'any great devotion to the assembly'; the Field of Cloth of Gold. The ambassador could only reply, lamely, that Katherine had 'none other joy and comfort in this world' than to promote anything at all which might stand with her husband's pleasure.

In fact, reports said Katherine of Aragon was making no secret of her disapproval of the planned meeting, and finding a receptive audience for her complaints among the traditionally Francophobe English. 'There is no doubt that the French interview is against the will of the queen and of all the nobles', Charles was told. It was, however, dear to the heart of Wolsey, who was now (in the words of one Italian observer) 'the man who rules both the king and the entire kingdom'. But in a sense the international situation played into Katherine's hands. Henry's position as the counterbalance between France and the Holy Roman Empire – the man who could make the shape of Europe – was too good not to enjoy.

As Charles V expressed a burning desire to meet his 'uncle' Henry (and his aunt Katherine), Charles's other aunt, Margaret of Austria, arranged a high-powered delegation to England, including several of her closest men, who arrived at the start of April, pointing out that Henry could be the first European monarch Charles would meet since his elevation to the imperial role. It was in Katherine of Aragon's room that, in a meeting with Henry and Wolsey, England decided to agree. Henry's anxious assurances to his wife suggest the strength of Katherine's part in the decision.

Shortly afterwards, Henry VIII's ambassador in France was asking that the meeting with François I be delayed for a week. François refused, saying Henry should be at Calais no later than 4 June, on the reasonable plea that his wife Claude would be in the seventh month of her fifth pregnancy. But the meeting with Charles almost did fall through on the grounds of time, as his journey from Spain to England was delayed by contrary winds. As Charles wrote to Katherine from Coruna:

> We have been told of the effort and will that you have put into arranging these meetings. But as the sea is so changeable that men cannot always do what they want . . . we beg you, if there is some delay, that, as you have already done, you try to make our brother and uncle, the king of England, wait for as long as is possible.

Charles V finally arrived on English shores on 26 May, the day after Henry and Katherine arrived in Canterbury on their way to the south coast, the day on which they should have sailed the other way. But, galloping to Dover Castle to greet his guest, Henry kept his whole mighty cavalcade waiting for four more days. Charles was greeted by the archbishop in Canterbury Cathedral, then taken to the archbishop's palace next door, where a tense Katherine was waiting, royally dressed. She broke into tears after she embraced him, the representative of her family. His huge retinue, including two hundred ladies dressed in the

Spanish fashion, an evocative sight for Katherine of Aragon, were entertained for three days in Canterbury; three days of banqueting, dancing and games of courtly love in which the Spanish noblemen excelled. (One went so far as to swoon at one lady's beauty and had to be carried out of the room by his hands and feet.) As the two trains, English and Spanish, left Canterbury for the south coast, the meeting had been a rehearsal of what lay ahead at the other, the Anglo-French, party.

Katherine and Henry set sail from Dover on 31 May and, after a brief few hours' crossing, landed at Calais. The encounter was to take place on the plain, the Val d'Or, between the English citadel of Guisnes and the French town of Ardres, so that each king could sleep in his own territory. Four days later they set off for Guisnes. The first meeting of the two kings was scheduled for 7 June, the feast of Corpus Christi.

An extraordinary sight greeted their eyes; one that had been months in the preparation. England had sent more than six thousand workmen, two thousand of them to work on Henry's temporary palace, a *trompe l'oeil* fantasia whose solid foundations and dazzling array of newfangled glass windows were topped off by canvas painted to look like brick. It was a combination of utter luxury and practicality. Or parsimony. As one observer noted, the whole thing could be dismantled and taken home again for reuse for no more than the cost of its transport. But there were statues of Cupid and of Bacchus, from which flowed claret cup and malmsey, with silver cups for the drinking. (None were stolen, it was remarked by contemporaries.)

Suites of tents – blue and gold, gold and scarlet, topped with heraldic beasts – were linked by curtained passageways to resemble the layout of a palace. Like the rooms of a permanent palace, they were scented with flowers and furnished with tapestry, while the royal chapel was stuffed with holy relics. Katherine's oratory had in the centre a large shield bearing the arms of England and, possibly provocative under the circumstances, of Spain.

There were other tents, some three hundred of them, striped in the Tudor colours of green and white, for the kitchens and dormitories and painted or embroidered for the courtiers. Not that accommodation could be provided for everybody; even some 'knights and ladies' were forced to sleep outdoors in the hay.

The French party approached the accommodation problem differently. In Ardres, work was done on the king's lodging, which was attached, by a gallery of clipped box plants, to a large banqueting pavilion, whose ceiling was made to look like the night sky. But they too brought in master tent-makers to erect fabulous creations in the Field itself, made of stout canvas which was covered in more luxurious fabrics: silk, velvet and damask, in blue, violet and crimson, with the royal livery colours of tawny, white and black. Claude's pavilion, and Louise of Savoy's, were dressed in *toile d'or* and *toile d'argent*, with *fleurs de lis* in gold thread strewn on, respectively, violet and crimson satin, alongside the two women's own heraldic emblems. However, unseasonable weather blew down many of the French tents.

In between the two camps a nine-hundred-foot tournament ground boasted an artificial tree of honour, decorated with hundreds of silk or satin flowers representing English hawthorn and French raspberry, on which the challengers could hang their emblazoned shields. But women could not play a major part in the chivalric encounters that were the first order of the day.

The two kings did not compete against each other; or not officially. There was an impromptu bout of wrestling, which saw François throw Henry. (He would seize another such advantage of surprise when, disregarding the protocol that surrounded their normal meetings, he arrived in Henry's bedroom one morning, insisting that he himself would be the English king's valet.) Henry's brother-in-law, Charles Brandon, did not distinguish himself in the joust, having hurt his hand, but Bonnivet was one of the chief organisers of the French side.

The ladies were to have their ceremonial part in the tourney. The two queens met on 11 June, in a royal pavilion where they could receive the homage of the knights. Queen Claude, dressed in cloth of silver over an underskirt of cloth of gold, rode in her coronation litter, made to match. She was followed by her ladies, in three coaches draped in silver, and the likelihood is that the ladies included Anne Boleyn. Louise of Savoy wore black velvet and was followed by 'an infinite number of ladies' in crimson velvet, with sleeves lined in cloth of gold. She was said to have purchased 'a whole emporium' of the dazzling stuff.

Katherine of Aragon too had been buying fabric for months. She, of course, had already had her nephew's entourage to dazzle, in cloth of gold lined with violet velvet, black 'tilsent' sparkling silk, crimson tissue 'pirled' with gold and 'rich cloth of gold tissue'. Even her fifty-five footmen wore white satin and green velvet, with Spanish 'feathers of arrows' embroidered on their doublets; her seven henchmen wore orange boots, black velvet cloaks, coats of green and russet velvet and doublets of yellow. It was noted that Katherine wore a headdress in the 'Spanish fashion', with her hair hanging down over her shoulder. A point was being made here, silently.

Clothes wars notwithstanding, the women came into their own away from the tourney. Etiquette decreed that the two kings should be feasted not by each other but by each other's ladies. Henry and François ate together less formally on a handful of occasions but at the great banquets – on 10, 17 and 24 June – two kings at one board might give rise to awkward questions of precedence, so nothing could be left to chance.

Surviving reports (from French, Venetian and Mantuan observers) record the two kings leaving their lodgings at the same time, announced by the firing of cannon. They encountered each other briefly on the tournament ground and passed on. François (on the 10th, the first occasion), was received by Katherine of Aragon in her huge chambers to dine from gold plate, under a cloth of state, surrounded by tapestries. Beyond the royal party, a long hall was divided into two, one half for 134 ladies to dine and the other for some two hundred gentlemen.

Each of perhaps three courses consisted of fifty dishes, sweet and savoury together, topped off by a 'subtlety', an elaborate and often allegorical creation in marzipan or spun sugar. Account books record that in the course of their visit the English camp consumed almost thirty thousand fish – in which list was included a dolphin – more than six thousand birds and almost a hundred thousand eggs. After the meal there was dancing in the main hall, led by the king's sister, Mary Tudor, partnering a French nobleman, after which François – who like Henry was an impassioned dancer – had a masquing dance performed 'in the Italian manner'.[1] Henry, for his part, was being entertained by the French in a hall decked with pink brocade, with twenty-four trumpeters playing as he waded his way through a solid four hours of eating before the dancing.

On the second occasion, the 17th, Louise of Savoy came to join her son François, while his sister Marguerite partnered Henry VIII. Both kings slipped out of the hall to don their costumes for the masque; François and his companions donning long gowns with plumes and hoods to dance 'in the Ferrarese fashion'. Henry had brought three companies of masquers with him: fake beards and gowns described as being in the Milanese style for himself and his fellows, black velvet doctors' costumes for another group of noblemen, and yet another group boasting purses and girdles of sealskin to dress as visitors from 'Ruseland or farre Estland'. Henry loved to dress up (at home, no one was supposed to admit they recognised him) and by the sound of it, François did, too. For the third and last banquet both royal parties wore masquing costumes from the beginning. Nine worthies headed the English party – soldierly heroes from Alexander to King Arthur – led by Hercules with a club covered in green damask and a lion's pelt made from cloth of gold.

The whole long international encounter was as choreographed as a masque. When the two queens met at an open-air mass in the tiltyard, they each tried to insist that the other have the first chance to kiss the Gospel but wound up embracing each other instead. Contemporaries recorded the precise ceremonial; how 'the English King dined with the French Queen and the Duchess of Alençon at Ardres . . . kneeling with one knee on the ground, his bonnet in his hand, he first kissed the Queen, then Madame [Louise of Savoy], then the Duchess of Alençon [Marguerite of Navarre]'.

Even the gifts exchanged were carefully recorded: the English queen gave the French one several hobbies and palfreys, with their appurtenances, presenting also a saddle and harness to Louise of Savoy. Claude gave Katherine of Aragon a litter of cloth of gold ('as well as mules and pages'). Louise of Savoy gave Wolsey a valuable jewelled crucifix, while he gave her a small cross of precious stones, with a piece of the True Cross inside it.

But behind the scenes, serious business was going on. At Guisnes, even before the kings began their joust, Wolsey visited the French camp and arranged that he and Louise of Savoy should settle matters between

England, France and Scotland. One of the victors of these festivities was indeed Wolsey, honoured as the pope's own representative (in which capacity he could treat even François as an equal), talking to everybody. Marguerite of Navarre had begun to address him as 'father', while he described her as his daughter or god-daughter: *'filleule d'alliance'*. Margaret of Austria would write to Wolsey as to her dear son.

The two groups parted on 24 June and the next day the English made their way back to Calais. Here Henry VIII waited, until 10 July. François, too, stayed in the vicinity. For in that summer of 1520, the Field of Cloth of Gold was followed – as had been arranged in May – by another meeting. Henry and Katherine of Aragon went on to the coastal town of Gravelines, on the border with the Netherlands, and there met Charles V and Margaret of Austria, who accompanied them back to Calais for a few days of more restrained festivities. François made it known he was just a day's ride away and would come over to join in the debates without ceremony if asked. He wasn't, but several of his gentlemen made use of their English friends to gatecrash the parties.

Margaret of Austria, in her brief Spanish marriage, had lived at close quarters with Katherine of Aragon. Now, the two reaffirmed their girl-hood bonds over a supper. Charles V showed his particular mettle: while Henry had been competitively on edge with François, and left far from sure he had got the best of the encounter, Charles offered him a modest air and a welcome flattery, stressing Henry's importance in keeping Europe's balance. While Wolsey was in pursuit of that 'universal peace' so long aspired to – a church-sponsored Anglo/Imperial/French alliance against the infidel Turks who were menacing Europe's eastern borders – Charles wanted an alliance with England against France.

He didn't get it, or not immediately, but for all that, the Gravelines meeting, like the Field, might be considered to have gone well. Perhaps it was a triumph for Wolsey's subtlety. He managed to seem to promise everything to everybody without technically breaking his word to anybody, for to the best of our knowledge (no exact record of the discussion survives) nothing agreed at Gravelines contradicted the Anglo/French agreement for a marriage between François's son the dauphin and Henry's daughter Mary.

The mood at the French court, as everyone returned home, was positive, at least where François was concerned, with an allegorical book singling out the 'wise knowledge and divine way of achieving of Our Lady Concord': Louise of Savoy. Louise herself had put a good face on things. The Venetian ambassador reported her telling foreign envoys that the French king and the English king had parted with tears in their eyes; that they planned to build a chapel to Our Lady of Friendship, and a palace where they could meet every year.

But while spending the summer in the lovely settings of Blois and Amboise Louise must have been more conscious than her son of the cost of the recent venture – may have been all too aware that the real winner of the summer had yet to be decided. François I or Charles V? In the end (just as had happened with the contest to become Holy Roman Emperor) it would not be the French party.

14

Repercussions

The Netherlands, France, 1520–1521

ONE OF THE winners, again, was Margaret of Austria. In the autumn of 1520, she and her nephew Charles travelled from Gravelines to Maastricht, where he reappointed her his regent in the Netherlands. On 18 September he signed over to her, for life, the town and territory of Mechelen, with two hundred thousand gold florins. Together, aunt and nephew moved on to Charles's German territories, where on 23 October, at Aix-la-Chapelle, he was crowned into the office to which he had been elected the previous year, that of 'King of the Romans' and Holy Roman Emperor-Elect.[1] The German princes swore fealty, Charles V promised to uphold the rights of the Empire, and those of the church, and was girt with Charlemagne's sword, while Charlemagne's crown was placed on his head.

Margaret of Austria had a prominent place in the cathedral, as well she deserved. She had even stripped her home at Mechelen of its tapestries and silver plate to make a good show at the coronation festivities. Fleuranges wrote a description to Louise of Savoy.

In France, meanwhile, all the 'trinity' were at a loss. In the winter of 1520–21 François had three accidents: a fall from a horse, a prank that ended in a fire, and a mock battle that got out of hand. Although none caused him any lasting injury, the last shave was close and made Louise palpitate over how easily she might have been wholly lost; *'femme perdu'*.

That was even before he went back to the Italian wars. Power in Italy was still a huge bone of contention between France and the Empire, particularly the disputed territories of Milan and Naples. Largely hemmed in by Charles' territories to the south, east and north, François was alarmed by the way Charles's new imperial title gave him also an Italian foothold.

In the spring of 1521 France made several incursions into foreign territory; French aggression was followed by Imperial retaliation and it was clear that England, abandoning its position of neutrality, would be forced into the conflict. In August 1521, Cardinal Wolsey crossed the Channel to Calais to act as a mediator between Charles and François. The French sent wine; Margaret of Austria (knowing his distaste for riding) sent a red velvet litter, lined with green satin, against which his cardinal's robes would stand out clearly. More importantly but less tangibly, both sides had long been raising their voice to get him the papacy. But any talk of peace was unavailing. Instead, the cardinal moved on to Bruges for another round of diplomatic discussions with the emperor.

Ever pro-English, Margaret of Austria, '*la bonne Angloise*', rushed to join them, supplementing the substantial presents of money made to the English suite with more domestic courtesies, including a daily breakfast delivery of fresh rolls, sugar and wine. She sent Wolsey candles to light his bedroom, while his musicians played at her parties; the upshot was that England entered a covert alliance with Charles V. The alliance between Charles and Henry was to be cemented at a future date by *his* marriage to Henry's daughter Mary, disregarding the previous match made between Mary and the French dauphin. Margaret of Austria was one of the two signatories on the emperor's behalf. She indeed had thrashed out the details with Wolsey. And in the summer of 1521, as Charles prepared for war with France, it was his aunt Margaret whose speech to the Netherlands' governing body raised him men and money.

The war that was to dominate the next four years would be cripplingly expensive for both sides. But in France, there was simply no money. A visiting Englishman, William Fitzwilliam, wrote of how 'the King borrows of any man that hath any and if any man refuse to lend he shall be so punished that all other shall take ensample from him . . . They eat up all they have, to their shirts.' In this crisis, both François and Louise of Savoy would turn to expedients that divided them from powerful nobles, and even, briefly, from each other.

It was all tied to the ageing Anne de Beaujeu. Despite all the noble girls to whom she had been mentor and surrogate mother, Anne had born just one surviving child, a daughter, Suzanne (the addressee of Anne's *Enseignements*), who had herself died at the end of April 1521. This left her husband Charles, the great Duc de Bourbon, a childless widower. Suzanne had been his kinswoman as well as wife; her claim to the Bourbon inheritance had been united with his. But now the question was what of the Bourbon lands he or his children by any second marriage could still inherit, for Charles de Bourbon came from the younger branch of the Bourbon family, Suzanne having been the last representative of the senior. Now Charles's claim might be challenged, since both Louise of Savoy and François I also had Bourbon blood in their veins, through Louise's mother, while the king could reasonably claim that the terms under which the lands had been granted saw them revert to the crown on the failure of the male line.

It was perhaps in an attempt to cut through this Gordian knot that Louise of Savoy took an extraordinary step. She, who had always fought so hard against remarriage, sent an envoy to Bourbon suggesting she should marry him. That way, since she was past childbearing age, the lands should still ultimately revert to her son's crown.

The proposal is recorded only in a seventeenth-century continuation of the chronicle originally written by Bourbon's secretary, so one cannot know for sure whether Bourbon really called her 'the worst woman in the realm, the dread of all nations'. He would not marry her 'for the whole of Christendom', he added; Louise, when she heard, vowing that his words should cost him dear. King Henry, in England, made a personal story out of it, telling Charles V's ambassador: 'There has been much discontent between the King Francis and the said Bourbon, since he has refused to marry Madame the Regent, who loves him very much.' More surely, Bourbon was discontented, feeling he was not given his right place in the realm.

Trouble at home was matched by disaster abroad, in the ongoing Italian wars. Six years earlier, the Battle of Marignano had given France control of Milan but in November 1521 the French lost the city again. To add another turn of the screw (reported one contemporary, Jean du Bellay), when the defeated general responsible for Milan's loss came to explain himself to the king, he protested furiously that the problem had been lack of money, which had lost him his mercenaries. François roared that he had sent the money; the treasurer Semblançay answered that he had got the money ready to send but that it had been taken by Louise of Savoy, who claimed it in payment of a debt. It blew over of course but not before son confronted mother in a scene unparalleled in their history.

In the Netherlands by contrast, Margaret of Austria was prepared to pawn her jewels to fund her nephew as, in the spring of 1522, he prepared to set out again towards his Spanish territories. There, the 'Revolt of the Comuneros' had seen Castilian rebels rise against Charles, a man they saw as a foreigner, and attempt to make his incarcerated mother Juana, nominally still co-ruler with Charles, once more the active head of state. Margaret's hand is all over her nephew's policy of the first years of the 1520s and her loyalty was not without its reward: Charles had informed the States General that in his absence they would be governed by his aunt 'who for so long has shown by her praiseworthy, memorable services and great experience, that she well knows how to honourably acquit herself of the said government and administration'. Charles also settled the question of Margaret's claim to her father Maximilian's estates, which she surrendered in return for two hundred and fifty thousand pounds, payable in ten yearly instalments.*

Margaret's task would not be easy. The Netherlands were rife with problems – financial, structural and religious – as the years ahead would prove. Nonetheless, as a woman who sought her family's advance and who welcomed authority, she was flying high. If there were a contest between the mother of the French king and the aunt of the Habsburg ruler, then Margaret of Austria and the Habsburgs, seemed again to have won.

That said, there was one cavil. The Habsburgs, even more immediately than the French monarchy, had to deal with an unexpected threat, the ramifications of which, although they can hardly have realised it, would

---

* He had also settled his brother Ferdinand's position, by giving him control of Maximilian's hereditary Austrian lands and regency in Charles's absence of the German territories. This marked the start of the division of the house of Habsburg into two branches: the Spanish, of which Charles (and later Charles's son Philip) was the head and the Austrian.

come to dominate their century. In 1520 Martin Luther's questioning of the pope's authority led to a Papal Bull, or edict, that condemned him as a heretic. Luther publicly burned the Bull, along with volumes of canon law but his very estrangement from the church encouraged him to take his own thinking in more revolutionary directions.

Luther was moving towards the idea of justification by faith alone; that man's salvation lay purely in his faith, not in any good works he might do – a central tenet of the reformed religion. At the same time, Luther's refutation of papal authority imposed from distant Italy was already becoming identified with political discontent.

In March 1521 Charles V offered Luther a formal hearing at the Diet (or Assembly) of Worms, a town on the Rhine. It led not to agreement but to the formalising of a position of opposition. 'Here I stand. I can do no other', Luther was reported to have said; while Charles for his part declared that 'My predecessors . . . left behind them the holy Catholic rites that I should live and die therein . . . I have therefore resolved to stake upon this cause all my dominions, my friends, my body and my blood . . .'

Margaret of Austria had herself been one of the great ladies critical of the 'infinite abuses' in the Catholic church and of the pope's attempts to exercise secular authority in her territories; had numbered humanists and moderate reformers among her friends, had hosted Erasmus at her court. The Netherlands, the old Burgundy, had been the home of the *devotio moderna*, the more spiritual model of religion, particularly attractive to aristocratic ladies, to which Margaret's godmother Margaret of York subscribed.

But after a papal legate arrived in Antwerp in the autumn of 1520, Margaret saw men such as Erasmus (and some of her own aides) publicly attacked in sermons; saw books burnt. The Papal Bull against Luther had been first published in the Netherlands. She issued the orders which, in 1523, ended with two reforming Augustine monks burnt and their monastery razed to the ground. Martin Luther had been an Augustinian friar and the monastery was believed to be a centre for the dissemination of his ideas.

'The heresies of Martin Luther', as Margaret wrote to the Prior of Brou, 'are a great scandal to our Holy Mother Church'. It seems likely that her first priority was and would remain to damp down controversy, so far as was possible. But in a comparatively short space of time it would be evident that Luther had opened Pandora's box, and he himself would be horrified at some of the beliefs and new creeds that flew out.

In France, Marguerite of Navarre had long been interested in the reform, with a small 'r', of the Catholic church. So, even, was her mother Louise of Savoy, to a degree, as had been Anne of Brittany and her daughters Queen Claude and Renée, while Marguerite's brother François at this point was interested in anything which kept him one step ahead of the papacy. (Pope Leo had already sided with Charles and would in 1522 be succeeded by Pope Adrian, a prelate who had been Charles V's tutor.) Lutheranism was never an option but for a brief period early in the 1520s, Marguerite's way would be the goal of all the trinity: reforming the church from the inside, orienting it more towards the Bible, towards trained preachers, towards less emphasis on ritual and worship by rote.

But as the 1520s got under way, Marguerite was coming to a time of personal crisis. Her life since her brother's accession had seen her juggle the great ceremonies of court life with more personal and spiritual concerns. A visit made by the king and queen to her house in 1517 had been followed by the grant of the rich duchy of Berry, that not only made her financially independent of her husband but (most unusually for a female, rather than a male, relative of the king) gave her the status of a *prince capétien* and the right to sit on her brother's councils. The wording of the lengthy grant explicitly spells out that this was to be territory under Marguerite's own governance, save only for a feudal allegiance to France. There was no mention of her husband anywhere in the document.

The return visit for the betrothal of the baby dauphin to Henry VIII's daughter Mary, at the end of 1518, saw Marguerite seated beside François in the courtyard of the Bastille, on a dais covered in cloth of gold, under a bower of flowers and greenery. A canopy of blue, spangled with stars and hung with gold balls, made the courtyard into a roofed room, while Louise of Savoy and Queen Claude sat in one of the galleries. While the king appeared with his male masquers in a white satin robe embroidered in gold, the ladies handed sweetmeats.

In the spring of 1519, Marguerite took a sponsor's role in the christening of what would prove an important boy: a second son for her brother King François, named Henri. Holding him at the font with Marguerite, representing his master for whom the child was named, was England's new ambassador to France, Thomas Boleyn, whose daughter Anne would have been present (though unnoticed or at least unrecorded) at the engagement festivities. But when Marguerite set about reforming the local convent of Almenesches, winning over the pope to her choice for the new abbess, she took care to have a small lodging built for herself within the convent grounds.

In the early years of her brother's reign Marguerite visited Lyons with the royal party and it is in the notably reformist Lyons, in the church of Saint-Jean, that she set the story in novella seventy-two of her *Heptaméron*. In this story, the Duchess of Alençon ('who later became queen of Navarre', as did Marguerite herself) overhears the sobs of another worshipper: a pregnant nun, who had been seduced by a monk. In the story, the duchess promises to take up the nun's cause and institute reforms very much of the kind Marguerite was making in real life.

It is possible that in the autumn of 1519 Bonnivet launched another sexual assault upon Marguerite, although once again the suggestions are almost wholly literary. That autumn François, accompanied by his mother, sister and a group of nobles including both Marguerite's husband and Bonnivet, set off on a leisurely progress towards Cognac. They stopped at the king's new building project, Chambord, at Chatellherault and, in January 1520, at Bonnivet's new Italian-style creation, Neuville-aux-Bois. The royal party left after just four days, leaving Bonnivet behind.

In novella four of the *Heptaméron* the heroine is in bed, and presumably undressed, when 'without further ado, he jumped into bed beside her.' Her first thought is to denounce her attacker and demand that her brother order his head struck off. But the heroine's lady-in-waiting (who the Seigneur Brantôme's writings identified as Madame de Châtillon, Marguerite's former governess) warns that everyone would say 'this poor gentleman . . . could not have attempted it without great encouragement. Everyone will say it has not been without fault on your side'. Madame warns the heroine to be more careful in the future, since 'many women who have led lives more austere than yours have been humiliated by men less worthy of love than he'.

It seems as if, around this point in her life, Marguerite of Navarre suffered some sort of emotional trauma. In the early summer of 1521 Marguerite penned an extraordinary letter, the first of many, to Guillaume Briçonnet, the reforming Bishop of Meaux, a man at war with medieval superstition but at home with the mysticism to which Marguerite was drawn. (Meaux would become the centre for a group of progressive clergy, several of them connected with Marguerite, and all eventually to come under attack by the Catholic church, from which, however, none had at this stage any thought of splitting.) 'I must deal with countless matters that cause me to be afraid and thus ask that you take up my cause and bring me spiritual succor', Marguerite wrote.

Some of the things she wrote were in tune with the new tenets of religion: 'Knowing that there is need of only one thing, I turn to you, entreating you to make yourself the means of reaching him [God] through prayer.' Some were more personal: in her second letter to Briçonnet, she wrote that she felt 'very much alone . . . Take pity on me . . . I beg you at least to visit me in writing and stir up the love of God in my heart.' Her repeated insistence that she was 'unworthy', 'useless', 'worse than dead' must be seen in the context of reformist theology, which believed humans were unworthy without God's grace. Nonetheless, it is hard not to read into her letters something more when Marguerite begs Briçonnet to help kindle her 'poor heart covered with ice and dead from cold' and when Briçonnet, a few years later, congratulates her on having obeyed his rule 'of telling everything without fear'.

She wrote frequently of her 'sterility'. Thirteen years of marriage and, at thirty, she had not yet born a child. In 1522 she believed she was pregnant but found herself mistaken. She was also nursing Louise of Savoy, who was suffering increasingly serious bouts of gout. Briçonnet, twenty years older than she, offered himself as her adoptive son and both took seriously the relationship (to sixteenth-century eyes a genuine one, made 'par alliance'), Marguerite signing herself as 'your sterile mother'.

Briçonnet, however, had other concerns from the first: that Marguerite should recruit her mother and brother to her spiritual quest, so that 'from you three will come forth as an example of life, a fire to burn and illumine the rest of the kingdom'. When she failed to do so quickly enough, he reproached her: 'you have not taken your gloves off. I do not yet see any flames issuing from your hands.' In fact, by the end of 1522, the attempts made by Briçonnet's deputy Michel d'Arande to instruct Louise of Savoy were causing the king's confessor to complain to the theologians at the university; the first red danger sign of troubles ahead.

Anne de Beaujeu, the last of her generation, died on 14 November 1522, just five weeks after François had settled the larger part of the disputed Bourbon lands on his mother Louise. Anne's reaction was to bequeath to her son-in-law Charles, Duc de Bourbon, her own personal properties, in recompense for the 'good, great, praiseworthy and recommendable services and pleasures' he had rendered her and her late daughter Suzanne. Bourbon had now a daring, even treasonous, scheme: to marry Charles V's sister Eleanor and thus ally himself with François's enemy.

Such dissent in the French ranks was the more serious for the fact that in the summer of 1522, England had fulfilled the promise made earlier to Charles V – the fruit of all that eager diplomacy – and played its part in keeping the balance of power in Europe by declaring war on France. There had been a hint of future storms at the beginning of the year, when King François tackled Cardinal Wolsey on what might seem a trivial matter: the family of one of his wife's maids, young Anne Boleyn, had decided she should come home. What; did they feel that France was no longer safe for Englishwomen?

Wolsey attempted to reassure the French king. It was no such matter, he said. Merely, a marriage had been arranged between Anne and her kinsman James Butler, the Irish Earl of Ormonde. But of course, Anne Boleyn's future was not to pan out that way.

PART III

1522–1536

Nor should you be melancholy or discomfited if you find yourself in some foreign or unpleasant alliance, but praise God and believe that He is always just and never does anything but what is reasonable. Therefore, my daughter, if it is so ordained and it happens that you have much to suffer, have complete patience, finding in whatever awaits you the will and pleasure of the Creator . . . if you want to live with peace of mind, protect yourself from stumbling into the snares of jealousy.

Lessons for my Daughter,
Anne of France (Anne de Beaujeu)
published 1517–1521

15

'Wild for to hold'

England, Scotland, 1522–1524

SPRING 1522 IN London. At Cardinal Wolsey's palace of York Place, the pre-Lent festivities were celebrated with more than usual splendour. The pageant might have come from the old Burgundian court: an assault on the *Château Vert*, the Green Castle or Castle of 'Vert'ue. The castle was made of wood and green tinfoil, sturdy enough for its towers to support eight ladies dressed in white satin, each representing a virtue, with her character or 'reason' picked out in yellow. The knights, led by King Henry VIII himself, and their spokesman, Ardent Desire, were dressed in cloth of gold and blue satin and were warded off, for a judicious interval, with a barrage of sweetmeats and rosewater.

In the end, of course, the masculine attackers prevailed; the colder female virtues warmed by masculine ardour, and everyone danced happily. But no one, for a few years yet, could guess how telling the pageant would prove to be. The lady representing Perseverance – newly come home from France – was Anne Boleyn.

The Anne Boleyn who appeared at the English court in 1522 would have been a very finished product. Not beautiful, perhaps, but surely compelling; sophisticated, and with the all-important gloss of difference. Later reports show her as 'very eloquent and gracious, and reasonably good-looking.' 'Not one of the handsomest women in the world' as a Venetian diplomat would put it, when the time came that ambassadors took note of Anne Boleyn, she was 'of middling stature, swarthy complexion, long neck, wide mouth, a bosom not much raised and eyes which are black and beautiful'.

But her years abroad had given her wide experience in the ways of a court. Indeed, if, as seems likely, she had been called on to act as an Anglo/French interpreter she may have gained not only experience of the queen's, the women's, rooms, but also an unusually direct appreciation of political dealings, more so for the fact that her father was for a time also attached to the French court.

Anne Boleyn's very 'Frenchness' would have been a novelty to the English courtiers. It is hard to realise now, after centuries in which French has been the *lingua franca* of diplomatic and social circles, that it was not so in the early sixteenth century, when Latin was the universal language.

As the writer, cleric and diplomat Lancelot de Carles described Anne: 'no one would ever have taken her to be English, by her manners, but a native-born Frenchwoman'. By contrast, Katherine of Aragon was now thirty-six, not young by the standards of the day. Repeated pregnancies had taken their toll and the ever-watchful ambassadors had for some time resorted to praising the beauty of her complexion, rather than her figure. Her five years' seniority to her husband was beginning to show.

As long ago as 1514 a rumour had gone the rounds of Europe that Henry VIII 'meant to repudiate his present wife ... because he is unable to have children by her'; premature at the time, but seeming less so with every year that went by. It was probably in 1522 that Henry took Mary Boleyn – Anne's sister – as his mistress. She, all too appropriately, represented Kindness in the York Place pageant. But whatever personal distress the relationship may have caused Katherine of Aragon, assuming she knew, this was not one to threaten her position as queen. Indeed, Henry was at this point, publicly at least, still very much the married man, moralising over the comportment of his sister Margaret Tudor in Scotland.

We last encountered Margaret on her return to Scotland some five years earlier, complaining bitterly (in an anachronistic but very Tudor fashion) that her husband Angus no longer loved her. Henry VIII and his wife Katherine were horrified, urging the sanctity of marriage on Margaret. But Scotland's affairs, which implicitly meant those of Margaret Tudor, had been a point of issue between Wolsey and Louise of Savoy at the discussions scheduled to follow the Field of Cloth of Gold.

The friar that Henry and Katherine of Aragon had (again) sent north tactfully blamed certain of Margaret's councillors for having seduced her into seeking 'an unlawful divorce from lawful matrimony directly against the ordinance of God and utterly repugnant to man's law'. But Margaret was having none of it. 'I had no help of his Grace my brother, nor no love of my lord of Angus and he to take my living at his pleasure and despoil', she wrote to Henry VIII's representative, Lord Dacre. 'Methink my lord, ye should not think this reasonable, if ye be my friend.' Her allegiance had often wavered between her natal and her present country; she had often been torn. But now: 'I must cause me to please this realm, when I have my life here.'

When the Duke of Albany returned from his visit to France in November 1521, Margaret Tudor welcomed him warmly. Though they had in the past been rivals for power in Scotland, she had perhaps learnt that there were worse evils. When he reached Edinburgh, and the constable handed him the keys of the castle, Albany courteously handed them back to Margaret. It must have been balm to her wounded spirit. While Margaret and Albany set about joint rule, as queen mother and regent, it was the turn of her estranged husband Angus to flee into French exile. It was probably Angus's Douglas clan who first started the rumour that Margaret and Albany were having an affair.

Soon Henry VIII was also complaining of Albany's 'dishonourable and damnable abusing of our sister, inciting and stirring her to be divorced from her lawful husband for what corrupt intent God knoweth'. Margaret wrote to Wolsey complaining of false reports; Wolsey advised Henry that Margaret had clearly been suborned. But meanwhile, England's borders with Scotland were fortified.

Anglo-Scottish relations were the worse for the fact that in one sense Katherine of Aragon was now riding high. England's European interest at this point no longer lay with France – Scotland and Albany's old ally – but with the Habsburgs. The end of May 1522 saw the arrival of Charles V in England for a six-week visit, celebrated with extraordinary splendour, to affirm his English alliance and, with his future marriage to his cousin the Princess Mary, a permanent binding of

England into the Habsburg hegemony. Charles and Mary's children would, if Henry himself had no sons, inherit an empire that stretched from England to the Mediterranean, to say nothing of Spain's colonies across the Atlantic. This, however, was for the moment secret, given that Mary was still officially betrothed to the French dauphin.

At Greenwich Charles was greeted by Mary and her mother, and asked for his aunt Katherine's blessing. Mary danced and played the virginals, and ambassadors reported that she was likely to become 'a handsome lady, although it is difficult to form an idea of her beauty as she is still so small'. There were masques and Masses, jousts and banquets. One of the most successful entertainments was a reading of the list of grievances Henry VIII had sent to the French king. The treaty between the two allies declared that in 1523 Charles would invade France from Spain and Henry from Calais.

Much though she might have longed for it, Katherine of Aragon was not without concern about the alliance between her husband and her nephew. Though Henry might dream of claiming his 'antient right and title to the crown of France', Katherine had witnessed Henry's rage when, years earlier, her father Ferdinand had made an alliance only to let him down. Did she suspect that this time he would not forgive her the sins of her Habsburg connections so readily? In January 1523 she told Charles's ambassador 'vehemently' that Charles had to deliver all he had promised: 'It was much better to promise little and perform faithfully than to promise much and fail in part.'

Her anxieties were all too justified, for the Anglo-Habsburg 'Great Enterprise' of 1523 against France was a disaster. Margaret of Austria offered Habsburg troops to the English, but nowhere near the three thousand horse and five thousand foot the English demanded. And even those she offered, she could not find the money to pay. The English troops sent to capture Boulogne marched instead on Paris but were turned back by foul weather and lack of supplies. Charles (distracted by French successes on the Spanish frontier) failed to keep to his part of the plan. And the French general the Duc de Bourbon, now in open rebellion against the king, who had promised to join Charles and Henry, failed to turn up at all, fleeing instead to Italy.

Margaret had to take the recriminations of Henry VIII and Wolsey, the latter declaring that they would not have expected a lady of her wisdom to have tried to excuse herself 'by inventions and compasses, by paraboles and assimilations'. By October Henry was secretly contemplating breaking his daughter's betrothal to her cousin Charles and instead allying her to her cousin on the other side, the young King of Scots, James V, Margaret Tudor's son.

This would certainly remove one thorn in England's side. The summer of 1522 saw skirmishes between England and Scotland. Albany led forces south, but the Scottish troops, remembering Flodden, refused to cross the border, and Henry was quick to cash in with the offer of a five-year peace. The following summer, Margaret Tudor caused to be read out in public a speech her young son had written in his own hand, urging that he should be allowed to make peace with his uncle of England. The Scottish authorities veered between waiting on Albany's guidance and clamouring for their young king to be set free from Albany's over-close tutelage; Margaret's own popularity ebbed and flowed. As England burnt the Scottish town of Jedburgh, as Margaret fed them information about Scotland's military dispositions, even her former supporters complained that she was 'right fickle'. In October 1523 Albany again tried to invade England with French and Scottish troops, only to be roundly defeated.

The Anglo-Habsburg alliance still, theoretically, stood; Margaret of Austria was certainly determined that it should. The English ambassador to the Low Countries reported her as saying she had always been 'utterly inclined' to Henry's good. But the following March Katherine of Aragon would warn Charles's ambassador that Henry was 'very discontented' and it is notable that she had to send her confessor secretly to do it.

It would, the ambassador said, be 'regrettable' if the communication came to the ears of 'certain English'; Wolsey was 'very restless' whenever he spoke to Katherine of Aragon, and frequently interrupted his discourse with her.

Wolsey had been further alienated from the Habsburgs when, on the death of Pope Adrian, Charles V's old tutor, in September 1523, after less than two years in office, Charles and Margaret of Austria failed to win him the papacy. (It went instead to another Medici, Clement VII.) But however far the ever-more powerful Wolsey might be from falling in with Katherine's plans, he had time left to annoy another woman, too.

There is a widespread belief that the enmity between Anne Boleyn and Cardinal Wolsey sprang early in her English career, when he was personally responsible for putting an end to her love match with a young English nobleman, and that much of what followed in the next decade sprang from this injury. It may be true, but the source that describes it, a book written by Wolsey's gentleman usher George Cavendish, was at once both partisan and crafted some time after the event, as the few sources for this early stage of Anne's career tend to be.

Anne Boleyn's name was linked to three men before Henry VIII, but we have little certain knowledge of any of the relationships. She had been brought home from France to marry her kinsman James Butler, heir to the disputed Irish earldom of Ormonde; a match proposed by her powerful Howard relatives, and one which might have sorted out several difficulties, since the Boleyns also claimed the earldom. It would moreover, from the viewpoint of Wolsey and his king, bind the powerful Butlers more closely to English interests. But the marriage did not take place. The question is why. There may have been some reluctance on the Butlers' part but it is also possible that Anne herself intervened.

As Cavendish tells it, while at court in attendance on Katherine of Aragon, Anne became acquainted with Henry Percy, heir to the great earldom of Northumberland, who was living in Wolsey's household. Accompanying Wolsey to court, Percy 'would fall in dalliance with the queen's maidens, being at the last more conversant with Mistress Anne Boleyn than with any other, so that there grew such a secret love between them that at length they were ensured together intending to marry'. But when Wolsey found out, he instantly upbraided Percy with his 'peevish folly'. Those of his rank were not supposed to marry for love. Wolsey had planned another, politically advantageous, marriage for him with a girl from the equally prominent Talbot family. And *if* Cavendish is to be believed, Henry had his eye on Anne already, though this last is perhaps unlikely.

Percy's father came roaring down to London, declaring his son was 'a proud, presumptuous, disdainful, and very unthrifty waster'. Although the words are from Cavendish, the earl did certainly make an unscheduled visit to London in June 1523; the long-arranged Percy-Talbot match was for a time postponed. Percy was forbidden to see Anne Boleyn again and, browbeaten, complied. Anne, in Cavendish's tale, swore that 'if it lay ever in her power, she would work the cardinal as much displeasure'.

The third relationship was with the poet and courtier Thomas Wyatt, whose family was a neighbour of the Boleyns in Kent. No question of marriage here: Wyatt was already married, albeit very unhappily, but that only gave more impetus to his expression of the courtly love fantasy. In the great game of courtly rivalry, one story has Wyatt (like Charles Brandon with Margaret of Austria) capturing a jewel from Anne and later flaunting it before Henry. The story itself is a useful pointer to the competitive court context in which the king's interest was first aroused. Another story – that Wyatt tried to warn the king that Anne had been unchaste with him, but was ignored – seems unlikely.

It is impossible to be sure exactly how many of the poems Wyatt later wrote were written with Anne Boleyn in mind, though she is surely the 'Brunet' who 'set our country in a roar'. But one gives a striking testimony to Anne's allure:

> Whoso list to hunt: I know where is a hind.
> But for me, alas I may no more;
> The vain travail hath wearied me so sore,
> I am of them that farthest cometh behind.
>
> . . . graven with diamonds in letters plain
> There is written her fair neck round about:
> 'Noli me tangere, for Caesar's I am,
> And wild for to hold, though I seem tame.'

The poem paints Wyatt himself as the unsuccessful suitor, and Anne, the hind, as evasive and chaste. It also breathes the kind of edgy romantic glamour guaranteed to make Anne a star and a quarry for the young men of the court, and to the not-quite-so-young man who led them. Even if, or perhaps especially because, that man was already married to the now less than glamorous Katherine of Aragon.

It was probably in 1524 that Katherine of Aragon's sexual relations with Henry came to an end. She was thirty-eight and Henry, himself five years younger, can no longer have felt that there was any point in trying to get another child on her. The queen's energies would from now be devoted to raising her only child, the Princess Mary. 'Daughters', Anne de Beaujeu had written, 'are a heavy responsibility – when they are young, you must watch over them carefully.'

The well-educated Katherine helped teach her daughter Latin, French and some Spanish. A fine musician and dancer, Mary was also educated in penmanship, as well as needlework. Katherine also obtained the advice of the Spanish-born scholar Juan Luis Vives, who in 1523 she commissioned to write *The Education of a Christian Woman*, and who, while advocating a certain amount of classical reading, nonetheless believed a woman should know only 'what pertains to the fear of God'.

To Vives, the question was not of women's mental inferiority, or otherwise; it was in the physical that their vulnerability lay. 'In the education of a woman the principal and, I might say, the only concern should be the preservation of chastity.' A better education might indeed lead to more strength in virtue but it is hard to feel that Mary was encouraged to let her mind run as free around the new humanist learning as, a decade or two later, her half-sister would be.

In Scotland, meanwhile, Katherine of Aragon's sister-in-law Margaret Tudor was also contemplating her offspring's maturity. Her ally (or lover) Albany had never succeeded in establishing undisputed control of the turbulent country, and in May 1524 he retired to France, where Margaret's estranged husband Angus now also lived, stirring up trouble for his rivals in Scotland wherever he could.

Margaret Tudor seized power, with the support of certain powerful allies within the nobility. It was in everyone's interest (whatever terms Albany and Margaret had or had not been on) to end the absent Albany's regency. He himself had insisted, before leaving Scotland, that 'the Queen should be obeyed in all her rights'. Margaret's solution was to declare her twelve-year-old son James of age and able to rule his own territory. With the help of his mother, naturally.

In England, Henry VIII was anxious to distance Scotland from the French connection that Albany's 'usurped' powers represented. It was at this all too opportune moment that Angus managed to make his way back across the Channel to the English court. Henry and Wolsey were happy to back a plan by which Angus should assume an Anglophile rule of Scotland, with young James V as nominal ruler, and his mother likewise exercising a largely ceremonial function. But endless letters from Margaret declared that rather than this, she would turn to France for help, and that Angus would create 'great jealousies'.

On 26 July James was brought from Edinburgh to Stirling and, despite the fact that Scottish sovereigns were not supposed to assume rule until the age of fourteen, formally invested with the crown. Henry sent his nephew a jewelled sword, made him a member of the Order of the Garter, and suggested that he might marry his cousin Princess Mary: a plan with which Margaret Tudor was delighted to concur.

But Henry also sent James's stepfather Angus north towards Scotland with a force. 'It is right to use the Queen of Scots as an instrument in this matter, but not so as all shall depend on her', Wolsey wrote. 'A good archer should have two strings to his bow, especially when one is made of threads wrought by woman's fingers.'

A reconciliation between Margaret Tudor and her husband Angus seemed the obvious next step. Obvious to everyone except Margaret. Angus was instructed 'to endeavour to recover the Queen's favour'; Margaret was urged that this reconciliation would be for the good of the country, that her personal feelings were not the point.

Despite Margaret's furious protest, Angus crossed the border into Scotland. As parliament sat in Edinburgh, Margaret closed the city gates. Angus and his supporters scaled the walls of the city, declaring in time-honoured fashion that they were the young king's loyal subjects, seeking only to sit in parliament as their ancestors had done. Down the Royal Mile, at Holyrood with her son, Margaret hastily assembled a matching force and, to the English ambassador's dismal bleating about her 'willfulness', ordered the cannons to be trained on her husband. At the young king's command Angus and his allies retreated. Margaret and her son went in a torchlight procession up the hill into the greater security of Edinburgh Castle, whence Margaret sent a firmly worded request that her brother in England should not interfere in Scottish affairs.

Parliament confirmed her regency but if Margaret Tudor had now demonstrated an unfeminine defiance, worse was to follow. The early months of 1525 saw Margaret ever more determinedly seeking a divorce from Angus. She ignored all her brother's protests that marriage was 'divinely ordained', the more so since she was by now in love with Henry Stewart, a young man of the royal household, eleven years younger than she but promoted from the king's carver to captain of the guard. A letter from her brother Henry VIII provoked an hour-long storm of tears, and a protest that such 'had never been written to a noble woman'. That summer, she accepted for form's sake the appearance of a reconciliation with Angus, but as parliament was reopened, with the king and his mother heading the procession while Angus carried the crown, some two thousand of Angus's clansmen ranged outside Edinburgh's walls faced Margaret's guns within.

A deal was struck, whereby four parties – Angus and three other nobles – would each in turn have custody of the young king. But at the end of 1525, after his three-month stint, Angus refused to give the boy up. James was forced to write an official letter saying he wished to remain in his stepfather's care, but he sent another in secret, begging his mother to rescue him. She gathered an army and rode to Edinburgh but when Angus brought James out of the city beside him, her men dared not fire on 'the person of their Prince'.

James V was to spend the next two and a half years in what by his mother's report amounted to polite captivity, while attempt after attempt at rescue failed. Is it unfair to say that in Scotland the game was in men's hands? Margaret had been born royal, had tried to claim every power of queenship, had fought her way back from overthrow after overthrow. She had faced an impossibly difficult situation in Scotland, but her choices had contributed to her problems. She had proved herself something of a wildcard (just as, at the English court, Anne Boleyn was beginning to do). Perhaps the game of queens was not one she was ultimately fitted to play.

16

Pavia

Italy, France, the Netherlands, Spain, 1525

I N FRANCE ANOTHER woman was about to come into her own.
Two other women, perhaps. Louise of Savoy had fantasised (with
fear and perhaps also with hope?) that the future of her whole
house would come to rest on her shoulders. She was about to find that
dream come true. By contrast, Louise's daughter Marguerite had
known all her life that she was, in her own words, the least useful of
their family trinity. But that was about to change.

The trigger was, as so often, a twist in the endless wars between
France and the Empire. The 1523 Anglo-Habsburg invasion might
have fizzled out but that was far from the end of the story. The revolt of
the disaffected Duc de Bourbon and the consequent trial of his allies
had left a bad taste. He had roused much sympathy in a populace angry
about the money mulcted from them to pay for François's Italian wars.
The French army that tried (under Bonnivet's command) to capture
Naples in the spring of 1524 was soundly defeated. But that summer
François decided once more to venture his hand in Italy; determined,
he said, to win 'nothing less than the entire state of Milan and the kingdom of Naples'.

In that summer, Queen Claude was clearly seriously ill. François
declared that, 'Never could I have believed that the bond of marriage
enjoined by God would be so firm and difficult to break.' He nevertheless
set off for the south, accompanied by his wife and sister. Louise of Savoy,
who in the past year had suffered two bad bouts of pleurisy, was soon in
a state of collapse, as her daughter Marguerite reported: 'What with the

fatigue of the roads and the extremity of worry which she has to bear, [she] has had a flux of bleeding from all parts, just as in her bad fever.'

That autumn Queen Claude died, followed just weeks later by her daughter Charlotte. Marguerite nursed the little girl, and tried to keep the news of her granddaughter's death from Louise of Savoy, already distraught at the thought of her son's departure. But in October, François appointed his mother as regent once more and led his army over the Alps, despite all Louise could say.

To maintain a campaign through the winter season was a challenge. François insisted on camping beside the city of Pavia, some twenty miles from Milan. In the last week of February 1525, matters came to a head. When, on 24 February, a Spanish-Imperial army attacked and succeeded in dividing the French army, the four-hour battle saw the French suffer the greatest loss of noblemen since Agincourt, with Bonnivet among the fallen (having, it was said, ridden out to seek his own death after urging François to fight that day). In the catastrophic French defeat, one of the few to evade either death or capture was Marguerite's husband Alençon but François himself was taken into imperial captivity.

Nothing was left to François 'but my honour and my life'. He wrote to his mother immediately, begging her not to lose heart, 'but to exercise your accustomed prudence'. Louise of Savoy forced herself to write reassuringly back, while her daughter Marguerite wrote to one of his companion noblemen, Montmorency, a Marshall of France: 'All my life I will envy you because I cannot perform for him the duties you are now performing; for although my will to do so is greater than yours, it is impossible, since fate has wronged me by making me a woman.' Montmorency, in return, asked Marguerite to write often, since news of herself and her mother was 'the only thing which gives [the king] the utmost pleasure'.

François was never going to be treated other than honourably. Soon, one of the noblemen who shared his captivity wrote to Louise that he required not only money, but silver plate. There was, however, concern about François's desire to fast several days a week; soon his sister was writing to say that if he would not eat meat and eggs in Lent he should remember fish did not agree with him. (In the end he observed the meat-free season by eating tortoises.)

Some three months after his capture, François was taken to Spain, reaching Madrid at the beginning of August, royally entertained the whole way. Meanwhile, his mother was left to deal with the effects of his captivity. 'Being so unfortunate', François wrote to his subjects, 'I have had no greater satisfaction than to know of the obedience which you have shown to Madame, as loyal subjects and as good Frenchmen. I recommend her to you.'

'Come soon, for never had I such longing to see you', François wrote to his mother. But this was impossible. Louise of Savoy had too many other problems to manage: primarily to ensure that Charles V (or his ally Henry VIII) did not follow up the French defeat by invading France itself. Burgundy – now French, but the ancestral home of Margaret of Austria's family – was a particular concern, since Charles had a special interest in recapturing this part of his heritage. More ships were commissioned, and the returning remnants of François's army paid and heartened. She had, moreover, to defend the crown itself against any incursions, under these circumstances, on royal authority. Murmurings that the regent should be not the king's mother but his nearest male kinsman quickly died when the said nobleman instead accepted a place on her council, but the Paris *parlement* had still to be won round. Louise had to use all her tact.

One specific cause of complaint was that the royal family had been too lax on religious unorthodoxy, had expanded their privileges at the expense of the church's authority. Here Louise, naturally more conservative than either of her children, or perhaps simply more fearful, made some concessions: she needed the new pope's support more than ever against Spain.

Across Europe, 1525 was something of a turning point in religious affairs. In Spain the Inquisition clamped down on the mystically-oriented 'Illuminati' within its ranks; in Germany, Luther's divergence from the main humanist reform movement became apparent. In this year the first of a growing number of German princely rulers followed where the cities were leading and joined hands with the Lutherans. Conversely, when peasant revolt broke out across Habsburg lands, it was linked, not altogether to Luther's pleasure, to the religious Reformation. It was also in this year that the more radical Swiss reformer, Ulrich Zwingli, both introduced a new liturgy to replace the

Mass, and dedicated his *Commentary on the True and False Religion* to the King of France.

An important tenet of the new faith was that ordinary people should be able to read the Bible in their own language, rather than having it confined to priestly Latin. But in this new climate the publication of Bibles in vernacular French was banned. Marguerite's mentor Briçonnet escaped heresy charges only because of his court connections. Nonetheless, wrote Chancellor Duprat to King François, Marguerite's mother 'manages so well that she has completely rehabilitated the realm'.

Louise of Savoy had real success with her foreign policy. On 30 August the Peace of the More (with Cardinal Wolsey as one of the prime negotiators and Thomas Boleyn one of the signatories) restored harmony with England. She also sent envoys to the Ottoman sultan in Constantinople, Suleiman the Magnificent, warning that if he did not come to France's assistance Charles V would soon become 'the master of the world'. But one of her overtures brought trouble for another lady.

Margaret of Austria greeted the news of Pavia with a public display of rejoicing: fireworks, processions and prayers. She was, however, concerned that the vulnerably placed Netherlands might be threatened by an alliance between France and England. And she was receptive when Louise of Savoy sent her secretary to the Netherlands to arrange a six-month truce. But Charles was furious when he heard that Margaret had arranged an armistice for those territories under her authority, without waiting to hear his overall plan: 'I cannot conceal from you, madame, that I have found it very strange, and very far from satisfactory, that this should have been done without knowing my intentions, and without receiving instructions on this behalf, and powers from me', he wrote on 15 August. His own treaty concerning the cessation of hostilities was to be published immediately, and her own should be regarded as 'null and void . . . for it is my express intention that it should not be held of the smallest force or value'. She was still his 'good mother and aunt', but all the same . . .

Wolsey was likewise annoyed that Margaret of Austria had concluded peace with France without consulting him: 'I should never have thought that, after so many stipulations, promises, and declarations made by madame, she would have been the first to break through them,' he told the imperial envoys. 'The perplexity and doubt by which madame is said to be assailed, and which have induced her to take this step, are no excuse . . .'

By contrast, the imprisoned François greeted the letters brought to him by Margaret of Austria's envoy with compliments and gratitude. He referred all questions to his sister Marguerite of Navarre, travelling to Madrid to negotiate the peace and François's freedom. François had refused to negotiate with his captors while imprisoned, insisting everything should await his sister's arrival. This was Marguerite's chance and she would, she said, 'throw the cinders of her bones to the winds' to do her brother service.

She was by now free of other ties. Her husband Alençon, almost the only noble to escape from Pavia, was jeered at by the crowds as he made his way back to France; variously blamed for having ordered a retreat when none was needed and for having fled the field. Marguerite wrote that he, 'the prisoner of his freedom', now found his life 'a living death'. Whether or not she blamed him (as it seems her mother did), she nursed him in the fatal illness which followed and on his death wrote to François that her grief 'made her forget all reason'. Three days later, however, she was carefully composing her face so as not to upset Louise: 'I would feel miserable, seeing I am of no use to you', she told François, 'if I were to disturb the person who is doing so much for you and for what is yours.'

In July, she received her safe conduct to travel through the emperor's lands, and wrote again to François (the trinity kept up a speedy interchange of letters and poems) that 'fear of death, prison, or any other ill have now become so familiar that to me they are liberty, life, health, glory and honour, since I believe that through them I could share your fortune, which if I could I'd bear alone'. But by the time she could set sail at the end of August, the Mediterranean waves were so bad her whole retinue was seasick. When she landed, riding across Spain with an honour guard sent by the emperor behind her, she heard that François was gravely ill; news that made her pick up the pace still further, travelling ten or twelve leagues a day until most of her servants were left behind. 'I cannot get over my fear of being inadequate', she wrote.

As she drew near to Madrid she sent off another note to François's companion Montmorency, that 'never did I know what a brother is until now; and never would I have thought I could love him so much!' On her arrival on 19 September she found the doctors had given François up for lost. Not so Marguerite. One of Louise of Savoy's envoys in Madrid described how she:

> asked all the gentlemen of the king's household and her own, as well as the ladies, to pray to God. They all took communion and afterwards mass was said in the king's chamber . . . After the mass, my lady the duchess had the Blessed Sacrament presented to the king so that he might adore it . . .

François managed to swallow a piece of the sacred wafer, and Marguerite took the rest. From that time François's fever abated. (It seems likely the abscess in his head had burst.) Marguerite despatched a messenger, with orders to press his horse until it foundered under him, to their mother, from whom the news of François's illness had hitherto been kept. Louise wrote back to Marguerite of her 'resurrection'; the idea of François's danger had thrown her into 'passion and death'.

Marguerite's nursing – or her prayers – may have saved François, but as she began peace talks with the emperor at Toledo, her diplomacy was less successful. Charles V had been warned against himself receiving Marguerite: 'being young and a widow she comes . . . to see and be seen'. Charles ordained that the two should meet 'alone in a chamber with one of my ladies to guard the door'. Marguerite found him 'quite cold'; putting her off by saying he had to consult with his council. She got on better with his sister Eleanor, one of the children Margaret of Austria had raised, the now-widowed Queen of Portugal who had returned to live at her brother's court. The two women spoke late into the night but when in subsequent days Marguerite tried to use Eleanor as a conduit she found her unresponsive: 'they keep her on a tight rein'.

None of the proposals Marguerite was able to put to Charles V was acceptable. The talks were suspended and Marguerite spent her days visiting convents for prayer and consolation. Another attempt, almost a month later, again failed. The stumbling block was always France's reluctance to return Burgundy, while Charles made it clear he had no intention of ransoming François simply for cash. At the beginning of December, with the truce almost expired, Marguerite was forced to leave for France again, without promise of her brother's release, sending with almost hysterical frequency as many as several letters as day to be sure her brother did not want her to return. [**see note on sources**]

She was greatly distressed at having failed in this, the most important mission of her life, writing to Montmorency that 'the farther I go, the unhappier I am to know that I am not worthy to serve the one who so deserves it'. The journey itself was exhausting, the stringent terms of her safe conduct meaning 'that every day for a month I was on horseback at six o'clock in the morning and did not arrive at my destination until night'.

It was Louise of Savoy who decided that even Burgundy (along with François's Italian claims and other border territories) was a price worth paying to free François from what was beginning to look like perpetual captivity. Earlier, the imperial ambassador had written that she was the one who might be in any degree flexible in this, although Marguerite, on her journey north, was likewise urging François: 'do not be held back by lands or children, for your kingdom needs you'. The treaty of Madrid, signed in the first weeks of 1526, ordained that the French king should immediately be set free, that he should marry the emperor's sister Eleanor and that his two eldest sons, aged six and eight, should be sent to Charles V as hostages.

Meeting Eleanor, his future bride, François's deportment was everything courtly but he had already made a secret declaration disavowing any promises made under duress. He had no intention of fulfilling the terms of the treaty. Nonetheless, on 17 March, by careful negotiation, two boats rowed towards each other across the border river of Bidassoa. On a barque moored in the middle they exchanged passengers: François travelling on to Bayonne where his mother, sister, and ministers were waiting, and his two small sons into Spain, to take their father's place in captivity.

17

'a true, loyal mistress and friend'

England, 1525–1527

EVENTS IN EUROPE, inevitably, had also their effect in England, and on two women close to Henry VIII. The first to feel it was Katherine of Aragon. Henry's first reaction to the news from Pavia early in 1525 was, of course, delight. His ally's victory was, Henry assumed, a fulfilment of the long-held dream: the rebirth of English power in France. An equally delighted Katherine of Aragon wrote to her nephew of her 'great pleasure and content', reminding Charles V that her husband had been, she said, his 'constant and faithful ally', and urging that 'from the continuance of such friendship and alliance the best result may be anticipated'. But the rejoicing proved premature.

Instead, it quickly transpired that the new adjustment of power in Europe, with the Habsburg Charles so clearly in the ascendant over a humiliated France, meant that Henry had lost his precious, precarious position as the keeper of the balance. Charles no longer needed him (and was aware, moreover, that Henry had contributed neither men nor money to the victory from which he hoped such gains). That summer, Charles demanded that Henry's nine-year-old daughter, Mary, should either be sent to Spain, to be educated in the ways of the country in preparation for her marriage, or that he should be released from the contract. Mary's age was a part of the problem, as Charles was careful to explain. Not only was he, at twenty-five, eager to get on with fathering a family but an adult bride was (given the Habsburg proclivity for female regents) the best answer to his immediate problem: who should be his regent to govern Spain while he was absent in Italy?

Charles V now sought to marry his cousin, the well dowered 21-year-old Isabella of Portugal: 'Were this marriage to take place, I could leave the Government here in the hands of the said Princess', he wrote to his brother Ferdinand. To Henry he explained: 'my subjects are pressingly requesting me to marry a princess who may fill my place, and govern during my absence'. His marriage to Isabella took place the following year, in March 1526.

Henry VIII, of course, was never going to see the force of these arguments. His disenchantment with the Habsburg alliance, which Katherine represented, may explain what came next. If Mary was no longer to marry Charles, then the future of England could no longer be left in a son-in-law's hands. In June Henry created his illegitimate son (by Elizabeth Blount) Duke of Richmond; Richmond being a title with particular importance to the Tudor dynasty, since the young Henry VII had borne it. Now also nominally Lieutenant-General of the North, the boy was to be addressed henceforth in official documents as 'the right high and noble prince Henry'.

Katherine of Aragon made her views clear; encouraged, so the Venetian ambassador reported, by three of her Spanish ladies. All she achieved was to provoke the king, who dismissed the ladies: 'a strong measure', the Venetian admitted, 'but the queen was obliged to submit and to have patience.' Inevitably there was speculation that Henry was planning to make the boy his heir but his intentions were far from clear. Just weeks later Princess Mary was sent to Ludlow as nominal Governor of Wales, with a household even grander than Richmond's, kitted out in her livery colours of blue and green, and with instructions from her father that she should be treated as to 'so great a princess doth appertain'.

Ruling a miniature court as a small queen, she was to be educated in Latin and French 'without fatigacion [sic] or weariness', to enjoy a diet 'pure, well-prepared, dressed and served with comfortable, joyous and merry communication'. It must have been a grief to Katherine in one sense, to be deprived of her daughter's company: 'the long absence of the King and you troubleth me', Katherine wrote to her daughter, but also an honour, surely.[1]

It is uncertain whether, with Katherine of Aragon's childbearing clearly at an end, Henry already contemplated setting her aside. But there was no thought of the shocking and controversial turn the king's marital career would next take. However, in the course of the summer peregrinations of 1525, Henry's interest in Anne Boleyn may have begun.

In the summer of 1525 Anne's sister Mary Boleyn became pregnant; whether by her husband William Carey or by Henry VIII it is impossible, now, to say. Either way, her pregnancy would have made Mary less attractive to Henry. One school of thought holds that her family effectively put Anne forward as an alternative, another female pawn who could be brought into play to ensure that the king's face still turned the Howard/Boleyn way. The exact nature of the mating dance that would soon be performed between several forces – dynastic necessity, Henry VIII's affections, Anne Boleyn's will and the impact of the new religion – remains one of the most debatable topics in history. Exact facts and precise chronology often cannot be found. But two things should perhaps be said.

First, the pattern of European events – Henry's turning away from things Spanish and towards things French – provided a context. There was widespread concern at Charles V's dominance and especially his pre-eminence in Italy where, in May 1526, an alarmed Pope Clement joined in a 'Holy League' with France, Venice, Florence and Milan (a league which had England's tacit support) against the Holy Roman Emperor. Second, on a personal level, Henry's initial pursuit of Anne – his attempt to make her (in several different senses) his mistress – can be set within what you might call another European context: the long fantasy of courtly love.[2] This was enacted in the masques and tournaments, the game played out in poems and pageants: the cruel superior mistress and the yearning lover who must always obey. Born in the courts of Provence and finding its English apogee in the days of Eleanor of Aquitaine, it had enjoyed a late rebirth in the fifteenth century under the Burgundian aegis. Modelled on the devotion man owes to God and the service a feudal vassal owed his lord, courtly love might yet allow a measure of masculine violence at this later, more cynical, stage of its development, anyway. That is what lay behind Margaret of Austria's poetry, and behind the warnings Anne de Beaujeu had issued so clearly. But for better or for worse, this was the game which, significantly, those of Margaret of Austria's court loved to play. And Henry VIII too was besotted with all the games of chivalry.

It is possible that Henry Tudor's initial pursuit of Anne Boleyn had an element of competitiveness in it. Anne, fresh from the continent, would provide an arena in which to compete not only against his own courtiers but against the French king: a field of cloth of gold in her own person, you might say. (The trouble, in years ahead, would perhaps be that she tried to keep up that spirit of rivalry.) Just so did François compete with cronies like Bonnivet.

Early in 1526 Henry began to sound out opinion on his marriage but there is no reason to suppose this was directly connected to any approaches he may have made to Anne Boleyn. At the Shrovetide jousts in February 1526, Henry rode under the device 'Declare I dare not', which has often been seen as an approach to Anne. But at the banquet which followed, in his role of gallant, he waited on Katherine. Many a queen (Katherine's mother among them) might be expected to tolerate her husband's infidelities, so long as he paid tribute to her position in public. 'You owe [your husband] nothing less than compliance and obedience so that you do not provoke his folly; God and the world expects nothing less of you', Anne de Beaujeu had written.

Henry VIII's letters to Anne probably started slightly later that year.* In the first of them he describes himself three times as Anne's true servant, while she is the 'mistress', in the controlling rather than the carnal sense; a distant unattainable star whose resistance only increased her desirability.

Henry's next letter repeats the theme: clearly Anne had protested her duty of service to the king. 'Although it doth not appertain to a gentleman to take his lady in place of a servant, nevertheless, in compliance with your desires, I willingly grant it to you . . .' Another is more revealing. Its lengthy and closely reasoned argument is the more striking for the fact that Henry was notoriously reluctant, under normal circumstances, ever to write:

---

* None of Henry VIII's letters to Anne Boleyn are dated, nor is there any agreement among historians as to their chronology [**see note on sources**]. None of Anne's letters to him survive.

> Debating with myself the contents of your letter, I have put myself
> in great distress, not knowing how to interpret them ... praying
> you with all my heart that you will expressly certify me of your
> whole mind concerning the love between us two.

He has been now, he writes, 'above one whole year struck with the dart
of love, not being assured either of failure or of finding place in your
heart and grounded affection'.

It is the last point, he says, that prevents him 'from calling you my
mistress, since if you do not love me in a way which is beyond common
affection that name in no wise belongs to you, for it denotes a singular
love, far removed from the common'. Henry had obviously started out
by trying to have Anne Boleyn as his partner in just another affair; the
kind of mistress Katherine of Aragon would have accepted, and the
kind Mary Boleyn had been. But now he seems to be adjusting his
offer:

> If it shall please you to do me the office of a true, loyal mistress and
> friend and to give yourself up, body and soul, to me ... I promise
> you that not only shall the name be given you, but that also I will
> take you for my only mistress, rejecting from thought and affec-
> tion all others save yourself, to serve only you.

Though the double sense of mistress is confusing, Henry seems to be
making the subtle, to modern eyes, but important difference of offering Anne the position of *maitresse en titre*.[3] Perhaps the offer was a
tribute to Anne Boleyn's French years. The question was why she did
not accept. But the experience of Marguerite of Navarre, and of
Margaret of Austria before her, taught that a woman was not necessarily a winner if once she engaged in the *guerre d'amour*. Nor had Anne's
sister Mary walked away with any great gains from the king's favour.

We cannot, in the nature of things, have any sure information as to
when the relationship became sexual. The picture may be of seven long
years' frustration, traditionally seen as being imposed by Anne but it
has to be admitted as a possibility that they had sex at the start of the
relationship, before marriage and legitimate children became the ultimate goal, and then later refrained; a restraint in this case at least as

likely to be imposed by Henry. The answer to the perennial question – how they managed it? – may lie in the question of what we mean by sex. Or rather, what was considered sex in the realm of courtly love.

Courtly love permitted an extended experience of what we would call foreplay but which could be accepted as an alternative to full intercourse. A manual written for one of Eleanor of Aquitaine's daughters, by a monk, instructed that a lover might enjoy the embraces of his lady naked in a bed as long as 'the final solace' was denied them. Indeed, given the patterns of late marriage (and only the most limited contraception) prevalent in sixteenth-century England, this seems to have been the practice well beyond courtly circles.

Courtly love, in essence adulterous, was never meant to end in marriage; it produced ecstasies but no heirs. This, ultimately, would be why the game had to end: it could not give Henry all he wanted. Again, we cannot know exactly when Henry's interest in Anne changed its focus; when the idea of marriage was first mooted between them but in the course of 1526 things took a serious turn.

By the December of that year Katherine of Aragon was isolated at court. When Charles V's new ambassador, Inigo de Mendoza, arrived he found it impossible to see Katherine, finally hearing from her that any interview would have to be arranged through Wolsey and conducted in his presence, and that the utmost discretion would have to be preserved. After their first meeting in the spring, Mendoza concluded that to seek another would merely 'add further damage to what might be said' about the Spanish queen.

It was probably to celebrate the New Year of 1527 that Anne Boleyn sent Henry VIII a gift he received with delight. The 'fine poésies' of the letter that came with it – the 'too humble submission', as the lovesick king protested – have long since been lost but the message is still plain to see. The gift is a jewel, once hung with a diamond, representing a ship on which a damsel is borne above a stormy sea. The diamond is the heart; hard but steadfast, as the myths of courtly love had it, and the damsel was surely Anne, the giver. Was Henry to be her refuge from the storms of life? Even if it meant another woman, the king's loyal wife, would be cast adrift on the sea?

At some point Anne seems to have withdrawn herself to Hever. One of Henry's letters to her laments that she 'will not come to court, neither with my lady your mother, and if you could, nor yet by any other way'. It may have been tactics, a strategic withdrawal on Anne's part, since Henry protests in wounded tones that he marvels at her decision, since he is sure he has committed no fault. (This may be a more complex statement than it seems: in courtly parlance the sinful lover was supposed to derive vicarious moral benefit from his mistress's virtue.) It was around Easter 1527 that the king informed Wolsey he had serious 'scruples' about his marriage.

Conversely, however, Princess Mary was brought back from Ludlow, to be displayed as a suitable bride for one of King François's sons. (The match would be the less welcome to Katherine of Aragon, it was reported, for the fact the French king's mother was 'a terrible woman'.) Curiously, Anne Boleyn played a part in entertaining the French envoys, dancing with the king while the French ambassador danced with Mary. If it were a snub to Katherine of Aragon's Spanish affections, it was also a sign Mary was still publicly seen as England's princess. But the end of April saw the Treaty of Westminster, an alliance made between England and France against Katherine's nephew.

In May 1527 Wolsey – surely by arrangement with his king – summoned Henry VIII to appear before an ecclesiastical court, to discuss matters affecting the 'tranquillity of consciences'. The court was held in the greatest secrecy at Wolsey's residence but Katherine was not wholly ignorant of it. 'Spanish ladies spy well', as Francis Bryan, a kinsman of Anne Boleyn's, once said. The day after the first meeting of Wolsey's inquiry, Charles V's ambassador de Mendoza was able to report on it, adding that 'though the queen herself has not ventured, and does not venture, to speak to me on the subject, that all her hope rests, after God, on your imperial highness'. She was communicating with Mendoza through a third party 'who pretended not to come from her, though I suspect he came with her consent'.

Two different strands of debate were raised about the validity of the king's original marriage contract: the theological interpretation of the Bible and the validity of the dispensation granted for Henry to marry Katherine at the beginning of the century; a dispensation so hedged around by the parents, Ferdinand and Isabella and Henry VII, as to leave several anomalies.

In the book of Leviticus, the Bible says: 'If a man shall take his brother's wife, it is an unclean thing: he has uncovered his brother's nakedness. They shall be childless', which, Henry was easily persuaded to believe, meant without male child. Although the book of Deuteronomy conversely urged that a man had a positive duty to marry his deceased brother's widow ('and raise up seed for his brother'), much of the debate centred on the question of to what degree Katherine had really been Henry's brother's wife; on whether she and Arthur had consummated their relationship. But Katherine was in any case unlikely to be impressed by Henry's suggestion that their marriage was incestuous and therefore cursed. Just recently, in 1525, her niece Catalina had married King João of Portugal – whose father Manuel had married one of Catalina's sisters, and two of her aunts.

Henry and Wolsey must, however, have had real hopes of papal sanction for the ending of his inconvenient marriage. Earlier in the spring of 1527 Clement had finally granted Margaret Tudor an annulment, while her sister Mary's husband Charles Brandon had received two. Events, however, were to overtake them, and in the most dramatic way. The proceedings of the inquiry were abruptly broken off when news filtered through of what was happening in that European bearpit, Italy.

In the pursuance of Charles V's Italian wars, the peninsula was now overrun not only by Spanish troops but by the emperor's unpaid German mercenaries and the French traitor Bourbon's men. Advancing southwards into the Papal States, on 6 May the famished furious soldiers surged into Rome itself, forcing the pope to flee and committing, in the words of Spain's own diplomat, 'unparalleled atrocities'. The slaughter raged for more than ten days, and it has been estimated that as many as twenty thousand died; eight thousand on the first day alone. Nuns were raped, St Peter's sacked and unburied corpses piled high in the streets.

Katherine of Aragon had been prophetically accurate to say that 'all her hope' rested on her nephew Charles V. After the sack of Rome the emperor held the pope's fate in his hands. How likely was the pope to give a judgement against Katherine, the emperor's aunt?

Forced to act on his own initiative, on 22 June Henry VIII at last confronted Katherine and told her he wanted a formal separation. Katherine's reaction was an outburst of tears, followed by the steadfast denial that her marriage with Arthur had been consummated. This, the physical rather than the legal, was to remain the bedrock of her case. If Anne Boleyn's story was now openly political, Katherine's body was a battleground. Wolsey sent instructions that his representative should tell the pope of 'certain diseases in the queen defying all remedy, for which, as well as for other causes, the king will never again live with her as a wife'.

That summer of 1527, Henry VIII and Anne Boleyn agreed to marry, as evinced by the terms in which, in September, a dispensation was requested from Rome. Henry sought permission 'to marry a woman with whose sister he had already had sexual intercourse' (presumably Anne's sister Mary) or 'one with whom he had himself had sexual intercourse'. This second proviso begs the question of whether Anne had indeed preserved her chastity as rigorously as is usually supposed, or whether she and Henry had in the early days consummated their relationship, only to pull back when the question of marriage, and with it the legitimacy of any child Anne might bear, arose.

In September Wolsey, returning from a mission abroad, found himself effectively summoned by Anne into the king's presence; a sign of how power was shifting. In October Henry asked Thomas More, who was rising rapidly as a politician and administrator, respected for his ethical principles as well as his sharp legal brain, his opinion on the passage in Leviticus. In November, he invited a number of scholars to Hampton Court.

Wolsey had been pressing the pope to help Henry, and Clement had been persuaded to issue a somewhat anomalous document: permission for Henry to marry Anne if his marriage to Katherine were dissolved, without saying how that goal might be attained. In February 1528 new envoys were sent towards Rome, with instructions to call, on their way, on Anne, who had withdrawn to Hever.

The last two years had seen dramatic changes in the positions of Katherine of Aragon and Anne Boleyn. Anne had now to be regarded as the king's future bride. But there was a danger.

The rules of the new chess declared that a lowly pawn, winning through to the enemy's back row, might itself become a queen, with all the powers that implied. But half a century earlier, a Catalan poem, 'Scachs d'Amor' (Chess Game of Love), had made a stipulation. No pawn could be 'queened' until the queen of its colour had been taken: there could not be two white, or two black, queens at one time.[4]

18

New pieces on the board

Scotland, the Netherlands, Hungary,
Italy, France, 1526–1528

I N ENGLAND A new phase of the story had begun. But the last
years of the 1520s were something of a turning point for every
one. Some actors would leave the stage, while others waited in the
wings for a new act of the play.

In Scotland two rescue attempts in 1526 failed to get the young
James V out of his stepfather Angus's hold but in June 1528 James
escaped. Colourful stories made a legend of it: the boy-king getting his
custodian drunk, dressing as a groom, and galloping away to Stirling
where his mother was waiting to raise the drawbridge once he was safe
inside. With Angus and his cohorts forbidden to come near his person,
at sixteen he would begin ruling in reality.

He was younger than François I had been when he inherited
France but Margaret Tudor was no Louise of Savoy. On 3 March
that year Margaret had married her young lover, Henry Stewart,
whom James created Lord Methven 'for the great love that he bore
to his dearest mother'. (Margaret's brother Henry VIII, by contrast,
would continue – with sublime disregard for the proverb about
pots and kettles – to call Margaret 'a shame and disgrace to all her
family'.)

James V gave his mother his blessing. What he withheld was
power. While Margaret's third marriage came to prove her unhap-
piest yet, she would have comparatively little political influence
in the years immediately ahead. From the end of the 1520s,

Margaret Tudor's would be largely a personal, rather than a political, story.

However, in each of the great European dynasties, new pieces were appearing on the board. In 1526, Charles V had married his cousin Isabella of Portugal. In the same year his widowed sister Eleanor, another of Margaret of Austria's nieces, became engaged to François during his captivity, although the marriage did not immediately take place. And 1526 also brought momentous change for another of Charles V's siblings, and evidence that the pattern of European power would soon be changing under the pressure of a new threat.

Mary 'of Hungary', as she would come to be known, the fifth child of Philip of Burgundy and his Spanish wife Juana, had been betrothed while in her cradle to Louis Jagiellon, the eldest son of the Hungarian king. At first raised at Margaret of Austria's Mechelen court, Mary was sent to the court of her grandfather Maximilian in Vienna before she was ten years old. There, she lived in company with the Hungarian king's daughter, who was herself betrothed to Mary's brother Ferdinand. The double alliance was intended to secure the Habsburg interest in the extensive kingdoms of Hungary and Bohemia, which were especially important as Europe's frontier with the Turks.

In 1521 Mary went to Hungary as its queen, and within three years the teenager had won considerable influence, placing herself at the head of one of the great political factions. This was, however, a turbulent kingdom. The Hungarian nobility were in a perpetual state of warfare with each other, with their peasantry and with the Ottoman Turks under the great Suleiman. In 1526, Suleiman broke through the Hungarian frontier; at the Battle of Mohacs at the end of August the Hungarian army was devastated and Mary's husband was killed.

Mary sent urgently for her brother Ferdinand (who claimed Hungary through his wife) but instead of travelling to her side, Ferdinand appointed her as his regent in Hungary.[1] Mary kept the throne for Ferdinand, engineering his election as King of Hungary in the teeth of any rival. By the time he arrived a year later she had, however, already asked for, and been refused, leave to resign her regency. This lack of appetite for power was to be a characteristic of her next few decades, which were permeated by the ever-growing Ottoman threat.

Another of Margaret of Austria's nieces, Isabella, was also unlucky in her spouse. Married to Christian of Denmark, Isabella had arrived in that country to find any place she might have hoped to occupy taken by her husband's Dutch-born mistress and her mother. Moreover Christian ('Christian the Tyrant' as he was known in Sweden, over which he also briefly reigned) was not a man who could make the friends needed for success in the elective monarchy of Denmark and Norway. In January 1523, he was deposed by his uncle Frederick. In 1531 he attempted to regain his throne, was captured, and eventually ended his life a prisoner. Isabella and the children she had borne him were taken back into the care of her family.

Isabella herself died in 1526, and Margaret of Austria was determined to bring up Isabella's daughters, her great-nieces, Dorothea and Christina. Margaret took a firm line with Isabella's errant spouse, refusing even to transmit letters between Christian and Charles, from whom he hoped to get troops to regain his kingdoms. The year saw also the start of marriage negotiations for yet another child being raised in Margaret of Austria's care; one whose future would be intertwined with the Netherlands. The illegitimate issue of Charles V's youthful fling with a Flemish servant, Margaret 'of Parma' was acknowledged by her father and in 1527 was betrothed to the pope's nephew (or more probably illegitimate son) Alessandro de Medici.

The rise of the Florentine banking family of Medici began during the late fourteenth century and gathered pace under Cosimo de Medici in the fifteenth. The artistic patronage they extended led to the great flowering of the Florentine Renaissance but their assumption of dynastic power angered the old noble families. The beginning of the sixteenth century saw them cast into exile but in 1512 they once again seized power, while the election of a Medici to the papacy as Leo X in the following year gave them even greater prominence. Now another Medici sat on the papal throne, as Clement VII.

But when, in the spring of 1527, imperial troops sacked Rome and took Pope Clement prisoner, the hostilities of necessity involved the pope's whole Medici family. In a riot of violence – a chair thrown from a palace window smashed the arm of Michelangelo's *David*, recently installed outside the Palazzo Vecchio – the Republic of Florence threw off the Medici yoke. One family representative, however, remained inside the city: the eight-year-old Catherine de Medici.

Her father was Lorenzo de Medici, Duke of Urbino, the pope's nephew, who had died weeks after Catherine's birth; her French-born mother had died of puerperal fever. During the short time they were with her, her parents, according to one contemporary, had been 'as pleased as if she had been a boy'. Nevertheless, hers was a difficult start even by the standards of the day. But now Catherine was being raised under the auspices of a formidable aunt, Clarice Strozzi, of whom Pope Leo X said that it would have been 'well for the family if Clarice had been the man'.

When, in May 1527, Florence turned against the Medici, most of Catherine's male relatives fled, but the child was left behind as a hostage for her family. She was placed in the Santa Lucia convent for her security but this was an establishment at odds with the Medici family. At the end of that year, amid a visitation of the plague, she was moved (veiled, and at dead of night, to avoid aggression from the Florentine people) to the more sympathetic Murate convent. But the European politics that made Italy a battleground still made Florence dangerous territory for her.

In France too – the country with which Catherine de Medici would be so much associated – there was also a new generation on the way. Late in 1526 François I asked his sister Marguerite to help him by marrying Henri d'Albret, the King of Navarre, a small but strategically important neighbouring kingdom of which the larger part had been annexed by Spain in 1512.[2] The provisions made for her security were exceptional, the marriage contract stipulating that she would have joint control, with her husband, of any territories François might give him, that she would retain control of any territories she already possessed or that Henri might give her and, in the event of his death, control of any children, without the male guardianship that had so troubled Louise of Savoy. Marguerite accepted the not-disagreeable young man, nine years her junior, and the match proved happy. In autumn 1527 they set off south on a visit to his kingdom and although Marguerite came to feel isolated, so distant from the French court, she wrote with a typically cautious optimism that her marriage was going so well 'up to this point . . . that I congratulate myself upon it'.

Perhaps she was better off at one remove from Paris. She had been in the highest favour after François's release from Habsburg captivity; his ally in the continued international negotiations through which he sought to talk his way out of the treaty he had signed with Charles. But the months during which François was in Spain had seen the conservatives harden their grip on religious affairs. On his return François, it is true, had moved to protect the reformers once again – Marguerite wrote promising to maintain their cause – but the conservatives did not give up easily.

An example of the difficulties was the plight of Louis de Berquin, the scholar Marguerite of Navarre esteemed 'as much as if he had been myself'. During François's captivity Berquin had been arrested and accused of having committed heresy for a second time, a lapse which carried the death penalty. On the king's return, he was reprieved only through Marguerite's intervention; she was, after all, still actively encouraging the production of works – the translation of the Scriptures into the vernacular – which the religious authorities condemned.

In the spring and summer of 1528 she was back at court, and pregnant, after the 'sterile' years of her first marriage. She wrote to François that she had felt the baby stir for the first time while reading a letter from him, and 'now I sleep contented, and wake up feeling so well that with my whole heart I praise the one who has not forgotten us'. As the birth came closer, however, she wrote frankly to her brother about her qualms: 'the suffering that I fear to undergo, as much as I desire it'. She longed for his presence at the birth.

When labour began it was indeed long and difficult but on 16 November she was delivered of (as she herself had always expected) a daughter. This baby, Jeanne d'Albret, was her father's heir presumptive since Navarre, unlike France, was not governed by the Salic Law. Henri had himself inherited Navarre from his mother, Catherine de Foix, albeit her accession in 1483 had been challenged by her uncle, who claimed that the Salic Law should apply in Navarre as in France; a challenge followed by a long period of civil war.

'Finally, my daughter', Anne de Beaujeu had written, 'as good counsel and as a general rule, make sure that all your desires, works, wants, and wishes are in God and to His credit, meanwhile awaiting His grace and just dispositions in great humility of heart'. But she wrote at a time when God's wishes had not seemed a matter of such uncertainty as those that her readers faced a few decades into the sixteenth century.

Religious dissent was growing more acute. In France, on 1 June 1528, while Marguerite was occupied with her pregnancy, extremist reformists defaced a public statue of Virgin and Child; an act of vandalism which caused a widespread and violent outrage. When, amid this climate, the trial of Louis de Berquin was resumed a few months later, Marguerite wrote to her brother on behalf of 'poor Berquin'. He was, however, sentenced to life imprisonment and to having his tongue pierced. Berquin made the mistake of appealing to the Paris *parlement*, which ordered that he should be executed. Since François was away at the time, Marguerite's hands were tied. Berquin was burnt alive, together with his books. Marguerite remained a good Catholic, albeit of the reforming variety. Although some of the Meaux circle of reforming Catholics she supported would join the new faith, others had denounced Luther as early as the start of the decade. The moderate position, however, was becoming harder to maintain.

In the Netherlands Margaret of Austria was also having to clamp down on Lutheranism, forbidding the meeting of groups to study the Bible, which she believed distanced the people from 'the reverence due to the sacraments, the honour due to the Mother of God and the saints'. At the beginning of the decade she had seen off a chief inquisitor of the Low Countries she regarded as too cruel and autocratic but in 1525 new inquisitors were appointed, with greater powers. The next year, 1526, her ambassador was instructed to tell Charles that his aunt 'had the greatest pleasure' in trying to extirpate the Lutherans.

Religious dissent within Christendom perhaps gave the rulers of Europe a reason to break off their great game of internecine warfare, which had exhausted everyone's country and everyone's treasury. So too, more forcibly, did the ever-mounting threat from without: the Islamic Ottoman Empire, on Europe's Eastern frontier.

Early in 1528, Wolsey urged Margaret of Austria to use her influence for a general peace. Yet the initial moves may have come from elsewhere. In October Margaret's state secretary, while in Paris, was summoned to see Louise of Savoy, who told him of her great desire for peace; a desire he was to communicate to Margaret. Louise also sent her own secretary, Bayart, to Mechelen.

Margaret of Austria played hard to get; perhaps from a genuine lack of interest (her nephew Charles V was doing better in the wars than Louise of Savoy's son), or perhaps simply because she was the better tactician, manoeuvring Louise into the position of supplicant. In dubious tones, she told the English envoy to her court that 'considering the odious writing of the Princes to each other, she thought the matter was not so soon to be pacified'.

Two days later, when the French emissary saw her again, she would only allow that if by any chance she should change her mind, she would need Louise to provide very good reasons why the emperor should listen to her. Five weeks later, Bayart was back in Mechelen with definite proposals from Louise and her suggestion that she and Margaret should meet.

The negotiations went backwards and forwards. Louise of Savoy's first (and second) proposals for the peace terms were described as 'captious and ambiguous' by Margaret of Austria's council; Louise's changes to the amended version were vehemently rejected by the Netherlands envoys. Even when a compromise was reached between the two women or their negotiators, Louise had to try to explain the Netherlanders' presence in Paris to her son, whom she had not yet consulted, and the envoys, making their way on to Spain with difficulty, had still to persuade Charles.

But Charles, perhaps unexpectedly, gave his aunt all authority. Peace – at least a ladies' peace – was clearly an idea whose time had come.

'ladies might well come forward'

The Netherlands, England, January–June 1529

THROUGHOUT THE CRUCIAL year of 1529, in the small arena comprising two sides of the English Channel, two dramas ran in tandem. Both were focused on women, extraordinarily. In continental Europe, two women came together in search of peace. And in England, two others were locked in a personal war.

On 3 January 1529 Margaret of Austria wrote a letter to her chief steward, specifically expounding the idea that peace between her nephew the emperor and France would stand a better chance if discussed by ladies. Neither of the two sovereigns, Charles V or François I, she wrote, could compromise his dignity by being the first to talk of reconciliation but, 'On the other hand, how easy for ladies . . . to concur in some endeavours for warding off the general ruin of Christendom, and to make the first advance in such an undertaking!' No less an authority than Christine de Pizan had declared that peace was women's special province.

The male rulers might fear loss of honour if they showed themselves too ready to forget the causes of the war, Margaret said, 'but ladies might well come forward in a measure for submitting the gratification of private hatred and revenge to the far nobler principle of the welfare of nations'. The King of France and the emperor, moreover, would have to answer to their friends and allies (notably England) for anything to which they might agree, but allowing their womenfolk to do it for them would 'take away all responsibility'.

Margaret of Austria's phrase the 'general ruin of Christendom' is perhaps key: the Ottoman threat was looming large in everyone's mind. Indeed, when the fighting season began again later that spring, the Turkish advance on Europe would lend the whole matter more urgency. That spring, Margaret was busy trying to draw everybody in. On 15 May she told a potentially suspicious Henry VIII that Louise of Savoy had often urged her to talk of peace and she had come to feel she had no choice but to listen. She had 'no doubt' that King Henry would be pleased to hear the news. On the 26th she wrote in cipher telling her nephew a meeting with Louise of France had been agreed but that it was important to keep England happy.

In a postscript the next day she added that a messenger had just arrived from Katherine of Aragon, saying that Henry was pushing ahead with the judicial proceedings to try his marriage and that Katherine urgently needed Margaret to send her lawyers. At this point, any overt partisanship for Katherine might well have embarrassed Margaret's diplomacy; nevertheless, she sought advice on Katherine's behalf. On 26 May she wrote to Charles V that she was 'sending to Malines [Mechelen] to obtain the opinion of experienced lawyers in that place . . . the poor Queen is very perplexed, and there is no one in England who dares take up her defence against the King's will'.

But the story of the ladies' peace was intercut, in England, with two other women's stories.

In England, in 1528, the dreaded sweating sickness almost brought an end to the vexed question of Henry VIII's love life. In the middle of June, one of Anne Boleyn's ladies fell sick and Henry, always terrified of disease, sent Anne hotfoot down to Hever, writing to her that his doubts about her health 'disturbed and alarmed me exceedingly'. He ended by saying that 'I wish you in my arms, that I might a little dispel your unreasonable thought'; an illuminating glimpse of their relationship. A couple of days later Henry heard that Anne had fallen ill. 'The most afflicting news that could have arrived' was how he described it, adding with equally illuminating precision that he would gladly bear 'half' her illness to make her well.

But in July a recovered Anne was back at court and the question of Henry's plans for her was still on the pope's plate. While a French success in Italy might have relieved the necessity for the pope to appease the emperor, in June 1528 Charles had started winning, and from then on the pope's fear of Charles's armies in Italy would be a dominant feature of the case. Nonetheless, the pope appointed a representative to look into the validity of Henry's marriage: Cardinal Campeggio, who arrived in England in October 1528.

Campeggio went to Katherine of Aragon, suggesting she retire to a nunnery, relying on her 'prudence' and 'example of a queen in France who did the same and is still honoured by God and that kingdom'; Louis's first wife, Jeanne. This would, with a little fudging, have allowed Henry to marry again, since Katherine could be seen as dead to the world and yet offer no implications for their daughter's legitimacy.[1] But Katherine was having none of it.

She saw Henry the next day and demanded, as she had earlier, some 'indifferent' (that is, impartial, not English) counsel. The next day she was with Campeggio again. Obsessively running over past events, she declared 'on her conscience' that her marriage to Henry's elder brother Prince Arthur had left her as 'intact and uncorrupted as the day she left her mother's womb' and that they could tear her 'limb from limb' before she altered her intention 'to live and die in the estate of matrimony'. Campeggio, at the end of it all, could only report feebly that 'nothing more occurred to me' to say.

And Katherine of Aragon had a trick up her sleeve. Among the papers of the late Spanish ambassador de Puebla was found a copy of the document the pope had sent to Katherine's mother Isabella on her deathbed, meaning that Katherine was free to marry Henry whether or not she had slept with Arthur. In it, declared Charles V's current ambassador Mendoza, 'consists the whole of the queen's right'.

At the Christmas celebrations, while Henry and Katherine displayed a public front of unity, Anne Boleyn was in a lodging nearby. As Campeggio put it: 'The king persists more than ever in his desire to marry this lady [Anne], kissing her and treating her in public as though she were his wife.'

Matters were reaching a crucial point. At the end of April 1529 Charles's envoys in Rome presented the pope with a formal petition that the case should be tried in Rome, since Katherine of Aragon 'would never obtain justice' in England. But on 31 May Campeggio's summons to appear at a hearing at Blackfriars went out to the king and queen.

On 14 June Henry and Katherine moved to Greenwich, a few miles downriver, in readiness. But two days later Katherine made what was in effect a pre-emptive protest, recording (in her own lodgings in the presence of two notaries), her appeal to Rome. She knew, Mendoza reported, 'that instead of calming her husband's irritation against her, she has increased it by her act'. But she felt she had no choice.

The royal couple were summoned to make a first formal appearance at the legatine court at Blackfriars, in person or by proxy, on Friday 18 June. Henry VIII sent proxies but Katherine took everyone by surprise when she made her entrance surrounded by advisors, four bishops, and a swarm of her ladies. 'Sadly, and with great gravity' she read the appeal to Rome she had recorded two days before. She was told that her appeal against the jurisdiction of this English court would be answered on Monday 21 June.

Katherine of Aragon had not always been a dramatic figure, but when Monday came, this was one scene she knew how to play. Henry himself spoke briefly; then Wolsey, to declare that he and Campeggio would judge the case on its merits, despite all the favours he had received from the king. Then Campeggio, formally rejecting the protest Katherine had lodged, and then the crier: 'Katherine, Queen of England, come into the court!'

Later writers (during the reign of Katherine's daughter Mary) were fond of figuring Queen Katherine as a Patient Griselda, an endlessly suffering *mater dolorosa*. But there was method in her display of marital meekness. Setting aside the chill formality of the legal process, and rising from her seat, she crossed the floor and knelt at her husband's feet. 'Sir, I beseech you for all the love that hath been between us, and for the love of God, let me have justice.'

Observers noted that after all her years in the country she still, under this stress, spoke in broken English; but what she said, as Wolsey's former gentleman and biographer George Cavendish recalled, was eloquent:

> Take of me some pity and compassion, for I am a poor woman and a stranger born out of your dominion. I have here no assured friends, and much less impartial counsel.

Alas! Sir, wherein have I offended you, or what occasion of displeasure have I deserved? I have been to you a true, humble and obedient
wife, ever conformable to your will and pleasure . . . I never grudged
in word or countenance, or showed a visage or spark of discontent.

She had born the king 'divers children, although it hath pleased God to
call them out of this world'. Then came the crunch:

When ye had me at the first, I take God to be my judge, I was a true
maid without touch of man. And whether it be true or no, I put it
to your conscience.

If there be any just cause by the law that ye can allege against me,
either of dishonesty or any other impediment to banish and put
me from you, I am well content to depart to my great shame and
dishonour. And if there be none, then here, I most lowly beseech
you, let me remain in my former estate.

She invoked the memory of the old kings – Henry's father and her own
– who had made the match. She spoke bitterly of the 'new inventions'
of this new court. She asked Henry's permission to write to Rome to
which he, taken by surprise, could do nothing but agree. She rose to
her feet, off the knees from which Henry had twice tried to raise her,
made a low curtsey and, instead of returning to her seat, marched
towards the door.

Once again the crier called to her: 'Katherine, Queen of England,
come into the court' but she did not pause: 'it is no indifferent court for
me, therefore I will not tarry'. Though the trial dragged on, with elderly
witnesses describing what (they thought) had or had not happened in
Katherine and Arthur's wedding bed all those years ago, the process
never recovered.

The common people of England were with Katherine; the women
especially. Outside the court, the French ambassador noted, 'If the
matter were to be decided by the women, the king would lose the
battle, for they did not fail to encourage the queen at her entrance and
departure by their cries.' But Katherine of Aragon was looking
elsewhere.

Her appeal was that the case should be heard in Rome. The supporting documents were rushed over to Brussels, where Mendoza sent them on to the Vatican by express messenger. When agreement to Katherine's request was wrung from a reluctant and distraught pope, copies of the papal decision were sent back to Flanders, some for posting there, and others for Margaret of Austria to send on to Katherine.

In one meeting with Wolsey and Campeggio, Katherine warned that the king and his ministers should consider the reputation 'of her nation and her relatives'. It was a declaration of the importance of Katherine of Aragon's blood legacy; her fortitude was perhaps inherited from her mother Isabella.

'Remember that whatever great alliance you achieve, you must never out of some foolish pride fail to value highly your own ancestors, those from whom you are descended – to fail in that would be against right and reason', Anne de Beaujeu had said. This summer of 1529 was the one in which women were inclined to stake their claim most assertively.

On 5 June, as Katherine of Aragon was readying her case, Margaret of Austria's envoy to England reported that Wolsey had asked him 'to declare on his word of honour whether he really thought the two Duchesses were in earnest' in their plans for peace. The envoy declared 'that he could answer for one of them; as to the other, time would tell'. Margaret of Austria's meeting with Louise of Savoy was set for July, in the border town of Cambrai. All Europe was watching. Mendoza wrote to Charles V: 'some think that the meeting of the two ladies will come to nothing' but in his humble opinion 'it cannot do harm, even if things do not immediately turn to good'.

As the meeting at Cambrai neared, the flurry of messages on the precise stages of both ladies' journeys resembled the behind-the-scenes work of a modern summit. Louise of Savoy declared her intention of bringing her chancellor, and the women of her chamber, but none of the French nobility. As she said to Margaret of Austria's envoy, 'You may tell my sister [Margaret] what my plans are, and that I hope we may hear of each other daily. Write also to her boldly that we must necessarily contend and argue, but that I sincerely hope it will be without anger or ill-will.'

Margaret of Austria had been warned not to go to Cambrai, for fear King François would take her prisoner but she said that 'if any of her councillors or courtiers were afraid, they might go home'. Told that she should at least take a strong escort, she replied that 'if she brought one single armed man in her suite, people might imagine she was going on a warlike enterprise, and not on a work of peace . . .'

Machiavelli had advised that war was of supreme importance for a ruler, but this was of course irrelevant or even damaging advice for women who could not lead their own armies into battle. But he also stressed the importance of presentation; and there they were surely even ahead of him.

The game of chess, with its all-important queen, was both popular, and an acknowledged metaphor of rule, in the fifteenth and sixteenth centuries. Sofonisba Anguissola painted her sisters playing chess (above). Both Isabella of Castile, pictured with her husband Ferdinand (below left), and Anne de Beaujeu (below right) were notable players.

The young Margaret of Austria (far left) could not have known that she would one day be seated across the conference table opposite her erstwhile playmate Louise of Savoy (left). Louise's daughter, Marguerite of Navarre (right) was also an important player in the great game of international diplomacy, as seen at the spectacular festivities of the *Field of the Cloth of Gold* (above).

The Tudor dynasty was split by the contest between Katherine of Aragon (below) and Anne Boleyn (above right) – the first and second wives of Henry VIII. Henry's sister Margaret Tudor (above left), married to the King of Scots, also got drawn into the debate.

The personal and religious conflict between Anne Boleyn and Katherine of Aragon would be inherited by their daughters Mary (above right) and Elizabeth (above left). *The Allegory of Succession* (below) – adapted in Elizabeth's reign from an earlier painting – shows the Protestant Elizabeth I attended by the goddesses of peace and plenty, and the Catholic Mary by the god of war.

While in Scotland Marie de Guise (above left) fought to maintain Catholicism, religious divisions were also clear on the continent. As Regents of the Netherlands both Mary of Hungary (above right) and Margaret of Parma (below) were compelled to crack down on Lutheranism. Margaret is pictured fishing for goods in a river of blood as Protestant rebels are condemned to death.

In France, Jeanne d'Albret (above left) became the heroine of the Huguenots, while Catherine de Medici (above right) was widely blamed for the Massacre of St Bartholomew's Day (below).

Two queens in one Isle… Elizabeth I and Mary, Queen of Scots were divided not only by personal rivalry but by the warring religions that made Mary a contender for Elizabeth's throne. Mary's execution at Elizabeth's hands was a final move in the sixteenth century's Game of Queens.

·MARIE·STVART·REYNE·DESCOSSE·
VEVFE·DE·FRANCOIS·SECOND·
ROY·DE·FRANCE·

The Ladies' Peace

Cambrai, England, July–December 1529

WOMEN – CASTIGLIONE had written in *The Book of the Courtier* – 'have often corrected many of men's errors'. This was the unspoken thought behind the interchange of letters between Margaret of Austria and Louise of Savoy, and this was the spirit in which they set out towards Cambrai. On Monday 5 July, Margaret of Austria was the first to arrive, carried in a magnificent litter and surrounded by twenty-four black-clad mounted archers, to take up her residence in St Aubert's Abbey. Two hours later Louise of Savoy arrived, accompanied by her daughter, Marguerite. A Venetian envoy sent back a report: Louise arrived 'in great state being clad in black velvet, with four ladies' litters, and with her daughter the Queen of Navarre, and ladies on horseback. The Lord Chancellor preceded her and ambassadors followed . . .'

Louise of Savoy had, in the event, brought across France some leading members of her son's council and indeed her son the king, although he stayed some little distance away and spent the days hunting. Perhaps she didn't feel quite as confident in her own experience of diplomacy as did Margaret of Austria (whose nephew Charles was many miles away).

Louise had also her priests and her painter, her choristers, and the keepers of her furs and her silver. A chronicle describes the 'triumphant' sight of the train of clergymen and ladies: 'it stretched from our House for half the road to St Pol and after them came hackneys and mules, very well appointed'. The town, struggling to feed and lodge all these people, had laid down rules for these huge and splendid retinues: no carrying of arms and serving men required to observe a curfew.

Louise and Marguerite were taken immediately to Margaret of Austria, with whom they spent two hours, before taking up residence in the Hotel St Pol opposite. It must have been an emotional moment for Margaret and Louise, meeting after so many years. Marguerite of Navarre's official role was to act as hostage for the imperial side, to guarantee the safety of Margaret of Austria. It is unclear whether she played any more active part. By now her interests were no longer necessarily identical with those of her brother and mother's France. She had also responsibilities to her husband, whose prime goal was the restitution of that part of Navarre which Spain had annexed.

The discussions took three weeks, and took their toll on both sides. Louise of Savoy was seemingly the fragile one, retiring each night in pain from the gout that had long plagued her, but when the Venetian envoy went to visit Margaret of Austria he found her, too, 'in bed, dressed, having a slight pain in her leg'. Margaret began by making lots of demands; she was operating from the position of strength given her by her nephew's recent victories.

All Europe was watching, nervously. England, Venice and Florence were afraid France would make a peace with Charles that would leave them in the cold. King François was edgy, writing to his mother on 17 July that since the emperor valued his friendship so low, Louise should remind him that he could be just as strong an enemy. He was desperate to get away to where his soldiers were assembled for the war he still believed was coming but he dared not leave without Louise's assent.

On 24 July peace was declared, prematurely. Margaret of Austria caused a hitch with a last-minute demand for certain border towns, Louise of Savoy and her daughter ordered their bags packed, and the papal nuncio had to intervene. Margaret offered concessions, relinquished some of her demands and engaged personally to arrange the return of François's sons, the French princes, still held hostage in Spain. In the closing days of July, a treaty was ratified at last.

On 1 August the three ladies – Margaret of Austria, Louise of Savoy and Marguerite of Navarre – went to Vespers in the abbey, receiving the congratulations of the men on both sides and, as the contemporary chronicle records, 'taking each other's hands, a beautiful thing to see'.

On the 5th, the peace was celebrated with a huge public Mass in Cambrai Cathedral and a sermon on the text of 'Blessed are the peacemakers'. The Treaty of Cambrai would become better known as the *Paix des Dames*, the Ladies' Peace.

The terms were definitely favourable to the emperor's party; 'so advantageous to the Emperor', reported an ambassador gleefully, 'that some deception is suspected'. So advantageous, indeed, that François was reported less than happy with what his mother had done; although in the last resort, as always, he had vouchsafed to 'place myself in your hands, to do what you think best'.

Charles V agreed not to press his claims to Burgundy, accepting a hefty ransom in its place, while François's sons, still hostage, would be released from their Spanish captivity on the payment of a further sum. François gave up his suzerainty over Flanders and Artois and his Italian claims. To cement the deal, it was agreed that the marriage of François to Charles's sister Eleanor, promised after Pavia, should soon be solemnised. The role of England as the emperor's long-term ally had not featured in the negotiations. Wolsey, who had been invited to attend and longed to go, was kept in England by a Henry VIII intent on the Blackfriars hearing. But at the last minute it was included in the deal.

The choir sang a *Te Deum*, alms were thrown to the crowd, and wine flowed from the conduits. On 9 August King François came to join the party, and the emperor Charles sent Margaret of Austria his congratulations, as well he might.

Meanwhile in England, on 23 July, the cardinals Campeggio and Wolsey were to have given their verdict. But instead, Campeggio formally referred the case to Rome. It was a triumph for Katherine, of a sort, but it proved to be a very hollow victory. On 11 September both cardinals formally relinquished their authority in the case. A month later came something that would once, in Wolsey's recent heyday, have seemed unthinkable. The great minister was arrested; the Venetians reporting that 'he has at length found fortune irate and hostile beyond measure ... ruin, which may be said to exceed his late fame and elevation'.

There is no doubt who Wolsey himself saw as responsible for his downfall, speaking of 'a continual serpentine enemy about the king'.

Later, he urged his supporters that everything should be tried in order that 'the displeasure of my Lady Anne be somewhat assuaged . . . this is the only help and remedy. All possible means must be used for attaining of her favour'.

On 3 November Henry opened what would come to be known as the Reformation Parliament. A month later Thomas Boleyn was made Earl of Wiltshire, and at the banquet which followed the ceremony, Anne was given precedence over all other ladies (even the king's sister Mary).

Katherine of Aragon, though still queen, cannot have looked back with any satisfaction as this momentous year came to an end. But neither, altogether, can Anne Boleyn. When, at the end of November, Henry and Katherine had an open confrontation about Anne, Anne's furious response made her insecurity clear:

> Did I not tell you that whenever you disputed with the queen she was sure to have the upper hand? I see that some fine morning you will succumb to her reasoning and that you will cast me off . . . alas! Farewell to my time and youth spent to no purpose at all.

It was a stalemate.

Exits and entrances

The Netherlands, France, Italy, 1530–1531

I N CONTINENTAL EUROPE, neither of the protagonists of the 'Ladies' Peace' lived long to enjoy their triumph of diplomacy.

In February 1530, after a triumphal progress through Italy, Margaret of Austria's nephew Charles V was formally crowned by the pope's hands as Holy Roman Emperor. It was Margaret's triumph. The children she had nurtured, her brother Philip's progeny, and their offspring, held the reins of power across Europe, from Valencia to Vienna, Lisbon to Louvain.

A letter she wrote to Charles in the months after Cambrai, concerning the state of the Habsburg Empire and her advice for his dealings with it, shows she was still active. But Margaret was nearing fifty. She had already thought of relinquishing her responsibilities and retiring to a convent near Bruges. She wrote to the mother superior, putting in place her financial provisions for the convent and adding that 'the time approaches, since the emperor is coming, to whom with God's help, I will render a good account of the charge and government which he has pleased to give me . . .' But she was not to have the opportunity.

According to the account of one Augustinian monk, in November 1530 a maid dropped a glass goblet near her bed and Margaret got a splinter in her foot. The tiny wound became infected, then gangrenous, and an amputation was decided on. Agreeing to it, she shut herself up for four days in prayer and preparation, receiving the Sacrament and revising her will. But the dose of opium given to her was so strong that, on 1 December 1530, she died before the operation.

Her work on behalf of her nephew Charles – she proudly wrote to him in a final letter – had been such that she might hope for 'divine remuneration, contentment from you, monseigneur, and the goodwill of your subjects'. Her last wish was that Charles should keep peace with France and England. Her heart was briefly placed in the tomb of her mother, Mary of Burgundy, before being taken south to join that of her last husband Philibert, at Brou, in the mausoleum she had so carefully rebuilt.

For Louise of Savoy, meanwhile, the Ladies' Peace meant the return from long captivity of her grandsons, the French princes. During their four-year captivity the conditions in which they were kept had become more and more miserable, held in a poorly furnished cell, without entertainment or French-speaking company. Margaret of Austria, as well as the French royal women, had become concerned about it and had written to her nephew to expostulate. But at the start of the 1530s, Louise's trinity set out towards Bayonne, where the boys were to be handed over to François, together with the emperor's sister Eleanor, now François's bride by the terms of the Ladies' Peace.

Marguerite of Navarre, pregnant once again, had to be left behind at Blois; 'banished', as she put it, because of her 'massive and too heavy belly', while the other two who made up the 'perfect triangle' went on without her. This time she was convinced that the child would be a boy but the thought did not seem to bring her joy, as witness some of the poetry she addressed to her absent brother: 'You tell me to take comfort / in my child, but I cannot . . . it is he who keeps me from doing my duty / to those I love a thousand times more than him'.

Another poem, to her mother, resentfully recalled how much she, Marguerite, had done to bring about the release first of François and then of her nephews; and now she could not be present at the consummation. 'How vexing it surely is, for a brave heart / that is unvanquished, / to be brought low by a mere baby.'

Perhaps, as so often, guilt played a part in her complex tangle of emotions. Guilt at what the boys had suffered, or possibly about the way she was now divided from her brother by the interests of her husband, Henri of Navarre, whose infidelities added to her distress. On 15 July she gave birth to a boy, Jean, only for the child to die on

Christmas Day. Marguerite wrote of the will of God but from that time on she wore only black.

Early in 1531 she was (most unusually for a woman, and a royal woman) preparing the text of one long poem she had written for publication; not only that, but publication by an evangelical publisher, Simon du Bois. Marguerite's lengthy religious *Miroir de l'âme pécheresse* (Mirror of a Sinful Soul) was later translated by Elizabeth Tudor as a gift for her reforming stepmother, Katherine Parr.

In it, as Elizabeth paraphrased, Marguerite 'doth perceive how of herself and of her own strength she can do nothing that good is or prevaileth for her salvation, unless it be through the grace of God'. Its description of the sinful soul redeemed by grace may have spoken of something in Marguerite's nature but salvation by grace alone (rather than devotional rituals or even good works) would also become the central piece of Protestant doctrine. This was dangerous territory: in 1530 the Diet of Augsburg had tried and failed to settle the divisions within the church. The next year, 1531, saw the formation of the Schmalkaldic League, an alliance of the Lutheran princes within the Holy Roman Empire.

Marguerite's health continued to give cause for concern. Pregnant again, she miscarried the baby. Her failure to provide more male babies to serve her brother seems to have been yet another arrow in the quiverful of guilt she carried. March 1531 saw the French royal family celebrate the coronation of François's new queen, Eleanor. But Louise of Savoy's health was failing fast.

Louise had long suffered from painful and debilitating bouts of gout and 'the gravel' (kidney stones). Marguerite had been her nurse as much as her advisor at Cambrai. By the end of the summer it was obvious Louise's condition was serious. Marguerite wrote frantically to her brother François, begging he should come ('because she is not content with me') but to her distress, and that of Louise, he stayed away. Only Marguerite was present when, on 22 September, Louise died at the age of fifty-five. Saying – or so Marguerite later wrote in *Les Prisons* – that the sight of Marguerite caused her to feel pleasure and attachment to this world, when she needed to think only of God and the next, Louise sent Marguerite out of her presence at the last.

* * *

Meanwhile, three hundred miles away in Florence, a convent had not long disgorged a frightened young girl. For Catherine de Medici, the repercussions of the Ladies' Peace had not been happy. Charles V, eager to confirm his position as the dominant influence in the Italian peninsula, had entered into negotiations with the pope, whose pre-occupation was to restore his Medici family's influence in Florence. The results would be terrifying for the eleven-year-old Catherine de Medici.

Catherine had spent the last three years tranquilly and happily in the Murate convent, where the aristocratic nuns treated her with every show of affection. The Florentine authorities 'would gladly see her in Kingdom Come', noted the French ambassador, who (Catherine's mother having been a Frenchwoman) kept a protective eye on her. He added – interestingly, in terms of Catherine's future – 'I have never seen anyone of her age so quick to feel the good and ill that are done to her.' And on 20 July 1530, great ill seemed to have come.

Charles V had placed at the pope's disposal an army, which in October 1529 began what would prove a ten-month siege of the city, with the aim of restoring Medici rule. Catherine's male relations had fled when the city established a republic two years before. Now came that danger of which the French ambassador had warned, a hammer-ing in the middle of the night on the doors of the Murate. The child inside the thick walls, however, had herself already decided how to combat this new threat. While the mother superior persuaded the men to come back in the morning, Catherine – convinced the summons could only be to her execution – cut off her hair and donned a nun's habit, shouting that no one would dare take a bride of Christ from her monastery.

She was wrong. As one of the nuns wrote, such force was used 'that we had to give her up'. But in the event, the city authorities did nothing worse than to set her astride a donkey and escort her through the baying crowds back to the convent where she had first been placed three years earlier. There had been calls for the child to be stripped naked and suspended from the walls, or placed in a military brothel for the amusement of the soldiery. Even after the city surrendered a few weeks later, contemporaries noted that she never forgot – could not stop talking about – her ordeal. It is something to remember when, in Paris four decades later, Catherine de Medici would once again be faced with the fear of violence ripping through her city.

When peace, and the Medici, were restored to Florence, Catherine went back to visit the nuns of the Murate, and celebrate with them. She would send them money and letters for the rest of her life. But her uncle the pope had plans for her beyond convent walls. Moving her to Rome, and placing her in the house of a relative instructed to give her a cosmopolitan gloss, he managed (with the promise of half a dozen Italian cities, Pisa among them, as her dowry) to betroth her to the French king's second son Henri, to cement the mood of all-round accord.

The 'greatest match in the world', the pope called it, and he was something of a connoisseur, having also betrothed the new young Duke of Florence (his nephew or illegitimate son) to Charles V's illegitimate daughter, Margaret 'of Parma'. In the spring of 1533 the fourteen-year-old Catherine de Medici would have the duty of welcoming the ten-year-old Margaret of Parma into Florence.

Catherine de Medici and Margaret of Parma were perhaps the first representatives of another generation of women; the one that would be associated with the latter half of the sixteenth century. But of course the generations did not divide so neatly. In the Netherlands, in 1531, Margaret of Austria was succeeded by another female regent: her twenty-five-year-old widowed niece Mary of Hungary.

After successfully holding Hungary for her brother Ferdinand, King of Hungary, Mary had refused his offer of a second regency in 1528. Such affairs needed 'a person older and wiser', Mary said. Her reluctance was understandable: it was the turbulence in Hungary that encouraged the Ottoman Empire to launch the campaign that culminated, just weeks after the Ladies' Peace, in the Siege of Vienna. That campaign almost cost Ferdinand all he had won and struck a terrifying blow deep into Habsburg heartland.

But Mary was undoubtedly able. A Hungarian correspondent had written to Erasmus: 'I wish that . . . the queen would become the king: the fate of the homeland would then be better.' And the Habsburg Empire was ever greedy for loyal lieutenants. 'I am only one and I can't be everywhere', Charles V would later complain to Mary. As Ferdinand said, telling Mary of their aunt Margaret's death in December 1530, her life might now 'take a different course'. The next month, Charles did indeed ask Mary to assume the regency of the Netherlands.

Family duty impelled agreement. Mary was now 'Mary, by the Grace of God, Queen of Hungary, of Bohemia, etc., governor of the Netherlands for His Imperial and Catholic Majesty, and his lieutenant'. Like Margaret of Austria before her, she was determined not to allow her family to marry her off again. But neither did she wish to remain as a queen without kingdom, income, role or offspring. Margaret of Austria herself had once, before she found her role as regent, lamented that she might 'be left to wander about the world like a person lost and forgotten', or so her father recalled.

Mary of Hungary continued, however, to display a more ambivalent attitude towards responsibility than her aunt Margaret, complaining a few months into the Netherlands job that it felt like having a rope around her neck. She did not, she said, perhaps pointedly, wish to act 'like those women who interfere in many things which are not demanded of them'. Conversely, it was said of her that she ruled by rigour whereas Margaret had done it by charm.

The Venetian ambassador to the Hungarian court had written that 'by reason of her natural volatility and from too much exercise' – Mary was notoriously obsessed with hunting and falconry – it was generally assumed she would never have children. He added a description; that she was 'of diminutive stature, long and narrow face, rather comely, very spare . . . lively, never quiet either at home or abroad'. The late sixteenth-century writer Brantôme described her as '*un peu homasse*' (a little mannish), adding that 'she made war well, sometimes through her lieutenants, sometimes in person, always on horseback, like an Amazon'.

Her brother Charles V told her on another occasion that she did 'not react in such a feminine manner as others of your sex, who are of a more delicate disposition'. Later, in 1537, when the French were attacking the Netherlands, she appeared in a black leather jerkin, fitted with eyelets that would hold a cuirass, swearing she would show François I 'to what purpose God can give a woman strength'. She had strength, and she would stand in need of it, as, in their different ways, Louise of Savoy and Margaret of Austria had; as Catherine de Medici would continue to do.

22

'Thus it will be'

England, 1530–1531

IN ENGLAND, ANNE Boleyn launched into her own battle, metaphorically picking up the weapons herself, once it had become all too apparent that Henry VIII's divorce would not be obtained the old clerical way. As she did, she had two great allies: the new reformed faith and the French upbringing which had given that country a stake in her success.

Generations of historians have chosen to see Marguerite of Navarre as a mentor, a mother figure if you like, to Anne Boleyn. There is no evidence to support the suggestion (made by some near-contemporaries, as well as subsequently) that Anne had been in Marguerite's service during her time in France. But there would shortly be evidence that Marguerite was a role model for Anne, and in this, their common interest in religious reform was key.

One of the many debates about Anne Boleyn remains the precise nature of her religious stance. Later, in the reign of Anne's Protestant daughter Elizabeth, the Protestant martyrologist John Foxe would declare of her: 'What a zealous defender she was of Christ's gospel all the world doth know.' The Scots reformer, Alexander Ales, told Elizabeth that, 'True religion in England had its commencement and its end with your mother.'

Certainly Anne was in the habit of both studying and speaking about the Bible. She even supported the illegal trade in vernacular Bibles. But then so too had Marguerite of Navarre, and she managed to remain a Catholic. The books Anne owned included several by writers close to Marguerite and indicate a strong interest in the new learning, including a French psalter with a translation credited to the unfortunate Louis de Berquin and a French Bible translated by another of the Meaux circle, Jacques Lefèvre d'Etaples. When the poet Nicolas Bourbon, whom Marguerite had made her daughter's tutor, found France too hot to hold him, he fled to England, and Anne's protection.

In the years ahead Anne Boleyn would undoubtedly be active in seeking out abuses in the Catholic church but then so was Marguerite of Navarre. It was, for example, Anne's emissaries who revealed that the blood held up for veneration at Hailes Abbey – supposedly holy blood – was in fact that of a duck. Anne would be sufficiently active in promoting the appointment of reformers in the church to be able to speak of 'my bishops'. But although some of the clergy she supported would continue to move further towards a new faith, it was not true of all. There is no reason to doubt the sincerity of Anne's beliefs but the question was how far her enthusiasm for purity in religion might take her.

A sermon later preached by her almoner, John Skip, would describe the 'little ceremonies of the church' – anathema to any radical reformer – as 'very good and commodious', as long as properly used. Nor were her religious practices stripped of all the old ways. She would plan a pilgrimage, put faith in a prophecy; say, near her death, that she would go to heaven because she had done good deeds, and spend her last night praying before the consecrated bread and wine. All these things belonged to the old brand of faith, not the new. But perhaps (only fifteen years after Luther's voice first made itself heard on the European stage) we should not be surprised that Anne, like many of her contemporaries, could not easily set aside all the traditions among which she had grown up. Heaven knows, Henry's beliefs and practices would be even more complex, or contradictory.

Even before the Blackfriars showdown, Anne Boleyn had shown Henry VIII passages in an illicit book, *The Obedience of the Christian Man and How Christian Rulers Ought to Govern*, published by the exiled William Tyndale. Famous for his translation of the New Testament with Lutheran prologues, Tyndale had taken refuge in the Netherlands, where the regents were, for as long as possible, turning a blind eye to this cuckoo in their midst. The book was a defiance of papal authority, declaring that the subject is accountable to the ruler, and the ruler to God alone. It was the idea Henry had been looking for: 'This book is for me and all kings to read.'

If the traditional function of a woman behind a powerful man was to be advisory, intercessory, the conduit through which ideas as well as clemency could flow, then Anne fulfilled it very successfully, in that her ideas won through. But these ideas began to give a more overtly religious framework to the question of King Henry's marriage.

A timely new introduction at court, in the months after the hearing at Blackfriars, was the Cambridge scholar, Thomas Cranmer. He suggested that Henry's was not a case of canon law but a theological problem of the pope's right to dictate to princes, and that theologians (at the universities of Europe as well as England) should thus be canvassed. He was sent away, in the care of the Boleyn family, to formulate his ideas.

Through the following spring one theological authority after another was persuaded to give Henry VIII the answer he wanted until at last (once King François's sons were safely back in their own country) even the University of Paris gave way. In June 1530 Henry was handed the *Collectanea satis copiosa*, a bank of biblical and historical material suggesting the pope was not necessarily supreme; in August, he summoned his council to another conference at Hampton Court. In September, warned by a newly arrived papal nuncio that the Vatican trial of the marriage Katherine of Aragon had requested would have soon to begin, Henry issued a proclamation forbidding any suit to Rome.

Charles V's horrified ambassador Eustace Chapuys warned that if 'the Earl and his daughter' (Anne Boleyn and her father) remained in power, they would 'entirely alienate this kingdom from its allegiance to the Pope'. In October, Henry suggested to his gathering of clerics and lawyers that his Archbishop of Canterbury should be empowered to decide the divorce suit, although the idea did not immediately bear fruit.

It was now a propaganda war, and some of the weapons were women's. Anne Boleyn, angered to learn that Katherine of Aragon was still stitching Henry's shirts (as her mother Isabella had once embroidered Ferdinand's), insisted she should – briefly, as it proved – take over the task. She would have learnt the traditional female arts in Mechelen, where Margaret of Austria's personal possessions included a distaff and spindle with which to spin. Margaret once sent her father Maximilian some shirts she had helped to make. 'Our skin will be comforted with meeting the fineness and softness of such beautiful linen, such as the angels in Paradise use for their clothing', Maximilian wrote in the chatty letters they exchanged.

Before Christmas 1530 Anne ordered a new livery for her servants, bearing her recently adopted motto: 'Thus it will be, Grumble who will'. It had been the motto of Margaret of Austria's court. Chapuys reported that Anne, on New Year's Day 1531, declared 'that she wished all Spaniards were at the bottom of the sea . . . that she cared not for the queen or any of her family, and that she would rather see her hanged than have to confess that she was her queen and mistress'.

In February, Henry VIII demanded that the church authorities recognise him as 'sole protector and supreme head of the English church and clergy'. Anne Boleyn, Chapuys reported, made 'such demonstrations of joy as if she had actually gained Paradise'. In fact her marriage to Henry was far from certain. Many of those who had backed Anne as a political counter to Cardinal Wolsey still baulked at the prospect of her as queen. But the situation was worsening dramatically for Katherine of Aragon.

At the end of May, Henry's emissaries had a final attempt at persuading Katherine to see reason. She refused, with a fortitude that belied her description of herself as 'a poor woman without friends or counsel'. Anger at her recalcitrance brought, at last, an end to those strange two years in which Katherine had retained her place as queen, moving around the country at the king's side, even though Anne might be one of the party. Early in July they were all three at Windsor; on the 14th Henry and Anne rode away to hunt at Chertsey Abbey, with Katherine ordered to remain behind. Some days later Henry's council, in the first letter not to address her as queen, rejected her request she might bid her husband farewell.

Her husband was not the only member of the family from whom Katherine of Aragon was to be separated. Her daughter Mary had been with her at Windsor but when Katherine was sent away to one property, Mary was sent to another some miles away. There are some indications that Henry may have been forced, by pressure of public opinion, to allow a brief visit in 1532 but it is certain that mother and daughter would never be allowed to live together again.

For the moment at least Katherine of Aragon kept her state. A Venetian visitor reported that she had thirty maids of honour around her as she ate and a court of two hundred people. But she regarded herself as a prisoner, telling the imperial ambassador Chapuys she would rather be in the Tower and overtly locked up. The Venetian also gave it as his opinion that the people would accept no other queen.

Keeping Katherine and her daughter apart was a punitive measure. But there was a genuine fear that Katherine – 'a proud, stubborn woman of very high courage', wrote Henry – might, in her defence of Mary's interest, 'quite easily take the field, muster a great array, and wage against me a war as fierce as any her mother Isabella ever waged in Spain'. In fact, had the authorities but known it, Katherine wrote that war 'is a thing I would rather die than provoke'. Told, she said, that 'the next parliament is to decide whether I am to suffer martyrdom', Chapuys wrote to Charles V that the queen was 'so overscrupulous' that she preferred to suffer.

In the event, the very separation became a perverse reinforcement of the bond between mother and daughter; a hatred of the forces that had kept them apart, a harsh and unyielding commitment to her rights and her religion, would be Mary's hallmark. The game of queens was an unforgiving one.

'a native-born Frenchwoman'

England, 1532–1535

I N 1532, ANNE Boleyn had the chance to deploy another weapon in her armoury. Politically, as well as in her religious tendencies, she had long made a point of playing up her French connections: the fact that she seemed, as the French diplomat Lancelot de Carles had put it, 'a native-born Frenchwoman'. Indeed, in 1530 the imperial ambassador Chapuys had written that it was her alliance with Henry VIII 'on which alone depend the credit and favour the French now enjoy at this court'.

By 1532 a French alliance had become a more general goal. It was, after all, the French who were likeliest to assist Henry in putting pressure on the pope to grant his divorce. Practical control of the king's 'Great Matter' was now largely in the hands of the new man on the scene, Thomas Cromwell. Rising from the ashes of his erstwhile master Wolsey, Cromwell had been a member of the Privy Council since the end of 1530. Now he would mastermind the process by which, this spring, first parliament and then the clergy were persuaded to ratify Henry as sole head of the church.

But in the latest negotiations, Anne Boleyn was still the key. As the French ambassador De La Pommeraye accompanied the English court on the summer hunting trip *cum* progress, King Henry discussed his private affairs with the envoy and took 'as much trouble to give me good sport as though I were some great personage', De La Pommeraye reported proudly. He was often stationed 'quite alone' with Anne, who had given him a new set of hunting gear, complete with hound, for the occasion.

Henry VIII had determined to further his goal of an Anglo-French alliance by meeting his brother-king face to face in Calais, in the autumn. Anne took the plan further. She was an ardent friend to France, she told De La Pommeraye, but many of Henry's advisors felt differently. Would it not be best if she too were present at the meeting? De La Pommeraye was persuaded, writing home that François I 'should request King Henry to bring Lady Anne with him to Calais', adding 'but then the King [François] must bring the queen of Navarre with him to Boulogne'.

The French ambassador told Chapuys that Anne Boleyn's services to France were more than could ever be repaid. But the debt did not go only one way. French backing gave Anne, the commoner, a measure of credibility. There was even a notion that she and Henry might marry during this summit, in Calais, with King François present at the ceremony. Katherine of Aragon was, Chapuys said, very much afraid of it, although Anne declared she wished the ceremony to be 'in the place where queens are wont to be married and crowned'. Nonetheless, the idea was persistent. Well after the French trip had got under way, Venetian reports still declared with confidence that the marriage would take place the following Sunday.

In September Henry declared that Katherine of Aragon should hand over her jewels, even those she had brought from Spain, to deck Anne for the forthcoming encounter. Katherine retorted that it was 'against her conscience to give her jewels to adorn a person who is the scandal of Christendom', but that if Henry sent a direct command, she would comply. Anne got her jewellery, and Chapuys reported that 'the Lady', as he called her, was also busy buying costly dresses. On 1 September, Henry created Anne Lady Marquess of Pembroke, to raise her status for the encounter ahead. Immediately afterwards – no coincidence – came ratification of England's treaty of mutual aid with France, in the event of any Habsburg aggression.

The plans meant that Marguerite of Navarre had to make a difficult diplomatic decision. The French queen, Eleanor, Katherine of Aragon's niece, never wished nor was expected to attend. But at the last minute, Marguerite too withdrew. She may have been ill – the diplomatic excuse – or she may, as one report said, have come to see Anne not as a fellow reformer but as a figure of scandal. The decision may not have been wholly her own: although French reforming thinkers believed their country should stand with Henry and Anne, there was a strong and divisive counter-opinion.

Chapuys reported to Charles V that Henry VIII was 'vexed that Madame d'Alençon will not come' and that François instead suggested bringing another lady, who might be accompanied by some of the more disreputable elements of the French court. 'These people [Anne and Henry] cannot see the mountains in their own eyes and wish to take the straw from the eyes of others', added Chapuys acidly.[1]

Perhaps, in the last resort, Marguerite of Navarre was more of a royal than a reformer. It was a pity, Anne recalled looking back two years later: 'there was no one thing which her grace so much desired . . . as the want of the said queen of Navarre's company, with whom to have conference, for more causes than were meet to be expressed, her grace is most desirous.' As queen, Anne would not forget her goal of contact with Marguerite of Navarre; would send word to Marguerite herself that 'her greatest wish, next to having a son, was to see you again'.

When October came Anne Boleyn was greeted in Calais with every sign of pleasure (and a very valuable diamond) when François and the men of the French court visited from Boulogne, where the bulk of the encounters between the two kings had taken place. She had, after all, known these men a decade earlier. And it was almost certainly either at that meeting in Calais or on the way home, forced by a massive storm to dawdle for days after the formalities had ended, that Anne and Henry VIII started sleeping together. It was perhaps Anne's throw of the dice; a pregnancy would force an end to all delays.

Anne was indeed pregnant by the time she and Henry married, at the end of January 1533, in a secret ceremony. In February Anne, surely intentionally, let the cat out of the bag with a public joke about her great longing to eat apples; a fancy for a particular food being known as a sign of impending maternity. By end of the month Chapuys was spreading the news. Katherine of Aragon was informed that she was no longer to be addressed as queen and her state and income were to be greatly reduced. That Easter, Anne was prayed for as queen. In the Netherlands there was a rumour that the emperor, with certain English nobles, would go to war for Katherine; would 'assist her from field to field . . . with her crown upon her head'. But short of that, there was nothing anyone could do.

The old Archbishop of Canterbury had died the year before, and on 30 March Thomas Cranmer was consecrated in his place. In April, the Act in Restraint of Appeals forbad appeals to Rome on any matter, which meant Katherine's fate was now entirely in Henry's hands. On 23 May, Cranmer used his new power to declare Henry's marriage to Katherine of Aragon void and five days later, to validate that of Henry and Anne Boleyn.

On 1 June Cranmer was able to crown Anne in a deliberately resplendent public ceremony. The official entry of a queen into her city was supposed to reflect the assumption of the Virgin Mary into heaven, and this one did. The new emphasis on classical, as well as biblical mythology, however, may have been something Anne had gleaned from the French court. Anne was dressed in the French fashion, and in white, for the procession to Westminster Abbey; a procession headed by the French ambassador's servants, in blue velvet and white plumes. The report Chapuys sent to the Netherlands declared that the crowd had withheld any sign of pleasure. But the crown of St Edward, hitherto used only for monarchs, was placed on her head.

'Queen Anne, when thou shalt bear a new son of the King's blood; there shall be a golden world unto thy people!' the pageants at the coronation declared and both parents seemed confident in the prophecy. But when Anne's child was born on 7 September, at three o'clock in the afternoon, it was, disappointingly, a daughter, who was nevertheless named Elizabeth after the king's mother (and Anne's).

The official line was that the birth of a healthy daughter was surely a pledge that a healthy son would follow. Although the tournament planned for the arrival of a prince was cancelled, the pre-written letters of announcement were sent out with 'prince' altered to 'princes'[s], and the French ambassador was once again guest of honour at the splendid christening.

If Anne Boleyn's baby had been a boy, her position would have been unassailable; she would have won. With only a daughter in the cradle, everything was still to play for.

A daughter was certainly enough to ensure Anne's unremitting hostility to that other mother and daughter who might stand in her, and Elizabeth's, way. She sent orders not only that Katherine of Aragon's daughter Mary should come to attend on her daughter Elizabeth, when the baby heiress was given her own household, but that if Mary should insist on being called princess, Elizabeth's attendants were to box her ears 'as the cursed bastard that she was'.

No doubt her aggression sprang in part from fear. 'She is my death, and I am hers', Anne is reported to have said. On several occasions Anne made conciliatory gestures towards Mary, which would always be rejected; an attitude very actively endorsed by Katherine of Aragon. Perhaps Henry, and Anne, were right when they were both separately, credited with attributing Mary's obstinacy to her 'unbridled Spanish blood'.

On 23rd March 1534, ironically the very day that the pope tardily declared in Katherine's favour, parliament passed the first Act of Succession, declaring Anne Boleyn Henry's lawful wife and their children the heirs to the throne. Everyone of consequence was asked to swear to it. Princess Mary had been bastardised, and mother and daughter knew that Mary would be asked to renounce her title.

'Daughter, I heard such tidings today that I do perceive, if it be true, the time is come that Almighty God will prove you; and I am very glad of it', Katherine of Aragon wrote, in terms that reflect her belief their very lives might be in jeopardy. 'If any pangs come to you, shrive yourself; first make you clean; take heed of His commandments, and keep them as near as He will give you grace to do, for then you are sure armed . . . we never come unto the kingdom of Heaven but by troubles.'

That November the Act Respecting the Oath to the Succession required swearers 'to be true to Queen Anne, and to believe and take her for the lawful wife of the King and rightful Queen of England, and utterly to think the Lady Mary daughter to the King by Queen Katherine a bastard, and thus to do without any scrupulosity of conscience'. It also required that they abjure any 'foreign authority or potentate'.

At the end of the year Henry opened parliament to pass the Act of Supremacy, declaring that Henry VIII was and always had been 'the only supreme head on earth of the Church of England'. Henry, and Cromwell, were determined to crush any opposition but Anne has certainly got much of the blame.

For a woman to be the scapegoat was perhaps the reverse side of a queen's traditional intercessory function; the same distancing of responsibility from the monarch that had allowed Margaret of Austria and Louise of Savoy to make peace more easily than their men. But in June 1534 Chapuys reported fears that if Henry went abroad Anne swore – were she left in authority during his absence – she would have Mary's life.

The interesting thing is that Anne Boleyn assumed she would be given these regent's powers; that she would follow in the footsteps not only of Katherine of Aragon, but of the great and potent European women she had known.

24

'inclined towards the Gospel'

France, the Netherlands, 1533–1536

CROSS THE ENGLISH Channel, as in England, religious divisions had hardened in the year or so that followed the deaths of Margaret of Austria and Louise of Savoy. In France, when Gerard Roussel, chaplain to the king's sister, Marguerite of Navarre, preached a Lenten sermon at the Louvre he became an overnight star, to the fury of the Catholic conservatives. But Roussel (as the French-born reformer John Calvin angrily wrote to him) was, like his patroness, treading an impossibly fine line between evangelical ideas and continued loyalty to the Catholic church.

As both sides carried placards through the streets, moderates blamed the University of Paris for the hysteria of their response, while conservatives spoke of Lutheranism and accused Marguerite and her husband Henri of Navarre alongside Roussel. King François intervened but Roussel was arrested. Marguerite had to rush to his defence, eventually finding him a bishopric safely within her husband's territories. Nothing Roussel had said was heresy, she protested. How could it be? He was in her service and she would never have listened to 'such poison'.

When Marguerite of Navarre was viciously mocked in a farce at the university, François took the insult on himself. When, in February 1534, an orator accused her of being the spokeswoman for the reformers, François demanded the speaker's imprisonment. Marguerite's first instinct was not to sound the retreat; instead, she pressed for a political alliance against the emperor with the German princes, Protestant as well as Catholic, and attempted to bring to France the scholar Philip Melanchthon, Luther's close associate. But the French court was splitting along religious lines.

One unlikely recruit to the reformist faction was a new arrival in France; the pope's young niece, Catherine de Medici. In the autumn of 1533, escorted by the Duke of Albany (who was married to her mother's sister), Catherine arrived in Marseille to marry François I's second son, Henri.

An entire district of the city was blown up to make way for the accommodation of her retinue and that of the pope, her uncle. Catherine brought with her a staggering wardrobe and an unparalleled array of jewels, as well as Marie the Moor and Agnes and Margaret the Turks, captured 'in expeditions against the Barbary'. For the marriage ceremony, she wore gold brocade and violet velvet, trimmed with ermine and thick with gems; a handsome enough figure despite her strong features and protruding eyes. 'She is a beautiful woman when her face is veiled,' said a courtier later, ungallantly.

The holiday atmosphere of this seaside wedding reputedly had a loosening effect on the already lax morals of the French court but Catherine de Medici and her spouse Henri must have found the wedding night an ordeal: François insisted on remaining in the nuptial room and afterwards (Brantôme writes) declared that both the fourteen year olds had performed well in 'the joust'.

Catherine received a more understanding welcome from Marguerite of Navarre, but her early years at the French court were difficult. When in September 1534 her uncle the pope died, the value of the Medici alliance plummeted, causing François to complain in horror, when the new pope refused to pass on Catherine's promised dowry, that his son's bride had come 'toute nue' (stark naked). All too obviously uninteresting to her youthful husband, she was sneered at by the French courtiers as the descendant of merchants.

Marguerite of Navarre's position, too, was becoming ever more challenging. October 1534 saw the 'Placard Affair', when the inhabitants of Paris and a handful of other cities woke up to find placards nailed in the streets attacking 'the horrible, great, and insufferable abuse of the papal Mass'. Legend says there was even one affixed to the king's bedroom door. When the reformers (or, as Marguerite later swore, conservatives trying to discredit them) began insulting even the sacraments, it was war. Amid widespread panic, a special commission was set up to try suspects, and when in January 1535 the protesters managed the dissemination of a radical tract, the authorities clamped down yet further. Marguerite, perhaps wisely, had by this time withdrawn to her husband's estates in Béarn, and though she clearly distanced herself from those behind the *'vilains placards'*, her closeness to her brother seemed, in the years ahead, to go into slight eclipse.

The publication of 'Lutheran' texts was banned, although many of the dissidents now followed not Luther's teachings but those of the far more radical Swiss, Ulrich Zwingli.[1] Many of Marguerite of Navarre's former associates found it prudent to flee abroad. Those who harboured heretics were to be punished as severely as they. One who suffered the ultimate penalty, burning at the stake, was the man who had published the second edition of Marguerite's *Miroir*. The book had attracted hostility from the University of Paris, although when it was briefly placed on the list of banned books, François once again intervened.

In July 1535 François ordered an end to the persecution, and the release of all religious prisoners (who had, however, only six months' grace in which to renounce their views). He and his sister were soon back together again, and united in trying for Marguerite's old dream, an alliance with the German princes against the emperor. At the start of 1536, when the pope (still in pursuit of that Christian alliance against the Turk) organised peace talks – which ultimately failed – between François and Charles V, Marguerite attended as France's representative.[2]

In the years ahead Marguerite of Navarre spent increasing amounts of time in the south, writing. Even Marguerite's husband, if the recollections attributed to her daughter are accurate [**see note on sources**], seems angrily to have warned her off her dangerous experiments of faith. Her prodigious output saw her turn increasingly to secular texts, albeit often with a moral or even a religious message under the surface. Crucially, almost none would be published in her lifetime.

In the Netherlands, Mary of Hungary, likewise in her earlier years accused of too much sympathy with Protestants, was rumoured to be a 'bonne luteriene' (good Lutheran). She greatly admired the human-ism of Erasmus, who wrote admiringly of her, and had also spent formative years in the Germanic circles where Luther's teachings were most in currency. When she became Queen of Hungary she aroused controversy by appointing the Lutheran Conrad Cordatus as her preacher; he then launched an attack on the papacy in front of the whole court.

In 1526 Luther had dedicated four psalms to Mary, having heard that she was, as he wrote, 'inclined towards the Gospel', despite anything the 'godless bishops' of Hungary could do to dissuade her. Her brother Ferdinand wrote to reprimand her but Mary wrote back that she couldn't control what Luther had to say, without, however, dissociating herself from the connection.

When the question of the Netherlands regency first arose, Mary had been anxious – for all her loudly professed aversion to the post – to reassure her other brother Charles V that she still held firmly to the family faith and would prove it by dismissing any possible Lutherans in her train. Charles, for his part, warned that he would send even his closest relative – parent, child, or sibling – to the stake rather than condone heresy. But perhaps in the end their attitude was not so dissimilar. For Charles, certainly, this was less a matter of conscience than of civic order. 'By turning away from the Catholic faith, people will at the same time turn away from loyalty and obedience to their ruler,' he said.

Once in place in the Netherlands, Mary of Hungary proved a reasonably successful governor, making her court a centre of luxury and culture and eventually building a wonderful Renaissance palace at Binche as her home. Just as Mary and her sisters had themselves been raised by Margaret of Austria, so Mary continued the work, looking after those of her nieces who were already in Margaret's care. In 1533, when Christina of Denmark was, at the age of eleven, married to the Duke of Milan, her uncle Charles agreed she should immediately assume her wifely duties. But Mary, like Margaret before her, first protested and then stalled: 'you may endanger her life, should she become pregnant before she is altogether a woman', Mary wrote. She begged her brother to forgive her for speaking out, but 'my conscience and the love I bear the child compel me'. Forced to send Christina to

Milan immediately after her twelfth birthday, Mary fell ill and asked to resign her post.

Like other women in power, she found that stress took a physical toll, and the times remained taxing. In 1534, religion was once again the problem. In the neighbouring German duchy of Westphalia, Anabaptists seized the town hall of Münster and declared the new Jerusalem, founded on common ownership and the equality of man. When they called on the faithful to join them, many in the Netherlands heeded the call and set out up the Rhine.

Besieged by its expelled bishop, Münster fell only in June 1535, so it was against this background, and heightened Franco-Imperial tension, that Charles V finally agreed to something for which his sister Eleanor, Queen of France, had long been pleading: that, after many years apart, she and her sister Mary of Hungary might meet.

In the summer of 1535 the two sisters met, at Cambrai, where Margaret of Austria and Louise of Savoy had faced each other just six years before. But this time Charles had decreed that no politics were to be discussed and though Eleanor came with a great retinue, at least some of whom surely hoped for diplomatic discussion, Mary unyieldingly followed her brother's script.

A sign of the changing times, perhaps? Or of very different personalities? Certainly no great results were achieved by *this* meeting at Cambrai.

'to doubt the end'

England, 1536

'TAKE GREAT CARE to live well so that you have no reason to doubt the end, and so that you have the grace of God in this world and in the next', Anne de Beaujeu had warned. The game of queens was played for high stakes, and could carry a deadly penalty. The first half of 1536 saw the death of not one but two English queens. Before the corn was ripe in the fields, Katherine of Aragon's painful battle was ended and her rival Anne Boleyn had knelt in the straw of the scaffold to await the executioner's sword.

Like Katherine, Anne Boleyn had failed to produce another child. She probably miscarried in the summer of 1534 and possibly again in 1535. But Henry VIII's concern over what was perceived to be her lack of fertility would pick up shocking speed in 1536.

Katherine of Aragon died on 7 January, probably of cancer of the heart. She had been transferred sixty miles north, to Kimbolton in Huntingdonshire, where she continued the dismal practices she had followed in her previous place of imprisonment: having her meals prepared by the few old servants she trusted, for fear of poison, and refusing to leave her room. She eschewed the new servants Henry had put in place, whom she regarded as 'guards and spies'. In the hours before she died she wrote a last letter to Henry – 'My most dear lord, king and husband' – urging him to prefer the 'health and safeguard of your soul' to worldly matters and to 'the care and pampering of your body'.

She said she pardoned him everything and prayed that God would do the same. 'Lastly, I make this vow, that mine eyes desire you above all things.' The defiant signature was that of 'Katherine the Queen'. Henry VIII and Anne Boleyn celebrated the news of Katherine's death with a party but Anne was acute enough quickly to realise that for her at least, the celebrations may have been premature.

The evidence is contradictory as to whether Henry and Anne's marriage was already in trouble or whether the events of 1536 came out of a clear blue sky. Was the marriage on the rocks? The imperial ambassador Chapuys reported it was, but he had, in a hopeful spirit, been saying that for years. There continued to be regular reports of the couple as 'merry', and if there were also stories of squalls that, certainly in the early days, had been the nature of their relationship. Even Chapuys admitted that some of their broils may have been mere 'lovers' quarrels'.

It is possible that what attracted Henry in the mistress came to repel him in the wife. And if the king's attraction faltered, Anne Boleyn, unlike Katherine of Aragon, had no ruling European family behind her. Anne de Beaujeu had written wisely: 'Nor should you talk too much or too sharply, like many foolish and conceited women who want to attract attention and, to be more admired, speak boldly and in a flighty way . . .'

Shortly before Katherine's death Henry had said to Chapuys that if she died, Charles V would have no cause to trouble himself about English affairs. Crudely and callously put, perhaps, but it was true that Henry could now renew his relations with Charles without having to take Katherine back as part of the price. On the contrary, it was now the Francophile, intrusive Anne, rather than the wounded figure of Katherine, who stood in the way of a new imperial alliance.

Anne Boleyn was as identified with the French interest as if she were indeed a Frenchwoman. After Anne's death, Mary of Hungary, despite their childhood acquaintance at Mechelen, remarked that she had been a Frenchwoman and thus the Habsburgs' enemy. And almost as though she had been a French princess, married off and then abandoned, like others in this story, she found herself caught between the two sides.

France had long been ambivalent about the new situation in England. Henry VIII certainly believed François supported his search for an annulment, but France had proved unwilling to confront the pope to secure it. In 1535, Anne Boleyn had been shocked when

France suggested a match between the officially illegitimate Mary and the dauphin, more so when it proved lukewarm about the marriage of the baby Elizabeth to even one of François's younger sons. France's mounting persecution of reformers, moreover, alienated Anne's reforming friends.

Anne thought she had a trump card to play: she was once again pregnant. But on 29 January 1536 – the day of Katherine of Aragon's funeral – Anne Boleyn miscarried again, disastrously. She blamed it on the shock, five days before, of hearing that Henry had been injured in a joust. She had, as Chapuys reported 'miscarried of her saviour'. 'I see that God will not give me male children,' Henry told her ominously, later adding to a male courtier that he had been 'seduced by sortileges [enchantments]' into the marriage.[1]

No wonder Chapuys wrote to the emperor that Anne's reaction to Katherine's death had not been unmixed joy. She had, when she paused to think, begun to fear she would meet the 'same end'. In mid-January she changed tack, or at least tactics, in regard to Katherine's daughter, writing to those in Hatfield, where Mary had been transferred to join the baby Elizabeth's household, that Mary should no longer be pressured to acknowledge Elizabeth as her superior in rank. She must have been aware that Henry was attracted to Jane Seymour, one of her ladies-in-waiting: a woman pale, passive, wholly English; a much more traditionally submissive model of femininity.

But the signs were contradictory. And Anne Boleyn herself must have found them so. On 18 April Chapuys was persuaded, or manoeuvred, into doing what he had for so long avoided and acknowledging Anne, in her capacity as queen, as she passed through chapel – exchanging the 'mutual reverences required by politeness' as he put it – making Katherine's daughter Mary 'somewhat jealous' when she heard. That King Henry should insist the ambassador of the emperor, Queen Katherine's nephew, should acknowledge Katherine's supplanter as England's queen surely suggests that Henry was not at this moment actually intending to put Anne away. Although conversely, having won this point may have meant that his ego was no longer so closely tied to having Anne accepted.

Henry VIII had come to doubt whether Anne Boleyn would give him a male heir, and he wanted Jane Seymour. But there was another chain of dissent. On 2 April 1536 Anne's almoner, Skip, preached a sermon in front of the king's councillors, describing how King Ahasuerus was almost persuaded to the massacre of the Jews by his evil counsellor Haman, and was saved from the deed only by his wife, Esther. At her coronation, Anne (like, ironically, Katherine) had been compared to Esther; and Haman could easily be identified as Thomas Cromwell.

At the very end of Anne's life Chapuys wrote of 'the heretical doctrines and practices of the concubine – the principal cause of the spread of Lutheranism in this country'. But it is possible that reform was proceeding along lines she had not envisaged. In 1535, there had been a general inspection ('visitation') of the monasteries under Cromwell's aegis, with some smaller institutions scheduled for suppression. But it was obvious the process would pick up speed. And Anne may have clashed with Cromwell over where the proceeds of the dissolution of the monasteries should go: into education and social reform, as Anne wanted, or into the king's coffers.

However, the accusations made against Anne in the spring of 1536 were framed in terms of sexual misbehaviour. After Anne Boleyn's death Lancelot de Carles, secretary to the French ambassador, said that Lady Worcester, a member of Anne's household, herself accused of lax morality, had exclaimed in her defence that her own faults were nothing compared to those of the queen and that the queen had had carnal knowledge of her musician Mark Smeaton, of one of the king's favourite gentleman Henry Norris and of her own brother, George.

On 30 April Mark Smeaton was taken to Cromwell's house for questioning and – possibly under torture or the threat of it – confessed to having three times had sex with the queen. Anne herself described a recent exchange of words which seemed to show him languishing after her; languishing, perhaps, in the tradition of the game of courtly love which, however, his lowly rank did not allow him to play. Other remarks she made to other men might seem to suggest the game of courtly love gone sour but the point is that Smeaton's confession, true or false, put a new complexion on all subsequent inquiries, which would now operate from a presumption of Anne's adultery.

Henry was surely told of this. The Scottish reformer Alexander Ales later told Anne's daughter Elizabeth that he remembered, after

Smeaton's confession, 'your most religious mother carrying you, still a little baby, in her arms and entreating the most serene King, your father, from the open window . . . the faces and gestures of the speakers plainly showed that the King was angry'. The scene shows Anne and Henry in distress but surely still also in uncertainty. Henry decided to postpone his planned and imminent trip with Anne to Calais for a week but the jousts to celebrate May Day the next day were still to go ahead.

Anne Boleyn must have sensed where she was vulnerable. Also on 30 April she begged Norris to swear before her chaplain that she 'was a good woman'; a reaction to another incident capable of a deadly interpretation. Asking Norris, who was betrothed to marry one of her ladies, why he had not yet gone ahead with the match, Anne suggested a scandalous reason: that Norris hoped to marry Anne herself. 'You look for dead men's shoes; for if ought came to the king but good, you would look to have me.' Under the Treason Act of 1534 words which intended harm to the king were treasonable.

As Henry VIII and Anne Boleyn attended the May Day jousts at Greenwich. Henry still showed Norris every sign of favour. But when the king abruptly left the festivities, something at which 'many men mused but most chiefly the queen', the king began questioning Norris, promising him pardon if he would but speak the truth. Norris stoutly maintained his innocence but the next day he was taken to the Tower, where Smeaton was already being held, together with Anne's brother George.

Four others were also arrested, accused of adulterous relations with Anne, including her old admirer the poet Thomas Wyatt and Sir Francis Weston, a gentleman of the king's privy chamber. Weston had been in a flirtation with a lady of Anne's chamber but said that he loved another there better and, when she pressed him as to who, said 'it is yourself'.

'Thus, my daughter, whatever your age, guard against being deceived and remember what I told you before because you can be blamed even for something very slight . . .' Anne de Beaujeu had warned.

All this must have been running through Anne Boleyn's head. She surely had some inkling of trouble ahead: in the last week of April she asked Matthew Parker, her chaplain, to have a special care of her daughter.[2] But it was a stunning blow when, on 2 May, she was arrested, accused of having had sexual relations with Norris, Smeaton and one other. She said that 'to be a Queen, and cruelly handled was never seen', and hoped that the king was doing it only to 'prove' her; a regular trope of courtly love.

Taken to the Tower, Anne asked if she would be placed in a dungeon. She was told that she would be housed in the royal lodgings she had used before her coronation. She fell to her knees, crying 'Jesu have mercy on me.' The indictment drawn up preparatory to the trials said that she 'following daily her frail and carnal lust, did falsely and traitorously procure by base conversations and kisses, touchings, gifts, and other infamous incitations, divers of the King's daily and familiar servants to be her adulterers and concubines'. More explicitly yet, she 'procured her own natural brother to violate her, alluring him with her tongue in his mouth, and his tongue in hers, against the commands of Almighty God and all laws human and divine'. This was how a queen could be brought low; as Anne herself protested in a memorable image, with accusations she could only deny 'without I should open my body'.

On 12 May the four commoners actually charged were tried (Wyatt and another having been suspected but released). Smeaton again confessed his guilt and the others pleaded not guilty. They were, inevitably, all four sentenced to a traitor's death. Three days later, on the 15th, Anne Boleyn and her brother George were each tried separately before a jury of their peers.

She entered the Great Hall of the Tower of London 'as though she were going to a great triumph', an eyewitness wrote. In front of some two thousand spectators, she answered firmly 'Not guilty' to each charge. 'She made so wise and discreet answers to all things laid against her, excusing herself with her words so clearly as though she had never been faulty to the same', recorded the Windsor Herald Charles Wriothesley.

When George Boleyn's turn came, he both confused the issue and upped the stakes by reading aloud the accusation that had been written down for him: that he and Anne had laughed together over the king's lack of virility. But inevitably, all twenty-six peers found them guilty. Anne's uncle, the Duke of Norfolk, pronounced the sentence: that she should be burned or beheaded at the king's pleasure. Two days later the five men were executed, and on the same day Anne's marriage was annulled.

On the 19th Anne Boleyn herself came to the block. In those agonising days in the Tower, she had cried out that her fate would be the death of her mother, the blood mother who figures so little in the stories of Anne. But otherwise she seemed, so the Lieutenant of the Tower reported, to have 'much joy' in death.

Why did Anne Boleyn have to fall? At the time the obvious assumption was that she was guilty of the crimes with which she was charged. As one John Hussey wrote: 'if all the books and chronicles . . . which against women hath been penned . . . since Adam and Eve, those same were, I think, verily nothing in comparison of that which hath been done and committed by Anne the Queen'. But Archbishop Cranmer, as the Scottish reformer Ales reported him, walking in the gardens of Lambeth Palace in the early hours before Anne's execution, protested that, 'She who has been the Queen of England upon earth will today become a Queen in Heaven.'

One theory, of course, continues to be that Anne was guilty of adultery, if not quite as charged. But it has few subscribers, the more so for the demonstrable inaccuracy of much of the detail of the accusations, such as the fact that she and her supposed lovers were often not even in the same place on the alleged date. And also perhaps for the fact that Anne repeatedly swore to her innocence in the face of her death, 'on peril of her soul's damnation'.

Anne Boleyn herself said that she 'believed there were some other reason for which she was condemned than the cause alleged'. Another, far more palatable theory, sets her erstwhile ally Thomas Cromwell as the agent of her destruction. It is wholly credible that once Cromwell and Anne had fallen out, he feared for his safety if she remained in place; the more so if he, like so many, saw her as having engineered Wolsey's fall.

Yet another theory sees Cromwell as the tool of his royal master Henry VIII who – whether genuinely convinced of Anne's guilt or cynically cruel enough merely to be seeking an excuse to be rid of her – ordered Cromwell to substantiate a case. Henry announced his betrothal to Jane Seymour the day after Anne's death and married her with indecent haste. Even Chapuys, on 18 May, noted public anger that the king was so happy 'since the arrest of the whore'. Here, essentially, is the great problem for historians of these years: that Henry appears as either mutt or monster.

Perhaps there is a fourth, compromise position, which allows for an element of confusion – of self-deception, rather than deception by a third party – in the English king's reaction. Perhaps Anne died for an idea; not an idea of the reformed religion but the old ideal of courtly love. The game she had learnt in the European courts, the game that permitted – demanded – a measure of freedom with the men around her. The game with which she had at first enchanted Henry, the game she had never learnt when *not* to play.

Early in her queenship Anne's chamberlain had written: 'as for pastime in the queen's chamber, [there] was never more. If any of you that be now departed have any ladies that ye thought favoured you and somewhat would mourn at parting of their servants, I can no wit perceive the same by their dancing . . .' 'Servants' is the term from courtly love but perhaps by this late stage in the long courtly tradition, the term could only be used cynically.

Anne Boleyn was not born to be a major player in that other game, the game of queens. She was a pawn 'queened', who had won for herself the right to move with a queen's freedom. And if she had found that that freedom had definite limits, so had others, better-born than she. Katherine of Aragon had been born into queenly rank, daughter of the woman whose authority seemed to offer a lesson for the century. Yet she too had wound up in actual fear of her life and dying in a state which would have seemed absurd in her heyday.

If Anne was in so many ways a transgressive figure, Katherine had played by the rules throughout her marriage, transgressing only in her refusal to end it quietly. Yet her fate, like Anne's, served to show how conditional was a woman's power, a woman's privilege, in the first half of the sixteenth century. Conditional on a man's will, conditional on not being betrayed, in any one of a number of senses, by the vulnerability of her body, whether exposed in terms of her chastity or of her fertility.

Anne Boleyn's rise to queenship revealed the powers of the role but also its ultimate vulnerability. On the chess board the queen had assumed new powers and yet the safety or otherwise of the king was still all that mattered, ultimately. In the years ahead St Teresa of Avila, in *The Way of Perfection*, would use the chess queen as her model for humility, because of her commitment to her lord.

These decades saw a number of women exercise great authority. But with the sole exception of Isabella of Castile, all had exercised it conditionally: in the temporary absence or incapacity of a son, nephew, husband or brother. This made palatable a woman's exercise of power. In the latter half of the century a new set of female monarchs – queens regnant, not regent – would present a new set of challenges, different not just quantitatively but qualitatively.

In England, both Henry VIII's daughters had now been declared bastards, by the new Second Act of Succession. Bastards like Bessie Blount's son, Richmond. As Chapuys reported, it might well have been decided that a male bastard trumped a female one. But on 23 July, Richmond died.[3]

'Illegitimate' though they might now be, time would not leave the Tudor sisters Mary and Elizabeth in obscurity. They carried their mothers' rivalry and, as religious divides continued to harden, their mothers' religious legacies into the second half of the sixteenth century.

France too, in the summer months of 1536, saw the unexpected death of the dauphin, its heir. Contemporaries suspected, surely wrongly, that the emperor had had him poisoned; other suspicions lighted on Catherine de Medici, more so since the servant suspected of doing the deed was an Italian who had come to France in her retinue. This left François's second son Henri as the new heir, and meant that Catherine de Medici, formerly the disregarded wife of a mere younger son, was now the future Queen of France. Truly, a new generation was on the way.

PART IV

1537–1553

My lord Gaspar shall not find me an admirable man, but I will find you a wife or daughter or sister of equal and sometimes greater merit.

The Book of the Courtier, Baldassare Castiglione, 1528

26

Daughters in jeopardy

England, Scotland, 1537–1543

THE MIDDLE YEARS of the sixteenth century represent something of a hiatus in the story of powerful queens or regents. Across France and Spain, and in England, women resumed their traditional place behind a powerful man. There were two notable exceptions: Scotland and the Netherlands. Coincidentally or otherwise, these were also among the lands where in these decades the Reformation battle was fought most fervently.

In England these years represent the gap between the deaths of Katherine of Aragon and Anne Boleyn and the accession of Katherine's daughter Mary. Henry VIII's marital adventures continued with the birth of his son Edward, and the death of Jane Seymour, in October 1537; his marriage to and divorce from Anne of Cleves in 1540, followed hard by his marriage to Katherine Howard (Anne Boleyn's kinswoman) and Katherine's downfall and execution in 1542.

The tales of all Henry's wives are among British history's most dramatic personal stories. But if they offer a lesson in this context it is, if anything, how disposable royal women could be. Henry's third, fourth, and fifth wives showed no sign of being active players in the political story.

What of his daughters? Elizabeth was a toddler, not yet three, when her mother died in 1536. For all her noted precocity, she was a child during all her father's lifetime and not required to make any particular accommodation with his policies. But for Mary Tudor, turning twenty when her mother died, it would be a different story.

The Act of Succession passed in the summer of 1536 decreed that the throne should go only to Henry VIII's children by Jane Seymour or any subsequent wife. Elizabeth Tudor, like Mary, was 'illegitimate . . . and utterly foreclosed, excluded and banned to claim, challenge or demand any inheritance as lawful heir'.

If they were bastards, they were royal bastards: Mary stood as godmother at the new Prince Edward's christening, while Elizabeth (herself still so small she had to be carried) held up the end of his christening gown. And when the baby Edward in his turn was sent away from the court for his own health and safety, it was to join his sisters in Hertfordshire, with Mary as pseudo-parent in a communal royal nursery.

At Hatfield, Hunsdon, Ashridge and Hertford Castle Elizabeth began to be educated in Latin, French, Italian, Spanish and even Flemish; in history and geography, astronomy and mathematics, as well as dancing and riding, music and embroidery. A fine humanist education, of the sort that might be given to a boy. Elizabeth was not given any specific training for the throne, of the sort that had briefly been given to Mary at Ludlow but then, as a female bastard, why should she?

The problem was to know what future could be planned for Henry's discredited daughters. Even Henry's council noted that the girls were unlikely to be marriageable abroad unless they were made 'of some estimation' at home. But first, in Mary's case, came the question of submission to her father's authority.

Hard on the heels of Katherine of Aragon's death, Henry's men came to Mary, demanding that she sign a document declaring her acceptance that her parents' marriage had never been valid; that it 'was by God's law and Man's law incestuous and unlawful'. They had often before tried to wring such an acceptance from both mother and daughter; but now the mother was gone.

Mary at first refused, but the pressure mounted. She wrote to her father begging him to consider 'that I am but a woman and your child'. Finally, terrified for the lives of her friends, and indeed her own life, Mary capitulated and signed. The same document forced her to declare that she did 'recognise, accept, take, repute and [ac]knowldege' her father as head of the church in England and refute 'the Bishop of Rome's pretended authority'.

She saw her capitulation as a weakness. Mary Tudor probably never forgave herself for an action which helped to shape her as much as her mother's firmness did. It did, however, signal the start of a new rapprochement with Henry. On 6 July 1536 Henry's 'dear and well-beloved daughter Mary' rode secretly to join the father who had not spoken to her for five years. She received gifts and monies, and precedence over all but Queen Jane. Her position was curious and double-edged. On the one hand, she was favoured; on the other, she was watched, and closely.

Some around her suffered after the uprisings of 1536 and 1537 against Henry's religious changes. The Catholic rebels of the 'Pilgrimage of Grace' demanded she be reinstated as her father's heir. But if Mary lamented their failure, and the savage penalties the rebel leaders suffered, she did so silently. In 1538, she was warned by Cromwell about the 'lodging of strangers' at Hunsdon. In 1539, the discovery of a supposed Yorkist plot against King Henry resulted in the execution of, among others, the 68-year-old Margaret Pole, the kinswoman and former governess whom Mary had called her 'second mother'. As Chapuys commented bitterly: 'It would seem that they want to leave her as few friends as possible.'

Mary made the best of what personal relationships were left to her. Late in 1536 she wrote to her father that Elizabeth was such a child 'as I doubt not but your Highness shall have cause to rejoice of in time coming'. She got on well with her father's fourth wife Anne of Cleves (despite the fact that the latter's marriage had been made to cement a Protestant alliance); badly with the flighty Katherine Howard, not only Anne Boleyn's cousin but nineteen to Mary's twenty-three. As 1543 dawned, she must have been relieved when news came of the king's impending and, as it turned out final, nuptials to a cultivated and self-controlled widow of thirty.

Katherine Parr had been a member of Mary's household while Henry was courting her and her mother had served Katherine of Aragon. Katherine of Aragon may even have stood godmother to her namesake and eventual successor. Now, ironically, Katherine Parr, like Katherine of Aragon before her, would come to represent the English side in the long story of the Scottish wars.

In Scotland, Margaret Tudor was now completely estranged from power under her son James V's rule. Her dream of an English alliance had never gone away. In the early months of 1536 she had been preparing for what in fact would never happen, a meeting between her son and her brother. But she could only watch as her third husband, Henry Stewart, cuckolded her and squandered her money. She tried to escape across the border into England, only to be brought north again. Something between an irrelevance and an embarrassment to both countries, Margaret Tudor could be found grumbling to the English envoy Sir Ralph Sadler that she had no letter from Henry: 'though I be forgot in England, shall I never forget England. It had been but a small matter . . . to have spent a little paper and ink upon me.'

Margaret's relationship to James grew a little easier in her new role of grandmother (to two short-lived boys, not to her famous granddaughter Mary). In 1537, to reseal the 'Auld Alliance' with France, James V married King François's daughter Madeleine. He went to France to woo and wed her himself; as royal marriages go, it was a romantic story. But Madeleine (already ill with tuberculosis) died seven weeks after her arrival in Scotland. James needed a new bride, but King François was reluctant to commit his younger daughter to the Scottish climate. Luckily, there was an alternative; a young widow from an already-prominent French family.

Marie de Guise (Mary of Lorraine) was born, on 20 November 1515, into a clan rising quickly through the French territories. Her father Claude, Duc de Guise, was from the start of the reign a contemporary and crony of François. Claude's father owned the huge independent duchy of Lorraine, as well as large estates within France itself, and laid claim to the kingdoms of Naples and Jerusalem. He was thus descended from the family that had produced Margaret of Anjou, wife of England's Henry VI, and the woman who had played so controversial a part in the Wars of the Roses.

Claude's mother, a cousin of François's mother Louise of Savoy, was herself a famous figure. Philippa of Gueldres, a noted beauty in her youth, ignored the pleas of her family and retired into the austere embrace of the Poor Clares when the youngest of her thirteen children was still only twelve. Not only Claude and his elder brother Anthony, but also King François himself braved the convent walls to consult her.

Claude became a hero of François's first Italian campaign, wounded almost to death at the Battle of Marignano but sufficiently recovered to ride at François's side as the king entered Milan in triumph. From that time, the Guise star was in the ascendant. When François's wars took him back to Italy in 1525, he left Claude as principal advisor to Louise of Savoy. When German reformers took advantage of François's preoccupation to invade Lorraine, Claude was advised by his mother Philippa that while some illnesses could be cured by gentle care, heresy was a gangrene that had to be cauterised by fire or sword. From now on Claude (created duke on François's return) was seen as a Catholic hero.

One of the biggest influences on Claude's daughter, the young Marie de Guise, was probably her mother, the forceful and devout Antoinette de Bourbon, although the Guise and Bourbon clans were to be dramatically at odds later in the century. Antoinette was left to run the family estates in her husband Claude's frequent absences. Their eldest daughter, Marie, may have been intended for the church, since when she entered her teens she was sent to join her grandmother Philippa in the convent of the Poor Clares. But it seems to have been her budding charms that, after two or three years, decided her uncle Anthony that she could be better deployed for the advantage of her family.

After Marie's debut at court in 1531, she was soon treated by the king almost as one of his own daughters. There may have been some thought (in her family's mind at least) that she might marry one of François's sons but a few weeks after Henri was betrothed to Catherine de Medici, Marie was instead betrothed to the Duc de Longueville, one of France's premier peers. The marriage was happy and Marie soon gave birth to a son. She was back at court in time to be one of the principal guests when her friend Madeleine married the Scottish king. Just four weeks before Madeleine's death, Marie de Guise's husband Longueville died, and a month later she gave birth to their second son.

The French king offered Marie to James V before her husband was two months buried. Marie was appalled, and the match beset with difficulty, not least about how much of her dowry should come from the Longueville estates, to the disadvantage of her sons. Rumour said François's son Henri wanted to put Catherine de Medici aside in Marie's favour. And soon another suitor entered the lists, in the increasingly portly shape of Henry VIII of England. Henry was attracted by everything he had heard of Marie, not least her large physique. 'I may be big in person,' she famously retorted, 'but I have a little neck.'

At this stressful moment, Marie's second son died, at just four months old. Letters between Marie, her father Claude and mother Antoinette agreed that nothing should be done without Marie's consent; Marguerite of Navarre offered to mediate with her brother King François, but Marie (once an advantageous contract had been drawn up) took the sensible course. She set sail for Scotland in June 1538, leaving her surviving son, and the Longueville estates, in her mother Antoinette's care.

Arriving in Scotland, Marie de Guise, encouraged by an exchange of lovely letters with her mother, did everything right: saying politely that James V's new castles were the equal of anything on the Loire, befriending his illegitimate children and making a friend of Margaret Tudor, her new mother-in-law. The extent of Marie's influence is unclear, unless we take anything from the fact that James resisted his uncle Henry's efforts to urge him towards making his own break with Rome, but the marriage could be accounted, broadly speaking, successful. There were hints of personal dissent. In May 1540, Marie gave her husband a son, with another born just eleven months later. Within weeks, however, both babies were dead, to the great distress of both parents and their grandmother Margaret Tudor (who would die of a stroke that November).

Soon, there came another problem on the horizon: a renewed threat from England. Henry VIII's attempt to assert a historic overlordship of Scotland failed, but when James V tried to ward off a military assault by himself invading England, he found that too many of his nobles had been bought off with English gold. Nevertheless, he pressed ahead, and while he was not himself present at the disastrous Battle of Solway Moss in November 1542, some stories say news of the defeat overset his already fragile reason. Nor was Marie in any position to help him, being by now in the final months of another pregnancy.

On 6 December 1542 James V took to his bed; on 8 December Marie de Guise was delivered of a daughter. Legend has it that James, hearing the news, murmured that 'it cam' wi' a lass and it will gang wi' a lass'. (The Stewart family had inherited the crown through Robert the

Bruce's daughter, Marjorie.) On 14 December he died, leaving the throne to be inherited by his six-day-old daughter, Mary Stuart.

Marie de Guise was not left in the officially sanctioned position that Margaret Tudor had held. Her husband had left no will naming her as protector, and insofar as Margaret Tudor might be regarded as a precedent, it was not an encouraging one. Protocol, moreover, required Marie to remain in her apartments, both as mourning royal widow and newly delivered royal mother. Meanwhile, the dominant position on the regency council was a bone to be fought over between the Earl of Arran (who, if the baby died, would inherit the throne) and the Archbishop of St Andrews, Cardinal Beaton.

Marie let it be known she sided with Beaton. Not only were his anti-English policies closer allied to her French interests but she probably had qualms about allowing Arran, himself so tantalisingly close to the throne, sole control of her vulnerable infant. Within a month of James V's death Arran was proclaimed lord governor of Scotland, but Beaton was to be lord chancellor.

Among themselves, they had to find a way of confronting the ever-present English threat and holding the throne for the infant Mary, Queen of Scots. Henry VIII proposed his solution: to marry the infant Queen of Scots to his son Edward, and have her raised at his own court, thereby securing control of her country. There was a real fear that if his proposal were refused outright he would launch an invasion. Marie de Guise could only play for time.

The first thing Marie did, amid fears that either England or Arran (vacillatingly in support of the English match) would kidnap the baby queen, was to get herself and Mary out of what was effectively Arran's custody and into the greater security of Stirling Castle. Soon, Marie, with every sign of pleasure in the forthcoming alliance, was proudly showing her infant to Henry VIII's envoy, Ralph Sadler. On 1 July the Treaties of Greenwich agreed to peace between Scotland and England during the lifetimes of Henry VIII and Mary Stuart, to a marriage between Mary and Henry's son Edward to be concluded when she was eleven and to Arran, in the meantime, remaining as Scotland's governor.

But Marie had no intention of ever seeing these plans fulfilled and she derived considerable support from their extreme unpopularity with the majority of Scots. A deal was struck which saw the infant Mary placed in the custody of four lords, rather than of Arran; Antoinette, in France, wrote to congratulate her daughter on her escape from 'such a great and long captivity'. The baby Mary, Queen of Scots was crowned at Stirling on 9 September 1543.

It was the French ambassador, La Brosse, who helped Marie de Guise and Cardinal Beaton find an excuse – Henry VIII's seizure of some Scottish ships, a breach of the peace – to declare void the Treaties of Greenwich made only months before and to formally renew the alliance with France. The summer of 1544 saw the start of the so-called 'Rough Wooing', a years-long and punitive campaign launched by an infuriated Henry to pay back the Scots for what he called 'their falsehood and disobedience . . . putting man, woman and child to fire and sword'.

The ensuing devastation was no advertisement for Arran's leadership of the country and Marie de Guise decided to launch a bid for the regency. Though the council agreed, the bid failed in view of the greater military power Arran could wield, but Marie won a role as leader of the special council that would now advise the lord governor.

Anne de Beaujeu's advice – that widows should strive to keep power in their own hands – might have been ringing in her ears. Marie de Guise had preserved her daughter's throne. But in England it remained unclear whether Henry VIII's daughters could find such a female protector or role model – whether they would be as lucky.

Pawns and princesses

The Netherlands, France, 1537–1543

As THE INFANT Mary, Queen of Scots assumed a throne she was too young to recognise and Henry VIII's daughters faced an uncertain future, in France and the Netherlands, other princesses' lives seemed set on the traditional path: to be moved like pawns for the advantage of their family.

In the Netherlands, Mary of Hungary scored a small but telling victory on behalf of one of her quasi-daughters when, in 1538, she supported her niece Christina of Denmark – a widow at sixteen – in her urgent desire not to make a second marriage with Henry VIII. The Holbein portrait painted in the course of the courtship gives little hint of the strong character behind Christina's reputed declaration that if she had two heads, one of them would be at the King of England's disposal.

Perhaps she got her trenchant tongue from Mary of Hungary, for when Mary heard that Henry had married again after Anne Boleyn's execution, she wrote to her brother Ferdinand:

> It is to be hoped, if one can hope anything from such a man, that if this one bores him he will find a better way of getting rid of her. I believe that most women would not appreciate it very much if this kind of habit becomes general, and with reason. And although I have no inclination to expose myself to dangers of this kind, I do after all belong to the female sex, so I shall also pray God that he may protect us from such perils.

Mary's work in centralising the government of the various Netherlands provinces was too often hampered by the financial and military demands made by her brother Charles V. To pay for his Italian wars, taxes were raised across the Empire and in 1539 the citizens of Ghent rebelled, their violent uprising put down only when Charles himself arrived with an army. He paraded the rebellious burghers with halters around their necks, only to pardon them at Mary's public request: an exercise of a queen's traditional intercessory function equivalent to the one in England two decades before when three queens had pleaded for the apprentices' lives. After the revolt was quelled, Mary of Hungary begged her brother to relieve her of her post but instead, her appointment was renewed.

In France, meanwhile, François had from the first largely ignored his new queen, Charles V and Mary of Hungary's sister Eleanor. Yet the ghost of the Ladies' Peace never quite went away. Eleanor was present at the peace negotiations between Charles and François in 1538, and took a more active role in 1544, when she met Charles as well as Mary.

Eleanor's marriage to François remained childless. So, more seriously, did that of the heir to the French throne, Henri, and Catherine de Medici. Marguerite of Navarre comforted Catherine: 'God will give you a royal line when you have reached the age at which women of the House of Medici are wont to have children. The King and I will rejoice with you then, in spite of these wretched backbiters.'

Catherine won for herself the support of the older generation. King François was always fascinated by anything from Italy, the cradle of the Renaissance, and pleased by Catherine's membership of the '*Petite Bande*', the gang of hard-riding, hard-living young ladies with which he surrounded himself. When, in 1538, there were suggestions that the marriage might be set aside, Catherine spoke to her father-in-law, who assured her of his continued protection. The Venetian ambassador reported that she offered to go into a nunnery or to serve the lady who became her husband's next wife; behaviour diametrically opposite to that of Katherine of Aragon.

Catherine's husband Henri had never warmed to his bride. He was falling increasingly under the influence of Diane de Poitiers, the legendary court beauty who, despite the twenty-year age gap between them, became Henri's mistress.[1] Catherine de Medici, so the story goes, had holes sawn in the floorboards so she could watch, and learn from, what her husband and his mistress did in bed. (Ironically, over the next decade Diane would become one of Catherine's strongest supporters, believing the disregarded Italian wife to be less of a threat to her own position than another, better-loved, consort might be.) More certainly, a royal doctor was called in to examine both Catherine and Henri and found slight abnormalities in both.

His advice, sadly unrecorded, seems to have been some slight change of practice or position. It was successful: in the summer of 1543 Catherine de Medici at last became pregnant. The baby was born in January 1544 and named for his grandfather, François; thus beginning another, better-known, stage in Catherine's journey. (King François, present at the event, took such an urgent interest in the proceedings that he demanded to view the afterbirth.) Marguerite of Navarre wrote to her brother that this was 'the most beautiful, the most longed for, and the most needed day that you and your kingdom have ever seen'.

Marguerite had continued to be a force in French affairs, and an ardent ally of her brother, attempting even, in 1540 and subsequently, to mediate an Anglo-French peace, with or without François's knowledge. But she would find herself increasingly torn by the differences between her brother and her husband. By 1537 the Navarrese couple, attempting to regain that part of Navarre annexed by Spain, had entered into secret negotiations with the emperor Charles V, whose son Philip, they suggested, might marry their daughter, Jeanne d'Albret. Every letter to Marguerite's brother breathes, in its exaggerated protestations of love and loyalty, her anxiety about acting against his interests in this way and perhaps her desire to reassure him, for the battlefield of Marguerite's ever-troubled loyalties were about to see their most bitter conflict.

It is possible that Marguerite of Navarre's relationship with her daughter was affected by the difficult relation she had with her mother, Louise of Savoy. Jeanne was at first raised largely in Normandy, where her foster mother Aymee de Lafayette lived. Jeanne's father, Henri d'Albret, was occupied either at court or in his own southwestern territories, while Marguerite had always been preoccupied by her role as supervisor of her brother's royal nursery.

Mentions of Jeanne in Marguerite's letters are scarce; only two during the first seven years of her life, and in one of those Marguerite wrote that she needed to rest 'away from my daughter, who is too noisy and boisterous'. By contrast, there was mention of Jeanne's always-frail health when Marguerite was planning to take her away for a change of air in 1533.

In 1537, before she was ten years old, the question arose of how Jeanne might best be deployed as a marriageable pawn. Her father hoped she could be used to win the reunification of Navarre; her mother, deeply conflicted, wavered between supporting him or her brother, who had no wish to see the vital frontier state of Navarre thus allied to the Habsburg Empire.

That summer, François sent for his niece but the child was seriously ill with, as Marguerite of Navarre wrote, 'fever and looseness of bowels with blood, which was so fast and furious that if God had not brought down her fever after twenty-four hours her little body would have had more than it could stand'. But Marguerite added:

> I hope that He who put her in this world to be of service to you will give her grace to fulfil the desire of mother, father, and herself, which is rather to see her dead than [commit] any deed against your intention . . . On this I base my hope of her recovery.

The hope was not misplaced: Jeanne recovered and, with her parrot and her pet squirrel, was taken away to recuperate by her mother. From her tenth to her twentieth year Jeanne resided chiefly in Plessis-les-Tours, largely without either of her parents, on the orders of an uncle, François, determined they should not dispose of her to their advantage rather than to his.

While Jeanne d'Albret's parents were angling for the Spanish match that might reunite the kingdom of Navarre, François had very different plans. In January 1540 he received an offer for Jeanne's hand from the Duke of Cleves, a duchy in the Rhine. François was always keen to break the Empire's hold on the German states, a hope the more realistic for the fact that some were tending towards the reformed religion. The marriage contract was drawn up in July that year. Jeanne, informed of her uncle's plans in her mother's presence, declared herself 'content'.

It was understandable that her mother should delay as much as possible. Jeanne was still only twelve when, the following spring, Marguerite of Navarre wrote tearfully to the prospective bridegroom that the marriage was 'not yet ripe according to God and nature'. François, however, pressed for an early conclusion to the alliance and ordered her parents to bring Jeanne to court, where her Cleves bridegroom had arrived. Marguerite succeeded only in winning the hostility of both her husband, angered she had bowed to François's wishes, and her brother, irritated she had not done so more swiftly.

What happened next is a matter of conjecture. Only one report, from the Spanish spy Juan Martinez Descurra, survives. According to Descurra, Marguerite of Navarre suggested that her daughter should make a formal protest against the marriage before witnesses. With that protest in their pocket, Jeanne's parents could safely allow the betrothal to go ahead, insisting on keeping Jeanne with them until she was a few years older, trusting that time would make an alliance between France and Cleves less pressing. Henri of Navarre agreed, warning his wife that if she blabbed, and word of the plan got to her brother François, he would see that she had 'as bad an old age as any wife or woman ever had'.

The formal protest was safely stowed away, but with François himself bringing the duke to meet his bride, Jeanne d'Albret had to tell her formidable uncle that she had changed her mind. François asked who had coached her, and the angry conversation (which Descurra reports as an extended dialogue) saw Jeanne sobbing and shouting that she would rather throw herself down a well than marry the Duke of Cleves. François told her, and those around her, ominously, that 'heads will fall for this'. As Jeanne reiterated her threat of suicide, her parents received a letter indicating that the emperor had no immediate intention of offering his son as an alternative husband. Marguerite and her husband had little choice but to let the Cleves marriage go ahead, at least in its initial stage.

What happened next is a confusing and worrying story. Marguerite of Navarre wrote to her brother King François that she had learnt with horror of her daughter's defiance: 'my daughter, appreciating neither the great honour you conferred upon her by condescending to visit her nor realising that a good daughter has no right to have a will of her own, has been so foolish as to beg you not to marry her to the Duke of Cleves'. She, Marguerite, would be only too happy to punish anyone who had put such 'insolence' into her head.

By the end of May, François was preparing resplendent wedding festivities. On 13 June 1541, at the château of Chatellerault near Poitiers, the betrothal was celebrated, the king himself escorting the twelve-year-old Jeanne.

Both parties were asked for, and gave, their assent, although later in life Jeanne d'Albret would tell her historian, Nicolas de Bordenave, that when asked for the third time whether she would marry the duke, she said only, 'Don't press me'. She had made another lengthy declaration 'that the marriage proposed between me and the Duke of Cleves is against my will, that I never have consented to it, and that I never will'. Anything she might say to the contrary, the document continues, will have been spoken from fear. Fear of her uncle, of her father:

> and of my mother the Queen, who had me threatened and beaten by the Baillive de Caen, my governess. [She] has several times brought pressure on me at the command of the Queen my mother, threatening that if I did not do everything the King wished . . . I would be so beaten and maltreated that I would die, and that I would be the cause of the ruin and destruction of my mother and father and of their house . . . I do not know to whom to appeal except to God, when I see that my mother and father have abandoned me.

As the marriage was celebrated with great solemnity, Jeanne, dressed in crimson satin trimmed with ermine, a golden crown and a gold and silver skirt trimmed with precious stones, was observed not to take a step towards the altar: whether, says Brantôme, 'because she could not move under the weight of her costume, or whether she wished to protest to the last minute . . .' François ordered the Constable of France, Montmorency, to take her by the collar and carry her there.

The nuptial Mass was followed by dinner and masquerades but the putting of the couple to bed was purely ceremonial, the bridegroom putting only a single ritual foot between the sheets. A week later the duke set out for Cleves and Jeanne, seriously ill, was taken back to Plessis by her mother.

What had really been going on? Various historians, through the centuries, have put forward various explanations, but each has a problem. If we follow the spy Descurra's saga, we see a Marguerite of Navarre who first set up the pretence of Jeanne's refusal and then backtracked to protect her own position, leaving the child to bear the king's anger alone. If we give credence instead to Marguerite's letter to François, we see perhaps the most extreme example of her prioritising of her brother's needs over those of husband or child. If we believe Jeanne d'Albret's declaration, Marguerite had gone further than that, threatening to have her daughter beaten within an inch of her life. And this the woman whose lifelong writings proclaim the female cause! The kindest explanation is that it was all, to some degree, a put-up job, with Jeanne complicit in her parents' pretence, although this scenario would surely have required a good deal of a twelve-year-old's acting ability.

Jeanne herself gave a measure of explanation later in life, although it still leaves much unclear:

> The marriage was performed . . . against the will of the bride and of her father, who endured it rather than consented, in order not to anger the King. The daughter did not dare to oppose [it] openly, as much out of fear and respect for her uncle and for her mother (whom her brother had won over) as because of the embarrassment and simplicity of her age and sex . . .

The narrative Jeanne commissioned relates how she secretly drew up a protest: 'Whether she was advised to do so or whether she did it on her own initiative'. It is hard to imagine an unadvised twelve-year-old coming up with such a ploy. But it is easy, the more you read Jeanne's declaration, with its dramatic tale of threatened beatings, to suspect you are witnessing Marguerite of Navarre's ability with fiction. Perhaps what we are seeing here is a teenager set in motion by her parents but then unable to retreat from the stand she had taken, as a more experienced politician might be able to do. In all events, this was a wound which would fester. And this was not, with Jeanne technically now Cleves's wife, ever going to be the end of the story.

Small wonder that a letter from Marguerite to her son-in-law that winter describes Jeanne as still thin and ill: 'We are doing everything to fatten her up, but she does not gain weight.'[2] Jeanne herself wrote to her new husband: 'there is no medicine in the world which could do so much for my health as knowing that yours is good'. Perhaps she had learned how to dissimulate in a good, or a politic, cause. Or perhaps the coaching went on.

France and Charles V were once again at war when, early in 1543, Jeanne d'Albret was despatched to join her new husband, who was proving himself a valuable French ally. But she was still on French soil when word came that the Duke of Cleves had been forced to switch sides and renew his country's old allegiance to the emperor. François immediately demanded an annulment of the marriage and instructed Marguerite and her husband to provide the evidence.

Marguerite of Navarre produced Jeanne's signed protest declaring she had been married under duress. Marguerite and her husband would never have dared speak out, she claimed:

> if Cleves had behaved to you as he should have and as I hoped, we would never have entertained such a thought, and would have preferred to see our daughter die, as she said she would, rather than lift a finger to prevent her going to any place . . . where . . . she could serve you. Since he is so infamous we no longer fear to speak the truth . . .

Jeanne was forced to sign yet another witnessed declaration, this time with her uncle François's full approval. Even then, there was yet another coda to this story.

Although Cleves himself had decided instead to seek an alliance with one of the emperor's nieces, before the fraught annulment could finally go through the pope had to be convinced. Letters from Marguerite of Navarre in the spring of 1545 declared she had 'forsaken all maternal tenderness' to force her daughter into the alliance; those from Jeanne declared that 'my mother, the Queen, preferred obedience to the king to her own life, and to mine'.

The marriage was finally annulled in November. Whatever the truth of the affair, it is unlikely the fourteen-year-old Jeanne understood or forgave completely, and the bitterness she felt may have been a lasting legacy.

By contrast, Marguerite of Navarre and her brother François seemed to be back on their usual terms, apart from the ever-present religious question. A conference in 1541 attempted to find some common ground between Protestant and Catholic but its failure would see increased persecution of Protestants (as they would come to be called) both in the Low Countries and in France.

The mood of the times was growing ever harder. When in 1542 François resumed his war with the emperor Charles V, he dared not leave behind him a country split by any challenges to state or church authority. From her husband's duchy of Béarn, Marguerite wrote to her brother about the cruelties perpetrated in the name of eliminating heresy: 'a poor woman whose baby was aborted by torture . . . and many other things that should be heard by you alone'. She was, as so often, carefully treading a fine line; protesting not about the principle but rather the extremities of the persecution.

Complaining of a local bishop who was preaching that both the king and his sister supported heretics, Marguerite made a point of dissociating herself from those who attacked the 'real presence' in the Mass: 'Thank God, my Lord, none of our people has ever been found to be sacramentarians.' But she and her husband believed the local monks had 'found a way of putting poison in the incense' and were trying to do away with them.

She found herself at odds with her former protégé, the austere French theologian John Calvin, over her protection for two mystic preachers.[3] By contrast the pope – who had enjoyed discussions with Marguerite – was inclined to regard her as his spokesperson at François's court. All good Catholics had fresh reason to be hopeful in these years. The opening of the Council of Trent in 1545 signalled a new crusading spirit in the Catholic church, discussing the reform of corrupt practices as well as doctrinal decrees. But inevitably the 'Counter-Reformation' would itself be the pretext for aggression against dissenters in the years ahead. At the beginning of 1545

Marguerite was horrified when François, at the pope's request, author-ised the massacre of perhaps several thousand members (estimates vary wildly) of the unorthodox Waldensian sect.

Marguerite may, as she so often did, have found refuge in writing: encouraging those around her to undertake translations of Plato's dialogues while she herself began exploring the relationship between the kind of ideal love figured in the courtly romances and Plato's ideas. On her southern estates she surrounded herself with the talented and literary. Her writings, however, provide no clear answer to Marguerite of Navarre's continued ambivalence about her female role; an ambiva-lence the events of these years can have done little to diminish.

In 1544 she wrote to François of the desire she had had all her life to serve him not as a sister but as a brother. Conversely, she would write too of her wish that she might give birth to a hundred warriors to serve him. Perhaps that admixture of messages is something with which many women had to deal in the sixteenth as in any other century.

New winds

England, France, 1544–1547

IN ENGLAND IN 1544, Katherine Parr was, like Katherine of Aragon before her, left regent when Henry went away to war against France. When England's ongoing affrays with the Scots set her at odds with Marie de Guise, it was an echo in a minor key of the events of 1513, when Katherine of Aragon and Margaret Tudor had found their armies at enmity.

Katherine Parr's regency also allowed both of her stepdaughters, Mary and Elizabeth Tudor, to witness a woman successfully wielding power; a spectacle familiar on the continent which had not always come England's way.

Even religious differences seemed, at first, to be subsumed under the new Queen Katherine's reforming zeal. Katherine Parr had her own literary aspirations, producing first the anonymous *Psalms or Prayers* and then, under her own name, *Prayers or Meditations*, which made her the first queen to be a published author in English, if not French, history. The ten-year-old Elizabeth Tudor made Katherine a New Year's present of her translation of Marguerite of Navarre's *The Mirror of Glass of a Sinful Soul* but when Katherine Parr commissioned the translation into English from the Latin of some of Erasmus's *Paraphrases upon the New Testament*, Katherine's other stepdaughter Mary was one of the translators. Ill health prevented Mary from completing her translation of the *Gospel According to John*, but the final version nevertheless included a lengthy dedication to Mary as a 'peerless flower of virginity'.

Katherine Parr very nearly went the way of others of Henry's queens

when she fell under suspicion for the extent of her reforming tendencies.[1] Mary Tudor, by contrast, was able to accommodate to her father's
religious policies, which still included the supremacy of the Mass, the
celibacy of priests and the necessity of confession. In her brother
Edward's reign, it would be a different story.

At the beginning of 1544 Henry VIII, fifty-two, and with no sign of the
longed-for second son, laid down another Act of Succession. If he had no
further child and if his son Edward died without heir, then the throne
would pass to Mary. If she too died childless, then to Elizabeth. Both
sisters feature in the anonymous painting *The Family of Henry VIII*. In
the centre sits Henry, enthroned, the young Edward at his right hand, and
at his left the long-dead Jane Seymour, mother of the all-important boy.
These three are framed in a network of gilded pillars. Pointedly outside
the magic circle of legitimate royalty, framed by another set of rather less
conspicuous pillars, the two royal daughters stand separately; Mary, the
elder, to Henry's right, and Elizabeth to the left.

In December 1546, the message of the portrait was ratified by the
king's will, which confirmed the place in the succession of both Mary
Tudor and then (assuming neither her brother nor Mary left any heirs)
Elizabeth. But as 1546 turned to 1547; as Henry lay dying, that seemed
an unlikely contingency.

The early part of 1547 saw a general clearing of the decks. The death of
the obese and ailing Henry VIII on 28 January 1547 was followed,
barely two months later, by that of his old rival, King François.

Marguerite of Navarre had spent the last few months on her estates,
in pain from arthritis and apprehensive of the future. At the time of
her brother's death, she was on the road to try to meet – rescue, revive
– him, an echo of her dash to Spain twenty years earlier. She was staying at a convent in Poitou when the news of his death reached her: not
for several months could she bring herself to leave. 'O death, who
conquered the Brother, / come now in your great goodness / and pierce
the Sister with your lance', she wrote in the *Chanson spirituelle,* and:

> My life was filled with sugar and honey
> when it was sustained by his
> but now it is nothing but absence and bitterness
>
> (Le Navire)

The last few years had seen difficulties between brother and sister. But in the end he had, as she had recently written to him, supported her 'in the office of king, of master, of father and brother and of true friend'. François's death was not only a bitter personal, but also a practical, loss: a loss of influence, as well potentially of the pension François had made her. Small wonder that one source of friction between her and her daughter was the high expense of Jeanne's household, which Marguerite found, as she wrote to Jeanne's financial controller, 'insupportable'.

The new king, Henri II, relieved Marguerite of her financial worries but wrote of her dismissively as 'my good old aunt'. The new king's solemn entry into Lyons saw Marguerite of Navarre, who had once taken pride of place in every procession, grateful for a place in Catherine de Medici's carriage. ('I share your distress, as I always knew you shared mine', Catherine had written to her.) Catherine was now, of course, Queen of France.

The deaths of the men in this story brought all too often, for better or for worse, a dramatic change for their women. In England as in France, Henry VIII's daughters (and his widow) had to trim their sails to a new wind. The effects of the powerful kings' deaths spread like ripples from a stone in a pond. They would even be felt in Scotland, albeit that, for some years to come, the fate of Scotland would be bound to that of France ever more closely.

The death of Henry VIII brought no end to the Rough Wooing, which indeed, in September 1547, saw the disastrous Scottish defeat at Pinkie Cleugh. Amid real fears that the young Queen Mary would be kidnapped by the English, Marie de Guise contemplated a suggestion by the new King Henri II that the four-year-old Queen of Scots should marry his three-year-old son the dauphin and be raised in France. The plan was agreed and on 7 August 1548, with a numerous Scottish retinue (including her famous contemporaries and future attendants the 'four Marys'), the little Queen of Scots set sail for France and for what, it was assumed, would be her future country.

Accommodations

France, 1548–1550

EVERYONE, YOU MIGHT say, had to make accommodations in these years. In Scotland, Marie de Guise was certainly having to deal with the realities of practical politics. It was two years before the relief of a peace treaty, made in 1550 between England and France, and in which Scotland was included, allowed Marie to return to France for an extended visit. She was lucky: she might well never have seen her daughter again.

The English envoy to the French court wrote that Marie's work in Scotland 'is so highly taken here as she is in this court made a goddess'. It had been suggested that the Scots governor, Arran, should be replaced by a French governor, which would have allowed Marie a comfortable retirement but one account says she went to Henri and announced she wanted to rule Scotland.

She had the immense distress, during her visit, of losing her one surviving son, with whom she had so recently been reunited, the young Duc de Longueville. She also heard of a plot to poison her small daughter, the Queen of Scots. 'Our Lord must wish me for one of his chosen ones, since he has visited me so often with such sorrow', she wrote to her mother Antoinette. But she prepared to return to Scotland, acknowledging where her future lay.

The little Queen of Scots, meanwhile, was growing up very happily at the French court. The Scottish train with which she arrived had largely been sent away. The French complained the Scots were uncouth and dirty, and even the four Marys were sent to be educated at a convent near Poissy, since the aim was to make Queen Mary as French as possible. But she had come to a welcoming place. Henri II and his wife Catherine de Medici were devoted parents, constantly demanding reports and portraits when absent from their children, among whose number Mary was now included. There are records of the endless chain of pets brought into the nursery – mastiffs, and even a bear – and reports, as she grew older, of Mary and her attendants taking pleasure in playing at cookery.

She shared a bedroom with Elisabeth, the eldest daughter of Catherine and Henri. The king often wrote to Marie de Guise with 'tidings of our little household'. More significantly, Mary and the French princesses shared the same educational curriculum as the dauphin François: history and rhetoric, languages and poetry.

From the first, care was taken to foster the idea of love in the dauphin and his future bride or, in the slightly older and infinitely stronger Mary, of protectiveness. Care was taken, too, to pay due tribute to Mary's rank. Henri II was enchanted with his future daughter-in-law, and wrote that 'she should take precedence over my daughters. For the marriage between her and my son is decided and settled; and apart from that, she is a crowned Queen'.

With hindsight, it is too tempting to look back to Mary Stuart's childhood and ask what it was in her education that so signally failed to teach her how to rule. Mary had come to a country with a formidable tradition of female governance, for all that Catherine de Medici had not yet come into her own, and from one where her mother was already a leading player. But the question may be misguided, the answer lying in Mary's character and with lessons that cannot be consciously taught. The branches of study in which Mary excelled were embroidery (in years to come she would often sit and sew through Scottish council meetings) and dancing. She was taught what were considered the skills of rule but she never learnt the edgy arts, the awareness of danger and opportunity, that Elizabeth Tudor in England learnt during her difficult youth. She was expected to live her life less as ruler of Scotland than as consort of France and it is hard not to feel that, to her ultimate danger, that expectation shaped her.

It is a too-ready assumption that Mary Stuart's early consciousness of her status was a source of friction between her and Catherine de Medici, based on a tale that she spoke of Catherine as a merchant's daughter. But it is largely the work of fiction, extrapolating backwards from the later conflict between Catherine and Mary's Guise relations, to suggest that Catherine regarded the child with unremitting hostility. Catherine must anyway largely have been preoccupied with her continuous childbearing: ten children in twelve years, with Henri's mistress Diane de Poitiers assisting at the births.

In the first years of her husband's reign Catherine de Medici found that her new title did not in any way mean she could shift her husband's dependence on his mistress. Many years later, in a letter concerning her daughter Margot's marital problems, Catherine wrote that she had only 'made good cheer' to Diane for Henri II's sake, 'for never did a woman who loved her husband succeed in loving his whore'. In her capacity as overall superintendent of the royal nurseries Diane would have been a figure in the life of the little Queen Mary. But as Henri's reign wore on, Diane's influence was perhaps beginning to fade, while just the opposite was happening with Catherine de Medici.

By the start of the 1550s one observer noted that the king now treated his wife 'with so much affection and attention that it is astounding'. She had first been made nominal regent in 1548, when her husband needed to travel out of the realm to secure his interests in Italy. Four years later she was given rather more authority in a second regency, when the king went to war with the Habsburgs.

To her annoyance, she found she still had to share the power but what is striking is the zest with which she took to the duties, writing to Constable Montmorency over her task of raising troops and money for Henri: 'I shall soon be past mistress, for I study nothing else all day long . . . you may count on me to press and push.' She was, in other words, beginning to assume the posture that would see her set against another woman in another story of a clash of queens.

The question of a marriage for Jeanne d'Albret had survived her uncle King François's death: it was to be a source of friction between her cousin, the new king, and her parents, who still secretly hankered after a Spanish match. It was however, as before, the king's will that would prevail. On 20 October 1548 Jeanne was happy to be married to Antoine de Bourbon, France's premier noble, first in line of succession to the throne if Henri's sons should produce no heirs.

Antoine was an attractive man, whose bravery as a soldier perhaps masked a more fundamental lack of resolution in his personality. The hasty ceremonies were scanty compared to those which had marked the abortive Cleves match. But as King Henri noted: 'I have never seen a happier bride than this one, she did nothing but laugh', adding that Marguerite of Navarre, by contrast, was in floods of tears, which seemed not to trouble her daughter in the slightest.

A courtier noted that Antoine 'performs his marital duties very well both day and night. He says that the six couplings went off very gaily.' Contemporaries noted that Jeanne, later so austere and forceful, seemed besotted by her husband. Marguerite wrote to Antoine in the summer of 1549 that her daughter had 'no pleasure or occupation except in talking about or writing to you'. Antoine, for his part, wrote to Jeanne with surprising tenderness: 'I would never have thought that I would love you as I do. I intend another time, when I have to take a long trip, to have you with me, for all alone, *je m'ennuye* (I grow weary).' However, his military duties often kept him away and Jeanne spent time with her mother, in what would prove to be the last year of Marguerite's life.

Marguerite of Navarre had lived too long, as perhaps had Anne de Beaujeu before her. Though still only in her fifties, she was the last survivor of her generation, with even those who had been her protégées, such as Anne Boleyn, now gone. Retreating to a modest country estate, she ventured outside on a damp night, possibly to watch a comet, which caused the chill which brought about her death on 21 December 1549.

There had clearly been a degree of rapprochement, if such were needed, with Jeanne. In those last months, mother and daughter exchanged a series of verse letters expressing, albeit in highly stylised terms, ideas of love and loss when apart from each other. Jeanne d'Albret's reaction to Marguerite of Navarre's death is not recorded but in the years ahead she would come to take on her mother's mantle, as arguably Marguerite had taken on Louise of Savoy's, promoting certain of her mother's causes, however, in ways Marguerite could not have foreseen.

'device for the succession'

England, 1547–1553

I N ENGLAND TOO, with Henry VIII dead and a new boy-king
on the throne, the question of accommodation to new political
realities was coming sharply to the fore. Edward VI and his advisors were committed to the new faith in a way that would never have
occurred to Henry VIII. Those who clung to the old faith would find
the times growing ever more difficult. Notable among them was
Edward's 31-year-old half-sister, Mary Tudor.

Conservative Catholics might be pernickety enough to query a
marriage conducted without the pope's authority but when her father
died, Mary Tudor showed no sign of querying that her nine-year-old
brother, as a male, had a superior right to the throne.

Another woman had long been watching over Mary Tudor's safety:
the regent of the Netherlands, Mary of Hungary. After submitting to
her father and acknowledging her own bastardy, Mary Tudor was
forced to write to Mary of Hungary, as well as to Charles V, declaring
that she had done so freely. Mary of Hungary (like Charles's wife,
Isabella of Portugal) would be sent reports as to Mary Tudor's welfare.
Emperor and regent both refused to acknowledge Edward until sure of
Mary Tudor's position. As Mary of Hungary wrote to their ambassador: 'We likewise refrain from sending you any letters for our cousin,
the Princess Mary, as we do not yet know how she will be treated.'

She was, at first, treated remarkably gently, given enough lands to
make her one of the country's leading magnates, a generosity designed
to buy her complicity with the new regime. But nothing would buy her

complicity in the attacks on religious rituals which, under a regency council headed by Jane Seymour's brother Edward, soon to be Duke of Somerset, were shortly under way.

There is no doubt that the religious reforms had the active support of the young king. That fact, in a sense, gave Mary Tudor her opportunity. Writing to express her horror at the changes quickly imposed on the celebration of the Mass (communion in both kinds for laity as well as clergy, and a denial of the real presence), she insisted that she would 'remain an obedient child' to her father's ordinances, until such time as her brother should 'have perfect years of discretion': a waiting game. The more evangelical the doctrine propounded, the more furiously Mary's household practised according to the old forms. But for a time she was given a measure of leeway, with Edward's council ever conscious of her watchful Habsburg relatives.

When, late in 1549, 'Protector' Somerset was deposed from the pre-eminent position he had taken upon himself, there were rumours Mary would become her half-brother's regent. Instead John Dudley, a successful military commander and fellow reformer, thrust himself into power. As the new forces on the council struck an alliance with France, sidelining the Habsburg interest, Mary was placed under increasing pressure to cease having the Mass said, even in her private household.

Even before this, Mary had felt her position to be sufficiently precarious that she told the Habsburg ambassador she might need to flee the country. In 1550, it seemed that would indeed become a necessity, and a plot was hatched between Mary Tudor, the ambassador, and Mary of Hungary, who sent three ships to stand by off the Essex coast, waiting to snatch her away.

Edward VI wrote indignantly of how 'you, our nearest sister' wished 'to break our laws and set them aside deliberately and of your own free will . . . I will see my laws strictly obeyed'. By contrast, the Christmas celebration of 1550 brought the king's other sister Elizabeth to London 'with a great suite of gentlemen and ladies', escorted by a hundred of the king's horse and formally welcomed by the council. The point being, as the imperial ambassador bitterly pointed out, to show that she who had embraced the new religion had 'become a very great lady'. Elizabeth was preferred to Mary by the new elite, being 'more of their kidney'.

Elizabeth's image as a virtuous Protestant princess had been some-what besmirched, less than two years before, by the scandal of her 'affair' with Thomas Seymour, the brother of Protector Somerset, who had married the widowed Katherine Parr. It started out as a distasteful story of bedroom romps in which the forty-year-old Seymour smacked the teenaged Elizabeth's bare backside. But when Katherine Parr died after giving birth to Seymour's child, it became clear Seymour sought to marry Elizabeth, a girl with a claim to the throne.

The early months of 1549 saw what must, for the fifteen-year-old Elizabeth, have been a terrifying official inquiry, with her servants, including her governess and surrogate mother Kat Ashley, incarcer-ated in the Tower. She herself fought free, although Seymour went to the block. Elizabeth's famous comment that 'this day died a man of much wit and little judgement' is probably apocryphal but she had shown that when danger threatened, she could act not from the heart but from the head.

The Seymour affair may have reinforced the lesson her mother's fate could have taught her: that sex is dangerous. For the moment, she concentrated on displaying the kind of maidenly modesty that would speedily ensure her complete rehabilitation in the eyes of Edward VI's court. Kat Ashley's husband recalled the 'free talk' and 'trim confer-ences' which took place between Elizabeth and those she gathered around her, notably her tutor Roger Ascham. She appeared in the demure garb that befitted Edward's 'sweet sister Temperance', deliber-ately positioning herself in contrast to the Catholic Mary.

When, in March 1551, Mary came to London, she rode through the streets escorted by a host of gentlefolk, each carrying their rosary. The council reacted, at first, merely with a war of attrition against members of Mary's household. Soon, however, she was under such pressure that Mary of Hungary wrote to the imperial ambassador that if they took the Mass away from Mary Tudor she would have to endure it but if they tried to force her into 'erroneous practices . . . it would be better for her to die than to submit'.

Once again, however, all the participants drew back from the brink. This was in part because of continental troubles that entailed a need to secure England's wool trade with the Netherlands, although Mary of Hungary, afraid England would join with France, proposed invading

England to place Mary Tudor on the throne and secure the precious trade that way.[1] Edward's councillors were no doubt conscious that Mary was still, by the terms of their father's will, her brother's heir. This consciousness was about to grow more acute as 1552 turned to 1553 and Edward caught first one cold, then another, which he failed to shake off.

As his health worsened, the young king, committed to his position as defender of the reformed faith, was for obvious reasons determined his throne should not pass to Mary. If it did, Edward told a reluctant lord chief justice, 'it would be all over for the religion whose fair foundation we have laid'.

Less obviously, he determined that Elizabeth had also to be excluded, despite her adherence to the new faith. Elizabeth, he explained, was the daughter of a disgraced woman 'more inclined to couple with a number of courtiers rather than reverencing her husband, so mighty a King'. Perhaps the truth was that Elizabeth Tudor was too much her father's daughter to consent to the overturning of his will, or that John Dudley, now running England behind the cloak of the royal council, knew she would never be his puppet.

More probably, it was because, still unmarried, she could yet be married to a Catholic prince, and (such was the perception) thus find her country returned to Catholicism. If Edward's sisters married abroad, their 'stranger' husband would, as Edward put it, work to have the laws and customs of his own native country 'practised and put in use within this our realm ... which would then tend to the utter subversion of the commonwealth of this our realm, which God forbid'. Better the princesses should be 'taken by God' than that they should so imperil the true religion, thundered one of Edward's bishops supportively.

Instead it was Edward's intention 'to appoint as our heir our most dear cousin Jane'. The eldest daughter of Frances Brandon, eldest daughter of Henry VIII's younger sister Mary, Jane Grey was not only herself ardently Protestant but had recently been married to Guildford Dudley, John Dudley's son.

Not that Edward wanted to leave his throne even to Jane, a safely Protestant and safely married woman. The irony is that, because of the efforts his father and grandfather made to clear the Tudor path of any potential rivals, he had little choice. With Edward's death imminent, questions of whether a woman could succeed were irrelevant. The only question was which woman would?

A paper in Edward VI's handwriting, entitled 'My device for the succession', followed his father's will in excluding the Scottish line descended from Henry VIII's elder sister Margaret Tudor; a line which was now represented by the Catholic Mary Stuart. The line of Henry's younger sister Mary had likewise so far produced only females, since Frances Brandon had no sons. Edward's original 'device' had been that the throne should pass not to Lady Jane herself but to her 'heirs male'. Events, however, overtook him. In May, with the king's health visibly worsening, he altered 'the heirs male of the Lady Jane' to 'Lady Jane or the heirs of her body'.

The so-called gynocracy debate had not been silent in these years, as witness Sir Thomas Elyot's *Defence of Good Women*, written in the 1530s and published in 1540, which defended Katherine of Aragon and her daughter's right of succession. And witness too the English publication, in 1542, of the volume Thomas Agrippa had dedicated to Margaret of Austria. With the birth of Edward, the pamphlet debate had seemed an intellectual game, rather than a real consideration of political possibilities.

What had been a game was, however, about to become reality.

PART V

1553–1560

A Queen ought to be chosen when she shall be wedded of the most honest kindred and people. For oftentimes the daughters follow the teachings and manners of them that they be descended from ... A Queen ought to keep her daughters in all chastity. For we read of many maidens that for their virginity have been made queens.

The Game and Play of the Chess, William Caxton's translation of Jacobus de Cessolis, ?1474

'Herculean daring'

England, 1553 – 1554

MARY TUDOR'S HALF-BROTHER Edward VI had died on 6 July 1553, having survived their father Henry VIII by only six years and now another girl had been proclaimed queen. Lady Jane Grey, the granddaughter of Henry VIII's younger sister, had been nominated to the crown by Edward's will. But Mary Tudor, Henry's eldest daughter, was determined she should never be crowned.

The move that followed, wrote Robert Wingfield in his *Vita Mariae Angliae Reginae* (Life of Queen Mary of England) 'should have been judged and considered one of Herculean rather than womanly daring, since to claim and secure her hereditary right, the princess was being bold as to tackle a powerful and well-prepared enemy . . .'

For too many of her thirty-seven years, Mary Tudor had been able to mount only a passive, if stubborn, resistance to the blows life had dealt her. But in 1553 she had a chance to act. To act as her mother Katherine had wanted; and act as her grandmother Isabella had done. Most of her contemporaries thought she was mad when she unfurled her standard at the castle of Framlingham in Suffolk and had herself proclaimed queen. But everything in Mary Tudor's heritage told her the crown was a prize worth fighting for.

Mary set up her rival banner on the very day after the royal council proclaimed Jane queen. Many flocked to what they saw as the true Tudor monarchy. As the Genoese merchant Baptista Spinola reported: 'the hearts of the people are with Mary, the Spanish Queen's daughter'.

To cooler observers the thing seemed impossible. The Habsburg ambassadors reported that all the country's forces were in the hands of the men who had proclaimed Jane Grey. But as Mary rode hard across country, those hostile forces close behind her, the people rallied to her standard.

As it became clear King Henry's daughter would not passively accept what many saw as a perversion of the natural order, the magnates of East Anglia – Sir Richard Southwell and the Earl of Sussex, the nobles and the knights – came to join her, mustering their local forces. On 12 July she reached Framlingham, a castle she had only recently acquired and a great fortress that might have been designed for just such an eventuality. As the imperial ambassador triumphantly reported: 'A great concourse of people were moved by their love for her to come and promise to support her to the end.' Local justices came; ordinary people brought cattle instead of money. In Orwell harbour, a squadron of five ships went over to her when the common sailors mutinied against their officers. Mary Tudor issued a proclamation, 'not doubting that all our true and faithful subjects will so accept us, take us, and obey us as their natural and liege sovereign lady and Queen'.

In London meanwhile, even the members of the royal council who had pressed Lady Jane Grey to the throne were beginning to suffer 'a kind of remorse'. On 18 July the councillors holding the Tower, where Jane was lodged for safety, turned it over to the supporters of Queen Mary, only too relieved to abandon a policy of which they had never really approved. The next day, in London, Mary Tudor was proclaimed queen, and on the 21st, John Dudley – Jane Grey's father-in-law and the man behind her elevation to the throne – himself threw his cap into the air and hailed Mary's sovereignty. In the Tower, the trappings of sovereignty were stripped from Lady Jane

Enclosed at Hatfield, Mary's half-sister Elizabeth Tudor had taken no part in the affray. Instead, she wrote to Mary, offering her congratulations. To have staked a claim of her own to the throne would have been neither a practical nor, for her, ethical possibility. While many supported Mary from civil loyalty rather than Catholic faith, many of the Protestant party might have followed Jane rather than Elizabeth. More importantly, by the dynastic rules to which Elizabeth herself subscribed, the throne, for the moment, belonged to Mary; their father had willed it so. Although Elizabeth may already have hoped that the much older Mary would not hold it indefinitely.

Mary Tudor made her royal entry into London on 3 August, resplendent in purple velvet and satin, as a contemporary chronicle reported, 'all thick set with goldsmith's work and great pearls'. Elizabeth and her entourage rode directly behind her. There were also 'a great number of other ladies', a sign that under a female ruler the women directly around the monarch's person would come more to the fore.

Even at that moment Queen Mary's sex caused controversy. Some of Edward VI's councillors suggested the coronation should be postponed until parliament had confirmed Mary's legitimacy. England had not had a ruling queen since Saxon days. In 1135, when William the Conqueror's granddaughter Matilda had attempted to succeed her father, it sparked a long civil war with her cousin, Stephen. Matilda was never crowned, having in the end to be content with the title 'Lady of the English' and an agreement that after Stephen's death the crown would pass to her son, not his. The idea that women could thus transmit their claim to the throne, as Margaret Beaufort had transmitted hers to her son Henry VII, was much less controversial than the idea they might take it themselves.

Other powerful women in first half of the sixteenth century had been regents rather than queens regnant and the idea that a woman might deputise for (or exercise influence on) a man was more acceptable than the idea that she might rule in her own right. Even then, only a century earlier, the attempts of Margaret of Anjou to govern on behalf of her incapable husband had been met with chauvinistic horror.

Isabella of Castile represented a precedent that must have been ever-present in her granddaughter Mary's mind, but four centuries after Matilda, the Aristotelian concept of society as a family, ruled over by a father, still held sway in most Western societies. There wasn't even the language: a queen was a king's wife.[1] Both Mary and Elizabeth Tudor would describe themselves as 'princes', while a successful woman was often described as being no longer wholly belonging to her sex.

In these puzzling first days of Queen Mary's rule, care would be taken to declare she had the same authority as a male ruler. But, reported Simon Renard, the new imperial ambassador, when Mary summoned her council before embarking on the extensive coronation festivities, she sank to her knees before them. 'She had entrusted her affairs and person, she said, to them . . .' They were taken aback by this 'humble and lowly discourse, so unlike anything ever heard before'. Unlike anything they would have heard from her father Great Harry, or even from his son.

How to crown the queen; with what rituals and festivities? With those of a king – nearly. The ceremonial was taken from the usual manual for such ceremonies, the *Liber Regalis*, but with a curious admixture of messages. Where a king would ride through the streets on the day before his coronation, Mary Tudor was carried in a litter. Tudor women habitually kept their hair bound but hers was loose, as a consort queen's would be, in token of her fertility. Mary wanted to invoke the idea that she was married to her country.

A peer deputised for her at the ceremony to create fifteen new Knights of the Bath; it was obviously inappropriate for a woman to partake in the bathing and robing rituals that marked an important stepping stone of masculine chivalry. But the next day, 1 October, Mary proceeded to Westminster Abbey, with the Earl of Arundel carrying the sword of state before her; the same military symbol that had caused such controversy at the coronation of Mary's grandmother, Isabella, some seventy years before.[2]

Mary's garments were not notably different from a king's ceremonial robes. Like any male king, she prostrated herself on the floor of Westminster Abbey, was anointed 'on the shoulders, on the breast, on the forehead and on the temples', crowned and presented with all the ceremonial regalia. But she merely touched the spurs, instead of attaching them to her heels, and while she was given the king's sceptre to hold in her right hand she also held in her left 'a sceptre wont to be given to queens, which is surmounted by doves'. A queen consort, rather than regnant, traditionally had a pacific and intercessory role.

This coronation was always going to be something of a mish-mash and not only because of the sovereign's sex. In religious terms, Mary Tudor was determined to put the clock back to where it had been before her father's break from Rome but it would take time for her changes to come into effect.

An evangelical sermon preached one week outside St Paul's

Cathedral was followed by a strongly Catholic one the next; the Catholic preacher had, amid some difficulty, to be rescued from the furious crowd. On 18 August Mary issued a proclamation that while she herself would always practise the religion 'which God and the world knoweth she hath ever professed from her infancy', because 'of her gracious disposition and clemency her highness mindeth not to compel any her said subject thereunto unto such time as further order by common consent'.

No one can have thought it was going to rest there. Indeed, Mary told one foreigner she wished to restore papal authority but that, as yet, such matters should not be spoken of publicly. In August she wrote to the pope, professing that 'his Holiness had no more loving daughter than herself'.

Elizabeth Tudor later described the relationship between queen and country as a marriage. In Mary's case the honeymoon was over almost immediately, as too was the brief community of interest between the sisters. The imperial ambassador Renard was soon reporting that Mary wanted to disbar Elizabeth from the succession because of her 'heretical opinion and illegitimacy, and characteristics in which she resembled her mother'. Anne Boleyn 'had caused great trouble in the kingdom' and Mary was all too sure Anne's daughter would do the same 'and particularly that she might imitate her mother in being a French partisan'. Queen Mary, Renard noted, 'still resents the injuries inflicted on Queen Katherine, her lady mother, by the machinations of Anne Boleyn'.

As early as September 1553, Elizabeth felt it necessary to make the first move. Begging an interview with her sister, she pleaded mere ignorance of, rather than hostility to, the Catholic faith, 'having been brought up in the creed which she professed'. She requested instructors. A few days later she attended Mary's Chapel Royal, but made sure observers noted her ostentatiously 'suffering air'. Very soon, the Venetian ambassador noted that Mary was treating her sister with fresh hostility. When Mary Tudor had parliament declare her parents' marriage valid, old wounds reopened. As for the succession, Mary must have hoped that the problem would resolve itself naturally. When Elizabeth left court in December, her absence must have been the more welcome for the fact that her sister Mary was about to marry.

Mary would declare that she had never, as a private individual, sought marriage, 'but preferred to end her days in chastity'. Nevertheless Renard, at his first private audience, told Mary that his master Charles V was conscious that 'a great part of the labour of government could with difficulty be undertaken by a woman' and advised her to choose a husband quickly. But the question of consort was seen, with good reason, as being one of the central problems for a female monarchy.

The book of Genesis gave it as part of Eve's punishment: 'thy desire shall be to thy husband, and he shall rule over thee'. The fear was that the husband of a queen regnant would be master not only of her but of her country. Indeed, a preface to *A Glasse of the Truth* (a pamphlet in which Henry VIII was widely supposed to have had a hand, supporting his repudiation of Katherine of Aragon) had declared that if a woman shall chance to rule, 'she cannot continue long without a husband, which by God's law must then be her governor and head, and so finally shall direct the realm'.[3]

Mary Tudor faced the same arguments that would later revolve around the famously vexed question of Elizabeth Tudor's marriage: the dangers of faction if she married within the realm, and the danger that England would be subjugated to a foreign power if she married out of it. But in Mary's case the clamour seemed to sound less loudly. Not only if, but who, Mary would marry was decided quickly.

In her childhood Mary Tudor had been betrothed to her cousin Charles V, but although Charles was now a widower, his health made another marriage unlikely. Charles's son Philip, his father's regent in Spain, was a widower, having made a first marriage with his cousin, the short-lived Maria of Portugal. More than a decade younger than Mary, he was as Catholic as she. This last was important: the Counter-Reformation had given a new impetus to the international Catholic community. But Protestantism, too, was now more forceful. Lutheranism looked like yesterday's creed, and 'the wolves' were coming out of Geneva, with the harsher doctrines of Calvin on their lips.

Charles V proposed Philip as Mary's husband almost before the ink was dry on the letters that announced her accession and at the end of October 1553, Mary agreed. The Venetian ambassador reported that 'Being born of a Spanish mother she was always inclined towards that nation, scorning to be English and boasting of her descent from Spain'. The imperial ambassador, Renard, was quickly established as her secret counsellor, with Mary begging him ('If it were not too much trouble for you') to come secretly to her privy rooms under cloak of darkness. Mary of Hungary had sent both the able and ingratiating Renard to speed the matter and Titian's portrait of Philip to England.

Only a fortnight after Queen Mary agreed to marry Philip of Spain, parliament presented a petition that she would reconsider and marry within the realm. Mary's reply was singular, based less on the protection of a powerful Spanish alliance than on her personal preference. 'Where private persons in such cases follow their own private tastes, sovereigns may reasonably challenge an equal liberty.' In November a deputation of MPs tried, unavailingly, to dissuade Mary from the Spanish marriage.

There were, everyone agreed, to be provisos to the match. Mary told Renard that in her private capacity she would love and obey her husband, 'but if he wished to encroach in the government of the kingdom she would be unable to permit it'. This was essentially the deal Isabella of Castile had made but it would inevitably have practical difficulties. Isabella's partnership with Ferdinand of Aragon had worked not only because of personal compatibility, but because hers was by far the larger kingdom. Here, the balance of power lay with Philip of Spain.

In France, Henri II said that once Philip was married to Mary, 'he shall be King himself, and then what councillors will or dare counsel against his King's pleasure and will?' Henri told Mary's ambassador that 'a husband may do much with his wife', and that it would be hard for a woman 'to refuse her husband anything that he shall earnestly require of her', adding that he knew marital authority to be 'very strong with ladies'.

Henri was, naturally, partisan. It was the old problem: an Anglo-Habsburg alliance was a dangerous prospect for France, which would thus be surrounded. But his opinion was shared by many. Mary's ambassador was accordingly instructed by her council to stress that 'if the marriage took place the government of the realm should always remain in her Majesty and not in the prince'. Bishop Gardiner preached that Philip 'should be rather a subject than otherwise; and that the Queen should rule all things as she doth now'.

The final terms of the marriage treaty – published in January 1554 to allay popular concern and ratified by parliament in April – stipulated that Philip could not introduce foreign office holders, nor involve England in foreign wars. If Mary died without children, he would have no further role in English affairs. Should a child be born of the marriage, it would inherit not only England but the Low Countries. (Spain would go to Don Carlos, the son of Philip's first marriage.) Terms highly advantageous to England – in theory. But the practice might be a different story, not least as Philip, when he saw the terms, made a secret but solemn vow not to consider himself bound by them.

From the start, the Spanish marriage met the deepest public hostility. When an imperial embassy arrived in London in the first days of 1554, even the schoolboys in the streets threw snowballs at the ambassadors. Within weeks came news of the so-called Wyatt rebellion – a series of coordinated risings planned to take place across the country – the aim of which was to dethrone Mary and replace her with Elizabeth. But the plot leaked in early January, and it was only Sir Thomas Wyatt himself (the son of the poet, Anne Boleyn's admirer) who, at the end of that month, marched on London with a Kentish army.

Some of Mary's own troops went over to Wyatt, rather than be ruled by 'Spaniards or strangers'. But Queen Mary showed herself to advantage in this crisis, even asking to go and fight in person. Riding to rally her troops in the City, she had, she said, been wedded to her realm at her coronation, 'the spousal ring whereof I wear here on my finger, and it never has and never shall be left off':

> I cannot tell how naturally the mother loveth the child, for I was never mother of any. But certainly, if a prince and governor may as naturally and earnestly love her subjects, as the mother doth the child, then assure yourselves that I, being your lady and mistress, do as earnestly and tenderly love and favour you.

In the same sentence, Mary figured herself as a mother and as a prince. It was the same sense of a monarch's being above sex that allowed a king to be described as a nursing father. Mary promised, furthermore, that unless both houses of parliament were content that the marriage would be for the benefit of the whole realm, 'then I will abstain from Marriage while I live'.

London stood; Wyatt surrendered his arms and was taken to the Tower. In February, Mary reluctantly consented to the execution of the girl who had so briefly been raised up to supplant her, the hapless Jane Grey. In March Elizabeth Tudor, the intended beneficiary of Wyatt's plot, was charged as an accessory and found herself a prisoner in the Tower. She must have felt she was following in her mother's footsteps, in the most horrifying way.

But she admitted nothing. Such written evidence as existed proved nothing and when Wyatt was executed on 11 April, his speech from the scaffold exonerated her completely. The terms of her imprisonment became lighter. When fresh guards appeared at the Tower early in May, she was still in a terrified state, asking whether Jane Grey's scaffold had been taken away. But the guards were there to escort her away from the Tower, to house arrest in Woodstock where, warmed by the popular support shown her on the journey, she would spend a year in comfortable captivity.

The parliament of April 1554 confirmed that the status of a ruling queen was identical with that of a king and that Mary would remain 'sole and solely queen' after her marriage. But when, at the end of July, Mary married Philip in Winchester Cathedral (the ceremonies based on those that had tied Katherine of Aragon to Prince Arthur in an earlier Anglo-Spanish alliance), the old Catholic marriage service saw her promising 'to be compliant and obedient . . . as much in mind as in body'.

Once again, however, the messages were infinitely mixed. At the feast which followed the ceremony Mary Tudor was served on gold plate and Philip of Spain on silver. But she endowed Philip with her worldly goods, while he endowed her only with his movable ones; that is, not his territories.

As Philip moved into the rooms once known as the queen's apartments, with Mary taking the king's, it seemed as if Philip and his Spanish entourage were determined to prove that the worst fears of the English would not be fulfilled and to use his position as queen's consort tactfully. On a personal level his behaviour was positively emollient.

He had been warned to 'caress' the English gentry. Two days after his marriage, he assured the council that he was there to advise but that on any question 'they must consult the Queen, and he would do his best to assist'. Mary for her part insisted that – in his advisory capacity – Philip should always be informed of the council's discussions (by a note in Spanish or Latin, since he spoke no English), and that all Council papers were to be signed by him as well as her.

Habsburg negotiators insisted that his name should precede hers on official documents: 'Philip and Mary by the grace of God King and Queen of England'. They claimed that 'no law human or divine, nor his highness's prestige and good name' would allow otherwise. A newly minted coin featured both their images, at the same height, with a single crown floating above their head. The Spanish believed that Philip would provide an element necessarily lacking in Mary's female monarchy; that he would 'make up for other matters which are impertinent to women'. But parliament would neither grant Philip a matrimonial crown nor any official authority. Philip was angered by this, although Mary seems to have understood that her people would never accept any alternative.

In the autumn of 1554 Mary, ecstatic, was convinced she was pregnant with a child who would consolidate her marriage, confirm her husband's status and ensure a Catholic future for the country. The parliament of November, however, confirmed measures to define, and limit, Philip's powers as regent should Mary die in childbirth but leave a living child. Advised by a council of peers, he could have 'rule, order and government' of child and country during the child's minority but could not call parliament, declare war or arrange the marriage of the child without the consent of the peers. It was the deal Margaret Tudor had in Scotland, effectively. Should both mother and child die, the default heir was Elizabeth. Mary herself was said to prefer Margaret Douglas (yet another woman), the child of Margaret Tudor's second marriage but perhaps that was seen as an overthrow of the natural order, on the scale of Jane Grey.

One of the matters on which Philip wished to help his wife was the full restoration of Catholicism, and of the pope's authority. That was in part the reason he stayed in the country for a full year, considerably longer than had at first been expected. But here too Mary's signals were considerably less simple than her later reputation might lead us to expect.

Mary was not the backward-looking bigot of legend. She had been raised in the humanist tradition that pushed for reform with a small r; reform from within the Catholic church. Her concern to restore the Latin service and the centrality of the Mass did not prevent her placing more emphasis on preaching, education and the importance of good works than Catholic hardliners, who stressed the transformative power of religious ceremony alone, would allow. At the end of her reign she was still encouraging plans for a new English translation of the New Testament. She employed a number of Protestants in her service and remained close to Lady Anne Bacon, a noted Protestant.

One huge sticking point was the question of church lands. Those who had profited from the dissolution of the monasteries were in no hurry to give back their booty. That also went for the Crown itself, to a degree. Here, Mary Tudor differed even from the man who became known as her chief advisor. Reginald Pole was her kinsman, with Plantagenet blood in his veins. Long exiled for his faith, he had years before, in Italy, been one of the group that hoped to bring about an accommodation between the Lutherans and the Catholic church. But by the 1550s his view had probably hardened; certainly, *spirituali* views were out of synchrony with tougher times. Pole insisted, from abroad, that all ecclesiastical property should be returned and that parliament should instantly restore papal supremacy. Mary understood that this was a political impossibility. Not until November 1554 was Pole was allowed to return to England as papal legate, and by this time, it was possible for a prayer for the pope to be included in parliament's opening ceremonies.

When Pole attended the court ceremonies which celebrated the country's return to the Catholic fold, he made a speech praising Philip as a king of 'great might, armour and force' and spoke of how miraculously God had preserved 'a virgin, helpless, naked and unarmed': Mary. A few days later, at St Paul's, Bishop Gardiner preached a sermon with an interesting view on the same theme. 'When King Henry was head perhaps there was something to be said for it, but what a head was Edward . . . Nor could the Queen, being a woman, be head of the Church . . .' Women were openly assuming rule as never before; women were finding themselves at the forefront of opposing sides of the religious divide. But the two positions did not necessarily agree.

'not one year of rest'

Scotland, the Netherlands, 1554–58

A s Mary Tudor came to the throne, two other women – Marie de Guise and Mary of Hungary – occupied positions of power in western Europe. Neither, however, was finding her position easy.

Inevitably, the effects of Mary Tudor's accession and marriage were felt north of England's border. Marie de Guise wrote politely to the new English queen, expressing the hope for a continued peace, and Mary Tudor answered in kind. But that was far from the whole story. They shared a Christian name and a faith but in terms of the great power struggle of Europe, their allegiances were very different: Marie's to France and Mary's to the Spanish Habsburg family.

While Marie de Guise tried to steal support away from the governor of Scotland, Arran, and sought to recruit a powerful Scottish noble – the Earl of Lennox – to her side, Mary Tudor's government was urging Lennox to double-cross her: to 'secretly enter into communication with the Regent [Arran] against the Dowager, with a view not only to driving her from the country, but to making himself King if possible and throwing Scottish affairs into confusion'. So much for the sisterhood of queens.

Marie was to be the winner. In December 1553 she sent an envoy to the French court to discuss the Scottish situation. France needed to ensure that Scotland was ruled by an ally more secure than the ever-uncertain Arran. The result was that increasing pressure was placed on Arran to resign and cede the regency to Marie and on 19 February 1554 he signed an agreement to do so.

There were questions, also, as to the precise status and household of Mary, Queen of Scots in France, as she entered her teenage years. Marie's brother, Cardinal de Guise, proposed that at just eleven (considerably younger than the usual age) she should be declared of age and 'take up her rights', including the right to appoint her own deputy; her mother, naturally.

On 12 April 1554 Marie de Guise proceeded up from the palace of Holyrood to the Tolbooth, there to be solemnly invested with the Honours of Scotland: the sword, the sceptre, and the crown. In France, the young Mary, Queen of Scots wrote a neat showpiece letter to Queen Mary of England: 'May it please God, there shall be a perpetual memory that there were two Queens in this Isle at the same time, as united in inviolate amity as they are in blood and near lineage'. In Scotland, Marie de Guise, now officially her daughter's alter ego and Queen Regent of Scotland, rode back to Holyrood accompanied by all the accoutrements of male authority.

Significantly, the French ambassador, the Sieur d'Oysel, King Henri's representative, performed the ceremony. One of Marie's first acts – replacing Arran's choices with her own, mostly French, appointments – was to make d'Oysel lieutenant-governor. Once again a royal wife had to juggle the demands of her natal and her marital country; once again she saw them as identical. Once again, her Scots subjects would disagree.

Marie's concerns were to restore royal authority to a faction-ridden country, centralise government and improve the administration of justice (though she complained that Scotsmen, convinced the old ways were best, 'would not endure it'). As Marie would later write to her brother, Cardinal de Guise in France:

> It is no small thing to bring a young nation to a state of perfection and to an unwonted subservience to those who wish to see justice reign . . . I can safely say that for twenty years past I have not had one year of rest, and I think that if I should say one month I should not be far wrong for a troubled spirit is the greatest trial of all . . .

In 1555, on much the same note, another woman resigned her post. Recent years had been hard for Mary of Hungary, the regent of the

Netherlands, forced increasingly to act as amanuensis to her depressed and ailing brother Charles V, who was planning to set aside his titles and responsibilities and retire to a religious life. Mary had to assist him in his struggles to determine how best to bequeath his immense lands and to attempt to heal the breach this issue was making within the Habsburg family.[1]

Knowing that their widowed sister Eleanor, the dowager Queen of France, would join Charles in his retirement, Mary of Hungary was determined to make a third. Once, familial duty (to which she and Eleanor both subscribed) had seen them placed on opposite sides of Europe's great political divide. But now sisterhood trumped politics at last. Mary had asked to resign her position before but now she argued her case in an extraordinary letter:

> ... it is impossible for a woman in peacetime, and even more in time of war, to do her duty as regent towards God, her sovereign, and her own sense of honour. For in peacetime it is unavoidable, in addition to all the meetings and cares of daily affairs which any government brings with it, that whoever guides the government of these provinces must mix with as many people as possible, in order to win the sympathy of both nobility and middle classes ... For a woman, especially if she is a widow, it is not feasible to mix thus freely with people. Of necessity I myself have had to do more in this respect than I really wanted. Moreover, a woman is never so much respected and feared as a man, whatever her position.

> If one is conducting the government of these countries in time of war, and one cannot in person enter the battle, one is faced with an insoluble problem. One receives all the blows and is blamed for all mistakes made by others ...

It was a theme to which she would return: that 'as a woman I was compelled to leave the conduct of war to others'. It was one other female rulers knew.[2]

Mary of Hungary: 'a woman of fifty who has served for at least twenty-four years', she wrote, and served, moreover, 'one God and one master', was finally allowed to have her way. Her brother was retiring and to serve his son, Philip, would be to find herself 'learning my ABC all over again'. Philip of Spain had been slow to visit his Netherlands territories and Mary had already written to him tartly: 'Anything is better than to wait until your lands are lost to you, one by one . . .'

The ceremony by which, on 25 October, Mary quit her post and Philip took possession of the Netherlands, was emotive. Mary told the Estates General, with which she had so often been at odds that:

> if my capacities, my knowledge, and my powers had been equal to the good will, the love and the devotion with which I have given myself to this office, I know for certain that no ruler could have been better served and no land better governed than you.

Preparing to leave the country she had governed for almost a quarter of a century, Mary of Hungary made her will. She concluded by requesting, with unexpected softness, that a certain gold heart that she wore, which had been left her by her long-dead husband, should be melted down and the proceeds given to the poor. It had been worn by two people who 'though parted for a long time in body have never been so in love and affection', so it was fitting that on her death 'it should be consumed and change its nature as the bodies of these lovers have done'.

The following autumn Mary travelled to Castile with her siblings (not without qualms, since Spain was foreign territory to her), but only eighteen months later, in February 1558, Eleanor died, leaving her lonely. Bereft, and despite her conflicted feelings about the responsibilities of public life, Mary sought to find herself another role as advisor to her niece Juana, Philip's sister, who was acting as regent of Spain while he was in the north. But Juana rejected Mary's offer with some coldness, saying, probably with truth, that Mary's character would make it impossible for her to take the back seat.[3]

Charles V and Philip sought to persuade Mary of Hungary to resume the regency of the Netherlands. 'Explain to her what a support her presence will mean', Philip wrote to an intermediary. 'Finally, offer her a large income and great authority, and give her hope there will be peace, and that this will last a long time, as the rulers are all exhausted.' Mary's reluctant agreement was rendered irrelevant by her own death, eight months after her sister's.

33

Sisters and rivals

England, 1555–1558

MARY OF HUNGARY died on 18 October 1558. By that time, in England, another and far from reluctant woman was preparing to assume power. The second half of Mary Tudor's reign was in some sense a battle between Mary and her sister Elizabeth – between Catholic and Protestant – and it was far from clear who would win.

In the spring of 1555 Elizabeth Tudor was summoned from her imprisonment at Woodstock to Hampton Court, where her sister Mary triumphantly awaited the child who would sweep Elizabeth from the succession. There were rumours at the end of April that the queen had been delivered of a son, The bells rang out in joy. But it was a miscarriage – or worse, a mistake, a phantom pregnancy. Early in May the French ambassador heard that all the thirty-nine-year-old queen's symptoms had been the result of 'some woeful malady'.

Mary Tudor's mistake has been used to the detriment of her reputation; a sign of her obsessive personality, even a cause of comedy. But it would be fairer to blame the medical knowledge of the sixteenth century. Mary herself had only slowly been convinced by her doctors that she was pregnant – just as her mother Katherine had been convinced, on the occasion of her first miscarriage, that she was still carrying another baby.

Through May, June and July Mary waited in her birthing suite, quietly emerging in August to hear that her husband Philip of Spain was going away. The Habsburg Empire was once again at war with

France, and Philip was to assume his father's duties. As emperor Charles V resigned to Philip first the lordship of the Netherlands and then the two Spanish crowns of Castile and Aragon, he sent a message of congratulation to Mary on 'being able for the future to style herself the Queen of many and great crowns, and on her being no less their mistress than of her own crown of England'. But this was to make no distinction between the role of a queen regnant and of a consort.

It was beginning to look likely that Mary Tudor would die childless, which left the succession in jeopardy. Ironically Elizabeth (heretic though she may be) was, from Spain's viewpoint, a better candidate than the French-dominated Mary, Queen of Scots. A female could, after all – her brother Edward's point – be safely married to a Catholic prince and converted that way.

In November 1556 Elizabeth Tudor was invited to the court for Christmas but by the first week of December she was on her way back to Hatfield. She had almost certainly been instructed to marry a suitor of her brother-in-law Philip's choosing: the titular Duke of Savoy, cousin-by-marriage to Philip of Spain, whose dukedom, however, had been seized by the French in 1536.

Elizabeth seems swiftly to have refused. She never met the two Habsburg relatives (his cousin Christina of Denmark and his illegitimate half-sister Margaret, the Duchess of Parma), whom Philip sent over to persuade her. Christina, after her refusal to marry Henry VIII, and despite being in love with another man, had in 1541 been married off by her uncle Charles V to the heir to the duchy of Lorraine. Her husband had died early, however, and though Christina was regent for their young son, in 1552 the French had invaded Lorraine, taking the boy back to be brought up at the French court and causing Christina to flee back to the Netherlands and her aunt Mary of Hungary's protection.

Philip saw Elizabeth as a valuable pawn in Habsburg policy and his protection would shield Elizabeth for the rest of her sister's reign. That protection was increasingly needed. Whether or not Mary believed the failure of her pregnancy was a sign of God's displeasure, a sign that her country had to be cleansed, the fires of Smithfield, where heretics were burnt at the stake, have nevertheless defined 'Bloody' Mary's posthumous reputation.

It was the Protestants who had the chance to write the history but the facts cannot be denied. The reigns of the Protestant Edward and Elizabeth each saw two heretics burnt (although others died for other religion-related crimes, including some two hundred Catholic priests or sympathisers under Elizabeth). Mary burnt almost three hundred. Mary's initial instruction had been that the penalty should be exacted 'without rashness', but that obdurate heretics who refused to recant should die was an all but universal tenet. The former Archbishop of Canterbury, Cranmer, who himself famously died in Mary's fire, had prepared measures, at the end of Edward's reign, to punish obstinate Catholics in the same way.

The first man died in the fires on 1 February 1555. Some fifty women perished too, including the nightmare of the pregnant woman in the Channel Isles who gave birth at the stake only to have her baby flung back into the flames.

The crunch for Mary (as for Elizabeth) may have been the question of conformity to the law. Unfortunately Calvin was at this moment urging true believers to declare their beliefs openly. There was also a political element to the story: some who claimed to act for the Protestant cause had found an unlikely ally in Catholic France.

At the start of her reign Mary refused to accept that the interests of France and of the Habsburg Empire could never agree for long. Like the ladies of an earlier generation she had, within weeks of her accession, offered herself as a mediator. The French responded derisively but a year later, in 1554, Mary had by no means abandoned the idea; early in 1555 the French ambassador de Noailles believed her health had even been improved by hopes of a European peace. But when France and the Habsburgs finally agreed a short-lived truce in February 1556, Mary had played no role in the discussions, and now France was active in support of rebellion against Mary.

By the autumn of 1556 France and the Habsburgs were once again at war, with a French army attacking the Netherlands. By March 1557 Philip had urgent reason to seek English support. He arrived at Greenwich on 19 March, to resume his marital duties and to persuade England into the war. Parliament and council had long opposed Mary's desire to send troops and money to her husband's fight; something the terms of the marriage treaty had been designed to prevent. But French support for yet another minor rebellion in England helped to change the minds of the English government: a support so ill-timed that it has been suggested the whole thing was the work of Spanish agent provocateurs.

War against France, at this point, was war against the pope. Small wonder that the French ambassador commented that a distraught Mary was on the eve 'of bankrupting either her own mind or her kingdom'. But some of the rhetoric of war was interesting. Thomas Stafford, the rebel leader, used as justification for his act the theory that Mary had broken the terms of her father's will by marrying without the declared consent of the councillors Henry had appointed for the under-age Edward. (Absurd but noteworthy, in that it was not a charge ever likely to be levelled against a male monarch.) Mary, speaking to her council 'expounded to them the obedience which she owed her husband and the power which he had over her as much by divine as by human law'.

In June a herald was sent to the French court, to – literally – throw down the gauntlet. Henri II dismissively declared that:

> as the herald came in the name of a woman it was unnecessary for him to listen to anything further, as he would have done had he come in the name of a man to whom he would have replied in detail . . . 'Consider how I stand when a woman sends to defy me to war.'

But Philip was able to send to France a six-thousand-strong English army. He himself sailed from Dover on 6 July, never to return. The siege of Saint-Quentin was considered a notable Anglo-Spanish victory but the campaign went sour when, in January 1558, the French took Calais. England's last remaining continental outpost had been in her possession for two centuries and its loss was a humiliation for England abroad, and a personal failure for Mary. The Protestant martyrologist John Foxe reported that, in her unhappy latter days, she told her trusted lady, Susan Clarencius, that although she regretted the absence of her husband Philip, it was Calais the embalmers would find engraved upon her heart.

It was another lesson, and one Elizabeth Tudor was surely learning, that war was an evil to be avoided at all costs: a reason to be wary of foreign alliances, and foreign allies.

*   *   *

In January 1558 Mary once again informed her husband that his last visit had left her pregnant. He expressed proper delight but probably few this time thought it anything other than a phantom pregnancy. By April Mary knew she had been mistaken; and everyone knew her half-sister Elizabeth was likely to be her heir. The Venetian ambassador had written the year before that 'all eyes and hearts' were turned towards Elizabeth as Mary's successor, and that she or her people were found behind every plot. When in the late summer of 1558 it became clear that Mary was very ill, Elizabeth had a network waiting.

At forty-two, Mary Tudor had endured a lifetime of difficult health, often beset by stress-related problems; something that was true of many of the women in the latter half of this story. In early October the queen's condition worsened and on 28 October Mary added a codicil to her will. If she continued to have no 'fruit nor heir of my body', she would be followed by 'my next heir and successor by the Laws and Statutes of this realm': Elizabeth.

Philip's special ambassador, De Feria, rushed to Hatfield, where he found Elizabeth impatiently waiting. Wanting Elizabeth to acknowledge her debt to Philip and Spain, he instead heard her declare that the affection of the people would bring her to the throne; an affection Mary had lost 'because she had married a foreigner'. De Feria warned that 'she is determined to be governed by no one'. And so it would prove.

In the early morning of 17 November, Mary Tudor slipped quietly away. The blame game would quickly take over her memory. By 1588, the Protestant exile, Bartholomew Traheron, could write that she was 'spiteful, cruel, bloody, wilful, furious, guileful, stuffed with painted processes, with simulation and dissimulation, devoid of honesty, devoid of upright dealing, devoid of all seemly virtues'. Five years after Mary's death, in his *Book of Martyrs*, John Foxe would have his say.

The Venetian ambassador Michieli had written of Mary Tudor that:

in certain things she is singular and without an equal; for not only is she brave and valiant unlike other timid and spiritless women, but so courageous and resolute, that neither in adversity nor peril did she ever display or commit any act of cowardice or pusillanimity, maintaining always, on the contrary, a wonderful grandeur and dignity . . .

But his description was coloured by the fact he believed her sex 'cannot becomingly take more than a moderate part in government'.

The gynocracy debate had, moreover, just seen its most famous contribution. In the spring of 1558 the Scottish reformer John Knox published his *First Blast of the Trumpet against the Monstrous Regiment of Women*, claiming that to put a crown on a woman's head was as inappropriate 'as to put a saddle upon the back of an unruly cow': 'the subversion of good order, of all equity and justice'. It was, he wrote, 'a thing most repugnant to nature that women rule and govern over men'.[1]

Women in general, Knox declared, were 'weak, frail, impatient, feeble and foolish: and experience hath declared them to be inconstant, variable, cruel and lacking the spirit of counsel and regiment'. Mary Tudor was the 'horrible monster Jezebel'. Nor was Knox's the only voice; other writers, such as Christopher Goodman, Anthony Gilby and Thomas Becon, likewise linked their attacks on Mary's Catholicism with her sex.

But facts speak louder than words and the fact was that Mary Tudor had ruled England with a successful assumption of authority. As John Aylmer wrote in his 1559 refutation of John Knox (*An Harborowe for Faithfull and Trewe Subjectes, agaynst the Late Blowne Blaste, concerninge the Government of Wemen*): 'it is not in England so dangerous a matter to have a woman ruler as men take it to be'. Mary Tudor, granddaughter of Isabella of Castile, had proved it was a possibility. That was her legacy, her gift to the women who came after her. Although she never wanted it to be her Tudor half-sister Elizabeth, who would benefit most immediately.

34

'if God is with us'

France, 1558–1560

As MARY TUDOR died and Elizabeth Tudor came to the throne, in France the three women who would one day be called upon to take charge of a realm still saw their future as subsumed in a husband's authority. But Europe's religious divides already underpinned the fabric of their lives, whether or not the process was plain to see.

In April 1558, the fifteen-year-old Mary Stuart achieved the destiny for which she had been reared: marriage with François, the fourteen-year-old French dauphin. The recapture of Calais was a victory led by Mary's Guise family and this was their reward. The ceremonies were spectacular, albeit that Mary's vivid white-clad beauty showed up her new husband's puny frailty.[1]

'These nuptials really were considered the most regal and triumphant of any that have been witnessed in this kingdom for many years', wrote the Venetian ambassador, 'from the pomp and richness of the jewels and apparel both of the lords and ladies; or from the grandeur of the banquet and stately service of the table, or from the costly devices of the masquerades and similar revels'.

At the state banquet that followed the ceremony, six clockwork-powered mechanical ships with silver masts sailed over the billowing cloth waves of a painted sea. Each was captained by a royal man, who invited aboard the lady of his choice. King Henri II chose Mary herself and the dauphin his mother, Catherine de Medici. Marie de Guise, unable to leave Scotland to be present at the ceremony, appointed her mother to represent her in the negotiations. But the important deal was the one made behind the scenes.

The official marriage treaty (like those of Mary Tudor and of Isabella of Castile before her) carefully preserved the independence of the Scottish nation. But under the instruction of her Guise uncles the fifteen-year-old queen had some days earlier signed another, secret, treaty by which Scotland, should she die childless, would become the property of France. Would Elizabeth Tudor, even at fifteen, have signed away her country so blithely?

François would now be called the King Dauphin. Even more problematic, at the end of the year after Mary Tudor died in England, was the decision to blazon the heraldic arms of England together with those of France and Scotland on all Mary Stuart and François's goods. It was a clear declaration that France did not recognise the Protestant Elizabeth – a bastard, to Catholics – as queen. Instead they saw Mary Stuart, Henry VII's true-born great-granddaughter, as Mary Tudor's heir. By the following summer, ushers were calling out to 'make way for the Queen of England' as Mary Stuart went to chapel.

In fact, where the French government was concerned, cooler diplomatic counsels would prevail, and they soon were dealing with Elizabeth Tudor as England's queen. But between the two royal kinswomen, the question of Mary Stuart's rights to the English throne continued to be an issue until their dying days.

Catherine de Medici's star continued to rise through the 1550s. When Henri II backed Catherine's claim to inheritance in Tuscany, the Venetian ambassador Michele Soranzo wrote that 'the Queen will have all the merit should Florence be liberated'. (The same man also wrote that she was 'loved by all'.) When northern France was itself invaded in 1557, Catherine – once again regent while Henri pursued France's war with Philip of Spain – did much to calm the people of Paris and persuade them to give Henri men and money.

But Europe was growing tired of war, and the vital peace that was negotiated at the end of the decade would have another woman's fingerprints all over it. Christina of Denmark, the widowed Duchess of Lorraine (and one of the nieces Mary of Hungary raised) had, she claimed, for several years been trying to bring about a peace between the two great powers. She had felt the effects of the conflict at first hand; suspected in Lorraine because of her Habsburg connection and then forced into exile as a result of French action. In October 1558 she wrote to her cousin, Philip of Spain, that she was happy to act as mediator in any peace negotiations, but that he must provide for her safety 'not only because I am a woman, but because, as you know, I am not in the good graces of the French'.

The talks begun that autumn had to be halted, not least because of the need to mark Charles V's funeral and the deaths of Mary of Hungary and Mary Tudor. But in the spring of 1559, shortly after Christine's son the young Duke of Lorraine was married to the French king's daughter Claude, they began again in the small town of Cateau-Cambrésis, some twenty kilometres from Cambrai, where three decades earlier Margaret of Austria and Louise of Savoy had negotiated the Ladies' Peace. As her kinsman and representative Baron Howard of Effingham wrote to Elizabeth Tudor: 'the assembly hath been entirely procured by the Duchess's labour and travail . . . and she is continually present at all meetings and communications'.

Christina of Denmark sat at the head of the table, the French on her left, the Spanish opposite her and the English on her right. Just as at Cambrai all those years ago, the talks almost stalled several times, with Christina catching the ambassadors at the very door to prevent them walking out. As the Venetian Tiepolo wrote: 'The Duchess, regardless of personal fatigue, went to and fro between the Commissioners, with the greatest zeal, ardour, and charity, imploring them to come together again.' In April, finally, a deal was agreed.

The Treaty of Cateau-Cambrésis brought an end to decades of the Italian Wars. France essentially agreed to abandon its historic claims in the peninsula. This was greatly to Spain's favour but there was a downside to the agreement for Habsburg interest as a whole, since the concessions made to France cut the Holy Roman Empire off from Spain. Nevertheless, Spain itself emerged stronger.

Christina wrote to the French king that, 'I feel the utmost satisfaction in having been able to bring about so excellent an arrangement, and one which cannot fail to prove a great boon to Christendom.' She returned to the Netherlands a heroine; a worthy 'daughter' to Margaret of Austria, and Mary of Hungary, surely?

Ironically, it was probably her very roots in the Netherlands, her independent popularity in that country that, in Philip's eyes, militated against her gaining its regency; the post which had been up for grabs since Mary of Hungary's retirement, and which would instead be given to Margaret of Parma in June. Christina of Denmark spent the next nineteen years as advisor to her son in Lorraine, and a dozen more in a fiefdom of her own in Italy, never ceasing to keep a wary eye out for undue pressure being placed on either territory by either Philip of Spain or France, in the person of Catherine de Medici.[2]

The Treaty of Cateau-Cambrésis saw Catherine de Medici and Henri II's eldest daughter, the thirteen-year-old Elizabeth de Valois, promised in marriage to Philip of Spain (and the French king's sister Marguerite to the Duke of Savoy). But indirectly, the treaty would soon bring tragedy to the French royal family.

In the summer of 1559, at a joust to celebrate his daughter's marriage to Philip, his opponent's lance struck Henri II in the face. His visor shattered, a splinter entered his eye, and after nine days of agony, he died.

It was, unquestionably, a personal tragedy for Catherine de Medici. The perceptive Venetian ambassador had noted that 'more than anyone else she loves the King'. But arguably it was also an opportunity, or to put it more kindly, a challenge to which she dared not fail to rise. Had not Anne de Beaujeu, holding the throne for another boy-king of France half a century before, singled out widowhood as the time of a powerful woman's greatest responsibility – and autonomy?

The new king, Catherine de Medici's eldest son François II, was a sickly teenager, susceptible to influence. But Catherine's was not the only voice in his ear and in the first days of her son's reign she could take a seat at the table of power only by allying herself with the new Queen Mary's Guise family. As the Guises moved swiftly to take possession of the fifteen-year-old king, Catherine abandoned her husband's body to join them. Her presence lent them legitimacy; others who might have hoped to seize a measure of power, notably the Guises' great rival, the Constable of France, Montmorency, were left lamenting.

Once installed in the Louvre, Catherine de Medici allowed herself to relapse into the mourning seclusion expected of a French queen dowager. Her daughter-in-law Mary frequently joined her in her black silk-shrouded apartments. In a letter to her 'true friend, good sister and cousin' Elizabeth of England, Catherine wrote that her loss was 'so recent and so dreadful and brings such pain, regret and despair that we have need of God, who has visited us with this affliction, to give us the power to endure it'. A visitor described her as so 'wept out' as to bring tears to their own eyes.

Under Guise influence, the new king told Montmorency that he was 'anxious to solace thine old age'; effectively, that he was being pensioned off. Jeanne d'Albret's husband Antoine de Bourbon would, as first Prince of the Blood, have expected to head a regency council, but he too found himself sidelined, to the point where Catherine de Medici commented he was 'reduced to the position of a chambermaid'. Catherine herself, by contrast, got a speedy and lavish financial settlement. The title she claimed for herself – Queen Mother, rather than the conventional Dowager Queen – showed clearly that she considered her part to be about the future, not the past.

Although the English ambassador Sir Nicholas Throckmorton declared, in the first days after Henri II's death, that the 'House of Guise ruleth', a fortnight later he opined that Catherine had 'though not in name, yet in deed and in effect th'authority of Regent'. From the early days of her son's reign, his official acts opened with the words: 'This being the good pleasure of the Queen, my lady-mother, and I also approving of every opinion that she holdeth, am content and command that . . .' The challenges facing France – faction, the terrible debt caused by Henri's wars, and religious controversy – were enough to employ the talents of all François's possible advisors.

By now, Protestantism had reached its tentacles into every level of French society. Within a few years as many as two million people worshipped in a thousand congregations, while two of Constable Montmorency's nephews had converted, including notably (a name that would resound later in French history) Gaspard, Admiral de Coligny. King Henri II had taken a hard line against the dissidents but now it was not so easy.

The new faith was gaining a particular hold in the southwest and in the territories of Navarre and Béarn. The seeds were also sown (in France as in the British Isles) of a clash of two ruling women, Catherine de Medici and Jeanne d'Albret, one on either side of the religious divide.

In 1555 another female ruler had ascended a throne on France's southern borders. The first half of the 1550s saw Jeanne d'Albret, heiress of

Navarre, as a wife and a mother, her first child having been born in 1551. Sadly that son died just before his second birthday, but by that time Jeanne was pregnant again. Henri was born on 14 December 1553, in the family seat of Pau. The family legend surrounding his birth said Jeanne d'Albret's father promised to hand over a will in her favour if she sang, while giving birth, a local song to the Virgin, and if her baby were born without a cry. His conditions being fulfilled, he handed over the will but took the baby, saying 'That is for you, my girl, but this is for me.' When Jeanne was born a girl, the Spanish sneered that the 'the bull has sired a lamb'. Showing the baby to the people, 'The lamb has given birth to a lion!' he proclaimed triumphantly.

Jeanne's marriage to Antoine de Bourbon was a loving one, troubled only by Jeanne's insecurities. Antoine's letters are full of reassurance and perhaps a touch of exasperation: '. . . no husband ever loved a wife as I love you. I hope, my dear, that in time you will realise it, more than you have up to now.' She should rid herself of her fears concerning both his safety and his fidelity: 'I am saving everything I have for my spouse, praying her to do the same.' On another occasion he wrote that, 'I have offended neither God nor you, and have no desire to begin now. I am surrounded by trotting horses every day, I feel fine and feel no need for a mare . . .'[3]

Her father's death in the spring of 1555 made her Jeanne III. Antoine's letter to Jeanne during what proved to be her father's last illness breathes warmth, if also a clear measure of apprehension: 'I fear that your nature will cause you to *faire une démonstration* [to make a fuss] and I beg you to keep calm. I assure you that [if need be] you have a husband who will be father, mother, brother and husband to you.'

Jeanne d'Albret's marriage to Antoine – a prince expected to rule on her behalf – might well have been seen as one way to circumvent the anomaly of female rule. This was how things had worked for the country's first reigning queens, for Navarre did have some tradition of female sovereignty, even before the troubled reign of Jeanne's grandmother Catherine de Foix. But the equation worked out differently. Jeanne instructed the Estates of Béarn that she wished to rule jointly with her husband, since 'if she, who was their Queen and sovereign lady, regarded him as her lord, they should do the same, because the husband is lord of the person and property of his wife'.

By contrast, the Estates (who had to ratify by vote the selection of a new sovereign) declared that Jeanne was their 'true and natural Lady', while her husband, by their law, had only stewardship of her goods. It took them five days of debate to give in and accept a joint sovereignty. The ceremony that crowned her Jeanne III was based on that of Jeanne II and her husband in 1329.[4] The marriage remained a devoted one. 'You say you want to wear a coiffe next summer and I think you could not do better, it became you very well last year. I am sending by the bearer a golden chain', Antoine wrote.

Jeanne tried to smooth over concerns at the French court that Antoine (through the ubiquitous Descurra, the spy who had reported on Jeanne's first, Cleves, marriage) was intriguing with the emperor over the restoration of the part of Navarre that Spain had annexed, just as her mother Marguerite of Navarre tried to smooth over her husband's intrigues. Antoine was as desperate to do the deal as his father-in-law had been, but the Habsburgs played him in the same way. Finally, he began looking for another source of support and found it in the Protestant faction.

It is now impossible to be sure whether Jeanne or her husband first began the move towards Protestantism. It was Antoine, at this stage, who conducted the correspondence with Calvin, Antoine to whom the French Protestant (or 'Huguenot') community looked. Brantôme famously wrote of Jeanne that she 'loved a dance more than a sermon', and that he had heard 'on good authority' she reproached Antoine for his interest, saying that 'if he wanted to ruin himself she did not wish to lose her possessions'.

But some Protestant contemporaries were already thinking of Jeanne. On 19 July 1559 the new Queen Elizabeth of England (prompted by her minister William Cecil) wrote to both King and Queen of Navarre. To Antoine, she expressed herself 'anxious to please and serve'. To Jeanne her tone is at once more encouraging, and more that of one beleaguered sister addressing another: '*si Deus nobiscum quis contra nos?*' (If God is with us, who can be against us?) Elizabeth was anxious to have the pleasure of Jeanne's acquaintance but since distance did not permit that, it would have to be done in spirit and goodwill, honouring Jeanne 'not only for [your] rank in the world but even more for the true profession and sincerity of your Christian religion, in which [I] pray the Creator may keep [you] by His grace, and that [you] may continue a supporter of His Holy Word'. Religion was making bonds between powerful women, just as it would ultimately divide them.

35

'maidenly estate'

England, 1558 –1560

ELIZABETH TUDOR'S SEX, as well as her Protestant religion,
set the terms of her rule from the first; a perceived weakness that the 'Virgin Queen' would manage to make a
strength.

On the one hand, the long game she played, dangling the tantalis-
ing possibility of her hand in marriage, would prove to be one of the
best tools of her diplomacy. On the other, like other reigning queens,
Elizabeth did not present herself as a woman when it suited her not
to. The doctrine of the monarch's two bodies had been implicit at her
sister Mary's funeral, when the Bishop of Winchester described her
as: 'a Queen, and by the same title a King also' but the idea had its
clearest expression in Elizabeth's reign. Just three days after her
sister's death she told parliament: 'I am but one body naturally
considered though by [God's] permission a body politic to govern . . .'
A few years later (in relation to an obscure piece of property dealing), her lawyers spelled it out for her. A monarch, they said, was
'utterly devoid of Infancy, old Age, and natural Deformities or
Imbecilities, which the Body natural is subject to'. Including mortal-
ity and, presumably, femininity.

The very ideal of government – 'the king counselled' – gained added
impetus from the ruler being a woman. Even the supportive John
Aylmer wrote in his refutation of John Knox's tirade against women
rulers that Elizabeth's sex mattered the less because England was not 'a
mere monarchy', nor yet a mere oligarchy or democracy, but 'a rule

mixt of all three'. In other words, that Elizabeth's sex did not matter, because she was not that powerful, anyway.*

Knox's work, originally written to take aim at the Catholic rulers Mary Tudor and Marie de Guise, was now, all too obviously, potentially a slur on the Protestant Elizabeth. John Calvin wrote a private letter to William Cecil, in which he admitted he and Knox had discussed the problem. Calvin's feeling was that a female sovereign was 'a deviation from the original and proper order of nature ... to be ranked no less than slavery'. But there was, Calvin admitted, the biblical Deborah and also the idea derived from the prophet Isaiah that 'Queens should be nursing mothers of the church'. The idea Knox, and others, now employed was to figure Elizabeth as a reincarnation of Deborah; an 'extraordinary' woman, exempted from the 'proper order of nature' only by the 'special providence' of God.

It was assumed from the first that Elizabeth would, for better or worse, soon be sharing her authority with a husband. On 21 November 1558, within four days of the old queen's death, the Spanish ambassador De Feria wrote to King Philip that 'everything depends upon the husband this woman may take'. Meanwhile, every decision made was, in a sense, provisional. Even Elizabeth's mainstay William Cecil could in these early days be found reproaching a messenger for having taken papers directly to the queen, as 'a matter of such weight being too much for a woman's knowledge'. Cecil would be only one of the influential voices urging now and later that a husband was her and the realm's 'only known and likely surety': 'God send our mistress a husband, and by him a son, that we may hope our posterity shall have a masculine succession'. At the time, it still seemed likely.

Both Elizabeth and 'her people', De Feria warned, 'will listen to any ambassadors who may come to treat of marriage'. Three weeks later, on 14 December: 'Everybody thinks that she will not marry a foreigner, and they cannot make out whom she favours, so that every day some new cry is raised about a husband'. As well as Philip of Spain himself (reluctant but resigned), there was the persistent Eric of Sweden.

---

* Aylmer's treatise memorably contrasted Elizabeth with the bulk of womankind: 'fond, foolish, wanton, flibbergibs ... in every way doltified with the dregs of the devil's dunghill'.

Charles V's brother Ferdinand, the Holy Roman Emperor, offered one of his younger sons; Scotland proposed the Earl of Arran. Home-grown candidates included the Earl of Arundel, Sir William Pickering and of course the perennial frontrunner (as the next two decades would continue to prove him) Elizabeth's Master of Horse, Robert Dudley.

Certainly it was assumed that she must and would marry someone. There was, Elizabeth Tudor herself observed, 'a strong idea in the world that a woman cannot live unless she is married'. The Holy Roman Emperor's envoy agreed that she should ('as is woman's way') be eager 'to marry and be provided for. For that she should wish to remain a maid and never marry is inconceivable'. She herself would say that 'I have already joined myself to an husband in marriage, namely the kingdom of England'. It was the rhetoric her sister had used but Elizabeth would prove to take it more seriously.

The example of Mary Tudor offered Elizabeth a dreadful warning, just as, later, would Mary Stuart. Any marriage of a queen regnant offered an insuperable problem: whose would be the mastery? Elizabeth Tudor wrote hastily to fellow sovereigns on her accession to explain that she would not necessarily continue the quarrels of her sister's day. Then, 'nothing was done on the part of England but with the privity and direction of the Ministers of the said King [Philip]', Mary's husband. The unmarried Elizabeth, by contrast, was 'a free princess'.

John Aylmer tried to argue:

> Say you, God hath appointed her to be the subject to her husband . . . therefore she may not be the head. I grant that, so far as pertaining to the bands of marriage, and the offices of a wife, she must be a subject: but as a Magistrate she may be her husband's head.

She could be his inferior in 'matters of wedlock' and yet his leader in 'the guiding of the commonwealth', he claimed. But such a distinction would be almost impossible to make in practical terms.

On 4 February 1559, parliament drafted a petition urging Elizabeth to marry quickly, to ensure the succession. If she should remain 'unmarried and, as it were, a vestal virgin' it would be 'contrary to public respects'. She answered that 'from my years of understanding' – since she first was old enough to understand herself a servant of God – 'I haply chose this kind of life in which I yet live, which I assure you for mine own part hath hitherto best contented myself and I trust hath been most acceptable to God'. In the end, she said, 'this shall be for me sufficient: that a marble stone shall declare that a queen, having reigned such a time, lived and died a virgin'.

Where other powerful women accepted their coding within the usual social framework, as surrogates for or in at least some ways subordinate to a man, the unmarried Elizabeth Tudor challenged preconceptions to an almost unprecedented degree; Isabella of Castile being, ironically, the great exception to that rule. Perhaps it was in part her controversial position as an unmarried, Protestant, queen regnant, however, that drew Elizabeth towards a centuries-old established image, albeit one so central to the Catholic church: virginity.

Virginity – chastity – had in both ancient and medieval times been seen as offering entry into what was almost a third sex. Its importance was confirmed by St Augustine and St Jerome, by the whole monastic convention, and by early modern writers from Malory, stressing the (male) chastity of the *Morte d'Arthur,* to Petruccio Ubaldini, whom Elizabeth patronised and whose book on six celebrated women included an early female warrior queen whose virginity, like Samson's hair, was crucial to her military success. Medieval Scandinavia likewise had tales of maiden-kings who dressed as men and successfully led armies, until finally overcome by the man they would marry.

Elizabeth Tudor seemed to subscribe to this view of virginity, later writing to Ivan the Terrible (who had dared suggest that 'there be other men that do rule in England' while 'you flow in your maidenly estate like a maid') that 'we rule ourselves with the honour befitting a virgin queen appointed by God'. Not until later in Elizabeth's reign did her status as the virgin queen reach its apogee but even now, at this vulnerable early moment in her reign, she needed something to set herself apart from other women, even if it were the Catholic image of the Virgin Mary.

The religious question distinguished Elizabeth's rule not only from that of her sister but also from any previous female ruler of Christian

Europe (unless we count Jane Grey). She was not only a queen regnant but also one who did not see herself as subject in any way to the pope's authority and thus with an almost unprecedented autonomy.

It was obvious from the start that the religious aspect of her role might be a particular stumbling block. The first version of a frankly reforming bill Cecil prepared in the first months of her reign met with outrage, not least because of the role it accorded to Elizabeth. As the Catholic Archbishop of York Nicholas Heath put it: 'preach or minister the holy sacraments a woman may not, neither may she be Supreme Head of the Church of Christ'. The subsequent amendment declared that Elizabeth, in her humility, wished to be known not as supreme head of the church but as its supreme governor.

Meanwhile, Elizabeth Tudor was almost about to fall into the trap that lay in wait for any powerful woman, if (as Anne de Beaujeu had warned and as Anne Boleyn had found) she were the least bit unwary.

From the start of Elizabeth's reign, ambassadors had reported her closeness to Robert Dudley. His rise in the first months of Elizabeth's reign was extraordinary; so extraordinary that by November 1559 the outgoing Spanish ambassador, Feria, was reporting that the pair had 'a secret understanding'. His successor, De Quadra, two months later described Dudley as 'the King that is to be'.

That idea was dangerous for a queen who needed to preserve her reputation, her support among the English nobility and her foreign allies. Feria put it plainly: 'if she marry the said My lord Robert, she will incur so much enmity that she may one evening lay herself down as Queen of England and rise up the next morning as plain Madam Elizabeth'. De Quadra said there was not a man in England who did not 'cry out upon him [Dudley] as the Queen's ruin'. Other factors apart, Robert Dudley was of course a married man, even though he lived largely apart from the woman, Amy Robsart, with whom he had made a youthful match.

As the first year of Elizabeth's reign turned into the second, it is extraordinary how ready everyone seems to have been to assume that Amy Dudley was a problem that could be resolved. Feria had reported rumours that she had 'a malady in one of her breasts', and natural causes (or the effect of sixteenth-century medication) remains one possible explanation for what was to come. On a more sinister note, De Quadra spoke of Amy's being sent into eternity. This set the scene for what was to prove the first defining moment of Elizabeth's rule. On 8 September 1560, Amy Dudley was found dead at the bottom of a staircase in the Cumnor house where she was staying, her neck broken and with wounds to her head.

She may conceivably have fallen, through sheer misadventure or ill health, although the shallow nature of the steps makes that unlikely. She may have committed suicide; there is circumstantial evidence that she was in a state of desperation, although the same cavil concerning the stairs applies. Or she may have been murdered, either by someone anxious to see Robert Dudley take the blame, or simply by Robert Dudley. On existing evidence, no case can be proven but what matters in this context was the effect on Elizabeth's reputation.

If a sexual scandal was the obvious way to attack a powerful woman, no powerful woman could give a better excuse for an attack. The English ambassador in Paris, Sir Nicholas Throckmorton, wrote of how his very hair was standing on end at the 'dishonourable and naughty reports' which were being relished by 'the malicious French'. The French queen, he reported, had joked that the Queen of England was to marry her horsemaster, who had murdered his wife to make way for her. More seriously, 'the cry is that [the English] do not want any more women rulers'.

Elizabeth's reaction was crucial. She sent Robert away from court, pending an inquiry. When a coroner's court found Amy had died by misadventure, when the scandal had finally died away, still she did not marry him. The question, of course, is why.

In 1560, contemporaries certainly assumed that Elizabeth Tudor wanted to marry Robert Dudley. It is only hindsight that encourages us to ask whether, when it came to it, she really found marriage an emotional possibility. Whether she had been too deeply scarred by the scandal of her youthful relationship with Thomas Seymour, by her mother's fate, by the deaths in childbirth of two of her stepmothers and several of her leading courtiers' wives; or whether she simply saw no way to combine wedlock with the retention of her authority.

Certainly, over the years, she spoke with what sounds very much like a visceral fear of marriage and of childbirth, while in the short term she behaved towards Robert Dudley with an increased freedom, as if the very fact she could not for the moment marry him had perversely given her the freedom to enjoy him more completely.

But in objective terms Elizabeth had behaved correctly, authoritatively, impeccably. Behaved as Margaret of Austria had done over the scandal with Charles Brandon. Behaved in a way designed to set her aside from the scandalous sisterhood John Knox had so vividly described.

36

Trouble in Scotland

Scotland, 1558–60

WHEN ELIZABETH TUDOR acceded to England's throne, once again English affairs had an effect in Scotland. Marie de Guise's French-backed rule had become deeply unpopular. In 1557, when Henri II declared war on England's ally Spain and told Marie he required her to invade the north of England as a diversionary tactic, she had no choice but to agree. She and Mary Tudor, who had been forced into war by her Spanish allegiance, were essentially caught in the same trap at the same moment. Ironically, when in April 1558 Mary, Queen of Scots was married to the French dauphin, some Scots even hoped that in Mary's teenage husband they would find an alternative to her mother Marie's governance.

As the Protestant Elizabeth took the English throne, Scottish Protestants took courage. Marie de Guise was convinced that their demands – the right to hold services in the vernacular and to take both bread and wine at Mass – had a political motivation. She herself, like so many of these women, had long been in favour of internal reform of the Catholic church. In 1557, she had appealed for the pope to send a cardinal to reform Scottish abuses. But this was different and, in her eyes, a piece of English-inspired meddling. As her advisor, Sieur d'Oysel, wrote: 'You can never know here who is the friend or the enemy, for he who is with them in the morning is against them after dinner.' Both sides felt betrayed: the lords by what they saw as Marie's determination to make Scotland a virtual French province, Marie by the readiness of those closest to her to side with her enemies.

The winter of 1558–59 saw a series of petitions from the Protestants, including the so-called Beggars' Summons which, pinned on the doors of the Scottish friaries, called on the inhabitants to vacate the properties. At this all too opportune moment, at the beginning of May 1559, John Knox arrived back from Continental exile, declaring that the deeds of the French queen regent 'did declare the venom of her heart'. The sermon he preached at Perth on 11 May provoked a storm of rioting that saw locals smashing the church's images.

Marie de Guise summoned Châtelherault (the former Arran; a title now accorded to his son), saying that it was for him, as 'second person of Scotland', to act, since the lords 'stand in no awe of me because I am but a woman'. Her mixture of force and flattery did the trick, despite Châtelherault's rumoured Protestant sympathies, and they rode out together at the head of a small army. Too small, as it turned out, to face the forces mustered by their Protestant foes.

A deal was struck but the trouble was not really to be put down in Marie de Guise's lifetime. Effectively banned from using French troops, fleeing from Edinburgh to Dunbar on the coast, she had to worry more about her safety than about the dwindling chance of exerting her authority. A fresh deal gave Protestants freedom of worship in exchange for bowing to Marie's civil authority, but Marie was shocked when, in line with the austere tenets of the reformed faith, a revered statue of St Giles was stolen, hurled into the Nor' Loch, dragged out and burned. She might have been even more distressed had she known that Elizabeth of England was instructing her agent Ralph Sadler to stir up faction and force her to sign a treaty of perpetual peace with England, thus stymying the French.

Throughout the autumn the number of Marie de Guise's followers diminished almost daily, with Châtelherault chief among the quitters. In October, Marie was forced to flee to Leith, her regency – so the lords declared – suspended. In November, however, she was back in Edinburgh but fell ill with what was probably chronic heart disease, although Sadler reported that rumours of her death 'are too good to be true'. Her doctors advised her to shun cold damp climates (in Scotland!) and to avoid worry.

In January 1560, eight English warships sailed into the Firth and while Marie ordered Scotsmen to prepare for war with England, the

Scottish Lords of the Congregation had other plans. They went south to meet Elizabeth Tudor's representative and on 27 February signed the Treaty of Berwick, by which Elizabeth took Scotland under her protection and promised military help for the Scottish to expel the French. But Marie was never going to accept a treaty which sidelined her completely.

As an English force crossed the border, Marie de Guise entered the security of Edinburgh Castle on 1 April, the safer for the fact that Elizabeth's lieutenant, the Duke of Norfolk, believed Elizabeth would never countenance so directly personal an attack on a fellow queen. Stalling for time, writing desperately for French military aid, Marie met the English envoys. 'Madam, you have composed so many great differences, I beseech you to bring to the settlement of this one all the means in your power', one of them said.

The Protestant Scots 'think the Dowager does more harm than five hundred Frenchmen', the Duke of Norfolk said. Marie (writing to her Guise brothers that 'our troubles and affairs increase here by the hour') found the strain told badly on her health. Her leg so swollen that 'if any lay his finger upon it, it goes in as with butter' – with, it was said, only her tears keeping the watery swelling of dropsy at bay – she was losing lord after lord to the other side.

Her health was rapidly worsening. Just after midnight on 11 June, Marie de Guise died, with several of the Scottish lords she had seen turn from friend to enemy at her side. On 6 July Scotland and England (with France represented by the Guises) signed the Treaty of Edinburgh. All English and French troops were to withdraw, while in France, the young Mary, Queen of Scots would cease using the English arms.

For the duration of Mary Stuart's absence in France, Scotland would be ruled by a council of twelve lords, chosen jointly by the queen and by the Scottish parliament (one of whose first actions was to declare Scotland a Protestant country). If Mary and her husband François refused to ratify the Treaty, then England would intervene to protect the Scottish Reformation; a refusal the likelier for the fact that Mary, frantically mourning her mother, had not been consulted as to the treaty's terms.

With Mary apparently permanently based in France it seemed as if the council, headed by Châtelherault and Mary's increasingly ambitious half-brother Lord James, had things satisfactorily under their own control. But fate had a twist in store.

In her last letter, Marie de Guise wrote of her health that 'I do not know what will happen'. In fact, as regarded her impending death, she probably did have some idea. But she could not possibly have foreseen the overthrow that was about to come to her daughter Mary Stuart.

PART VI

1560–1572

The greater and better parts of Christendom would be very wrong to complain, seeing themselves presently governed by princesses whose natural intelligence, seasoned by long experience of good and bad fortune both in wars and domestic matters, have put a great many kings to shame.

Pierre de Ronsard
Mascarades et Bergeries 1565

37

'Rancour and division'

France, 1560–1561

FRANCE WAS BECOMING the theatre in which the religious conflicts of Europe played out most clearly. In March 1560 came the Conspiracy of Amboise, a Protestant plot to overthrow the Guises and the government. It may or may not have been supported by Elizabeth Tudor of England; some of the conspirators, under torture, implicated the Prince de Condé, the committed Protestant brother of Jeanne d'Albret's husband Antoine, and there were also suggestions about Antoine.

That summer Jeanne and Antoine, at home at Nérac, accompanied by Condé, requested Calvin to send them a preacher, Theodore Beza. Another minister wrote ecstatically of the atmosphere that awaited him in their territory: 'Preaching is open – in public. The streets resound to the chanting of the Psalms. Religious books are sold as freely and openly as at home [in Geneva].'

A letter from Beza to Calvin written on 25 August says that 'the ladies commend themselves warmly to you'. The importance of great ladies in spreading the reformed faith was universally acknowledged: Condé's wife, Eleonore de Roye, was another significant figure. Nothing, however, was yet to be done openly. Indeed, Antoine and Jeanne still sent an envoy to the pope, to assure Rome of their orthodoxy.

Catherine de Medici, meanwhile, was arguing forcefully that the way to forestall any more religious troubles was to allow a measure of tolerance of the French Protestants. Catherine was on the rise. Mary,

Queen of Scots was now Queen Consort of France, but by the start of 1560, there were mutters of discontent about the hold her Guise family had over the young king. Catherine de Medici's policy of allowing the Guises to take the political foreground, while she remained aloof as a sorrowing widow and mother, was paying off.

Catherine sought to make a distinction between those genuinely committed to the new faith and those disaffected with the Guise regime; between, even, those of Protestant beliefs, and those prepared to rebel to promulgate them. The Edict of Romorantin, of May 1560, was Catherine's doing: an edict that confined the trial of religious cases to the ecclesiastical courts, which could not impose the death penalty. She also urged, successfully, for peace with England and for France's withdrawal from active participation in Scottish affairs, the latter decision perhaps the easier for the death of Marie de Guise.

On the advice of the leading Protestant, Admiral de Coligny, Catherine de Medici called a meeting of the full council for August; a discreet move to curb the exclusive influence the Guises had at first enjoyed. She herself made the first speech, hoping the councillors might find a policy whereby the king 'could conserve his sceptre, his subjects find relief from their suffering and the malcontents find contentment'. But events would overtake the peaceable plan.

The first of these involved the Bourbons; Antoine, and particularly Condé, who preferred to put their faith in military might rather than Catherine's assemblies, prepared through the autumn for armed confrontation. Condé was arrested and his wife imprisoned, while there were stories the Guises, in league with the Spaniards, planned to seize Jeanne d'Albret and her son. But the second event was more definitive still. Young King François II, notwithstanding his passion for hunting, had always been frail and sickly, and on 9 November, after riding out in the cold, he fell ill.

It soon became clear that his condition was serious. Catherine de Medici wrote of how hard it was 'to see the terrible and extreme pain that the King, my son is suffering'. François II had an abscess in his ear, and sepsis set in. Everyone, even his mother, had to think of what would happen if the worst befell.

The heir, Catherine's next son, Charles, was only ten, so the Estates General would have to vote on a regency. Their choice was likely to fall on Antoine de Bourbon, for all that his brother Condé was now under sentence of death. This would leave no great place for Catherine. Boldly, she called Antoine de Bourbon into her presence (and that of the Guises) and accused him of having plotted, treacherously.

Terrified that the same sentence would fall on him as on his brother, Antoine weakly offered to give up his rights in the regency to Catherine de Medici; an offer with which she was quick to close, citing examples of other queen mothers who had ruled on behalf of a young son, notably the thirteenth century Blanche of Castile, mother of the revered Louis IX. The Guises were alarmed that they too would be called to account for their dubious part in prosecuting Condé and all too aware that their influence would suffer once their niece Mary was no longer queen. Catherine placated both parties, and made them embrace. Pitting her rivals against each other, she had seemingly emerged above the fray. She had become an operator. It was a triumph of her personal diplomacy.

François II died on 5 December 1560, after a reign of only sixteen months. This was Catherine de Medici's moment. An English diplomat wrote that, 'The Queen was blithe of the death of King Francis her son, because she had no guiding of him.' Calling a meeting of the council, she told them: 'Since it has pleased God to deprive me of my elder son, I mean to submit to the Divine will and to assist and serve the King, my second son [Charles IX], in the feeble measure of my experience.'

She had decided, she told the council:

> to keep him beside me and to govern the state, as a devoted mother must do. Since I have assumed this duty, I wish all correspondence to be addressed in the first place to me; I shall open it in your presence and in particular in that of the King of Navarre [Antoine de Bourbon], who will occupy the first place in the council as the nearest relative of the King . . .

Antoine gave his assent, protesting his loyalty, and so did the Guises. Both parties ascribed the actions which had produced their former enmity to the orders of the dead François II; Catherine de Medici colluded in the pretence, content with the situation she had set up. At forty-one, she had attained immense authority. The Venetian ambassador wrote that her will was supreme: 'it is she who will henceforth have her hand upon the most important negotiations'. Before the year was out, she had herself proclaimed Governor of the Kingdom, 'Catherine by the grace of God, Queen of France, Mother of the King'.

François II's early death would have huge consequences for his widow Mary Stuart, and thus, indirectly, for Elizabeth in England. Mary Stuart had been raised in the expectation that her role as queen consort of wealthy France would outrank that of queen regnant of obscure Scotland. But now, fewer than two years into her marriage, as she sat in the darkened room, custom prescribed for a mourning queen, she must have known her future had changed, completely and unexpectedly.

There was yet another woman, also in France, whose future would be profoundly affected by the ramifications of François's death. It was clear Catherine de Medici had used Antoine de Bourbon as pawn and cat's paw. Did the word of his humiliation, and his vacillation, persuade Jeanne d'Albret that she should take a stand? Calvinism, with its authoritarian logic, its insistence on a black and white simplicity, must have had an emotional appeal. At Christmas communion, at Pau, she publicly forswore Rome and, as her personal historian Nicolas de Bordenave recorded, 'having made a confession of faith, partook of Holy Communion according to the rites of the said Reformed Religion'. Bordenave later recorded that once the previously reluctant Jeanne had 'put everything in God's hands', she did so 'with such constancy that never again could she be turned from her course, no matter what assaults Satan and the world made upon her'.[1]

Jeanne d'Albret was hailed by other Protestant players on the international board. Calvin first wrote to her in mid-January 1561, declaring that he had no need to advise her, for 'when I see how the spirit of God rules you I have more occasion to give thanks than to exhort you'. Queen Elizabeth's ambassador Throckmorton had been told to congratulate Jeanne on her 'affection for the true religion', commenting that the time offered 'great opportunities to encourage those well-disposed'.

Both Calvin and Queen Elizabeth regretted the defection of Antoine, now declared Lieutenant-General of France, as Catherine had promised. The Florentine ambassador took his appointment as a sign of

Catherine's weakness, declaring that she had 'finally proven that she is only a woman'. But Antoine's reward was less than he hoped. When he suggested that, in the event of Catherine's illness, her responsibilities should devolve on him, her reply was uncompromising: 'I shall never be too ill to supervise whatever affects the service of the King my son'.

In the middle of 1561, delayed by the need to settle affairs in Béarn before she left (not least the protection of her Calvinist ministers), Jeanne d'Albret set out to join her husband at the French court. She hoped, perhaps, to stiffen his commitment to the Protestant faith.

The Spanish ambassador wrote that along the way 'everywhere the heretics await her coming as if she were the Messiah, because they are certain she will perform miracles on their behalf. Personally I do not doubt it, for wherever she goes she meets with no resistance'. Throckmorton told Elizabeth's minister Cecil, after Jeanne had moved on from Orléans, of how twenty-five religious ladies, 'the fairest of sixty', threw aside their habits and scaled the walls, so convinced were they now of 'the superstitions of the cloister, and the pleasures of secular company'. The Venetian ambassador called Jeanne a woman '*di terribile cervello*' (of a fearsome brain). Catherine, noted the Spanish ambassador, 'will have a hard time living with her'.

Jeanne d'Albret made herself a focus of Protestantism at the French court, setting up a religious council, welcoming new evangelists, winning a certain following among other young court ladies and regularly attending Protestant services 'with the doors open'. She also sent word to England that Elizabeth Tudor's 'credit is great, and the more so for standing so firmly in God's cause. [Jeanne] was glad to hear that the candles and candlesticks were removed from the Queen's chapel'. Her husband Antoine, by contrast, attended both Protestant and Catholic services in these months.

Antoine, as even Calvin in Geneva heard with profound disapproval, by now notorious as a ladies' man, was involved with one of the pretty young attendants around Catherine de Medici. Even Calvin became drawn into the attempt to heal Antoine's marriage to Jeanne, but nothing could weigh against the inducements held out by the other side. Spain even offered him ('in principle') another kingdom to compensate for the loss of Navarre.

'I have always worked for the advancement of [the Religion]', Jeanne d'Albret declared later in her memoirs. Her husband 'having with-drawn from the first zeal that he had had for it, was for me a tough thorn, I won't say in the foot, but in the heart.' By contrast, 'I have always, by the grace of God, followed the straight path.' The Venetian envoy wrote that Jeanne was harassing Antoine 'night and day', while he was trying to force her into at least outward conformity. Forbidden to hold Calvinist services in her apartment, she went to those in Condé's, and when Antoine confronted her as she was about to step into the carriage, the rows were 'so loud everyone in the château could hear'.

When Jeanne d'Albret's ever-fragile health gave way, Antoine changed tactics and sought to separate himself from her. A year after his wife's conversion, he openly set his face even against the measures of tolerance now proposed by Catherine de Medici, declaring his determination to 'live in closest friendship with the Guises'. His brother Condé, however, would take his place as leader of the threatened Huguenots. Meanwhile, in the spring of 1561, the anti-Protestant alli-ance of the Guises and Montmorency had the support also of Spain, the emperor, and the pope: an all-male conspiracy to which they were eager to recruit Antoine.

Catherine de Medici, by contrast, was strongly behind the Colloque of Poissy, which met that summer in what proved a vain attempt to reconcile religious divides. She issued an amnesty for all religious offences committed since her husband's death, delaying French churchmen from attending the Counter-Reformation's Council of Trent, but Catherine's toleration was a pragmatic measure aimed at preserving her son's monarchy. As she wrote to her reproachful son-in-law Philip of Spain, the experience of decades in France taught that 'violence only serves to increase and multiply [this infection], since by the harsh penalties which have constantly been enforced in this king-dom, an infinite number of poor people have been confirmed in this belief'.

Her edict in January 1562 allowed Protestants to practise their faith as long as it were outside town walls. But it was greeted with horror by domestic and foreign Catholic powers, despite her continued assur-ance that she and her children 'wished to live in the Catholic faith and obedience to Rome'. The *parlement* of Paris at first refused to register the edict, specifically, in their formal remonstrance, linking their refusal to Catherine's sex. 'Laws both sacred and profane insist that the woman is in holy bond to her husband and children in holy bond to their father, which is to say that the entire family is of the same religion as the father of the family'; that is, of the religion Henri II had followed. Failing to follow this, they said, produced 'nothing but contention, rancour, and division'. Deliberately, Catherine displayed herself, with her children, at every Catholic ritual.

To her daughter Elisabeth, Philip's wife, Catherine wrote word to ignore any rumours: 'I do not mean to change my life or my religion or anything. I am what I am in order to preserve your brothers and their kingdom.' But Jeanne d'Albret was cut from very different cloth. When Catherine de Medici asked Jeanne to moderate her Protestant behaviour, Jeanne's reply was uncompromising: 'Madame, if I had my son and all the kingdoms in the world within my hands, I would rather cast them to the bottom of the sea than lose my salvation.'

Catherine de Medici did not give up. She was still cultivating Jeanne d'Albret to a marked degree. As Jeanne prepared to leave the French court in the spring of 1562, Catherine kept her close as she and her son received foreign ambassadors; even going shopping in Paris together, 'disguised as bourgeois ladies in simple headdress'. Indeed, Catherine was identified with Jeanne's interest to the point where Elizabeth Tudor could instruct Throckmorton 'to encourage the Queen Mother, the Queen of Navarre, and the Prince of Condé to show their constancy [and to convey] her intention to stand by them'.

But it was no longer possible to resist the demands of Antoine, and of the Spanish ambassador, that Jeanne should be sent away from court. Her son Henri had been taken away from her, to be educated under his father's charge by conservative Catholic tutors. Jeanne, allowed to say goodbye to him, told the child that if ever he went to Mass she would disinherit him, or so the Cardinal of Ferrara said. The eight-year-old held out for several months before finally, predictably, being seen at Mass with his father and the royal family. By that time, the temperature of the religious conflict had risen in an alarming way.

On 1 March 1562 the Duc de Guise, while visiting family estates in the Champagne region, was riding to Mass through the small town of

Vassy, property of his niece Mary Stuart, when he heard the provocative sound of a Protestant service coming, illegally, from a building
within the town walls. Whether or not his armed escort actually began
what came to be called the Massacre of Vassy, it left more than seventy
Protestants dead and more than a hundred wounded. Small wonder
that Jeanne d'Albret secretly fled southwards to her own territories.
The First War of Religion, as it would become known, was under way,
with women prominent on either side.

'Two Queens in One Isle'

Scotland and England, 1561–1565

EVENTS IN FRANCE had radically altered the life of one young woman who had expected to live out her life there. Now that Catherine de Medici was the power in the land where Mary Stuart had expected to be queen, the Queen of Scots's eyes turned another way. After her young husband King François died, Mary, as a childless widow, had no role in France, while Scotland had no royal visible on the throne.

In August 1561 Mary, Queen of Scots landed at Leith, with the intention of governing her country. Just what kind of a fist she made of it is hotly disputed by historians; a question that goes right to the heart of the notion of the female ruler in the sixteenth century.

Mary made no attempt to consolidate her position in France. On the first day of her widowhood she handed the queen's jewels back to Catherine de Medici. A Scottish contemporary mentioned her next move as being motivated by Catherine's 'rigorous and vengeable dealing'. The forty days seclusion may have given Mary the thinking space she needed. Her Guise relatives were pushing for another marriage; pushing hard (through her aunt Louise who had many Spanish connections) for the Spanish heir Don Carlos, receiving offers from the kings of Denmark and Sweden, from the dukes of Ferrara and Bavaria. The Holy Roman Emperor Ferdinand offered one of his sons, while the Scots offered their leading noble Arran, Châtelherault's son. Philip's son Don Carlos was the prize but this was blocked by Catherine de Medici, who was writing in code to the Queen of England – who likewise had no wish to be caught between two jaws, northern and southern, of a Spanish vice – that this should be circumvented. Catherine's daughter Elisabeth, Mary's old playfellow, had married Philip II but was as yet childless; and Catherine did not want a rival at her court.

Mary herself was determined on returning to Scotland. The English envoy Throckmorton reported that Mary felt she could count on her family there; that she 'holds herself sure of Lord James and all the Stuarts'. It was, perhaps, a mark of her political naivety. Her half-brother Lord James Stuart – able, ambitious and quickly gaining control of a country where only his illegitimacy prevented him succeeding his father James V – would surely have preferred to see his legitimate but wholly inexperienced half-sister stay well away.

There was a perverse benefit in the very fact of Mary being a young woman whom the lords thought they could manipulate. Mary agreed that she would maintain the religious status quo, with Protestantism the official (if far from universal) religion, while she herself should be allowed to hear the Catholic Mass in her own chapel at Holyrood. It is unlikely, however, that she altogether understood the deal she was making. On her very first progress, it became clear that Lord James regarded the deal as extending only to Holyrood; not even to any other of her palaces where Mary might happen to be staying. And the problem was more fundamental. After the death of Marie de Guise in 1560, Scotland had reorganised itself into a country run by its lords, together with a Reformation Parliament which abolished the Mass and refuted the pope's authority. In England, letters were filed as coming from 'the States of Scotland', as if from a Scottish republic.

This was the rub. In the centuries ahead it would be speculated why Mary Stuart failed in Scotland while Elizabeth Tudor in England succeeded. One answer surely lies in the fact that Mary was eighteen when she began to rule. Elizabeth Tudor had been an unusually experienced twenty-five when she ascended the throne; her sister Mary thirty-seven. But too much altogether may be put down to personality, ability and training; too little to the fact that the Scottish nobles, and the Scottish church, had a very different concept of their relationship with their monarchy.

There is also the issue of her ministers. It is sometimes regretted that Mary had no minister as able as Elizabeth's Cecil. That is not altogether true; in William Maitland of Lethington she had 'Michel Wylie', the Scottish Machiavelli, who would become one of her chief officers. Maitland, like Lord James, was a Protestant, and his devotion to an increasing rapport with an England would eventually put him at odds with his queen, although for the first half of her reign, Mary's own eyes were turned England's way.

On the death of her husband François II, Mary Stuart told the Earl of Bedford, who brought Elizabeth's letters of condolence, that Elizabeth 'shows the part of a good sister, whereof she [Mary] has great need'. She reiterated that she and Elizabeth were (as she had written of Mary Tudor) two queens 'in One Isle, both of one language, both the nearest kinswoman that each other hath and both Queens'. She failed to realise that although Elizabeth told Maitland she was 'obliged' to love Mary ('as being nearest to me in blood of any other'), for the English, the question of Mary's claim to the English throne, stood – and would continue to stand – in the way.

That is why Elizabeth, asked to grant Mary safe conduct to travel home through her realm, rather than face the journey by sea, refused unless Mary ratified the Treaty of Edinburgh made between Elizabeth and the Scottish lords. Typically, Elizabeth changed her mind, offering the necessary conduct only too late. William Maitland, ever aiming at securing Mary's place in the future English succession, had been as anxious as Mary herself to bring about a meeting between the two queens, which, he said, 'shall breed us quietness for their times'. That meeting would never happen, although fictional writers have often imagined it, and Mary would continue to plead for it almost until her death.

Mary Stuart landed at Leith on 19 August 1561. As she made her official entry into Edinburgh a fortnight later, the welcoming pageantry suggested genuine pleasure at a queen's return, coupled with violent hostility to the Mass. A doctrine of hostility not necessarily felt by all the people but urgently propounded by men like the Protestant reformer John Knox.

On her first Sunday at Holyrood, Mary's Mass in her private chapel was interrupted by a noisy demonstration. She summoned John Knox, tackling him on his statement that a woman ruler was 'a monster in nature'. Knox's idea of an emollient reply ran: 'If the realm finds no inconvenience from the rule of a woman, that which they approve shall I not further disallow . . . but shall be as well content to live under your Grace as St Paul was to live under Nero.'

'I perceive that my subjects shall obey you, and not me', Mary told him, managing to wait until he left before bursting into tears. Small wonder that the English ambassador Thomas Randolph noted what would become a regular feature of Mary's life; a failure in health he called one of the 'sudden passions' that overtook her 'after any great unkindness or grief of mind'.

When Mary Stuart named her first council it was an inclusive blend of men. Seven out of the twelve were Protestants. Thomas Randolph wrote: 'I see the Lord James and the Laird of Lethington, Maitland, above all others in credit . . . She is patient to hear, and beareth much'. Maitland wrote to William Cecil in England that, 'The Queen my Mistress behaves herself so gently in every behalf as reasonably we can require', adding that she 'doth declare wisdom far exceeding her age'. He thought 'that the Queen your sovereign [Elizabeth] shall be able to do much with her in religion, if once they enter into a good familiarity'. A meeting was still Mary's passionate hope.

In the early spring of 1562, plans for a late summer meeting at York got as far as arrangements about the bureau de change to convert Scottish currency and agreement that Mary Stuart might bring a thousand attendants and practise her religion in private. There were advantages on both sides. Elizabeth's approval would ratify Mary in the eyes of her Protestant subjects, as well as holding out hope of the succession. But Mary's stock with Elizabeth Tudor was also high. Her rival in the English succession stakes, Lady Katherine Grey, sister of the nine days' queen Lady Jane, had recently blotted her copybook by contracting a secret marriage with the Earl of Hertford.[1]

But the plan fell through on news of the Massacre of Vassy, at which the Duc de Guise's men killed a party of the Huguenots. In the ensuing first outbreak of the French Wars of Religion, Elizabeth threw in her lot with the Huguenots, spurred by the hope of regaining Calais, which had been lost through her sister's Spanish sympathies.

Baulked of the trip to York, which put her 'into such a passion as she did keep her bed all that day', Mary Stuart set off on a progress into the north of Scotland. The Catholic Earl of Huntly, the so-called 'Cock of the North', made no secret of his disapproval of any pro-English policy, and showed, moreover, no disposition to bow to his queen's authority. The progress turned into something like a punitive expedition, and one in which Mary showed to advantage. Randolph wrote to Cecil that autumn of 1562:

> In all these broils I assure you I never saw the Queen merrier, never dismayed, nor never thought that stomach to be in her that I find. She repented nothing but that she was not a man, to know what life it was to lie all night in the fields, or to walk on the causeway with a jack and knapscall [a soldier's tunic and helmet], a Glasgow buckler, and a broad sword.

When one of Huntly's captains ordered Inverness castle to be closed against her, she had him hanged from the battlements; when one of Huntly's sons set out to kidnap Mary (and perhaps marry her by force), she had him executed. But the stress told. When she returned to Holyrood it was to a bout of illness, and to news from England that put a different perspective on many of her policies.

Elizabeth Tudor was ill, from an attack of smallpox so serious that her councillors were clustered around her bed in expectation of her death, terrified for the future of her country. 'Death possessed every joint of me', she later wrote. Mary Stuart was genuinely concerned, ordering her ladies to look out the recipe for a lotion used when she herself had had the disease in her youth, which had prevented the scarring every woman dreaded. But she must also have thought, what if?

When the answer came it was devastating. 'I have heard it whispered that in this late storm of yours a device was intended to prefer some other in the succession to my mistress, which I cannot think to be true, seeing none is more worthy', wrote Maitland to Cecil, disbelievingly. Elizabeth recovered from the smallpox but when the lords had felt impelled to discuss her successor, only one voice had been raised in favour of Mary.

This, in all its aspects, was the situation that would continue to bedevil Elizabeth and Mary's relationship. The succession was always the problem for Elizabeth. As she told Maitland: 'Princes cannot like their own children. Think you that I could love my own winding-sheet?' Over the years ahead the two queens would never cease to eye each other, and their relationship continued to employ a complex rhetoric.

Mary Stuart wrote of Elizabeth Tudor that, 'I honour her in my heart and love her as my dear and natural sister.' At moments they were mother and daughter; at other times they sent jewels and exchanged ardent verses, as lovers might do. In hopes of meeting with the English queen, Mary put all talk of suitors and a new marriage aside, joking that she would have no one but Elizabeth. There seems to have been a recurring fantasy in both courts that the two might marry, and although one thinks of Elizabeth as the masculine partner, it was the tall Mary who liked to roam the streets in male clothing.

In the first days of 1563, Mary heard that Cecil was planning to have parliament bar her from the English throne by an Act of Exclusion. Mary was forced to think of other plans; of marriage. But what seemed like a fresh possibility to her loomed as a threat for Elizabeth.

Elizabeth Tudor had long come under increased pressure from her council to marry and produce an heir, assuring parliament she would do so as soon as it might be done 'conveniently'. Her ambivalence is understandable. When Mary Stuart was first widowed, and the question of her remarriage mooted, Elizabeth's ambassador Throckmorton had written of the Queen of Scots:

> During her husband's life there was no great account made of her, for that, being under band of marriage and subjection to her husband (who carried the burden of care of all her matters) there was offered no great occasion to know what was in her.

It must have sounded more like a warning than an invitation.

Elizabeth was still toying with her chief favourite, Robert Dudley. In the spring of 1561 Cecil had written in confidence to Throckmorton: 'I know surely that my Lord Robert [Dudley] hath more fear than hope, and so doth the Queen give him cause.' But that same season Elizabeth could tell the Spanish ambassador De Quadra that she:

could not deny that she had a strong regard for the many excellent qualities which she saw in Lord Robert. She had not indeed resolved to marry either him or anyone; only every day she felt more and more the want of a husband . . .

By the summer of 1562, rumours were rife that Elizabeth had secretly married Dudley. But weeks later, the Swedish diplomat Robert Keyle reported the queen as telling Dudley, with 'a great rage and great checks and taunts' and in the presence of all the nobility, 'that she would never marry him, nor none so mean as he'.

This was in a sense a game; but it was play with a point, as all Elizabeth's marital games tended to be. In the decade ahead, Elizabeth Tudor would use Robert Dudley, with his enduring pretensions to her hand, as a stalking horse, an alibi for when any other foreign suitor got too close, a suitor to be safely spurned once they had retreated.[2] But the scare of her smallpox meant that, for the moment, her councillors were in no mood to play. The crisis had shown up the danger of the situation: the queen a childless woman with no near relations. The parliament that met in January 1563 was determined Elizabeth should marry. Both Houses united in sending petitions urging on Elizabeth the delight of beholding 'an imp of your own', whoever the father of the imp might be.

'Whomsoever it be that your Majesty shall choose, we protest and promise with all humility and reverence to honour, love, and serve as to our most bounden duty shall appertain.' It was effectively a mandate for Robert Dudley. But Elizabeth did not avail herself of the permission. Instead, at this moment, she broached a far stranger plan with Maitland: the possibility of Dudley's marrying the Scottish queen. It would be another year before anyone dared mention it to Mary.

The question of Mary Stuart's remarriage had never gone away but, as was also true at Elizabeth's court, her councillors could never all agree on whom she should marry. Maitland was willing to promote a match with Philip of Spain's son Don Carlos, since the threat of this grand alliance – of Spanish power on their northern border – might surely push England into making to Mary the counter-offer of a secure place as Elizabeth Tudor's heir. Mary wrote to the pope, expressing herself as his 'most devoted daughter'; effectively seeking a sign of warmth that would make her a more attractive proposition to Catholic suitors. Her Guise relatives were trying to promote another match with the emperor's third son, the archduke Charles of Austria, while Catherine de Medici used her influence as Philip of Spain's mother-in-law to oppose it, just as she opposed the idea of Mary marrying her youthful brother-in-law Charles IX, the new French king. Maitland wrote to Mary from the French court that the powers there 'care not greatly of your marriage or with whom it be, provided it bring with it no peril to this crown'.

The marriage with Don Carlos would eventually founder on reports of his insanity. But before that, two other people had decided to take a hand. One, with an unusually broad view of a subject's remit, was John Knox. Hearing that he had been speaking against her marriage plans from the pulpit, Mary sent for him and furiously demanded: 'What have ye to do with my marriage?' Alas, he was only too willing to tell her, declaring that if she married a Catholic the realm would be 'betrayed'.

When Mary was first widowed, Throckmorton had written admiringly of how Mary 'more esteemeth the continuation of her honour, and to marry one that may uphold her to be great, than she passeth to please her fancy'. But now Mary Stuart's Catholicism was being equated with the lustful urge to marriage, whence came the stereotype that she ruled from the heart not the head. Knox told his congregation at St Giles Kirk that the dogs would 'eat the flesh of Jezebel' and that dancing, of which Mary was so fond, 'is the vanity of the unfaithful, which shall cause the people to be set in bondage to a tyrant'.

Soon, Knox had a more reasonable cause of suspicion in the behaviour of one Chastelard, a French poet whom Mary had admitted to her court. Chastelard's sighing devotion to Mary came straight from the fantasy of courtly love, but perhaps Chastelard, like Knox, who claimed that while dancing Mary would steal a kiss from the poet's neck, confused fantasy with reality.

In the first weeks of 1563, Chastelard was twice found hiding under the queen's bed. The first time it was passed over as a drunken prank; the second, he was tried, sentenced, and executed. Chastelard had been found with sword and dagger, and one theory held he had been sent to assassinate Mary. Another held that he was an agent provocateur, intent on compromising her reputation. But Mary behaved as a queen should; behaved as Elizabeth in England had behaved, over the death of Amy Dudley.

The other meddler, of course, was Elizabeth. Elizabeth Tudor wanted Mary Stuart married off – an interesting sidelight on her view of the institution – but only under such conditions as she herself had, as Maitland put it, 'least cause to stand in fear'. Never mind the fact that Mary's marriage, and any alliance it might bring, had huge impli cations for the security of England's northern border, especially since Mary's claim to the English throne might well be taken as the most important part of her dowry.

Mary, however resentfully, seemed prepared to allow herself to be driven, demanding sarcastically just which husbands Elizabeth felt might be 'sortable' for her. Scotland had never been able safely to defy England without the French aid that Catherine de Medici was now unwilling to provide. And Mary wanted that place in the succession to the English crown.

In November 1563, England's definition of the 'sortable' candidate arrived. He should ideally be an English nobleman, committed to Scotland's friendship with that country. Failing that, a foreigner might, subject to specific English permission, be acceptable as long as he was prepared to live in Scotland after the marriage and did not come from Spain, France or imperial Austria. Only then could Mary be treated as Elizabeth's 'only sister or daughter'. No wonder that, in the ensuing months, Mary began formulating her own plans.

She neither acceded to, nor refused, Elizabeth's demand. Instead, she would call out to her courtiers that the English ambassador wanted her to marry in England. 'Is the queen of England become a man?', the courtiers would call back, in mocking query. She also asked, whom exactly Elizabeth did want her to marry? When the answer came, she was never going to be pleased.

In 1563 Elizabeth had first broached with Maitland the incredible idea that Mary should marry her favourite Robert Dudley but no one had felt it necessary to try the insulting idea on Mary. When, in the spring of 1564, Thomas Randolph brought himself to declare Dudley's name, Mary entered into the discussion with apparent seriousness but really she was never likely to 'so far abase my state'.

Mary Stuart was surely closer to reality than Elizabeth Tudor, especially when Elizabeth suggested that she, Mary and Dudley might all three live at the English court, at Elizabeth's cost and as one 'family': a virtual *ménage à trois*. But from Elizabeth's viewpoint the idea was perhaps logical: a loyal, Protestant candidate of her own on Scotland's throne and perhaps, just perhaps, a way to avoid actually marrying her favourite. If Elizabeth had ever wanted a husband, she told Sir James Melville, the urbane diplomat sent south from Scotland, 'she would have chosen Lord Robert, her brother and best friend, but, being determined to end her life in virginity, she wished that the Queen her sister should marry him'.

Melville, during his stay at the English court, was frequently called upon to prove how well he deserved the name of diplomat. Elizabeth quizzed him as to who was the fairer: Elizabeth was the fairest queen in all England, Mary in all Scotland, he said. Elizabeth's skin 'was whiter, but my Queen was very lovely'. Who made music more skilfully? Melville said that Mary played the lute and virginals 'reasonably, for a queen'; Elizabeth made sure he came upon her playing like an expert the next day.

More seriously, in one of their conversations Elizabeth told Melville that 'it was her own resolution at this moment to remain till her death a virgin queen'. He told her the information was unnecessary. 'I know your stately stomach. You think if you were married, you would be only a queen of England, and now ye are king and queen both. You may not endure a commander.' In Robert Dudley, she had a man – a subject – she could enjoy without fear of mastery.

Mary refused a proposal made by Catherine de Medici that while Elizabeth should marry King Charles IX, Mary should marry his brother Henri. Neither of the adult queens (thirty and twenty-one respectively) were eager for matches with boys of fourteen and thirteen. And having been a queen in France, Mary said, she could never return there in a lesser role. In 1564 she pretended to be considering Dudley, raised a little closer to her status when Elizabeth created him Earl of Leicester, although Melville spotted her tickling his neck during the ceremony. But the new Earl of Leicester was not eager for the match. The plan was a failure; Mary was now eyeing up other possibilities.

Mary Stuart's experience had taught her that marriage was a necessity – even though Elizabeth Tudor, in England, was drawing a different lesson. As Mary told Randolph early in 1565: 'Not to marry, you know it cannot be for me. To defer it long, many incommodities ensure.' But who was the lucky man to be?

He had already appeared on the scene. The way was clear for another candidate; not Dudley but another Englishman, the son of Margaret Douglas, newly arrived in Scotland. Like her mother Margaret Tudor, Margaret Douglas dreamt of uniting England and Scotland. But she dreamt of doing it in the person of her son: Henry, Lord Darnley.

Challenge and conciliation

France, 1562–1565

I N FRANCE, TWO other women also dreamt of unity. They faced each other across a religious divide but neither had abandoned the idea that something (their sex?) might still be a bond between them.

Jeanne d'Albret fled the French court in 1562, amid rumours that her husband Antoine was preparing to capture and imprison her. But Jeanne still had, she would later insist in her memoirs, the covert support of Catherine de Medici, herself anxious to escape from the influence of the Guises.

Catherine, Jeanne wrote, 'approved everything I had done and made an infinity of complaints against my husband'. Jeanne was the one who now withdrew, refusing to assist Catherine's negotiations with Antoine's committedly Huguenot brother, Condé. For the next few years she would be occupied chiefly in her own lands. 'God ... has always granted me the grace to preserve this little corner of Béarn, where little by little, good increases and evil diminishes.'

Diplomatically, she would attempt to steer something of a neutral path. Her son Henri was still in French hands, and an heir to the French throne, while the Huguenots had as yet insufficient military strength to stand against the royal armies. But within her own fiefdom, she made her stance clear. Antoine, she said, had sent orders to Pau that the *parlement* should cease all exercises of the Reformed Religion and exile any officials not Catholic. She in turn withdrew her permission for him to negotiate with Spain about exchanging Navarre for

Sardinia, saying it had been 'given through force and fear, not having dared refuse a husband':

> When I learned this, I used the natural sovereign power God had given me over my subjects, which I had ceded to my husband for the obedience which God commands; but when I saw that it was a question of my God's glory and the purity of his worship . . .

One way or another, the marriage was coming to an end.

The violence that followed the Massacre of Vassy in 1562 forced Catherine de Medici, however reluctantly, to put herself under the protection of the Duc de Guise, who arrived at Fontainebleu with a thousand cavalrymen. As the Protestants appealed to their co-religionists in Geneva, to the German Protestant princes and to Elizabeth of England, Catherine, with the Guises, was forced to find aid both from Philip of Spain and the papacy. Despite the wreckage of her policies, her personal courage remained high as she appeared on the ramparts above Rouen. 'My courage is as great as yours,' she told the men.

Another, too, showed bravery in these wars. Whatever his vacillations of policy, no one had ever doubted Antoine de Bourbon's physical courage. But, when he had merely wandered into the bushes to relieve himself, he was hit in the shoulder. The wound became gangrenous and he died a few weeks later, on 17 November. Catherine allowed Antoine's widow, Jeanne, to take control of her son's education, although for the next few years he would effectively remain a hostage at court.

In the following spring of 1563 Jeanne d'Albret wrote a long letter to Catherine de Medici:

> I trust, Madame, that you will not find that I have exceeded my duty by addressing myself to you on wings that fly above the heads of others . . . I am fully aware, Madame, of your perfect good will and friendship, and of your desire to further my son's welfare and my own, and I cannot ignore your acts, so praiseworthy that I kiss the ground where you walk. But forgive me, Madame, if I write as I spoke to you at St Germain, where you did not seem to mind.

Your good intentions are obstructed by the interference of those whom you know too well for me to describe them . . .

The letter also makes reference to a recent 'pitiful event', for Antoine's was not the only important death that season. In February 1563, to the grief of his niece Mary in Scotland, the Duc de Guise was assassinated. Catherine was suspected; she is said to have told Condé (who had been captured by her royalist party) that Guise's death 'released her from prison'. Ironically, however, it also made her by default the leader of the Catholic faction, while the Protestant one was led by Condé and Admiral de Coligny, supported by the emotive figure of Jeanne d'Albret.

There was a brief breathing space for everyone. In March the Edict of Amboise gave freedom of conscience, and limited freedom of worship, to Huguenots. In the summer of 1563, Catherine de Medici adopted the device that had earlier been used to confirm Marie de Guise's authority in Scotland, when she had her thirteen-year-old son Charles IX declared of age, despite the opposition of the Paris *parlement*.

The first act of the young king was to hand his mother the 'power to command', declaring that she 'would continue to govern as much and more than before'. When, some months later, Charles IX issued a decree maintaining a fragile peace between the Guises and the Colignys clan, his mother boasted that he had done so 'without anyone's prompting'. But that seems, to say the least of it, unlikely.

Jeanne d'Albret, meanwhile, was also consolidating her authority. The year 1563 saw the abolition in her lands of the traditional religious processions and the arrival of the extra ministers she had requested from Calvin. 'The Queen of Navarre has banished all idolatry from her domains and sets an example of virtue with incredible firmness and courage', wrote one. Many of Jeanne's nobles and officials were against her reform, and the reformer Jean-Raymond Merlin fretted that 'she is inexperienced . . . having always been either under a father who managed affairs, or under a husband who neglected them'.

A few months after Jeanne's imposition of Protestantism she was, Merlin said, '*épouvantée*' (aghast) at news the Spanish had stationed troops on her frontier, and that though he had pushed her into forbidding the Mass in one town, she was hanging back ('paralysed by fear') from repudiating the papacy entirely. The Spanish envoy, once again Descurra, had brought her a letter of remonstrance from the King of Spain. She replied:

> Although I am just a little princess, God has given me the government of this country so that I may rule it according to His Gospel and teach it His laws. I rely on God, who is more powerful than the King of Spain . . .

Philip had attempted to neutralise the widowed Jeanne by marrying her into his house but now he told his secretary of state that 'this is quite too much of a woman to have as a daughter-in-law'.

Next, frighteningly, Jeanne d'Albret received a letter from an emissary of the papacy, Cardinal d'Armagnac, sent from Trent to warn her away from the reformist path. But to that too Jeanne replied, with mounting indignation:

> I condemn no one to death or imprisonment, which penalties are the nerves and sinews of a system of terror – I blush for you, and feel ashamed when you falsely state that so many atrocities have been perpetrated by those of our religion. Purge the earth first from the blood of so many just men shed by you and yours . . . As in no point I have deviated from the faith of God's Holy Catholic church, nor quitted her fold, I bid you keep your tears to deplore your own errors . . . I desire that your useless letter may be the last of its kind.

On 28 September 1563 Pope Pius IV summoned Jeanne to appear before the Inquisition in Rome, on a charge of heresy. If she failed to appear she would be excommunicated and her lands declared free to anyone who could take them. She had six months to comply.

From this predicament she was once again rescued by Catherine de Medici; albeit Catherine's motives were not solely sisterly. The papacy's intrusion on French sovereign power had long been a bone of contention. In December, Catherine sent a special envoy to Rome protesting that the pope's actions were 'against the ancient rights and privileges of the Gallican Church'.

Philip of Spain, meanwhile, planned to kidnap Jeanne and deliver her to the Inquisition in Spain. But elements of the plan leaked out when an embroiderer employed by Catherine de Medici's daughter Elisabeth – Philip's wife – passed on word of what one of the agents had said while in his cups. The former French princess passed word to her mother's ambassador: an example either of natal trumping marital loyalties or of female solidarity.

'I put myself wholly under the wing of your powerful protection', Jeanne d'Albret wrote gratefully to Catherine de Medici. 'I will go to find you wherever you may be and shall kiss your feet more willingly than the Pope's'. Protection, however, had a price. Jeanne was summoned to the French court and Catherine wrote that she must moderate her religious policy 'in such a way that her subjects will not be led to rebel nor her neighbours to support them'. Jeanne should let her subjects 'all live in freedom of conscience and in the exercise of their own religion without forcing of any'. Jeanne's edict of February 1564 permitted a measure of Catholic as well as a measure of Calvinist worship and the pardon of all religious crimes that could not be considered lèse-majesté.

Jeanne d'Albret dawdled in obeying Catherine de Medici's summons to court; she had, after all, to arrange for her land to be ruled in her absence. But by the spring of 1564 it was Catherine herself who was setting out, taking her court and her son, the king, on a progress through France that would last for more than two years; ten thousand people on a twenty-seven-month journey, equipped with everything from portable triumphal arches to a travelling zoo. At the beginning of June, in Mâcon, Jeanne at last joined the royal tour, herself accompanied by three hundred cavalry and eight Calvinist ministers. From the start, her intransigence was clear.

The day after Jeanne's arrival, as the Corpus Christi procession passed under her windows, members of her suite shouted lewd remarks. In Lyons, a few days later, she attended Huguenot sermons, taking her son with her, until a provoked Catherine stopped the Calvinist services, took Jeanne's son Henri back into her own hands and swore she would cut off the head of anyone who did not attend Mass. But in some ways the progress had the unifying effect Catherine hoped for and, in Lyons, a joint procession of Catholic and Protestant children was staged to celebrate the current state of religious harmony.

As the journey wore on, Jeanne d'Albret often requested to be allowed to return to her own lands and to take her son with her. This was refused. Henri would continue to accompany the court. Jeanne, as a compromise, was instructed to retire to Vendôme; her own land but closer at hand and held in fief to the French crown.

Even Vendôme had seen conflict between the Calvinist lieutenants Jeanne had appointed and the royal agent the Protestants claimed was persecuting them. But Jeanne was to remain in its environs for some months. Everyone wanted her out of the way of the meeting that was looming at Bayonne, on the Spanish border.

There, Catherine de Medici hoped once again to see her daughter Elisabeth – a longed-for personal as well as a vital diplomatic encounter. But Philip of Spain, annoyed with Catherine's tolerant religious policy, and refusing to attend the meeting himself, had refused even to let his wife attend if Jeanne d'Albret and Condé were present; not wishing, he said, his wife to meet 'with rebels and fomenters of sedition'.

The meeting was a grand diplomatic spectacle and no doubt a rare personal pleasure for both Catherine de Medici and her daughter. But even here there was a conflict of interests. 'How Spanish you have become, my daughter,' Catherine said to Elisabeth, observing the latter's wholesale adoption not only of Spanish dress and manners but also of Philip's opinions. Philip had sent with his wife the Duke of Alba, a notorious hardliner and ardent Catholic, to dragoon Catherine into clamping down on the Huguenots. He failed, but conversely, the very fact of Catherine's having met him was taken by the Huguenot leaders as a worrying sign.

Immediately after the Bayonne meeting, Catherine de Medici, characteristically, once more set about appeasing the Protestant leaders. In the summer of 1565 Jeanne was allowed to leave Vendôme for Nérac (capital of the duchy of Albret, which gave her her name), there to receive the court on its homeward journey. Catherine urged Jeanne to return to the Catholic faith; Jeanne used the time to introduce her son Henri to leading Huguenots. When the royal circus finally reached Paris in early summer 1566, Jeanne d'Albret was with them but – so the Spanish ambassador complained – still behaving intransigently.

'Majesty and love do not sit well together'

Scotland, 1565–1567

I N THE SUMMER of 1565, Mary, Queen of Scots married her kinsman, Lord Darnley. What followed is one of the better-known tales in British history; a catastrophic chain of events and errors. Was Mary Stuart, like Jeanne d'Albret, a rebel against what those around her saw as good order and authority? Was she a fool for love? Or was she making what she saw as her best bid at keeping the rule of her country in her own (and a husband's) hands, however misguided her gamble proved to be? From the start, contemporary opinions were contradictory.

When Mary Stuart met, and to all appearances swiftly fell for Henry, Lord Darnley, she seemed to be fitting into the stereotype John Knox had used to discredit the whole idea of women's rule: infatuated, a prey to unbridled sensuality. As she told the English ambassador Randolph: 'Princes at all times have not their wills, but my heart being my own is immutable'. At eighteen, Darnley was tall (taller even than Mary's six foot), elegant, an expert in the manly arts and educated in a way which gave him a veneer of courtly civility, however illusory that would prove to be.

When, in February 1565, Mary went to greet Darnley on the Scottish coast, there was a subtext to any possible love story. The English parliament had objected to Mary's claim to the English throne on the grounds that she was a foreigner, as well as a woman and a Catholic. But if she could ally her claim to that of the English-born Margaret Douglas, Margaret Tudor's daughter and Darnley's mother, or to that of her son, it might be a different story.

This begs the question of why Elizabeth Tudor had agreed to let Darnley and his father Lennox go north to Scotland when they had asked permission the year before. The plausible reason was that Lennox needed to deal with his Scottish lands, but surely Elizabeth must have guessed what might happen? The idea of a match between Mary and Darnley had first been mooted long ago. Is it conceivable that Elizabeth was purposely handing Mary a poisoned chalice, knowing that Darnley would make Mary the worst of husbands?

It was Elizabeth Tudor herself who – inadvertently or otherwise – put the seal on the affair. Mary Stuart had been pressing for some definite commitment from Elizabeth regarding her place in the succession. In the middle of March Elizabeth's answer arrived; that 'nothing shall be done until her Majesty (Elizabeth) shall be married, or shall notify her determination never to marry'. No wonder it took the English ambassador Thomas Randolph two days to brace himself to deliver the message.

Within weeks Mary and Darnley were openly courting, with Mary defying convention to nurse him herself when he fell ill. When Elizabeth sent orders recalling Lennox and Darnley to England, Mary commanded them instead to remain. She was strengthened in her resolve by France's support, and by that of her former mother-in-law Catherine de Medici, whom it suited to have Elizabeth under pressure at this time.

Before the marriage, Darnley began to show himself as 'proud, disdainful and suspicious', drunken and violent. The question is whether or not Mary knew this; whether any infatuation she felt for him had already died. Throckmorton, sent to the Scottish court to bring Darnley home, found a queen 'seized with love in ferventer passions than is comely' even for 'mean persons'. But Randolph wrote to Robert Dudley, the Earl of Leicester, that Mary showed so much change in her nature 'that she beareth only the shape of the woman she was before'. A fool for love, or one already seeing love slip away?

'What shall become of her, or what life with him she shall lead, I leave it to others to think', Randolph prophesied gloomily. As Throckmorton quoted to Leicester and Cecil: 'Majesty and love do not sit well together, nor remain on one throne.' But Randolph was a partial witness, and royal marriages were not made for pleasure; and this one was going ahead whatever anybody said. Mary was unmoved by the disapproval of both her half-brother Lord James (now Earl of Moray) and Maitland. She was understandably disenchanted with their pro-English policy, while the fickle and ambitious Earl of Morton, another powerful player in Scottish affairs, was a kinsman of Darnley's.

'Greater triumphs there never were in time of Popery than were this Easter at the resurrection and at her high mass', reported Randolph grimly to Cecil at the end of April: 'She wanted now neither trumpet, drum, nor fife, bagpipe nor tabor ... Upon Monday she and divers of her women apparelled themselves like burgesses' wives, went upon their feet up and down the town, and of every man they met they took some pledge of money towards the banquet.'

Mary was riding high.

Elizabeth Tudor's attempt to forbid the match was countered by Mary Stuart with a mixture of wilful misunderstanding: Elizabeth had always said that Mary should marry an Englishman, hadn't she? and outright anger. 'You can never persuade me that I have failed your mistress', Mary told Randolph, 'but rather she to me; and some incommodity it will be as well for her to lose my amity as hers will be to me.'

The wedding took place on 29 July 1565, in Mary's private chapel, with Mary wearing the white dress of her widowhood. The ceremony was Catholic, although Darnley removed himself before the nuptial Mass. The heralds proclaimed him now King of Scotland: '. . . this Queen is now become a married wife', Randolph wrote to Leicester, 'and her husband, the self-same day of his marriage, made a king'. A king, however, 'so proud and spiteful, that rather he seemeth a monarch of the world than he that no long since we have seen and known the Lord Darnley'.

Darnley's kingship was in many ways an empty title. Mary never managed to procure him the Crown Matrimonial, which would have secured his position as a monarch of Scotland, independent of Mary, even in the event of her death. The great problem for reigning queens – the position of a consort – had caught out Mary. But it had also caught out Darnley.

In the first months of their marriage Mary and Darnley were able to subsume any anxieties into activity. They set out in force (and, in Darnley's case, in a specially-made gilt breastplate) to pursue and punish those lords who, under the leadership of her half-brother Moray, were now in open rebellion. Since battle was never really engaged with a fleeing foe, this became known as the Chaseabout Raid. But Mary showed to advantage, with loyal Scotsmen flocking to join her cause, more of them every day.

She sent Elizabeth word that she wanted no more interference in the affairs of her country; that she hoped she and her cousin could be the best of friends once more but only after Elizabeth had declared Mary her heir, she and Darnley. She reconciled most of the lords to her cause and split off the few rebels who held to Moray. When, at Mary's invitation, the Earl of Bothwell returned to the country and took command of the army, the rebels simply melted away. This, however, left the divisions in the royal marriage all the plainer to see.

On the one hand, Darnley was pressing not only for more power, but also for Europe's rulers to acknowledge his rights to hold the reins of the country. On the other, his unfitness for the role was becoming clearer every day. (Both his ambition and his outrages were reminiscent of the comportment of Margaret Tudor's husband Angus.) And there were two more jokers in the pack. One was that before the end of 1565, Mary Stuart must have known that she was pregnant. The other was that people were starting to talk about the favour Mary was showing to her Piedmontese private secretary, David Rizzio. 'To be ruled by the advice of two or three strangers, neglecting that of her chief councillors, I do not know how it can stand', Randolph wrote disapprovingly, calling Rizzio 'a filthy wedlock breaker'. Randolph warned Leicester: 'Woe is me for you when David son shall be a King of England.' This was surely an unfounded slander, but Mary's attitude to Rizzio could not but show up her very different feeling towards Darnley.

On 13 February 1566, Randolph told Leicester that 'I know now for certain that this Queen repenteth her marriage, that she hateth the King [Darnley] and all his kin' and that Darnley would be seeking to find a reason for that hatred. Darnley (prompted by a disaffected Scottish faction) had driven himself into a jealous fury, convinced Rizzio was the father of the child Mary now carried.

'I know that, if that take effect which is intended, David, with the consent of the King, shall have his throat cut within these ten days', Randolph predicted. It took a little longer, but on 9 March 1566 a party of nobles, Darnley among them, burst into Mary's chamber and hacked Rizzio to death almost before her eyes.

The bond signed by Lord Darnley declared:

> Be it known to all men by these present letters: We, Henry, by the grace of God, King of Scotland and husband to the Queen's Majesty . . . have thought pity to suffer her to be abused or seduced by certain privy persons, wicked and ungodly, especially a stranger Italian called Davie.

He and a group of lords had accordingly 'devised to take these privy persona, enemies to her Majesty, us, the nobility and commonwealth, to punish them according to their demerits, and in case of any difficulty, to cut them off immediately . . .' In this, as in many things, Darnley was the dupe of other, more resolute, men. But what was extraordinary was the insult to Mary.

Mary rallied sufficiently to persuade Darnley that his life as well as hers would ultimately be in danger from his collaborators; over-mighty subjects who had dared to kill her servant, almost in her very presence. Slipping out of the palace of Holyrood she escaped, taking him with her – a daring ride across country, despite her pregnancy, reminiscent of the journey her grandmother Margaret Tudor had undertaken. With Bothwell swiftly at her side she returned to Edinburgh in triumph and managed to regain a measure of control.

Elizabeth Tudor was genuinely horrified when she heard of the insults heaped upon Mary Stuart, telling the Spanish ambassador that Rizzio's killers had broken into Mary's chamber 'as if it were that of a public woman'. If this could happen to one of the two queens in the isle, it was all the harder for the other to preserve any sense of invulnerability.

While urging Robert Dudley on Mary, Elizabeth was half-heartedly contemplating her own marriage to the Archduke Charles, the emperor's son, although braced only for marriage 'as Queen and not as Elizabeth'. Then had come the suggestion of a French match – and there was always Robert Dudley. Even as Mary Stuart ordered her wedding clothes, Elizabeth Tudor was telling the Spanish ambassador that she would marry Robert if only he were 'a king's son', while the Holy Roman Emperor was sending another envoy. It seems likely that by 1566 Robert must have suspected he would never get anywhere with his hopes of marriage to the queen but, with him and at least one other, Elizabeth's matrimonial game had still some moves to be played.

The tempting possibility of her hand had become one of the best tools of her diplomacy. Almost forty years earlier, a Venetian observer had noted that the English used the young princess Mary as a hunter uses a lure to draw in birds. Elizabeth used her own hand in the same way.

In Scotland, incredibly, things were patched up after the debacle of Rizzio's death. With Mary expecting Darnley's child, they had to be. When she took to her birthing chamber in June, however, it was in Edinburgh Castle rather than any of her more commodious palaces. Edinburgh might indeed be a place steeped in Scottish history but it was also one of oft-proven security.

On 9 June she summoned the lords to hear her will, a sensible precaution for any women embarking on childbirth. The birth was long and difficult; so difficult that Mary, in the throes of labour, cried out that had she known the whole, she would never have got married, while the Countess of Atholl tried by 'incantations' to cast her pains on to another woman. But on 19 June the birth of a healthy baby boy, Prince James, set the seal on Mary's monarchy.

The Scottish ambassador to England took care to give Elizabeth all the gory details of the birth, telling her his mistress had been 'so sore handled that she wished she had never been married'. He did it, he said, 'to give her a little scare' off any marriage of her own. (It was obviously in Scotland's interest that Elizabeth Tudor should die unmarried, leaving Mary Stuart – or Mary's son – as her heir.) But that October, when in order to raise funds Elizabeth, was forced to summon parliament back after three years' absence, the members returned to London even more determined to tackle the question of the succession than before they had gone away.

Mary, when Darnley came to see his son, declared before witnesses that the baby was his. The extraordinary thing was that she should need to. Nevertheless, the summer of 1566, as Mary took time off to recover, saw some attempts at amity, sabotaged by the impossible Darnley. At Traquair there were plans for the royal couple to stag hunt the next day but Mary whispered in Darnley's ear that she preferred not to ride out. Another pregnancy was already a possibility. Darnley said loudly that never mind, if she lost this baby they could make another. It was a tiny incident, but it dramatised Mary's difficulties. His intransigence could only make her look favourably at other, more supportive figures.

In the autumn Queen Mary went to Jedburgh to preside over the justice assizes; one of those tasks she regularly undertook and which showed she aspired to be more than a pretty figurehead. While there, in the middle of October, she rode over to the stronghold of the Hermitage, where Lord Bothwell was lying ill, having been injured by Border raiders. The incident was later used to blacken her name, with the suggestion of an illicit affair between the pair but in fact Mary had taken a large party with her, including her half-brother Moray. The journey back was marred when Mary's horse threw her into a bog. The next day she fell ill, and soon her life was despaired of. The Bishop of Ross described it vividly: 'her Majesty became dead, and all her members cold, eyes closed, mouth fast, and feet and arms stiff and cold'.

She was brought round. But what is interesting is what the Venetian envoy in France heard as she recovered: that 'the illness was caused by her dissatisfaction at a decision made by the King, her husband'. Someone was going to have to do something about Lord Darnley.

As Mary began to recover her strength she moved, with a number of her lords, to Craigmillar, just outside Edinburgh, and it was probably there that a conspiracy was launched. Or perhaps several different conspiracies. Mary was persuaded to pardon even the Rizzio plotters; there was now only one real enemy. When his son was baptised on 17 December at Stirling Castle, Darnley, although present in the palace, did not attend the ceremony. Instead, foreign guests were welcomed by Lord Bothwell, who was gaining an ever-increasing ascendancy.

The first weeks of 1567 saw Darnley ill and undergoing medical treatment in Glasgow, heartland of his family's territory. His illness was almost certainly syphilis, and the fact that she might soon be called on to resume sexual relations with him was a factor in Mary's determination to be free. When Mary went to visit him there were huge concerns about her security and there had long been talk that Darnley might try to kidnap the baby James and rule as regent himself while holding Mary in captivity.

Just how far Mary's desire to be free carried her was and is a source of huge controversy. The bare facts are easily stated. At the end of January Queen Mary persuaded Darnley to return to Edinburgh with her where, by his own choice, he lodged at the nearby house of Kirk o'Field until his cure was complete. Mary visited him frequently; on 9 February she was there with a cheerful company, although she left early to attend a page's wedding party.

At 2 am on the 10th February, Edinburgh was rocked by the sound of an explosion. Mary, at Holyrood, sent at once to inquire what had happened, and soon heard that Kirk o'Field was rubble. The day's light, however, revealed Darnley's dead body not in the house but strangled, in the garden, whence he had apparently been trying to flee.

Volumes have been devoted to the murder of Lord Darnley and this is no place to weigh the evidence. Two things are important: Bothwell was immediately suspected by all sides of having cleared his rival out of the way and Mary was widely suspected of complicity. And perhaps a third: most historians today consider she was innocent at least of precise knowledge of the plan, although one of the skills of medieval or early modern monarchy might be to be able to express a desire that some obstacle be removed and take care not to know precisely how it would happen.

At Craigmillar Maitland had suggested a divorce or annulment but Mary was concerned that might affect her son's legitimacy. When Maitland seemed to say another way would have to be found, she cried out that nothing should be done against her reputation or her honour. To have failed subsequently to prevent what she should surely have guessed her lords were thinking was, if not a sin of omission, then at least an act of folly. But of folly, most would in the end have to declare Mary Stuart guilty.

Certainly Mary did now act foolishly. Her very unpreparedness to deal with this crisis perhaps suggests she had not anticipated it precisely. Instead of observing the strictest mourning as a wife, and as queen distancing herself from those suspected of the deed, she vacillated. She ordered black drapes for her chamber at Edinburgh Castle but stopped off as she travelled there, to attend another wedding party. She went to nearby Seton, several times, for a few days' holiday. She was observed, with the ever-present Bothwell, to be disporting herself at archery. Her mood was volatile, although she was distressed and angered by the placards blaming Bothwell for Darnley's death. One depicted Mary herself as a mermaid, a notorious symbol of harlotry.

Elizabeth, from England, wrote to her with extraordinary vehemence:

> My ears have been so astounded, my mind so disturbed and my heart so appalled at hearing the horrible report of the abominable murder of your late husband and my slaughtered cousin, that I can scarcely as yet summon the spirit to write about it . . . I will not conceal from you that people for the most part are saying that you will look through your fingers at this deed instead of avenging it . . . I exhort you, I counsel you, and I beg you to take this thing so far to heart that you will not fear to touch even him who you have nearest to you if he were involved . . .

Elizabeth was clearly afraid that Mary's actions would compromise the sisterhood of queens. If Mary failed to use such sincerity 'and prudence' that the world should pronounce her innocent, wrote Elizabeth on another occasion, then she would 'deserve to fall from the ranks of princesses and rather than that should happen to you, I would wish you an honourable burial rather than a soiled life'.

On 12 April, Bothwell was acquitted in a show trial; the verdict the surer both for the fact that Edinburgh was so packed with his men that Lennox, Darnley's father, dared not appear, and that Mary had waved him off to the hearing. A week later Bothwell went further, summoning the lords to a supper at Ainslie's Tavern. There, he demanded that they should all sign a bond. It called on the queen to marry and to marry a Scotsman. And who better than Bothwell himself?

Mary's next action was that of both a queen and a mother. She went to Stirling, where her son was being raised, to try to get possession of the baby. When Prince James's official guardian refused to give him up,

Mary was forced to set out once again towards Edinburgh. On 24 April she rode out from her birthplace, Linlithgow, to return to the city. The Spanish ambassador Guzman de Silva (writing home on 3 May) described what came next:

> On arriving six miles from Edinburgh, Bothwell met her with four hundred horsemen. As they arrived near the Queen with their swords drawn they showed an intention of taking her with them . . . She was taken to Dunbar, where she arrived at midnight, and still remains. Some say she will marry him . . .

Crucially, the ambassador continued: 'It is believed that the whole thing has been arranged, so that if anything comes of the marriage the Queen may make out that she was forced into it.'

Therein lay the rub. Although Mary's first reaction – ordering her men to ride for help – suggests she had genuinely been ambushed by Bothwell, her subsequent reaction is harder to understand. She remained at Dunbar for twelve days, by the end of which, from later evidence, she would seem to have been pregnant. Bothwell was absent for part of the time, arranging a hasty divorce from his wife, so as to free himself for a more advantageous marriage, and the conditions of her 'captivity', if one can call it that, were not such as to preclude Mary's escaping, if she really wished to.

The dark suspicion, as Maitland's friend Kirkaldy of Grange put it, was that Mary 'was minded to cause Bothwell to ravish her'; that to avoid the blame she would incur if she openly took up with the man believed to be her husband's murderer, she had helped to set up what was to be passed off as an abduction and ravishment.

Perhaps a more likely explanation is that Mary was indeed surprised and outraged by Bothwell's abduction but that he then won her round. She had, after all, come to feel in the last months that he was the only man in Scotland on whom she could really rely; who seemed to answer her desperate need for support and protection. If he told her he had been impelled to seize her for her own safety, and that her only hope lay in marrying him; if he showed her the Ainslie Tavern bond . . . That is the explanation Mary herself sent to her ambassador at the French court and the long circumstantial story makes convincing reading:

... seeing ourselves in Bothwell's power, sequestered from the company of our servants and others, of whom we might ask counsel . . . left alone, as it were, a prey to him, many things we resolved with ourself, but never could find a way out. And yet he gave us little space to meditate with ourself, ever pressing us with continual and importunate suit. In the end, when we saw no hope to be rid of him, never man in Scotland making a move to procure our deliverance we were compelled to mitigate our displeasure, and began to think upon that which he propounded.

... Albeit we found Bothwell's doings rude, yet were his words and answers gentle. As by a bravado in the beginning he had won the first point, so ceased he never till by persuasions and importune suit, accompanied not the less with force, he has finally driven us to end the work begun at such time and in such form as he thought might best serve his turn ...

The conclusion that would best serve Bothwell's turn was marriage with the queen, but she had her reasons for agreeing to the idea. Scotland 'being divided into factions as it is', she wrote (and it might have been her grandmother Margaret Tudor speaking), 'cannot be contained in order unless our authority be assisted and set forth by the fortification of a man'.

On 6 May they rode back into Edinburgh through sullen crowds, Bothwell leading Mary's horse. On 12 May she formally pardoned him for abducting her, and raised him to Duke of Orkney. On 15 May they were married, in a Protestant ceremony.

Once again, as with the marriage to Darnley, Mary's feelings appear to have been in conflict. Within days, the French ambassador Du Croc was writing to Catherine de Medici: 'The Queen's marriage is too unhappy and begins already to be repented of.' Mary had sent for him, after he had seen her and her husband at odds, and told him that, 'If you see me melancholy, it is because I do not choose to be cheerful; because I never will be so, and wish for nothing but death.'

'Yesterday, when they were both in a room, she called aloud for a knife to kill herself; the persons in the ante-chamber heard it,' De Croc reported. Bothwell, like Darnley but with greater force and abilities, was another man determined to rule as king. But the court was becoming a travesty from which men such as Maitland slipped away daily.

On 6 June, knowing the Earl of Morton and the lords were planning an attack, and determined on his overthrow, Bothwell took Mary away from Edinburgh, to a place of greater safety. On 15 June, a scorching day, the royal forces and those of the lords faced each other at Carberry.

Bothwell was ready to decide the matter by single combat. It was Mary who eventually intervened, knowing surely that this was no way to regain any useful control of her country. A deal was struck whereby she would be taken into honourable custody and Bothwell allowed to go free. But Mary was appalled by the reaction of the soldiers and, as the lords led her into Edinburgh, of the citizenry. Her dress torn, alternately sobbing and threatening, she listened to the crowds yelling, 'Burn the whore'. Was this the real romance gone wrong; the love Elizabeth never wholly lost in all her long marriage to her country?

On 17 June Queen Mary was taken, captive, from Holyrood to the island castle of Loch Leven, where she almost immediately miscarried, reportedly of twins.[1] On 24 June, still weak, Mary was forced to sign a document of abdication. Five weeks later her baby son was crowned James VI, with her half-brother Moray to act as regent during his minority.

Queen Elizabeth wrote yet again to her 'sister Sovereign': 'whatsoever we can imagine meet for your honour and safety that shall lie in our power, we will perform the same [so] that it shall well appear you have a good neighbour, a dear sister, and a faithful friend'. Elizabeth was aware that a blow to one monarch, and a female monarch, damaged any monarchy. 'You shall plainly declare to the lords that if they shall determine anything to the deprivation of the Queen their sovereign lady of her royal estate . . . we will make ourselves a plain party against them, for example to all posterity', she wrote to her ambassador in Scotland.

It may have been the fear of Elizabeth's wrath that kept Mary's lords from proceeding to any lethal extremity. Nonetheless, in Elizabeth Tudor's eyes Mary Stuart had committed an unforgivable crime. She had made all female rulers look foolish – exactly as men like John Knox had always suspected them to be.

'daughter of debate'

The Netherlands, France, England, 1566–1571

I N CONTINENTAL EUROPE too, religious divisions were hard-
ening. In the Netherlands Margaret of Parma, acting as regent for
her half-brother Philip of Spain, had from the start faced a situation even more difficult than that which had plagued her aunt Mary of
Hungary when she was regent for *her* brother Charles V.[1]

Charles V, who had been reared in the Netherlands, spent much of
his reign moving around his vast territories. Philip, although too
painstaking not to pay due tribute to the Netherlands and its culture,
was every inch a Spaniard, determined to rule from Madrid, or from
the vast new palace he was building nearby, the Escorial. This left the
Netherlands dissatisfied with their position as, effectively, a mere
colony and Philip with little real understanding of the seventeen very
different provinces that made up his northern holding. But it also left
Margaret of Parma, given far less authority than her predecessors,
trying to implement instructions sent from Philip, many weeks' journey away.

No one as yet spoke of the dissent in the Netherlands as a struggle
for independence. Instead, the trouble was cast in religious terms. The
Netherlands Council of State was coming under the leadership of the
Stadtholder William of Orange, who had been raised partly under the
influence of Mary of Hungary and was much trusted by her and by
Charles V. Now William, brought into alliance with the German
Protestant princes through a marriage with Anna of Saxony, electrified
the Council by expressing his continued opposition to Philip on

religious grounds. Himself a Catholic, he could not concede that a monarch had the right to decide his subjects' beliefs. Philip, horrified by the growing power of the Protestants in France, had earlier ordered Margaret of Parma to strictly enforce Charles V's *Placarten*, edicts imposing harsh penalties against heresy. William told the council that 'the king errs if he thinks that the Netherlands, surrounded as they are by countries where religious freedom is permitted, can indefinitely support the sanguinary edicts'.

In April 1565 a Confederacy of noblemen, William's younger brother Louis prominent among them, presented a petition to Margaret of Parma, requesting an end to the persecution of Protestants. The next year saw a wave of iconoclasm, as Protestants of various denominations swept through the Netherlands destroying Catholic images; exactly the kind of news most certain to appal Philip of Spain. Religious discontent was fostered by economic hardship: as one observer put it, 'It is folly to enforce the edicts while corn is so dear.'

Margaret's instinct was to agree to the demands of the Confederacy, as long as its members joined her in restoring order. In Italy, the counselling of the Jesuits' founder, Ignatius Loyola, had mediated in Margaret's troubled marriage to Farnese and her patronage had been vital in getting Loyola's nascent Society of Jesus off the ground. But, like Catherine de Medici and Elizabeth of England, she seems to have made a distinction between religious belief and civil disobedience. Also like Catherine de Medici, however, she would be thwarted in the attempt to act on any such belief. Elizabeth, in England, would hold out for longer.

The report Margaret of Parma sent to Philip sounded a despairing note. 'Everything is in such disorder that in the greater part of the country there is neither law, faith nor king.' Despite the sound of panic, she was taking steps successfully to deal with the situation. The noblemen, content their petition was to be forwarded to Philip, had for the most part rallied behind the regent, the country was calm and the effect of her words was surely not what she desired. Even as Margaret caused a triumphal medal to be struck, figuring her as an Amazon wielding both sword and olive branch, the hard-line Duke of Alba was despatched north from Spain to deal with what Philip saw as a rebellion, while the request that between ten to twenty thousand Spanish troops should be allowed to march through France, Netherlands-bound, was another source of alarm to the French Protestants and another thorn in the side of Catherine de Medici.

On his arrival Alba set up the Council of Troubles, a body directly under his control, to enforce the *Placarten* with the utmost stringency. More than three thousand people would be executed over the next five years. In June 1568 sixty Netherlands nobles, including a cousin of the French Admiral de Coligny, were put to death on the Grand Place in Brussels. But by then (in September 1567), Margaret of Parma had resigned her regency.

Margaret's resignation was a protest against Alba's powers, which were greater than her own and perhaps also against his policies, though it might be a mistake to assume her motives were humanitarian. Margaret retired to L'Aquila in Italy, where she was appointed governor of Abruzzo but she was still identified with the harsh rule of Spain. A 1622 picture in Berlin's museum of history, *The tied-up Dutch provinces before Duke Alba*, shows Alba enthroned in judgement above seventeen chained women, representing the provinces. Cardinal Grenville wields bellows to inflate Alba's fury while behind him Margaret of Parma fishes for their goods in a river of blood.[2]

Events in the Netherlands reverberated throughout Europe. In England, at the end of 1567, word of the Spanish activities finally saw an end to the proposal of a marriage between Elizabeth and the Habsburg archduke, the emperor's son. Moreover, William of Orange, now escaped to Germany, sought to drive the Spanish from the Netherlands. He would look not only to the German princes but also to the French Protestants for help in raising an army. As the French court arrived back from its 'Grand Tour' it became clear that one major source of dissent was going to be the desire of the Huguenots (and particularly of Admiral de Coligny, who had gained a quasi-paternal ascendancy over the young king, Charles IX) to aid their fellow Protestants across the border.

The clampdown in the Netherlands even affected Jeanne d'Albret. Throughout 1566, after the court's return, she remained in Paris, possibly in a house of her own rather than in the uncongenial atmosphere of the court itself. Eyeing the sexual licence of the French court, she wrote disgustedly. 'It is not the men who invite the women but the women who invite the men'. She was increasingly ill and increasingly at odds with other ladies of the court, notably Anne d'Este (the former Duchesse de Guise) and thus also with Anne's mother Renée, Marguerite of Navarre's former protégée. But she was also taking her son Henri on brief, seemingly innocuous visits to lands of her own nearby.

It apparently came as a surprise to Catherine de Medici when the Spanish ambassador told her, in the middle of February 1567, that Jeanne, with her son, had slipped back to the southwest and out of French control. 'This woman is the most *dévergondée* (shameless) and passionate creature in the world', raged Catherine.

Jeanne d'Albret recorded in her *Mémoires* how often she had cried for peace and how often Catherine and her son had tried to lure her back to court 'under the pretext of doing me the honour of making me the mediator between the King and his subjects of the Reformed religion'. But Jeanne's path led another way.

In September 1567 the Huguenot leaders Condé and Coligny, mistrusting the French crown's promise of religious tolerance, made an unsuccessful attempt to capture the young king. Six thousand Swiss guards were hired to escort Catherine and her son back to Paris but Condé and Coligny then embarked on a siege of the city. Their assaults were unavailing and they were forced to retreat southwards, but it is little wonder that in May 1568, weeks after a peace had finally been negotiated with the rebels, Catherine de Medici became gravely ill. When she recovered, it was to find Coligny and Condé in flight. Catherine's intentions were to 'run them to earth, defeat them and destroy them'. Would she include Jeanne in her hostility?

For that autumn, as Condé and Coligny rode towards the Huguenots' stronghold of La Rochelle, on the coast of the southwest of France, where Protestantism had gained the greatest support, Jeanne d'Albret had set out to join their party, with her daughter Catherine and fifteen-year-old Henri. 'Do not think . . . that I undertook this journey lightly', she said in the *Mémoires* she caused to be written some eight weeks into her stay. 'Believe me, it was not without conflict, with others and with myself . . . I not only had to fight outside enemies, I had a war in my entrails. Even my will was in league against me.'

She was to remain in La Rochelle – 'deprived of the pleasure of my own houses, but only too happy to suffer for my God' – for almost three years. She was, she wrote to Catherine de Medici, in 'the service of my God and of the truth faith'. But Catherine was unlikely to be mollified.

Jeanne d'Albret wrote also to Elizabeth of England, whose 'good will' she continued to laud. She also wrote propaganda pamphlets and ran a body called the Council of the Queen of Navarre, charged with the administration of the town and all not strictly military aspects of the campaign. She set the troops she had brought to work strengthening La Rochelle's fortifications. At the end of 1568 the Spanish ambassador was reporting that she 'continued to share the leadership' with Condé.

Then, at the Battle of Jarnac on 13 March 1569, the Prince de Condé was taken prisoner and then slain, leaving nominal command of the Huguenot cause to two fifteen-year-olds: Jeanne's son Henri of Navarre, and his cousin, the son of Condé. It was Jeanne who led the boys out to receive the acclamation of the Huguenot troops. It was Jeanne who wrote begging that Elizabeth of England would 'continue the affection you bear to so just and legitimate a cause . . . Amongst us, great and small are resolved to spare neither our lives nor our fortunes in the service of God's quarrel.' Although Catherine de Medici referred to her as 'marching with the Admiral', when Coligny and the boys went out on campaign Jeanne was left behind to cope with as many as sixty thousand refugees as people poured into La Rochelle.

Most among the Huguenot leadership were now thinking of peace. Not so Jeanne d'Albret, who was almost taken prisoner while outside the walls overseeing the construction of new fortifications. By the spring of 1570, it was Jeanne's determination that was continuing the fight. It would be Jeanne who later held out for freedom of worship as the price of peace, rather than Catherine's subtler and more pragmatic offer of freedom of conscience, with its suggestion of outward conformity.

Jeanne wrote to Catherine de Medici:

I can scarcely persuade myself having once had the honour of knowing Your Majesty's sentiments intimately that you could wish to see us reduced to such an extremity or to profess ourselves of no religion whatever, which must be the case if we are denied the public exercise of our own ritual . . . We have come to the determination to die, all of us, rather than abandon our God, the which we cannot maintain unless permitted to worship publicly, any more than a human body can live without meat or drink.

The war, in all directions, was becoming ever more bitter. Outside La Rochelle, Catherine's son Henri, Duc d'Anjou, leading the fighting on the crown's side, was behaving with terrifying savagery. There were rumours that Catherine, earlier in the troubles, had tried to kill Condé by means of a poisoned apple (a Snow White touch), and a man arrested on his way to Coligny's service was indeed carrying a packet of poison, while the Spanish ambassador reported Catherine had been trying to rid herself of the Protestant leaders by sorcery.

Catherine had been greatly saddened when her daughter Elisabeth, Philip of Spain's wife, died in childbirth in October 1568. This also meant she had no longer any special hold on Elisabeth's widower Philip of Spain, who had long been disgusted by her pragmatic religious stance. Catherine had written that she envied Elizabeth of England because 'all the subjects share the Queen's religion; in France it is quite another matter'. But in fact, Elizabeth Tudor might have greeted that with an 'if only'.

At the beginning of May 1568 the imprisoned Mary Stuart escaped from Loch Leven, and her lords' custody. Her supporters were defeated at the Battle of Langside on 13 May, and on 16 May she crossed the Solway Firth and fled across the border into England.

Mary had believed Elizabeth Tudor's protestations of sisterly solidarity; believed Elizabeth would immediately restore her to her throne. In many ways that was Elizabeth's first instinct: queenship called to queenship. But this was met with disagreement from most of Elizabeth's councillors, especially Cecil. Elizabeth's attitude was complex. As Mary sent an appeal to Elizabeth's fellow feeling 'not from a queen, but from a gentlewoman', Elizabeth was gloating over the purchase of Mary's famous black pearls – twenty-five of them, the size and colour of grapes – for which she had outbid Catherine de Medici.

Mary reluctantly agreed to Elizabeth's suggestion of an inquiry into her conduct, and into the rumours that she had been involved in her husband Darnley's death. The inquiry opened at York that autumn. The Scottish lords tried to ensure a 'guilty' verdict by producing the infamous 'Casket Letters'; letters purporting to prove Mary a murderous adulteress but which were almost certainly faked. Even with these dubious documents before them, the commissioners failed to reach any real verdict, leaving Mary to remain as the 'guest' of her 'dear cousin and friend' Elizabeth; locked into an indefinite genteel captivity.

The inquiry had repercussions of a different sort. The commissioners had been led by Thomas Howard, Duke of Norfolk, Elizabeth's kinsman and premier peer and a man with his own stake in the English throne. Norfolk had at first been horrified by the letters that seemed to prove Mary's 'inordinate' love for Bothwell. Norfolk's instructions from Elizabeth's government had included the clause that anyone plotting Mary's marriage 'shall be *ipso facto* acknowledged as traitorous and shall suffer death', but when one of Mary's lords suggested to him that the best way of neutralising Mary, and providing for the English succession, was to marry her himself, the idea took root in his mind.

The story of the next few months is uncertain, but Norfolk's aspirations were clearly something of an open secret at the English court. Dangerously, they became linked to the discontent felt by peers in the north of England, many of whom had never lost their Catholic faith. The result was the so-called Revolt of the Northern Earls in the autumn of 1569, which aimed to free Mary, if not actually to place her on Elizabeth's throne.

The rebellion failed, and many of the rebels suffered the harshest punishments. Norfolk was sent to the Tower, where he languished for some months. But what of Mary? The Queen of Scots had written to Norfolk as to her future husband; had made and sent him embroideries depicting a fruitful vine (Mary herself) and a hand clipping away the barren branch (Elizabeth). No direct reprisals were taken against Mary Stuart but she was kept in closer captivity.

In February 1570, the pope issued the bull *Regnans in excelsis*, depriving Elizabeth of 'her pretended right to her realm' and sanctioning any Catholic who attempted to depose her. This greatly raised the level of tension in England, both increasing and highlighting Elizabeth's vulnerability. In a poem she probably wrote in 1571, Elizabeth Tudor described Mary Stuart:

> The daughter of debate
> That discord aye doth sow
> Shall reap no gain where former rule
> Still peace hath taught to know.

Her words would prove prophetic.

In France, Catherine de Medici's goal was the reduction of tension, not its increase. On 8 August 1570 the Treaty of St Germain finally brought peace: freedom of conscience and freedom of worship limited to certain locations. But there had been other peace treaties and none had lasted. Jeanne d'Albret for one, during the long negotiations, had called this 'a peace made of snow this winter that would melt in next summer's heat'. Now Catherine had a plan to cement it. As early as May 1569 Sir Henry Norris told Elizabeth of England that Catherine de Medici planned 'to practice to withdraw the Queen of Navarre' by offering her daughter Margot in marriage to Jeanne's son Henri. Marriage was always Catherine's favourite way out of any diplomatic difficulty.

Catherine also had another marriage in mind. England had more reason than ever to pursue the safety of a French alliance against the increasing power and aggression of Spain. The summer of 1571 saw the 'discovery' of the Ridolfi Plot (of which Elizabeth's ministers may in fact long have known), to place Mary Stuart and the Duke of Norfolk on England's throne, with Spanish support and an invasion force headed by the Duke of Alba.

So Queen Elizabeth was amenable to Catherine's suggestion, in December 1571, that she might marry François, the Duc d'Alençon, instead of his elder brother, the reluctant Anjou. François, his mother Catherine coolly observed, was 'much less scrupulous' than his brother in matters of religion; sympathetic, even, to the Huguenots. Altogether less 'like a mule' as Elizabeth's envoy chimed in enthusiastically, and 'more apt than th'other' when it came to getting children.

England and France concluded the Treaty of Blois, whereby they agreed to support each other against the Spanish enemy. It now seemed more desirable than ever that this alliance should be cemented dynastically. In June came the formal offer of Alençon's hand. Elizabeth's ambassador (and later spymaster) Francis Walsingham feared that the small and pockmarked seventeen-year-old Alençon would never pass the crucial test, given 'the delicacy of Her Majesty's eye'. Nevertheless, as the court set off on its annual summer progress, the marriage seemed still a real possibility.

England and France had both seen trouble, but both might now hope the trouble had been successfully resolved. That hope would prove deceptive.

The Massacre of St Bartholomew's Day

France, 1572–1574

QUEEN ELIZABETH WAS at Robert Dudley's great castle of
Kenilworth when she had news of an event that shook her
world, one of those events which really do change history:
the Massacre of St Bartholomew's Day. The story had seemed at first to
lie between Catherine de Medici and Jeanne d'Albret but in the end,
the repercussions would reach out to touch everybody.

In the early months of 1571 William of Orange, the exiled leader of the
Netherlands Protestants, was trying to orchestrate an armed invasion of
the Netherlands from Germany. Although his brother was with the
Huguenot rebels in La Rochelle, Orange needed to draw the French
crown also to his side, invoking an old anti-Spanish hostility still arguably
more potent than religious division. The idea had immense appeal for a
young king anxious to prove his mettle in battle and soon Charles IX was
to be heard complaining that Catherine was 'too timid'. Newly married to
Elizabeth of Austria, devout young daughter of the Holy Roman Emperor,
Charles was beginning to resent his mother's dominance.[1] A few days
after the formal entry into Paris that celebrated his marriage in March
1571, Charles made a speech to his *parlement* commending Catherine's
'tireless work, energy and wisdom' in taking care of affairs of state for all
the time he had been too young to do so himself; the implication being
that such days were coming to an end.

Catherine de Medici was temperamentally opposed to expensive
warfare (yet another thing on which she agreed with Elizabeth of
England) but she was prepared to use the possibility of French support

for the Dutch Protestants as a lever to induce Jeanne d'Albret to agree to the marriage of her son Henri to Catherine's daughter Margot. (No one cared about Margot's reluctance to marry a heretic. Catherine threatened to make her daughter 'the most wretched lady in the kingdom' if she refused, but Jeanne's reluctance was another story.)

There was still, in theory, a personal bond between Catherine de Medici and Jeanne d'Albret. At the start of 1571 Jeanne wrote to Catherine of her reluctance to bring her son to the French court:

> ... I have a suspicious nature, Madame, as you well know, which makes me fear that, although your intentions are good – which I do not doubt – those who have been able to alter them in the past in regard to us ... continue to have credit with you ... I would fear to anger you by these words, Madame, if your kindness to me in my youth had not accustomed me to the privilege of speaking frankly and privately to you ...

Touchingly, she wrote *je suis ung petit glorieuse* ('I am a proud little thing' or 'a bit of a proud one'). She was indeed so; Biron, one of the envoys sent to negotiate with her, described to a colleague 'the scowling face in front of me'. An Italian wrote that 'the temper of this Queen is *molto fantastico* [very fantastical] ... She changes often and eludes you every minute. In the end she hopes to manage everything her own way.'

Jeanne d'Albret was under considerable pressure, not least from some of her own side. Admiral de Coligny's prime goal was to get French help for the Dutch Protestants; Jeanne's to preserve her inherited territories and her son's place in the French succession. On 31 August the papal nuncio reported that 'there is great discord between them because the Queen [Jeanne] wishes to conduct her own affairs by herself, without interference from the Admiral, while he seeks to make her obey the King'. While she was dubious about marrying her son to the Catholic Margot, she must have been alarmed, too, by Coligny's attempts to marry him elsewhere; even, for a few weeks in 1571, to Elizabeth of England.

That autumn Coligny arrived at court to negotiate, his safe conduct signed by Charles IX, by Catherine de Medici and by her next son, Anjou. His friends had warned Coligny not to go. His reception, however, went almost too smoothly. Coligny even accompanied Catherine to Mass, though he made a point of neither removing his hat nor of bowing to the Host. The young king Charles was soon back under Coligny's sway. The Spanish envoy described how Coligny told the king not to discuss his Netherlands plans with his mother, because these were 'not questions to be discussed with women and clerks. When the Queen Mother heard of this, she was on very bad terms with the said Admiral . . .'

Ever more pressure was being placed on Jeanne that she too should come to the French court. One indirect form of blackmail was the fear that her youthful marriage to Cleves could be recalled to discredit her marriage to Antoine de Bourbon and thus cast doubts on her son Henri's legitimacy. During the summer of 1571 Jeanne's health had given her a pretext to stall: 'I can never thank you enough for the honour you do me in wishing to see me', she wrote to Charles, 'but, to my great regret, Monseigneur, I have been obliged to yield to the exigencies of my health.' If she could no longer reasonably remain in La Rochelle, she could and did go to take the water cure at Eaux-Chaudes.

To Catherine de Medici's endless assurances of her safety if she entrusted herself to the French court, Jeanne d'Albret wrote testily from La Rochelle:

> I cannot imagine why you should find it necessary to say that you want to see me and my children, but not in order to do us harm. Forgive me if I laugh when I read these letters, for you are allaying a fear I never had. I have never thought that you fed on little children, as they say.

Eventually, her historian Bordenave related, Jeanne could no longer hold out. 'The leaders of her own religion were those who most urged her to do it.' She 'bowed to their will in order that they might not blame her stubbornness for keeping so many good things . . . from coming to pass'.

Jeanne said she would come to court, on certain conditions. One was that she wanted to negotiate directly with Catherine. Was it to be another kind of ladies' peace?

* * *

There were conditions on the other side, of course. The pope vowed he would lose his last drop of blood rather than grant the necessary dispensation for the marriage before the groom had returned to the Catholic church. But his envoy told him that most French, even Catholics, desired the marriage, 'comparing it to that of Clovis and Clothilde' – the Frankish king and the wife who persuaded him to convert to Christianity – while Catherine de Medici warningly invoked the example of Henry VIII.

In January 1572, in a carriage the size of a house, with a stove burning inside, and in no particular hurry, Jeanne d'Albret reluctantly set out to join the French court at Blois. The Florentine ambassador Petrucci wrote on 14 February that:

> today the Queen Mother [Catherine] went to Chenonceau to meet the Queen of Navarre. Embraces and salutations were exchanged . . . and the Queen of Navarre asked at once for something to eat. Immediately afterward the two queens retired into a room alone.

Jeanne's letters to the son she had left behind are revealing and sometimes appealing. She took to her prospective daughter-in-law: 'If she embraces our religion I may say that we are the happiest persons in the world.' Jeanne's thirteen-year-old daughter Catherine de Bourbon added her mite: 'I have seen Madame [Margot] and found her very beautiful . . . She was kind to me and gave me a little dog I like very much.'

Jeanne's initial attempts at optimism did not last. She suspected that Catherine and her son the king were trying to play her for a fool and she was probably right. A Huguenot contemporary describes Charles IX lavishing attention on Jeanne in public but then asking his mother in private if he was not playing his part well: 'Leave it to me and I will deliver them into your net.'

An ardent Catholic advised Catherine on how to handle Jeanne: 'as one woman to another, make her mad while staying calm yourself'. Petrucci described one long and fraught bout of negotiations, in which Catherine had suggested they allow their differences to be settled by deputies, to which Jeanne retorted that she trusted nobody but herself. 'This is no small break in the negotiations because *Navarra* is so obstinate . . . and no real results can be obtained without her agreement.'

On 8 March Jeanne sent a long and agitated letter to her son:

> I am in agony, in such extreme suffering that if I had not been prepared, it would overcome me . . . I am not free to talk with either the King or Madame [Margot], only with the Queen Mother, who goads me [*me traite a la fourche*] . . . She treats me so shamefully that you might say that the patience I manage to maintain surpasses that of Griselda herself . . . I have come this far on the sole understanding that the Queen and I would negotiate and be able to agree. But all she does is mock me.

Even Margot was not as she had been represented: 'she replied that when these negotiations begun we well knew she was devout in her religion. I told her that those who made the first overtures to us represented the matter very differently . . .'

Another letter to one of Jeanne's advisors three days later was even more agitated. 'I assure you I often remember your warning not to get angry.' She was fighting to keep her son away from the court while matters were still unsettled, fighting to convince the sceptical French courtiers that he was as committed as she to the reformed religion.

'As for the beauty of Madame Marguerite [Margot], I admit she has a good figure, but it is too tightly corseted. Her face is spoiled by too much makeup, which displeases me . . .' The corruption of the French court was a recurrent theme. Everyone was aware of the possibility of espionage and deceit. Jeanne swore holes were drilled in the walls of her apartment for the use of spies.

Jeanne d'Albret put her faith in the support of the English, claiming Queen Elizabeth would only make a treaty with France if the crown behaved properly over the Navarre marriage. But if it was important for Jeanne to feel the weight of international Protestant opinion behind her, international Protestantism also needed this alliance.

Acting as England's ambassador in France, Francis Walsingham found himself in a very special relationship with Jeanne. On 29 March he was writing to Cecil of how 'with the consent of the Queen-Mother, she had sent for us as the ministers and ambassadors of a Christian princess, whom she had sundry causes to honour, to confer with us . . . touching certain difficulties'.

Jeanne wished to confer with her co-religionists on some knotty points of doctrine concerning the marriage of a Catholic and a Protestant and also on the central issues of the two continuing in their separate religions. Her advisors urged her to stand firm on some points, but it remained vital that the marriage went ahead: 'upon the success of the Navarre marriage depends the enterprise of Flanders', wrote Walsingham.

Towards the end of March King Charles gave ground. As long as Henri of Navarre would come to Paris for the wedding, he would yield on all other points. Even the ministers to whom Jeanne appealed, asking if the marriage could be legal if it were not performed before a Calvinist congregation, declared that 'considering the urgent necessity of the case' it was.

Jeanne wrote encouragingly to Henri of how he should behave at the French court:

> be gracious, but speak boldly even when you are taken aside by the King, for note that the impression you make on arrival will remain . . . try to train your hair to stand up and be sure there are no lice in it.

'Your sister has a very annoying cough, which keeps her in bed. She drinks donkey's milk and calls the little ass her brother', Jeanne added, charmingly.

On 4 April the official decision was made to proceed. The next day Jeanne d'Albret wrote to Queen Elizabeth:

> I would not, therefore, Madame, lose time in informing you of the event, so that I may rejoice with you . . . I entreat you, Madame, to pardon the boldness which your goodness inspires, if I venture very earnestly to desire that I may soon have occasion to congratu-late you on a similar event personal to yourself.

The marriage contract signed on 11 April made no mention of reli-gious issues but only of the inheritance of various lands. This was based on a French conviction that Henri, if not Jeanne herself, would soon return to the Roman church. The Bishop of Mâcon saw it as Catherine's victory:

> The Queen Mother has chosen the best possible way . . . she has abased the haughtiness of the Queen of Navarre, overcome her instability, and made her accept conditions . . . we will soon see the Prince [Henri] returning to the bosom of Holy Church.

Jeanne, exhausted, set out for Vendôme to rest but soon the need to prepare for the forthcoming marriage sent her back to Paris. As Anne d'Este wrote to her mother Renée of Ferrara : 'The Queen of Navarre is here, not in good health but very courageous. She is wearing more pearls than ever.' Jeanne herself wrote to an absent Catherine late in May that, 'I have seen your Tuileries fountains, when M. de Retz invited me to a private supper. I have found many things for our wedding in this city during my excursions with him. I am in good form awaiting your arrival.' This last was not true.

Jeanne d'Albret's health had been poor since childhood and was growing worse; the chest problems from which she suffered were almost certainly a sign of tuberculosis. On 4 June, returning from a shopping trip, she felt tired and feverish. She took to her bed and two days later rewrote her will. Catherine de Medici, Margot and even Anjou came to visit her but she seemed resigned to her fate; she had, after all, found this life very trying: '*fort ennuyeuse*'.

Protestant chroniclers provide long hagiographic descriptions of her heroic last days: 'as soon as the pain increased she did not lose courage, showing an admirable confidence in the last fight and preparing herself gladly for death'. Like Katherine of Aragon, albeit from the other side of the religious divide, she urged that her daughter should 'stand firm and constant in God's service despite her extreme youth' and this instruction Catherine de Bourbon (like Mary Tudor before her) most faithfully obeyed.

Jeanne's last days were spent listening to expositions of Scripture and reading Psalm 31 and the Gospel of St John. The Calvinist ministers around her recorded with admiration and relief that she showed no concern for the worldly wedding arrangements that had been occupying her so completely. 'O my saviour, hasten to deliver my spirit from the miseries of this life', she prayed:

> ... and from the prison of this suffering body, that I may offend thee no more, and enter joyfully into that rest which thou hast promised and that my soul so longs for.

> Tell my son that I desire him, as the last expression of my heart, to persevere in the faith in which he has been brought up.

On 9 June 1572 she died. A suggestion that Catherine de Medici had poisoned her with a pair of perfumed gloves first appeared in 1574, in a vicious published attack on Catherine, but that was with the hindsight of what came next. The suggestion was not, even had Jeanne's state of health not made a natural death likely, mentioned by any strict contemporaries. But it was true that Jeanne's death, wrote the Venetian ambassador Cavalli, 'is causing the greatest possible setback to Huguenot affairs'.

The papal envoy praised God for the death of 'such an important enemy of His Holy Church', while the Spanish ambassador heard from home that 'all Madrid rejoices that the Devil has got her, at last!' But perhaps Jeanne d'Albret would prove lucky to have escaped the events of the next three months.

Catherine de Medici's energies were devoted to weaning her son Charles IX from his dependence on Admiral de Coligny, who she feared would lead the country into a war with Spain. She declared that she, with Anjou, would retire to her estates in the country, or even back to Florence, some said. Charles backed down (more frightened, recalled one observer, of his mother and brother than of the Huguenots). Amid scenes of 'mingled violence and tender reproach' he begged his mother not to retire from public life. An emergency council meeting on 10th August voted overwhelmingly for peace. But when the admiral warned that Catherine might regret what she had done, it must have sounded like a threat.

Catherine and Anjou decided that Coligny was too inimical an influence and had to be got out of the way, or so the *Mémoires* (produced by his son twenty years later) of the fanatically Catholic Maréchal de Tavannes, one of Catherine's advisors, declared, adding however that, 'this design was not imparted to the King'. But, typically practical, Catherine had first to finish with the wedding and its festivities.

After attending his mother's funeral at Vendôme, Henri of Navarre came on to Paris. Perhaps recalling his youth at the French court, he seemed to be getting on well with Charles as they waited through the summer's heat in a city increasingly filling up with wedding guests, with peasants from the surrounding countryside driven out of their homes by drought and famine, and with Huguenots.

Catherine de Medici (who had been visiting her daughter Claude) returned to find Catholic preachers fulminating from the pulpits and stirring up hatred of the Protestant visitors. She also found a Spanish ambassador demanding furiously why three thousand Huguenot troops had taken up station near the Netherlands border. It was clearer than ever to Catherine that Coligny had to be neutralised.

First, however, there was the wedding. On 16 August there was a betrothal ceremony at the Louvre and two days later, the actual marriage. As had been agreed by Jeanne d'Albret, Henri of Navarre did not attend the nuptial Mass; he was represented by the bride's brother, Anjou. One other hurdle had to be overcome: the assent of the bride.

When, in April, Catherine de Medici had asked her daughter for her formal consent, Margot recalled later in her memoirs, 'I had no will, no choice but her own.' She begged Catherine, however, to keep in mind the strong Catholic faith that made her reluctant to marry a heretic. She was moreover, as many a royal bride – a Margaret Tudor or a Katherine of Aragon – must have been, justifiably and prophetically anxious about an alliance which would, if things went wrong, place her on the opposite side to her family in a conflict.

Dressed in blue with 'all the jewels of the Crown', Margot took refuge in a passive resistance; going through the motions as she knelt beside Henri but making no answer when the cardinal asked if she took Henri as her husband. Finally, Charles IX stepped forward and pushed her head down, as though she were nodding agreement. (Later, she would use this lack of consent as grounds for an annulment; shades of Jeanne d'Albret and the Cleves match, some thirty years before.) There were to be four days of parties, with the king's masked ball boasting, as its centrepiece, a *pantomime tournoi* which saw Charles and his brothers first dispatching Navarre and his companions to hell, then rescuing them again.

By 22 August, the festivities were at an end. As Admiral Coligny walked back to his lodging from a council meeting at the Louvre, business having resumed that morning, he found a binding on his shoe was loose, and bent over to adjust it. Just as he did so came the sound of a shot. The bullet meant to kill him instead broke his arm and almost tore off a finger.

Catherine de Medici had just sat down to dinner with Anjou when the news was brought to her. Not even the watching Spanish ambassador could tell from her impassive face that it was not the assassination attempt but its failure that spelled disaster for her. Charles IX was on the tennis court when word came; finding himself confronted by his new brother-in-law Henri of Navarre and other senior Huguenots, he promised a full investigation and ordered that the citizens should not take up arms.

When Charles went to visit Coligny that afternoon, Catherine and Anjou went with him but Coligny indicated that he had words for the king's ears alone. As Anjou put it later: 'The Queen my mother has since acknowledged that never had she found herself in a more critical position.' They could not discover what Coligny had said but on the journey back to the Louvre it was clear that Charles was furiously angry with them.

No wonder Anjou, visiting his mother early the next morning, found she had not slept. They were desperate, he himself said later, to 'finish the Admiral by whatever means we could find. And since we could no longer use stratagem, it had to be done openly, but for this purpose it was necessary to bring the King around to our resolution.'

In the streets, people cried out against the king and Catherine de Medici; not on suspicion of murder but for allowing themselves to be surrounded by Huguenots. The Huguenots were already armed, having intended to go straight from the wedding to the fight in the Low Countries. Many Catholics now decided that they too needed to be prepared.

Opinions, contemporary and modern, vary wildly about who was to blame for the attempted assassination of Coligny. The Venetian ambassador wrote that, 'Everyone supposed it had been done by order of the Duc de Guise to avenge his family, because the window from which the shot was fired belonged to his mother's house'. But later he changed his mind, having learnt from various conversations 'that from start to finish the whole thing was the work of the queen. She conceived it, plotted it, and put it into execution, with no help from anyone but her son the duke of Anjou.'

Catherine's daughter Margot seemed to agree: at first the Guises were blamed but then it was revealed to Charles that his brother and mother 'had their shares in it'. At the lowest, Catherine de Medici and her sons (and the royal council with them) came to support the idea of Coligny's assassination once it had been introduced but it is unclear whether the Guise family were their evil geniuses or their scapegoats. Was Catherine Machiavellian enough to reflect that if the Guises suffered all the blame of these events then she would be rid not only of the Huguenot/Bourbon threat but also of the other great noble house that challenged her position as the power behind the throne?

On the evening of 23 August, Catherine sent one of her supporters to the king to tell him not only that his mother and brother had been aware of the attempt on Coligny's life, but that the entire royal family was now in danger. Charles was told also that the Huguenots were planning an attack that very night.

Catherine entered the fray, urging again and again that the Huguenots had brought nothing but trouble. Though he at first refused to believe them, finally the feeble young king was won over. 'Then kill them all', he is said to have cried. 'All', that is, of the senior Huguenots on a list Catherine had drawn up and which he now ratified, not all the Huguenots in Paris, or indeed in France.

At 3 am, the bell of the Palais de Justice was to toll to signal the start of the attack. By that time the militiamen had been alerted, all exits from the city closed, and chained barges linked cross the Seine. The Duc de Guise himself led the party which went to Coligny's house, stabbed the admiral to death and threw his body out of the window.

It was obvious from the first that no one was grand enough to be immune from this violence. The new bride Margot had been in her mother's apartments, together with her sister Claude, just arrived in Paris for the wedding, when it became obvious some sort of preparations were being made. But 'as for me no one told me anything about this', she wrote in her *Mémoires*. 'The Huguenots suspected me because I was a Catholic, and the Catholics because I had married the King of Navarre':

> I was at the *coucher* of the Queen my mother, sitting on a chest with my sister of Lorraine [Claude], who was very depressed, when my mother noticed me and sent me to bed . . . My sister said that it was not right to send me away like that to be sacrificed and that, if they [the Huguenots] discovered anything, no doubt they would avenge themselves on me. My mother replied that, God willing, I would come to no harm, but in any case I must go, for fear of awakening their suspicions . . . I left the room bewildered and dazed without knowing what it was that I feared.

In the quarters where the Protestant royal party lodged, her new husband Henri of Navarre sent Margot to bed. Woken by someone banging at the door and crying out for her husband, she found it was a stranger, one of Henri's gentlemen, wounded, pursued by four archers:

> To save himself, he flung himself on my bed, and I, with that man holding me, rolled into the passage and he after me, still hugging my body. I did not know who he was nor whether he meant to outrage me nor whether it was him or myself whom the archers were pursuing. We both screamed and were equally terrified.

The captain of the guards arrived just in time to grant Margot's request to spare the man's life before escorting her to Claude's apartment, where she 'arrived more dead than alive', ordered the man's wounds tended and changed her bloodied shift.

If none were too high to be troubled, none were too low as to be spared. The Huguenots, all too easily recognisable by their black and white clothes, were slaughtered. Violence against women featured heavily in the dreadful tales: of pregnant women with their wombs ripped out, of baskets of small children flung into the Seine.[2] Protestant, and admittedly partisan, sources told of a woman leaping out of a window to avoid capture, breaking both her legs in the fall, being dragged through the streets by her hair and having her hands slashed off at the wrists for the sake of her gold bracelets. Another woman, about to go into labour, was stabbed in the abdomen and hurled into the street below, where she died along with the child, its head protruding from her body. The killers then looted the house.

Even the Duc de Guise was so appalled by the scale of the killing (and by the fact that Catherine was according him the blame) that he could be seen defending Huguenots in the streets, and opening his house to give them sanctuary. The Spanish ambassador saw the mounting pile of bodies:

> While I write, they are casting them out naked and dragging them through the streets, pillaging their houses and sparing not a babe. Blessed be to God, who has converted the Princes of France to His purpose. May He inspire their hearts to go on as they have begun!

Priests encouraged the bloodshed but of the three or four thousand people killed in the capital not all were necessarily Huguenots. Some were killed in personal vendettas rather than for their religious faith, as the orgy of bloodletting took on a dreadful momentum.

Those on the list of high-profile victims, compiled by Catherine de Medici and Charles IX, were largely killed within the first two hours. But once kindled, the flame could not be put out. This was something the royal group had not foreseen. That afternoon Charles sent orders for the killing to cease but he was ignored.

It was another three days before Paris was quiet; by then, despite fresh orders from the king, the violence had spread to the provinces. It would be October before the storm cleared southern France, and across the country (although estimates vary wildly) some suggest as many as thirty thousand died. The royal family sheltered inside the Louvre while the slaughter was going on. Later (according to two sources) Catherine had recovered enough that on being presented with the head taken from Admiral de Coligny's disfigured and emasculated body, she had it embalmed and sent as a gift to the pope.

There could be, from this, no going back. 'You must clearly see that you cannot govern too wisely with kindness and diffidence', Anne de Beaujeu said three-quarters of a century earlier. This explosion of violence had ripped Europe apart, and left its divisions exposed all too clearly.

The French ambassador to Spain reported that Philip literally danced for joy when he heard the news. He certainly wrote to congratulate Catherine de Medici on 'this glorious event', admitting to the French ambassador that 'he owed his Low Countries of Flanders' to the French action. In the Netherlands, the Spanish general Alba's actions were becoming ever more brutal. That October, he allowed his men to sack and massacre the town of Mechelen, where Margaret of Austria had once lived in luxury. The pope ordered *Te Deums* sung, until he was informed that the massacre had never been intended and that the original assassination attempt had been a political rather than primarily religious story.

By contrast, the Queen of England was appalled. As Elizabeth wrote to Walsingham, the murder of the supposed Huguenot conspirators, without 'answer by law', was bad enough:

> We do hear it marvellously evil taken and as a thing of a terrible and dangerous example . . . But when more added unto it – that women, children, maids, young infants and sucking babes were at the same time murdered and cast into the river . . . this increased our grief and sorrow.

When Elizabeth at last consented to receive the French ambassador Fénelon, not a courtier would speak to or look at him as he approached the presence chamber. There, so the story goes, he found the queen, her ladies, and her privy councillors all dressed in mourning black. What the queen said to Fénelon was mild compared to the reproaches of the councillors. Cecil told him it was the greatest crime since the crucifixion. No one on the English side could now think of a marriage with the French royal family. If the French king had been 'Author and doer of this Act, shame and confusion light upon him', Leicester wrote to Walsingham. And the same would naturally be true of his mother.

The other marriage that had sparked the dreadful affair was completed. Henri of Navarre (and his cousin Condé) had been taken from the apartment where Margot was so rudely surprised and brought to the king, who assured them of their safety. Margot claimed she was asked by her mother whether the marriage had been consummated, since if not it could be dissolved. Margot, fearing Henri's life would be in danger, refused to comply with the clear suggestion, and said it had. The two Huguenot princes had, however, formally to be received back into the Catholic church. Catherine, perhaps overstrained, burst into rude laughter as they made the sign of the cross before the altar. Henri had, moreover, to return Béarn to Catholicism. Jeanne d'Albret was truly dead.

But Catherine de Medici too had lost; lost in reputation. She soon realised how much blame she would have to shoulder for the affair. Pamphlets against Catherine attacked the rule of women along with her other supposed iniquities; others harked back to her Florentine roots and recalled that Machiavelli's *The Prince* had been dedicated to her father.[3]

Her ambassador to Venice wrote that the massacre not only of the Huguenot leaders 'but against so many poor and innocent people' meant that the Venetians (though themselves Catholic) nevertheless 'cannot be satisfied with any excuse, attributing everything that has been done to you alone and Monsieur d'Anjou'.

She had moreover lost the chance of peace in France. Huguenots, believing the whole marriage had been a trap, now faced stark choices; driven now, as Elizabeth of England said 'to fly or die'. Those standing out in La Rochelle called on the protection of Elizabeth, now their 'natural sovereign princess for all eternity'. As royalist forces embarked on a long and bitter siege, the women of La Rochelle mustered on the walls to throw rocks at them.

Elizabeth's support of the continental Protestants remained partial and hesitant for some time to come. Not until 1585 was she finally persuaded to send an army to the support of the Dutch Protestants. Elizabeth even, although not without lengthy comment about the strangeness of the request, agreed to stand godmother to the daughter

Charles IX's wife bore him that autumn. She found it politic now to seem to believe French assurances that the king had merely acted against a Huguenot plot and that what followed had been a tragic accident. But talk of her possible marriage to Catherine's youngest son d'Alençon was off the table, for the moment, anyway.

Like her enemy and ally Catherine de Medici, Elizabeth Tudor (and Mary Tudor before her), was forged by fear. It was one reason they and Mary Stuart, the child who grew up the darling of the French court, would never be sisters in any real way.

For another queen had lost, here. Amid the fallout from the massacre, one thing that could be seen was a new consensus among Elizabeth's ministers as to the danger represented by the Scottish queen, Mary. In March 1571, Mary's agent the Bishop of Ross had written that the Queen of Scots's life was in great danger, with Cecil and others urging she should be put to death.

Elizabeth's councillors were almost united in believing that Mary (so recently the Catholic focus of internal rebellion) should be excluded from the succession, if not actually killed. It would be another fifteen years before the tussle between Elizabeth Tudor and Mary Stuart reached its climax, but the end was plain to see.

PART VII

1572 onwards

And nothing is firm or lasting in the gifts of Fortune; today you see those raised high by Fortune who, two days later, are brought down hard.

Lessons for my Daughter, Anne de France
(Anne de Beaujeu) published 1517–1521

43

Turning points

England, France, 1572–1587

THE EARLY TO mid-1570s represented a turning point in the history of women's rule in Europe. The question of Queen Elizabeth's marriage had retreated somewhat, only to have one final resurgence before finally it went away. The 'princely pleasures' of Elizabeth's 1575 visit to Leicester's house of Kenilworth signalled the last gasp of his long courtship, as well as promoting his bid to be allowed to help the beleaguered Netherlands Protestants. Elizabeth Tudor had turned forty; old for childbearing by the standards of the day. Her councillors must have been resigned to her determined virginity.

But an heir, however important, was not the only point of a royal marriage. The increase in Catholic activity on the Continent could only leave England more anxious for allies. The mid-1570s saw the start of the great Catholic infiltration of England itself, and of Philip of Spain eyeing opportunities in Ireland. And there had long been the idea of an alliance with a son of Catherine de Medici.

For a time after the Massacre of St Bartholomew's Day, and amid the massacre of her reputation, Catherine was preoccupied with the election of her favourite son Henri, Duc d'Anjou, to the vacant throne of Poland (shades of Louise of Savoy and the election to the Holy Roman Empire), a throne he would in due course abandon when that of France fell vacant. Her dying son, Charles IX, as he became ever more feeble, accused her: 'Madame, you are the cause of everything! Everything!' But nevertheless, on his deathbed, he ordered a new document to be drawn up, securing the regency to his mother until Henri could return from Poland. Charles died on 30 May 1574, holding her hand. As Catherine later said, 'After God, he recognised no one but me.'

The accession of her best-beloved Henri to the throne of France was at once a triumph and a problem for Catherine. She wrote that if she lost him, too, 'I would have myself buried alive', and that his return 'will bring me joy and contentment on contentment', while he wrote that he was her 'devoted servant'. The secretary of the English ambassador, in the first days of the new king's reign, wrote that Catherine's authority 'was as ample as ever'. But not everyone agreed. When Henri's dawdling journey home finally brought him back to France, Catherine found a young man whose ideas did not always match her own. She advised that in his new role as Henri III he should show who had the upper hand: he promptly put an end to the practice by which state papers might be shown first to her, although mother and son still held joint audiences and observers could still report that the queen mother 'commandeth very much'.

The religious divisions showed no sign of abating. As Henri III's younger brother François, the Duc d'Alençon, toyed with joining the Huguenots, Henri of Navarre escaped from the French court and back to his own lands in the southwest, where he abjured the Catholic religion to which he had been forced to convert after St Bartholomew's Day. The Huguenots were acting with virtual autonomy in several of the southern provinces of France. It was Catherine de Medici who, after a fragile peace was signed, had to carry the king's message into what was effectively enemy territory. She was still needed but also marginalised by the dissent within her family.[1]

Henri's accession left his brother François, long at odds with his family and long debating the idea of marriage as a way to bolster his position, more disaffected than ever.* In 1578 he allied with rebels in the Netherlands, accepting from the Protestants the title of 'Defender of the Liberties of the Low Countries against Spanish Tyranny'.

Elizabeth of England had spent much energy patching up relations between the Dutch Protestants and the said Spanish tyrant, and her first reaction was to send a message of solidarity to King Philip. The

---

* Alençon, confusingly, had himself become Duc d'Anjou when Henri succeeded to the throne. For clarity's sake, however, I shall continue to refer to him as Alençon.

right of monarchy always weighed with her more strongly than bonds of faith. But in the long term, for the English, the important thing was to be on good terms with anyone who held the harbours just across the sea. For Alençon, the important thing was to get English men and money. And in any game of alliances, marriage was still the best piece anyone could play.

But this last move in her long mating game was not wholly political, at least on Elizabeth Tudor's side. In 1579, first Alençon's personal envoy Jean de Simier, and then Alençon himself, arrived to conduct an overheated courtship, acted out on all sides with a kind of delighted fantasy. Catherine de Medici talked of visiting England, to sort this thing out; another of the meetings doomed never to occur. An on/off game for several years, it culminated in Elizabeth's publicly telling Alençon she would marry him, only to change her mind the next day.

In the spring of 1582 Alençon finally set out again for the Netherlands, with a hefty subsidy of English money. When he died in 1584 Elizabeth wrote to Catherine de Medici that even her grief as a mother could not be greater: 'Madame, if you were able to see the image of my heart, you would see the portrait of a body without a soul.' Nonetheless, the start of the 1580s effectively marked Queen Elizabeth's recasting of herself as the perpetual virgin. She would increasingly be figured as Diana, the ferociously chaste huntress.

The remaining female rulers continued to be, to some degree, aware of their sex as a potential bond. In 1578 Catherine de Medici was reported as praising Elizabeth Tudor's Christian love of peace: 'For her part, she also was a woman, and as became her sex, desired nothing more than a general quietness'. In her communication with Elizabeth Tudor she had often figured herself as a parent writing to a child, just as Elizabeth had in her letters to Mary Stuart. In June 1572 Catherine had told Elizabeth that 'I love you as a mother loves her daughter', and the maternal rhetoric resumed, in the light of the possible Alençon marriage, quite soon after the Massacre of St Bartholomew's Day.

Catherine also sponsored the 1570s *Discourse on the legitimate succession of women*, a defence of female sovereignty published in France by the Scot David Chambers. Brantôme would write of a private conversation in which she deplored the Salic Law and wished that her daughter Margot might inherit the kingdom 'by her just rights, as other kingdoms also fall to the distaff', since she 'is just as capable of governing, or more so, than many men and kings whom I know'. Sisterhood was also an ideal to which Mary, Queen of Scots never ceased appealing. But it had long ceased to have any reality in the relationship of Elizabeth and Mary.[2]

44

Prise

Fotheringhay, 1587

ANYONE WHO HAS ever been near a chessboard knows that if you manage to threaten your opponent's king you give a chivalrous warning: 'Check.' Learning to play chess in the latter part of the twentieth century, I was taught a partial survival of an older tradition: that if you manage to get into a position where your next move would let you take the other player's queen, then you must, by the same token, give a warning: 'Prise.' 'Prise' as in *en prise*, in a position to be taken. Up for grabs, you might say.

In one sense, of course, Mary Stuart had been *en prise* from the moment she put herself into Elizabeth Tudor's hands. But the danger would be that her actions – her very existence – caused Elizabeth herself to feel the same vulnerability.

Mary's plotting had never ceased. As the 1570s turned to the 1580s, with the overthrow and execution of the last of her enemies, the Earl of Morton, in Scotland, Mary had hoped she might soon be back in that country, perhaps ruling jointly with her son James VI, perhaps even with Elizabeth's agreement. But while nothing came of that, she – or those who supported her – had never ceased to eye the other, English, throne. And there would soon be no distinction made between Mary Stuart herself and those who perceived themselves as acting in her cause.

In 1584, after the assassination of William of Orange in the Netherlands, after several Catholic plots against Elizabeth, came the Bond of Association. The signatories swore not only to defend Queen Elizabeth but to kill anyone who attempted to harm her, and anyone 'for whom' such an attempt was made. Mary herself offered to sign it, ironically.

An act passed by parliament the following spring modified some of the Bond's more draconian elements, requiring at least a trial for the accused. But that same month, James VI in Scotland informed his mother Mary that, considering her captivity, he had no option other than that 'of declining to associate himself with her in the sovereignty of Scotland, or to treat her otherwise than as Queen-Mother'. Elizabeth, by contrast, his envoy assured her, could rely on James's affection for her 'as though he were her natural son'. Their letters continued to employ the rhetoric of parent and child, and Elizabeth was James's godmother, an important bond in the sixteenth century.

Mary reacted with a surge of distress. 'I pray you to note I am your true and only Queen', she wrote to her son. 'Do not insult me further with this title of Queen Mother . . . there is neither King nor Queen in Scotland except me.' To Elizabeth she protested: 'Without him I am, and shall be of right, as long as I live, his Queen and Sovereign . . . but without me, he is too insignificant to think of soaring.' She was ignored and when, a year later, James VI signed his treaty with England, she ceased to be valuable even as a pawn one side or the other might wish to play.

If Mary Stuart's life ceased to have value for others, so it now had only a conditional value for herself. She had no reason not to lend herself to another plot. Instigated by the young Catholic hothead Anthony Babington, it was a plot well-known to Elizabeth's spymaster Walsingham and a tool ready to his hand; a matter which, as he wrote to Leicester, if it be 'well handled, it will break the neck of all dangerous practices'. And of practitioners.

There could be no doubt Mary was guilty, yet when they came to accuse her in August 1586, she still protested that she had always shown herself Elizabeth Tudor's 'good sister and friend'. In October the case was tried, at the castle of Fotheringhay where Mary was held. Mary, after protesting that as a queen the commissioners had no right to try her, continued implausibly to protest her innocence: 'I would never make shipwreck of my soul by conspiring the destruction of my dearest sister.'

Crocodile tears? And yet it seems almost as if she did still half-believe. No wonder Elizabeth herself seemed almost puzzled. To

Mary's gaoler she spat that he should 'let your wicked mistress know how with hearty sorrow her vile deserts compels these orders, and bid her from me ask God's forgiveness'. But Elizabeth also swore that:

> if the case stood between her and myself only, if it had pleased God to have made us both milkmaids with pails on our arms, so that the matter should have rested between us two; and that I knew she did and would seek my destruction still, yet could I not consent to her death.

The judgment of 'guilty' was made public on 4 December. Queen Elizabeth's proclamation declared that: 'we were greatly and deeply grieved in our mind to think or imagine that any such unnatural and monstrous fact should be either devised or willingly assented to against us by her, being a princess born, and of our sex and blood'. But Elizabeth had still to sign the warrant for the penalty required by the act: execution.

In December the council were reluctantly forced to deliver to Elizabeth a letter from Mary herself, begging her cousin to 'favour your equal'; a letter which, in its requests about the fate of her servants, and the disposal of her body, was calculated to bring home the full enormity of the prospective death.

'Do not accuse me of presumption', Mary wrote 'if, on the eve of leaving this world and preparing myself for a better one, I remind you that one day you will have to answer for your charge . . . and that my blood and the misery of my country are remembered'. She signed herself 'Your sister and cousin, wrongfully a prisoner, *Marie, Royne*'.

Several years earlier, she had expressed to Elizabeth her readiness to shed her blood; telling the Spanish ambassador Mendoza that she hoped God would accept her death as an offering 'freely made by me for the maintenance of His church'. But that readiness did not mean Elizabeth was to be allowed to forget one jot of the horror of what she was doing.

Leicester wrote to Walsingham: 'There is a letter from the Scottish Queen, that hath wrought tears, but I trust shall do no further herein: albeit, the delay is too dangerous'. Elizabeth kept to herself as the new year came in but the antiquarian William Camden reported that she could be heard murmuring: 'Strike, or be stricken, strike, or be stricken.'

It was her kinsman Lord Howard of Effingham who finally, on 1 February, persuaded her to end this excruciating delay. She signed the warrant for Mary's execution, handing it over with just enough vagueness as to allow her later to claim she had never meant it to be acted upon. Her councillors, however, under Cecil's leadership, agreed to take upon themselves the responsibility for the warrant's being put into effect.

Machiavelli had advised his prince that crime, when necessary, should be delegated to others. Here and elsewhere Elizabeth seemed to have learnt his lessons, as well as those of Anne de Beaujeu. Elizabeth's motto was '*Video et taceo*': I see, but say nothing. Or, as Anne de Beaujeu wrote: 'you should have eyes to notice everything yet to see nothing, ears to hear everything yet to know nothing, and a tongue to answer everyone yet to say nothing prejudicial to anyone'. Least of all anything prejudicial to your own sovereignty.

On 7 February Mary was told she would be executed the next morning. She would die, she wrote, as a good Scotswoman and a good Frenchwoman – that odd dual role – but above all as a good Catholic. Her rule on earth had been a disaster, redeemed only (in the traditional, consort, model of a queen's role) by whatever successes her son James could win. But she had found her role as a martyr in heaven.

The scene of her execution is well known, in all its horror and pathos. A report sent to Cecil described how the executioners helped her women strip her of her ornaments and outer clothes and how she herself helped them make speed, 'as if she longed to be gone'. She had pleaded with Elizabeth that her servants should be allowed to be with her at the end, 'by the honour and dignity we have both held, and of our sex in common'. Briefly, the nobles escorting Mary to her death tried to ban her women from accompanying her but her frantic remonstrance prevailed.

All this time they were pulling off her apparel, she never changed her countenance, but with smiling cheer she uttered these words, 'that she never had such grooms to make her unready, and that she never put off her clothes before such a company' . . . groping for the block, she laid down her head, putting her chin over the block with both hands, which, holding there still, had been cut off had they not been espied . . . Then she, lying very still upon the block, one of the executioners holding her slightly with one of his hands, she endured two strokes of the other executioner with an axe, she making very small noise or none at all, and not stirring any part of her from the place where she lay: and so the executioner cut off her head, saving one little gristle, which being cut asunder, he lift up her head to the view of all the assembly and bade 'God save the Queen'.

Her lips, Cecil's correspondent wrote, 'stirred up and down a quarter of an hour' after she was dead.

Now she was dead she could safely be hailed as a Catholic heroine by the continental powers. Catherine de Medici told her ambassador: 'I am most grieved that you have been unable to do more for the poor Queen of Scotland. It has never been the case that one queen should have jurisdiction over another having placed herself into her hands for her safety.' (Shades of Jeanne d'Albret?) Philip of Spain wrote to his ambassador Mendoza that, 'You cannot imagine the pity I feel for the Queen of Scots.' But the fact was that he could now continue preparations for his great enterprise of England, his Armada, without having to question whether he really wished to place a queen committed to France on England's throne.

When the news was brought to Elizabeth early the next day, she 'gave herself over to grief', as Camden put it; a hysterical and histrionic paroxysm, meant to convince a watching Europe of her innocence, but doubtless springing from a real and complex cocktail of emotions.

It is perhaps not too over-dramatic to say that Elizabeth Tudor knew the sisterhood of queens had also died that day. Could it all have gone differently, looking back to the beginning? Could Elizabeth have, in effect, mentored Mary Stuart? Probably not: their religion, with all its implications for the rights to the English throne, was in the way. It would be overly simplistic to say that religion ended any real possibility of sisterhood among Europe's powerful women. There were, after all, plenty of powerful women within Catholic Europe among whom the game might still be played. But perhaps it had always been a fragile plant, capable of flowering only in very particular conditions. And towards the end of the sixteenth century, the climate was growing cold.

Postscript

'For myself, I was never so much enticed with the glorious
name of a king or royal authority of a queen as delighted
that God hath made me his instrument . . . There will never
queen sit in my seat with more zeal to my country, care to
my subjects, and that will sooner with willingness venture
her life for your good and safety, than myself.'

Elizabeth Tudor, the 'Golden Speech', 30 November 1601

FOR ELIZABETH TUDOR, the eighteen months after Mary
Stuart's death represented something of another turning point.
The Armada victory in the summer of 1588 might have owed
more to good luck and bad weather than to leadership and in a sense
it represented what she had always dreaded: a military crisis in which
she, as a woman, could not take direct command. Yet the speech she
made to her troops at Tilbury, with the Armada ships in the Channel
and Margaret of Parma's son planning an invasion from the
Netherlands, became the most iconic of her career.

I know I have the body but of a weak and feeble woman, but I have the
heart and stomach of a king and of a king of England too – and take foul
scorn that Parma or any prince of Europe should dare to invade the
borders of my realm. To the which rather than any dishonour shall grow
by me, I myself will venter my royal blood; I myself will be your general . . .

As so often before, she played on her femininity, her vulnerability,
making it into a strength. A text underneath a contemporary painting in

a Norfolk church has a variant on Elizabeth's words which tackles the issue more aggressively: 'The enemy may challenge my sex for that I am a woman, so may I likewise charge their mould, for they are but men.'

She made a point of leaving her ladies behind and rode among the troops with the sword of state carried before her: 'sometimes like a Woman, and anon, with the countenance and pace of a Soldier', as Camden put it two decades later. Yet Leicester, in the days before Tilbury, had told her that her person was 'the most sacred and dainty thing we have in this world to care for, a man must tremble when he thinks of it'. She was at once appealing to her subjects' chivalry and impressing them with her potency. If this were a great failure of the peace for which she and her sister queens had so often striven, it allowed to take unto herself the persona of the warrior, for which male rulers had chiefly been admired.[1]

Yet the last years of the 1580s marked, for Queen Elizabeth I, the start of a 'second reign' by no means as successful as what had gone before. On the wider stage the 1570s and 1580s saw an epic battle between Catholics and Protestants played across northern Europe; dividing France, threatening England, confirming Spain in its crusading Catholicism and stretching out long tentacles across the seas.

Elizabeth's long-time favourite and supporter the Earl of Leicester died within weeks of the Armada victory, to her great and solitary grief. She would lose another important councillor in each of the following few years. When William Cecil, by far the longest survivor, died in 1598, he left a son, Robert, to follow him as first minister but Leicester was succeeded as her prime favourite by his stepson the Earl of Essex, and this was a relationship which threw a profoundly unflattering light on her woman's rule.

Long indulged by Elizabeth, Essex's final descent into open rebellion was marked by a young and militaristic man's disdain for an old woman. 'The Queen's conditions are as crooked as her carcase', he was reported to have said once, unforgivably. In a decade of economic hardship and uncertainty about the future, Elizabeth's court in the 1590s was also rocked by a series of sexual scandals that not only reflected badly on her authority but evoked the old stereotype of a woman ruler surrounded by licentiousness.

Advancing age brought no halt to the slurs on Elizabeth's reputation. It was in the 1580s that the Catholic polemicist Nicholas Sanders brought out his scurrilous history of Anne Boleyn, a way of visiting the perceived sins of the mother on the daughter, and in the 1590s that Elizabeth's infamous interrogator Richard Topcliffe could fantasise aloud about having felt her legs and her belly. When, after her death, Robert Cecil wrote that the queen had been 'more than a man and, in troth, sometimes less than a woman', it was the reverse side of the coin to the idea of a ruler being above sex, which had once empowered Elizabeth's female sovereignty.

Elizabeth continued to be addressed in terms of courtly love but her looks had long faded. Anne de Beaujeu had warned her daughter that once over forty, no clothes can make the wrinkles on your face disappear. When Cecil – a loyal servant, but one anxious to secure both his own future and the succession – entered into correspondence with James VI of Scotland, he stressed the need for secrecy on the grounds of Elizabeth's age and infirmity, 'joined to the jealousy of her sex'. Even Elizabeth herself, taxing a Venetian envoy with the fact that Venice had failed to keep an ambassador at her court, asked bitterly if 'my sex hath brought me this demerit?' Her sex, she had to tell the man angrily, 'cannot diminish my prestige'.

In the last years of Elizabeth Tudor's life, even after Mary Stuart's death, several women were among the leading candidates to succeed to her throne. Philip of Spain insisted that the chief Catholic claimant was his daughter, the Infanta. In 1601, when Cecil had a list of claimants prepared, James VI of Scotland in first place was followed by Arbella Stuart (daughter of Lord Darnley's younger brother) in second; and James should, arguably, have been disqualified by reason of his foreign birth. For the crowd of careful international observers Arbella was interesting chiefly insofar as she might be married off to a man who could thus absorb her claim: anyone from Robert Cecil himself to one of Margaret of Parma's grandsons.

The trouble was (as the watching envoys reported) that England, for the moment, had had enough of queens. As a Catholic commentator on the succession, publishing as 'Doleman', put it: a woman 'ought not to be preferred, before so many men . . . and that it were much to have three women to reign in England one after the other, whereas in the space of above a thousand years before them, there had not reigned so many of that sex'.

In the end, by almost universal agreement, Elizabeth was succeeded by a man, Mary Stuart's Protestant son James VI and I. The proclamation made clear that he owed the throne to his female lineage, being descended 'from the body of Margaret [Tudor] . . . and of Elizabeth of York'. But James was a man whose imaginative concept of the monarchy was cast in wholly patriarchal terms. Kings are 'compared to fathers of families', he told the English parliament, 'for a king is truly *parens patriae*, the politique father of his people'.

James had, after all, been tutored in youth by George Buchanan, a Protestant who had played a leading part in blackening Mary's reputation. Buchanan wrote that it was as unbecoming for a woman 'to pronounce Judgment, to levy Forces, to conduct an Army' as it was for a man to spin wool or to perform 'the other Services of the Weaker Sex'. This was to be the theme of writing on (or rather, against) female succession in the decades ahead.

If Elizabeth were one of the two giant figures left standing at the end of the sixteenth century, the other, of course, was Catherine de Medici. One of the reasons Catherine had been so appalled by Mary Stuart's death was the impetus her martyrdom would give to the Catholic League led by the Guises, which had effectively replaced the Huguenots as the threatening rebel force within the land.[2] When in 1588 the Guises assailed Paris and made an attempt to kidnap her son Henri III it was Catherine who had to deal with them, first clambering over the barricades across the city and then remaining behind to liaise with the Leaguers while her son fled. But Catherine's 'authority and credit' with her son were now all but destroyed.

When her son, on his own impulse, ordered the assassination of the latest Duc de Guise, two days before Christmas of 1588, Catherine said he was 'headed towards ruin'. She was right. Just seven months later this last surviving, but childless, son was himself murdered by a Dominican friar, outraged that Henri III had allied himself with the Protestant Henri of Navarre. But Catherine did not live to see Jeanne d'Albret's son, whose marriage had been the trigger for the St Bartholomew's Day Massacre, declared Henri IV of France. She died barely a fortnight after the Guise assassination. Henri IV made her epitaph. 'What could the poor woman do,' he asked:

> with five children in her arms after the death of her husband, and with two families in France – ours and the Guise – attempting to encroach on the Crown? Was she not forced to play strange parts to deceive the one and other and yet, as she did, to protect her children, who reigned in succession by the wisdom of a woman so able? I wonder she did not do worse!

In 1593 Henri IV was received back into the church of Rome, having famously if apocryphally, declared that Paris was worth a Mass. What would Jeanne d'Albret have said? Henri's assassination in 1610 would bring another woman, his wife Marie de Medici, Catherine de Medici's kinswoman, as well as her successor, into power as regent of France. But Marie's attempts at rule never amounted to successful control of the country.

The closing years of the sixteenth century, and the first years of the seventeenth, saw some continued instances of female rule. Philip of Spain made his daughter the Infanta Isabella, with her husband, joint ruler of the Spanish Netherlands, a rule that ushered in the Netherlands's Golden Age. Queen Elizabeth 'says she wants to consider me as her daughter; just imagine how much profit I would get from such a mother!' said the Infanta, ambiguously. But the most famous female ruler of the seventeenth century, Christina of Sweden, would resign her throne, saying 'no woman is fit to govern', a sentiment later echoed by Queen Victoria, whose belief was that, 'We women . . . are not fitted to reign'. Appropriate, perhaps, that the dream of women's rule, which had progressed northwards through the sixteenth century, should die in the Baltic Sea.

From a northern European perspective at least, it is tempting to ask whether the end of the sixteenth century did not usher in a reduction in female autonomy: a reduction in the number of women to rule their country; a hushing of the gynocratic debate as to whether a girl should not be educated as well as a boy. Now, the Amazon queen, in Shakespeare's *A Midsummer Night's Dream* and elsewhere, was featured as tamed by man and marriage.

It is true that the Counter-Reformation had found one of its best weapons in a renewed and refreshed cult of the Virgin Mary, the Queen of Heaven. The Jesuits promoted the use of the rosary (and within it the 'Hail Mary'), restored shrines, and encouraged confraternities devoted to the mother of God. Mary was declared the true heroine of Lepanto, the great naval battle that in 1571 saw a Holy League organised by the pope and led by Spain defeat the Turks. The pope had declared the battle day, 7 October, as the Feast of Our Lady of Victory. But the Jesuits, who in their early days had relied so much upon the support of noblewomen, now preferred to turn to less controversial, male, patrons. Female religious orders had flourished during this period, and would continue to do so, but increasingly, the women who had joined them found themselves enclosed.

Not that things were any better for women in the Protestant community; far from it. The Protestants (and their largely married clergy) had long counterpoised the ideal of the family, with the father at its head, against the Catholic ideal of virginity. This left little room for the concept of the virginal woman warrior. In its early days the Protestant Reformation seemed to offer opportunities for women. But now these seemed to be dwindling.[3]

A century after the death of Elizabeth I, England again had a woman on the throne; another woman whose older sister had held it before her. But Queen Anne's older sister, Mary, declared that 'women should not meddle in government'. In theory, Mary reigned jointly with her husband, William; in fact, she ceded all control to him. Although, by contrast, Queen Anne relegated her husband, George of Denmark, to a background role, both Stuart sisters reigned over a nation that allowed the monarch far less power than Elizabeth had enjoyed.

On the Continent, women continued to play an important role. The Habsburg dynasty maintained its practice of using female relatives in a regent's role; in France, Louis XIV's mother and regent, Anne of Austria (born a Habsburg) was just one important figure. Nonetheless, in the mid-eighteenth century the power held by Maria Theresa, the Habsburg sovereign of Austria and Hungary, whose success in engineering her husband's election as Holy Roman Emperor gave her the title of 'Empress', represented something of a rebirth.[4] So too, of course, did that of the empresses who ruled Russia for much of the eighteenth century: Catherine I, Anna, Elizabeth and Catherine II – Catherine 'the Great' – but they were operating within a very different political system and playing by different rules.

Both Elizabeth Tudor and Catherine de Medici were chess players, as were Isabella of Castile, Anne de Beaujeu, Margaret of Austria and Louise of Savoy. Although Mary, Queen of Scots also played, she is not particularly associated with the game. Catherine, who learnt her game in Italy and promoted it when she came to France, was said to have sought to match herself against the great Italian champion Paolo Boi. Elizabeth, who had played against her great tutor Roger Ascham, was sufficiently aware of the symbolism of the game to have rewarded Sir Charles Blount, after a successful joust, with 'a Queen at Chesse of gold richly enameled', which he would wear tied about his arm.

But female participation in the game was itself in decline by the turn of the seventeenth century. The myriad medieval pictures of a man and a woman playing together dwindled away; by 1694 Thomas Hyde in his study of chess lamented that in a game of battle, to call the most active piece a queen was surely 'inappropriate'.

And yet, and yet . . . A tradition of female rule as strong as that seen in the sixteenth century cannot (however it may subsequently be overlooked) ever really go away. From then on, in the Western world, the tally card would record that it had been possible for women to control countries and that a number of them had done so very successfully. From then on, no one could say that was an impossibility.

Many of the battles these women fought are still relevant. Almost thirty years ago Antonia Fraser, in her groundbreaking book, *Boadicea's Chariot*, traced the line of 'warrior queens' from the ancient world to the Iron Lady, Margaret Thatcher. She identified several tropes of female leadership: the Chaste Syndrome and the Voracity Syndrome, the role of a woman as Holy (Armed) Figurehead, or as peacemaker, and traced them from Celtic mythology and the Roman Empire to the female leaders of her own day: Golda Meir, Margaret Thatcher, Indira Gandhi.

The women who ruled sixteenth-century Europe fit Fraser's patterns almost precisely, from the doublethink that reclassified a successful woman as an honorary man, to the number who reached power by what she called the Appendage Syndrome; as widow, mother, sister of a powerful male. Any look at the newspapers makes clear how well these tropes still work today.

The battles these queens and regents fought are relevant whenever it comes to the questions of women assuming power, and questions over whether women participating in public life might wield that power in a different way. None of these questions are yet wholly answered but they are being asked with new urgency. This book was written at a moment when in America a woman prepared to contest the world's most powerful office and when in Europe Theresa May, Britain's second female Prime Minister, entered negotiations with Scotland's First Minister Nicola Sturgeon and German Chancellor Angela Merkel. Though the defeat of Hillary Clinton dealt a blow to the dream that the Age of Queens had come again, we are nonetheless in an era when questions of women's relationship to power are debated with growing urgency. That gain – and the further gains which may yet lie ahead – is in part these earlier women's legacy.

> Now say, have women worth? or have they none?
> Or had they some, but with our Queen is't gone?
> Nay Masculines, you have thus taxt us long,
> But she, though dead, will vindicate our wrong.
> Let such as say our sex is void of Reason,
> Know tis a slander now, but once was treason.

> In Honour of That High and Mighty
> Princess Queen Elizabeth of Happy
> Memory, Anne Bradstreet, 1643

A note on sources

General and prologue

This book owes a particular debt to three others in particular –
besides, of course, Garrett Mattingly's *The Defeat of the Spanish
Armada* (Jonathan Cape, 1959) mentioned in the preface. My awareness of the role played in the sixteenth century by women ruling
beyond Britain's shores was heightened by William Monter's *The Rise
of the Female Kings in Europe 1300–1800* (Yale University Press, 2012)
– as too was my awareness that this was a subject our Anglocentric
popular history has been slow to address. I had long been interested
in the concept of inheritance from mother to daughter, and was
thrilled, halfway through my research, to discover that Sharon L.
Jansen, in *The Monstrous Regiment of Women: Female Rulers in Early
Modern Europe* (Palgrave Macmillan, 2002), had done so much to
explore the field. I envisage a somewhat different pattern from Jansen,
who traces coeval lines of inheritance through the royal families of
four different territories – but hers is an infinitely valuable body of
work, and itself a formidable legacy.

The same must of course be said of Antonia Fraser's groundbreaking *Boadicea's Chariot: The Warrior Queens* (Weidenfeld & Nicolson,
1988), which I reread as I was finishing this book, admiring once
again the dazzling virtuosity with which she explores patterns of
female leadership from ancient history through to the modern day. I
first met Lady Antonia many years ago, not in the context of any
historical work but as joint spectators – sufferers – of a freezing
springtime cricket match. I was grateful then for her generous offer

of a sip from her warming hip flask; I am infinitely more grateful today.

It would seem ungracious, too, not to make a more general acknowledgement of academic work now done in this field, notably through the Palgrave Macmillan series *Queenship and Power* edited by Carole Levin and Charles Beem, a series of which Sharon L. Jansen's book is one of the fruits. Other particularly relevant titles in the series include Beem's own *The Lioness Roared: The Problems of Female Rule in English History* (2008) and Elena Woodacre's *Royal Mothers and their Ruling Children: Wielding Political Authority from Antiquity to the Early Modern Era* (2015) – but everything they issue makes a valuable contribution to this ever-fertile field. Among a host of other books to address the subject, I should like to single out one further example, in particular: *A History of Women's Political Thought in Europe, 1400–1700* (Cambridge University Press, 2009) by Jacqueline Broad and Karen Green.

I should conversely also like to remind the general reader of the work being done in a very different context: on the Internet. The particular contribution made here is to set the sixteenth-century rulers in the wider context of powerful women across the world and down the centuries: among the exact contemporaries of 'my' women rulers, I shall always be sorry that the Rajput Rani who rode into battle on her own war elephant is outside the scope of this study.

Some suggestions for further reading

Preface

My conception of the changes in the game of chess was formed by Marilyn Yalom's *Birth of the Chess Queen* (Pandora Press, 2004). A wealth of information on sixteenth-century contributions to the gynocracy debate can be found in the notes to Sharon L. Jansen's book above, pp. 229–231 in particular.

Part I: 1474–1513

I have previously written about the English experience of these years in *Blood Sisters: The Women Behind the Wars of the Roses* (Harper Press, 2012). For Margaret Tudor (and her successors in Scotland) see Linda Porter's compelling *Crown of Thistles: The Fatal Inheritance of Mary Queen of Scots* (Macmillan, 2013), while Margaret and her sister Mary are the subjects of Maria Perry's *Sisters to the King* (Andre Deutsch, 1998).

The standard biography in English of Isabella of Castile is Peggy K. Liss' *Isabel the Queen: Life and Times* (Oxford University Press, 1992). See also Barbara F. Weissberger's article in Anne J. Cruz and Mihoko Suzuki eds, *The Rule of Women in Early Modern Europe* (University of Illinois, 2009). Julia Fox has written an important dual biography, *Sister Queens: Katherine of Aragon and Juana, Queen of Castile* (Weidenfeld & Nicolson, 2011). Katherine has also been the subject of a number of individual biographies, notably Giles Tremlett's *Catherine of Aragon: Henry's Spanish Queen* (Faber and Faber, 2010) and Patrick Williams's *Katharine of Aragon* (Amberley, 2013).

Margaret of Austria has been the subject of three comparatively modern biographies in English: Eleanor E. Tremayne's *The First Governess of the Netherlands: Margaret of Austria* (Methuen & Co, 1908); Jane de Iongh's *Margaret of Austria: Regent of the Netherlands* trans. M.D. Herter Norton (Jonathan Cape, 1954); and Shirley Harrold Bonner's *Fortune, Misfortune, Fortifies One: Margaret of Austria, Ruler of the Low Countries, 1507–1530* (Amazon, 1981). For Charles Brandon see Steven, Gunn, *Charles Brandon: Henry VIII's Closest Friend* (Amberley, 2015). Margaret's correspondence is published in Ghislaine de Boom, *Correspondance de Marguerite d'Autriche* ... (Bruxelles, 1935); see also André J. G. Le Glay, *Correspondance de l'Empereur Maximilien I et de Marguerite d'Autriche* (Paris, 1839).

Many of the royal women of France lack a solo biography in English but Pauline Matarasso's *Queen's Mate: Three Women of Power in France on the Eve of the Renaissance* (Routledge, 2001) is an authoritative consideration of Anne de Beaujeu, Anne of Brittany and (in her earlier years) Louise of Savoy. For Louise's later life see Dorothy Moulton Mayer, *The Great Regent: Louise of Savoy 1476–1531* (Weidenfeld &

Nicolson, 1966). *Anne of France: Lessons for my Daughter* by Anne de Beaujeu has been translated and edited by Sharon L. Jansen (L. D. S. Brewer, 2004). Louise of Savoy's *Journal* ed. M. Petitot in *Collection complète des mémoires relatifs à l'histoire de France* (Paris, 1826) can be found online.

I must also make special acknowledgement of *Marguerite of Navarre* by Patricia F. and Rouben C. Cholakian (Columbia University Press, 2006) for their development of the idea that passages in the *Heptaméron* are autobiographical: see below. The translation I used is Marguerite of Navarre, *The Heptaméron* trans. P. A. Chilton (Penguin, 1984). See also *Lettres de Marguerite d'Angoulême*, ed. F. Génin (Paris, 1841), and *Nouvelles Lettres* (Paris, 1842), and Pierre, Jourda, *Marguerite d'Angoulême, Duchess d'Alençon, Reine de Navarre* (Paris, 1930). Brantome's work on Marguerite is in Pierre de Bordeilles Brantôme, *Oeuvres complètes* (Paris, 1864–82).

'**Two long letters, signed simply "M"** ': The versions in the British Library's Cotton MS (Titus B. i. ff 142) are in the handwriting of Sir Richard Wingfield, the ambassador sent to the Netherlands to negotiate the proposed marriage between Margaret of Austria's nephew Charles, and Henry VIII's younger sister Mary. These are in English, presumably translated by Wingfield from the original French, and the BL will admit only that 'M' can 'probably' be identified as Margaret. From the internal evidence, however – the places, the occasions, the long interviews with the king – it is hard to see who else 'M' was likely to be. Wingfield had, moreover, endorsed the letters as having been written from 'Loivain', Louvain, Margaret's territory, and concerning 'Secret matters of the Duke of Suffolk'. See also John Gough Nichols, ed., *The Chronicle of Calais in the Reigns of Henry VII and Henry VIII to the Year 1540*, Camden Society, Vol. XXXV, London, 1846.

'**Heptaméron ... to some degree autobiographical**': See the Cholakians, op. cit., pp. 21–38. Earlier writers touch on the possibility of an entanglement between Marguerite and Bonnivet, in terms, however, of their own day. Francis Hackett, in his 1934 biography of Francis I, writes that Bonnivet watched Marguerite 'with guarded avidity while she, the regulator of nuns, tingled with his attention. She invited it, as Francis did his own form of violence, by the way she suffered and endured it'. Hackett, like Louise of Savoy's biographer

Meyer, also subscribed to the theory that Louise, 'the crafty and experienced matron', had fostered the affair, since Bonnivet could give Marguerite the child her husband couldn't. For sexual mores, and a possible autobiographical element in Marguerite's writings, see also Broad and Green op. cit. 70/1 and 79–89. Chilton, introducing *The Heptaméron*, notes that 'in periods when women show signs of assertiveness there is a corresponding preoccupation with violence against them': Marguerite may have been responding to a generally aggressive clime.

Part II: 1514–1521

In addition to the biographies cited above, see Antonia Fraser, *The Six Wives of Henry VIII* (Weidenfeld & Nicolson, 1992); David Starkey, *Six Wives: The Queens of Henry VIII* (Chatto & Windus, 2003); Alison Weir, *The Six Wives of Henry VIII* (Bodley Head, 1991). Also Glenn Richardson, *The Field of Cloth of Gold* (Yale University Press, 2013).

Part III: 1522–1536

The enigma that is Anne Boleyn has generated a huge volume of literature, though the single most comprehensive and authoritative biography remains Eric Ives's *The Life and Death of Anne Boleyn* (Blackwell, 2004). More controversial views can be found in *Anne Boleyn: Fatal Attractions* (Yale, 2010) by G. W. Bernard, chief exponent of the theory that Anne was, to some degree at least, guilty, and Retha M. Warnicke's *The Rise and Fall of Anne Boleyn: Family Politics at the Court of Henry VIII* (CUP, 1989). Alison Weir's *The Lady in the Tower: The Fall of Anne Boleyn* (Jonathan Cape, 2009) is a riveting forensic analysis of the circumstances leading up to Anne's execution, while Tracy Borman's *Thomas Cromwell: The Untold Story of Henry VIII's Most Faithful Servant* (Hodder & Stoughton, 2014) gives the other side of the story, and Suzannah Lipscomb's *1536: The Year that changed Henry VIII* (Lion, 2009) examines the year of her fall. I also found fascinating Nicola Shulman's *Graven with Diamonds* (Short Books, 2011), in which Thomas Wyatt serves as a prism through which to observe the court culture that saw Anne's downfall.

For the great religious struggle of which Anne Boleyn's story was but a part, see Diarmaid MacCulloch's great *Reformation: Europe's House Divided 1490–1700* (Allen Lane, 2003).

'**brother . . . wanting her to return**': It was possibly on her demoralised journey home that Marguerite wrote to her brother an undated, cryptic and desperate letter. She seems frantic to know whether François will send for her, tortured by the thought of what he may do, afraid he may 'abandon the right path', or afraid of what he may require her to do, by way of 'proof of surrender'. The letter, which Marguerite begs her brother to burn, breathes either the shame she seems so often to have felt, or a terrified awareness of the need for secrecy. Her great nineteenth-century editor, Génin, was in no doubt of what François was demanding, to her horror: that she make their relationship a physically, as well as emotionally, incestuous one. But it is hard now to see what in the letter compels such an extreme reading, which indeed hardly fits with Marguerite's reiterated offers to come to her brother, instantly. (Incest was, moreover, an absolutely favourite bugbear for writers of the first half of the nineteenth century.) Barbara Stephenson in *The Power and Patronage of Marguerite of Navarre* (Ashgate, 2004), p. 119, argues convincingly that the letter may have been written by another 'Marguerite'.

'**Henry VIII's letters to Anne Boleyn . . .**': There are quite literally as many different versions as there are writers on the subject of the chronology of Henry's letters, but I dwell too briefly on the subject to feel the need here to add to them. I find persuasive Eric Ives's theory as to which constitute the first three letters in the sequence, although otherwise I would differ slightly from his timetable.

'**if the recollections . . . are accurate**': A letter supposedly from Jeanne is quoted in full by Nancy Lyman Roelker, cited below, p. 127.

I am writing to tell you that up to now I have followed in the footsteps of the deceased Queen, my most honoured mother – whom God forgive – in the matter of hesitation between the two religions. The said Queen was warned by her late brother the King, François I . . . not to get new doctrines in her head so that from then on she confined herself to amusing stories. Besides, I well remember how long ago, the late King [of Navarre], my most

honoured father . . . surprised the late Queen when she was praying in her rooms with the ministers Roussel and Farel, and how
with great annoyance he slapped her right cheek and forbade her
sharply to meddle in matters of doctrine. He shook a stick at me
which cost me many bitter tears and has kept me fearful and
compliant until after they had both died.

Unfortunately, there have been questions as to the letter's authenticity,
see Broad and Green, op. cit., pp. 111/2.

Part IV: 1537–1553

The biography of Mary of Hungary has been written by Jane de Iongh,
trans. M.D. Herter Norton, (*Mary of Hungary: Second Regent of the
Netherlands* (Faber & Faber, 1959); that of Marie de Guise by Rosalind
K. Marshall, *Mary of Guise* (Collins, 1977). The most recent biography
of Mary Tudor is Anna Whitelock's powerful *Mary Tudor: England's
First Queen* (Bloomsbury, 2009), following Linda Porter's *Mary Tudor:
The First Queen* (Portrait, 2007), and Judith Mary Richards' *Mary
Tudor* (Routledge, 2008). The main biographical study of Jeanne
d'Albret in English is still Nancy Lyman Roelker's *Queen of Navarre:
Jeanne d'Albret* (Harvard University Press, 1968).

Parts VI and VIII

I have written twice before about the reign of Elizabeth I, in *Elizabeth
& Leicester* (Bantam, 2007) and *Arbella: England's Lost Queen* (Bantam,
2003). The bibliographies of those books provide a more extensive list
of reading and reference but there are books not then available of
which I have since had the benefit. To Alison Weir's *Elizabeth the
Queen* (Jonathan Cape, 1998) and Anne Somerset's *Elizabeth I*
(Weidenfeld & Nicolson, 1991) has now been added Lisa Hilton's
Elizabeth: Renaissance Prince (Weidenfeld & Nicolson, 2014), the
European perspective of which I found particularly valuable. John
Guy's *My Heart is My Own* (HarperCollins, 2004) remains the
outstanding biography of Mary, Queen of Scots.

To R. J. Knecht's *Catherine de' Medici* (Routledge, 1998) and Leonie

Frieda's *Catherine de Medici* (Weidenfeld & Nicolson, 2003) has now been added Nancy Goldstone's *The Rival Queens: Catherine de' Medici, her Daughter Marguerite de Valois, and the Betrayal that Ignited a Kingdom* (Weidenfeld & Nicolson, 2015). Several of the French primary sources are now available online: *Lettres de Catherine de Médicis* (Paris, 1880), *Mémoires et poésies de Jeanne d'Albret* (Paris, 1893), N. de Bordenave, *Histoire de Bearn et Navarre* (Société de l'Histoire de France Paris, 1873), *Mémoires et Lettres de Marguerite de Valois* (Paris, 1842).

While Christina of Denmark must join the long line of European women of whom there is no recent biography in English, Julia Cartwright's biography *Christina of Denmark: Duchess of Milan and Lorraine 1522–1590* (New York, 1913) is online.

Academic work I found particularly valuable included *High and Mighty Queens of Early Modern England: Realities and Representations* ed., by Carole Levin, Debra Barrett-Graves and Jo Eldridge Carney (Palgrave Macmillan, 2003); Rayne Allinson's *A Monarchy of Letters: Royal Correspondence and English Diplomacy in the Reign of Elizabeth* (Palgrave Macmillan, 2012) and *The Rule of Women in Early Modern Europe*, ed. Anne J. Cruz and Mihoko Suzuki (University of Illinois 2009): especially articles by Carole Levin on Elizabeth, by Mary C. Ekman on Jeanne d'Albret, and Mihoko Suzuki on Elizabeth and Catherine de Medici. (See also Susan Doran's essay on the same subject in Glenn Richardson (ed.), *The Contending Kingdoms: England and France 1420–1700* (Ashgate, 2008).)

Acknowledgements

This book might never have reached its present form without the help of one person in particular – my old friend (and unofficial editor!) Margaret Gaskin who, as so often before, came to my rescue and spent many hours helping me to mould a viable form out of some very challenging raw material. Her abilities make up for my deficiencies – thank you, Margaret. There is someone else I've had occasion to thank on every book I've done – the historian Alison Weir. Her unflagging support and enthusiasm never fails her friends.

A number of other historians have been kind enough to help me, by reading material or by answering queries. I owe an immense debt to the kindness of Dr Elena Woodacre at the University of Winchester, who organised a positive team of academic specialists to read parts of the text and ensure this generalist's book has as few errors as possible. I am indebted to Dr Jonathan Spangler, Dr Lucinda Dean, Cathleen Sarti, Rocio Martinez Lopez, Estelle Paranque and Una McIlvenny as well as to Aislinn Muller. I am also very grateful to Professor Carole Levin at the University of Nebraska-Lincoln, whose own work has been a source of inspiration and who supplied me with the *New York Times* quote which is the key to my preface. Thanks, too, to Dr Tracy Borman, Dr Linda Porter and Nicola Tallis, as well as to Dr Sara Wolfson and Professor Louise Wilkinson for their work in organising a conference on 'Premodern Queenship and Diplomacy in Europe', held at Canterbury Christ Church University in September 2014, which I found of the greatest assistance. Needless to say, any mistakes which remain in the book are my own responsibility entirely.

I want also to thank my agents, Peter Robinson in the UK and George Lucas in the US, and my publishers. In the UK, at Oneworld past and present: Fiona Slater for having commissioned the book with such enthusiasm, Sam Carter for having so kindly taken it over, and, especially, Jonathan Bentley-Smith for practical help and patience beyond the call of duty. In the US, at Basic Books, Lara Heimert and Leah Stecher for their acuteness and commitment. To all these and more – I only hope the book is worthy.

For more on the gynocracy debate and its relevance for women today, as well as some influential women only touched upon in this book, please visit the website:

gameofqueensbook.com

Notes

Preface

1. In Russia, where change came later, it was only in the eighteenth century, during the rule of Catherine the Great, that the chess queen really overtook the Vizier. By the same token, the chess queen's initial appearance in the early part of the millennium had also coincided, if that is the word, with a brief boom in female authority.
2. And beyond; as witness, for example, the 1915 Women's International Peace Conference that hoped to end the First World War.

Chapter 1: Entrance

1. The English ambassador often saw Margaret's nieces and nephews playing outdoors around a bonfire, or in winter with a sled rigged like a ship.

Chapter 2: 'Lessons for my Daughter'

1. The Concordia de Segovia, made weeks after Isabella took the throne of Castile, decreed that her arms would precede his on all chancery documents, however his signature would come first; a typical and effective, compromise. The Concordia was not without critics who held that Ferdinand – himself great-grandson of an earlier Castilian king – should now be Castile's ruler 'because he is a man'.
2. Many of the women in this story would, at the least, find it prudent in public to invoke their father's, rather than their mother's, legacy.
3. Whether these supposed womanly virtues do not, however, in themselves constitute a limitation on women remains an issue up to our own day.

Chapter 3: Youthful Experience

1. A device that would subsequently be used by several other French-educated queens.
2. The journal was less a diary as we know it than a note – possibly compiled for

astrological reasons – which at some point later in her life recorded all the significant events that had happened on particular days of the year.

Chapter 4: 'Fate is very cruel to women'

1. The third daughter, Maria, was, when Isabella also died early, called upon to step into her dead sister's shoes and in her turn marry Manuel.
2. Lemaire would eventually move from Margaret's service to that of Anne of Brittany; an example of how, intentionally or otherwise, interaction between women could be maintained by their officers.
3. Margaret's insistence on keeping Philibert's heart with her was not wholly unlike the behaviour that would have her sister-in-law Juana declared insane.
4. One seventeenth-century chronicler reported that 'for a moment' Anne de Beaujeu contemplated seizing the crown herself.

Chapter 5: Princess Brides

1. The sixteenth-century Scottish historian John Leslie said another possibility was mooted; that if Henry's male line should ever die out, Margaret's heirs would succeed to the English throne. If so, well and good, for 'England would not access unto Scotland but Scotland would access unto England,' said Henry prophetically. But at the time, with two of Henry's sons alive and well, that must have seemed unlikely.

Chapter 6: Repositioning

1. More appealingly, Ferdinand told his daughter that 'To be well married is the greatest blessing in the world . . . and source of all other kinds of happiness', an indirect tribute to Isabella of Castile.
2. The border town of Cambrai was the scene of Margaret's own later triumph, and a name that comes up time and again in this story.

Chapter 7: 'False imputations'

1. When the fourteen-year-old François was taken from his mother's care to live at court, Louise wailed in her *Journal* that his departure had 'left me all alone', for all that Marguerite remained with her. It is hard not to think of Henry VIII, although the father of a healthy daughter, considering himself childless in the years ahead.
2. Years later Anne Boleyn, arrested, would express the hope that Henry wished only to test her.

Chapter 9: Wheel of Fortune

1. When Eleanor's betrothal to the heir of Portugal fell through, she was instead married to his father, the Portuguese King Manuel himself, who had already been married to two of her Spanish aunts, Isabella of Castile's daughters. No wonder the results of Habsburg inbreeding would become notorious.

Chapter 11: 'One of the lowest-brought ladies'

1. Her granddaughter, Mary, would be similarly convinced that it was impossible for a woman to rule alone, unsupported 'by the firmness of a man'. And would choose as disastrously.
2. This baby, Lady Margaret Douglas, would grow up to be the mother of Lord Darnley, while her half-brother James would become father of Darnley's wife, Mary, Queen of Scots, so that Margaret was twice over the founder of the united British monarchy.
3. This may seem ironic, considering Henry's future history.

Chapter 13: The Field of Cloth of Gold

1. This may mean that, in contrast to the usual practice for a formal masquing dance, men and women danced together.

Chapter 14: Repercussions

1. Traditionally, no prince was officially entitled to call himself Holy Roman Emperor until crowned by the pope, in Rome. But Charles's predecessor Maximilian had broken with this tradition, winning from the pope the right to call himself emperor-elect. Charles would eventually be crowned by the pope – the last holder of the title so to be – but not for another decade.

Chapter 17: 'a true, loyal mistress and friend'

1. Mary was not formally created Princess of Wales but that was not a mark of personal disfavour. As a female she could only ever be heir presumptive, not heir apparent, since her father – if not by Katherine then by some future wife – might father a legitimate boy. The same issue was debated in the 1940s, when it was asked whether the future Elizabeth II could be invested as Princess of Wales, and it was decided, regretfully, that she could not. This situation changed only with the revision to the laws of succession in the twenty-first century.
2. A centuries-long movement 'compared to which the Renaissance is a mere ripple on the surface of literature', so CS Lewis wrote.
3. Though the phrase developed only slightly later, the reality could already be seen in

France. François was far from being a fool for love, but Anne d'Heilly, the mistress for whom he abandoned Françoise de Foix after his return from Pavia, could be seen openly at his side on state occasions.

4. The poem had possibly been influenced by the struggles of Isabella of Castile with La Beltraneja, her rival for the Castilian throne. But it still had resonance in Isabella's daughter's day.

Chapter 18: New pieces on the board

1. Or rather, in that westernmost section of Hungary that remained under Habsburg rule. Part was put under Ottoman rule and yet a further part became the separate principality of Transylvania, itself to enjoy a notable female ruler in the shape of Isabella Jagiellon, a great-niece of Caterina Sforza. Isabella Jagiellon would become the first ruler to issue an edict of universal religious toleration.

2. Henri had also inherited the large nearby territory of Béarn, and although Navarre would give Marguerite, and in time her daughter, the title of queen, Béarn was the richer property.

Chapter 19: 'ladies' might well come forward'

1. Legitimacy was, in any case, something the pope had the power to bestow. A child might be considered legitimate, as was Margaret Tudor's daughter, Margaret Douglas, even after divorce or annulment, if their parents had married in good faith.

Chapter 23: 'a native-born Frenchwoman'

1. Mary Tudor, Anne Boleyn's former mistress, was also absent. Her health really was poor; she would die within the year, amid rumours she was killed by the 'sorrow' of seeing her brother Henry abandon his wife. But her hostility was in contrast to the attitude of Henry's other sister, Margaret Tudor in Scotland, who would write to Anne, once queen, as 'our dearest sister', and who was happy to see her daughter Margaret Douglas welcomed to Anne's court.

Chapter 24: 'inclined towards the Gospel'

1. Though both Zwingli and by now Luther rejected the idea that the bread and wine consecrated by the priest during the Mass became literally the flesh and blood of Christ, Luther still held by Christ's 'real presence' at the ceremony, which was denied by Zwingli and his 'sacramentarians'.

2. In the war that followed, Marguerite – inspecting troops and reporting their condition, taking part in the interrogation of a spy – regretted that she could not do more,

since the emperor's iniquities were enough 'to make all women want to be men'. 'Since I cannot give you the help I would like to, being a woman, I will not stop assembling a battlefield of praying supplicants,' she wrote, in words that would be echoed in St Teresa of Avila's plan to restore the church with a praying army.

Chapter 25: 'to doubt the end'

1. The question has often been asked whether the foetus was deformed – a 'shapeless mass of flesh' in one later report – which would have raised the question, in the sixteenth- century mind, of witchcraft or satanic practices. Although the accusation of witchcraft had been levelled against several great ladies in the fifteenth century, notably Henry IV's widow Joan of Navarre and Elizabeth Woodville's mother Jacquetta, it was not an issue raised in Anne's day, nor did witchcraft feature in the formal accusations made against her.

   See Diarmaid MacCulloch, op. cit., pp. 561–70, for the role the fear of witchcraft played in the century and perhaps in the decline of women's power at the end of it. It has been said that the 'Age of Queens' also gave birth to the great age of the witch-hunt. Between 1400 and 1800, forty to fifty thousand people died in Europe and colonial North America on charges of witchcraft, the number mounting from 1560, when the burnings of heretics, as such, slowed. Witchcraft was seen as the natural successor to heresy, with the difference that it was particularly (though far from exclusively) associated with women. The *Malleus Maleficarum* (Hammer of Witches) published in 1487 specifically asserted that witches were more likely to be women, a 1484 papal bull gave approval to anti-witch activities, and in 1532 Charles V's *Lex Carolina* gave the death penalty to both heretics and witches. A crusade against witches was part of the Spanish attempt to impose order on the Low Countries in the 1560s.

2. Parker would become Elizabeth I's Archbishop of Canterbury.

3. Richmond's death was the more distressing for the fact that the king's niece Margaret Douglas – Margaret Tudor's daughter and another heir to the throne – had weeks earlier been detected in a secret betrothal to Thomas Howard and sent to the Tower.

Chapter 27: Pawns and princesses

1. Diane had a long court career behind her. Another woman raised partly under Anne de Beaujeu, she had served both of King François's wives, as well as his mother Louise of Savoy. She was related to Catherine through their shared descent from the La Tour d'Auvergne family.

2. Marguerite also instructed the French ambassador in England, Marillac, to intercede on behalf of Anne of Cleves, now in some sort her in-law.

3. Calvin would later be best known for his reforming ministry in Geneva and for the doctrine of predestination, which held that all events, and the fate of all souls, have been preordained by God.

Chapter 28: New winds

1. The Reformation in England had produced female martyrs on both sides: Elizabeth Barton the 'Holy Maid of Kent', who prophesied against Henry VIII's marriage to Anne Boleyn and was hung for it, and the Protestant Anne Askew, who was burned at the stake, having first been shockingly racked.

Chapter 30: 'device for the succession'

1. When, in October 1551, Marie de Guise visited Edward's court on her way home from France, Mary was invited to help entertain her. Sadly she declined, pleading ill health, afraid, perhaps, of more pressure. One of several meetings in this story one only wishes could have taken place.

Chapter 31: 'Herculean daring'

1. A king's wife might, however, enjoy the status of *femme sole*; that is, of a woman able to conduct financial and legal affairs in her own right, without going through a male protector.
2. The military aspect of a monarch's role was not the only one to be problematic for female rulers. Like her male predecessors, Mary Tudor would make a point of 'touching' to cure scrofula, the King's Evil, and other diseases; a huge symbolic importance was placed on what was believed to be the monarch's healing touch. The French had used the monarch's supposed healing power as one justification for the Salic Law, in that it showed monarchy to be a quasi-priestly role, which, self-evidently, no woman could exercise.
3. In the twelfth century Henry I, trying to ensure the succession of his daughter Matilda, had attempted to decree that her country would not be subject to her husband.

Chapter 32: 'not one year of rest'

1. In the event, Charles's son Philip would get Spain and its New World territories, and the Netherlands. The Holy Roman Empire, as well as the Austrian lands, would go to Charles's brother Ferdinand's branch of the family. This had not been Charles's original plan; he had wanted Philip to succeed him as Holy Roman Emperor. The painstaking memorandum Mary drew up concerning the future allocation of power, and defence of the Habsburg interests, shows just how divisive this issue was.
2. It would be one motive behind Elizabeth Tudor's famous pacifism.
3. Married off to her first cousin Joao, the heir of Portugal, Juana was summoned to take the Spanish regency after Joao died, just three weeks after the birth of their only son, whom she left behind in the care of his grandmother Catalina, Juana the Mad's youngest daughter, a former princess of Spain, and regent of Portugal. Charles V wrote to his son that Juana's instructions should be based on those given

to Mary of Austria: 'but as [Juana] is of a more active disposition . . . be sure to insist upon it that she and her advisors . . . forbear from those new interpretations of their instructions of which they have sometimes been known to be lavish'. Founder of the Convent of the *Descalzas Reales* (the Barefoot Royals), in Madrid, Juana is believed also to have been admitted to the Jesuit order under the pseudonym Mateo Sanchez.

Chapter 33: Sisters and rivals

1. Knox had earlier spent several years sentenced to row the French galleys as punishment for his part in an anti-French rebellion, something that surely helped harden his attitude.

Chapter 34: 'if God is with us'

1. She broke with tradition in wearing the white that suited her so well. White was, all too prophetically, the colour not of marriage but of mourning in the French royal family.
2. Christina's ambitions in another direction were also thwarted. On the death in prison of their father Christian of Denmark, his rights devolved on her elder sister Dorothea, who was, however, as a childless and ageing woman persuaded to cede them to Christina. She never won the help she needed to recover that throne but, from 1561, styled herself as rightful Queen of Denmark, Norway and Sweden. Her daughters would also be women of influence, the older becoming Governor of Siena, and the younger Regent of the Tyrol.
3. Less happily but perceptively he wrote to Jeanne that 'it is your natural tendency to torment your husband and all who love you' – to test them, in terms of pop psychology.
4. The concern of the Estates was that, in the event of Jeanne's death, Antoine should not become their ruler and that only Jeanne's children should inherit. It was the same distinction between king and king consort that had plagued Mary and Philip in England and that would deny the Crown Matrimonial to Mary, Queen of Scots's husband, Lord Darnley.

Chapter 37: 'Rancour and division'

1. Jeanne commissioned Bordenave to write a history of her provinces. She also commissioned a volume of *Mémoires* – or, more accurately, 120 pages of self-justification – to be written for her in the first person. Two lines in particular stick in the memory: that 'if I wished to undertake the defence of my sex, I could find plenty of examples'; and the opening line: 'I have always considered that if a person is not satisfied with herself in herself, the contentment that others can have of her is only a half in her conscience.'

Chapter 38: 'Two Queens in One Isle'

1. For much of Elizabeth's reign, all the possible candidates to succeed her were female. The Grey sisters and Margaret Clifford were descended from Henry VIII's sister Mary; Margaret Douglas and her granddaughter Arbella Stuart from Henry's sister Margaret.

2. She would use him as a foil through which she could show her resolute chastity. As Anne de Beaujeu had written: 'suppose a castle is beautiful and so well-guarded that it is never assailed; then it is not to be praised, nor is a knight who has never proven himself to be commended for his prowess. To the contrary, the thing most highly commended is that which has been in the fire yet cannot be scorched . . .'

Chapter 40: 'Majesty and love do not sit well together'

1. This has been used as evidence that she must (as her enemies alleged) have been sleeping with Bothwell before Dunbar, since otherwise the foetuses could not have been sufficiently developed to have shown themselves a pair.

Chapter 41: 'daughter of debate'

1. Margaret of Parma was unusual among female regents in that her (second) husband Ottavio Farnese was still alive. He, however, remained in Italy to govern his duchy of Parma, while their son Alexander accompanied Margaret to the Netherlands.

2. Later, Margaret would be advisor both to her much younger bastard stepbrother Don John, appointed Governor General of the Netherlands in 1576 and to her son, Alexander Farnese, who succeeded him. She was asked to act as co-regent with her son, dealing with civil administration while he, a commander of genius, took care of what was by now a full-scale military campaign but the two could not work together, and Margaret retired again.

Chapter 42: The Massacre of St Bartholomew's Day

1. The Holy Roman Emperor was now no longer Ferdinand, who had died in 1564, but his son, named Maximilian after his grandfather.

2. In this too the massacre was a precursor of 1789, which saw intensely sexualised violence directed against, for example, the Princesse de Lamballe.

3. Twenty years later Christopher Marlowe's play *The Massacre of Paris* cast her as a stage villain: 'Tush, all shall die unless I have my will:/For while she lives, Catherine will be queen.

Chapter 43: Turning points

1. Henri of Navarre, however, said to her, perhaps perceptively: 'This is trouble pleases you and feeds you – if you were at rest you would not know how to continue to live'.
2. Elizabeth in these latter years entered into correspondence with Safiye Sultan, the Albanian-born consort of the Ottoman ruler Murad III who, on his death in 1595, promoted their son Mehmed III to the throne and herself exercised such power the English ambassador could report that Mehmed was 'wholly led by the old Sultana'. Often Murad, whose own communication with Elizabeth was beset with difficulties of status, found letters from his consort a useful way to approach one he saw as being of the weaker sex. Actively promoting a rapport with England, Safiye described Elizabeth ('most rare among womankind and the world') as following in the steps of the Virgin Mary. The two exchanged gifts. Safiye sent Elizabeth 'a robe, a sash, two gold-embroidered bath towels, three handkerchiefs, and a ruby and pearl tiara'. Elizabeth sent her a carriage in which, to the horror of the locals, Safiye used to leave the harem and travel through the street. Joint military action between Murad and Elizabeth was even discussed, just as it had been between Murad's grandfather Suleiman, and Louise of Savoy. Was Louise another outsider willing to step outside the club of European male rulers in her need for allies?

Postscript

1. Her Netherlands allies, creating medals that depicted sunken Spanish ships, reportedly added the inscription: 'Done by a female leader'.
2. The Duchesse de Montpensier (daughter of François, the Duc de Guise murdered in 1563, and thus first cousin to Mary Stuart), was particularly rabid, carrying always at her belt a pair of scissors with which she threatened to tonsure the king and confine him in a convent.
3. To be reborn in England, in another time of crisis – the Civil War. Antonia Fraser's *The Weaker Vessel: Woman's Lot in Seventeenth-Century England* (Weidenfeld, 1984) details the importance on women's efforts on both sides. As Diarmaid MacCulloch notes in *Reformation*, p. 657: 'Female self assertion was possible in periods of uncertainty and crisis . . . When times quietened, there was a gradual reining-in of possibilities for women, together with a rewriting of history'.
4. Maria Theresa dictated an autobiographical account of her proceedings entitled, in a phrase reminiscent of Anne de Beaujeu, *Instructions drawn up from motherly solicitude for the special benefit of my posterity*. Advising her son that 'a mediocre peace is always better than a fortunate war' she nevertheless celebrated the recapture of Prague in 1743 with a spectacle known as the 'Ladies' Carousel', in which she engaged in a jousting contest with another noblewoman.

Index

References to notes and footnotes are indicated by n.